Mesoamerican Elites

Jim Selley

Mesoamerican Elites

An Archaeological Assessment

Edited by

Diane Z. Chase and Arlen F. Chase

University of Oklahoma Press : Norman and London

By Diane Z. Chase

(with Arlen F. Chase) *Investigations at the Classic Maya City of Caracol, Belize: 1985-1987* (San Francisco, 1987)

(with Arlen F. Chase) *A Postclassic Perspective: Excavations at the Maya Site of Santa Rita Corozal, Belize* (San Francisco, 1988)

(ed., with Arlen F. Chase) *Mesoamerican Elites: An Archaeological Assessment* (Norman, 1992)

By Arlen F. Chase

(ed., with Prudence M. Rice) *The Lowland Maya Postclassic* (Austin, 1985)

(with Diane Z. Chase) *Investigations at the Classic Maya City of Caracol, Belize: 1985-1987* (San Francisco, 1987)

(with Diane Z. Chase) *A Postclassic Perspective: Excavations at the Maya Site of Santa Rita Corozal, Belize* (San Francisco, 1988)

(ed., with Diane Z. Chase) *Mesoamerican Elites: An Archaeological Assessment* (Norman, 1992)

Library of Congress Cataloging-in-Publication Data

Mesoamerican elites : an archaeological assessment / edited by Diane Z. Chase and
    Arlen F. Chase. — 1st ed.
      p. cm.
    Includes bibliographical references and index.

    1. Indians of Mexico—Kings and rulers.   2. Indians of Central America—
Kings and ruler.   3. Elites (Social sciences)—Mexico.   4. Elites (Social
sciences)—Central America.   5. Mexico—Antiquities.   6. Central America—Antiquities.   I. Chase, Diane Z., 1953–   .   II. Chase, Arlen F. (Arlen
Frank), 1953–   .
F1219.3.K55M47   1992
972'.01–dc20

                                        91–40064
ISBN: 0–8061–2371–0 (cloth)   CIP
ISBN: 0–8061–2666–3 (paper)

2   3   4   5   6   7   8   9   10   11

For Adrian Sylvanus and Aubrey Marnyn

Contents

Illustrations

Figures

Tables

Preface

IN anthropology and archaeology, certain words have been overused to the point of losing at least some of their impact and meaning. "Culture" and "state" are such words. There are enough different definitions and usages of each to fill several books. Another amorphously used word is "elite."

Such key words are often neither precisely defined nor uniformly used in current archaeological research in Mesoamerica. Rather, their meanings and implications are simply assumed, even in areas of theoretical and definitional importance. Much like the subjectivity involved in the ascription of a type to a grouping of pottery sherds, individual researchers emphasize different aspects and see different things in the same term. Often, pivotal assumptions relating to the use of such words are left unstated and theoretical disagreements go unaired.

This book is an attempt to examine the use of one of those catchall words in Mesoamerican archaeology. In any description of Precolumbian society, the word "elite" almost always appears. Years ago—and to a large extent today—archaeologists tended to place anything unknown into a ceremonial context. Such a context was rarely defined, but rather served simply to explain the unknown. In Mesoamerica, "elite" had/has taken on much the same usage. If anything is foreign, elaborate, or unexplained, it often was/is termed "elite."

Yet this word (like the other words noted above) has very specific meaning in literature relating to the rise of and organization of society. There is no one-to-one correspondence between the theoretical use of the word "elite" and archaeological data. Rather, such transpondencies should require considerable contemplation and thought, much like a philosophical question. If, however, the word "elite" is indiscriminately used (as it is in danger of becoming), then it loses much of its theoretical meaning.

It was with thoughts such as these that we entered into this volume: What does "elite" mean? How can the term be operationalized archaeologically? And how do models of Mesoamerican society and archaeological data mesh? It appeared from the onset that one could ask more questions about elites than could easily be answered. Are there certain kinds of buildings, associations of artifacts, or specific modes of burial that characterize elites? Or are there no hardfast rules? Where do elites live—within the site center or in the suburbs? How many elites are there within any one site or society? Does a variation in the number or percentage of elites make a difference in the functioning or level of complexity of a society? Are all elite members of the ruling group? These papers are intended to stimulate an archaeological assessment of Mesoamerican elites by combining the differing data bases, research designs, assumptions, and interpretations of a broad spectrum of Mesoamerican archaeologists.

This volume illustrates that there is no agreement on what is and what is not elite archaeologically. But it also demonstrates that, if we do not understand this term, we cannot hope to understand Mesoamerican society—for our perceptions of this word color the way in which we view archaeological complexity. Yet research into elites was in danger of becoming obsolete. All too often an interest in anything elite was being portrayed in a negative light in the Mesoamerican field. In the search for "the common man" and "everyday life," elites were overlooked; it was assumed that archaeologists knew all that they needed to know about elites based on past work in the central areas of large sites. Settlement research, in fact, customarily excluded a consideration of elites from general research designs. We saw this emerging pattern as being in dire need of redress.

In order to encourage a discussion of these issues, we organized a session bearing the title of this book at the 86th Annual Meeting of the American Anthropological Association in Chicago, Illinois, during November 1987. Although at least one of us had previously sworn off edited volumes—especially given the thankless task of alternately pleading and berating participants into meeting submission and editing deadlines—we both felt that the topic was important enough once again to assemble a brain-trust of leading Mesoamericanists to examine this topic and then attempt to present this material in some coherent fashion so that it would be palatable to other colleagues, both within and outside of Mesoamerican archaeology.

With this in mind—and with the constraints imposed on the organization of sessions at the American Anthropological Association meetings—we assembled a diverse group of people. We knew from the outset that they would disagree on certain issues. What was unexpected was the discovery that a consideration of Mesoamerican elites would lead to the discovery and definition of two competing paradigms for explaining Meoamerican society. These existed independently of whether research was conducted in the highlands as opposed to the lowlands or in the core as opposed to the periphery or in central Mexico as opposed to the Maya area.

In brief, these two divergent points of view reflect a multiple-level as opposed to a two-class reconstruction of ancient society. Many of the distinctions made in the description of Precolumbian Mesoamerica lie in the researchers' unstated assumptions about one or the other of these paradigms and, even more importantly, in the nature of the archaeological data base that is being used or examined. Such points will become obvious to the reader of these papers.

As conceived, this volume seeks to provide both areal and temporal coverage of Mesoamerica (cf. Kirchhoff 1952) in considering elites. While the book is not all-inclusive because of the quantity of research being done in Mesoamerica, the major areas and periods are represented. Our hope was to provide enough coverage for both cultural variations and patterns to be revealed and discussed.

For the 1987 meetings, chapter 1 was circulated to all the volume partici-
pants both for their reaction and to provide a framework for their papers.
The individuals included in the 1987 session were divided into several areal
categories from our perspective: Maya lowlands, southeastern periphery,
Oaxaca, and central Mexico. Twelve papers were presented in the session.
Besides the introductory paper, presentations were made by D. Freidel
(Southern Methodist) on the Terminal Classic Northern Maya lowlands as
seen from Yaxuna and Chichen Itza; A. Chase (Central Florida) on the
Southern lowland Maya of the Classic period as seen from Santa Rita Coro-
zal, Tayasal, and Caracol; G. Tourtellot (Sayil Project), J. Sabloff (Pitts-
burgh), and K. Carmean (Pittsburgh) on Southern Maya lowland Seibal as
compared to Northern Maya lowland Sayil; W. Haviland (Vermont) and H.
Moholy-Nagy (Tikal Project) on Southern Maya lowland Tikal; D. Chase
(Central Florida) on the Postclassic Maya as seen from Mayapan and Santa
Rita Corozal; J. Henderson (Cornell) on the Maya of the southeastern pe-
riphery; K. Hirth (Kentucky) on Precolumbian exchange systems as related
to elites; D. Grove (Illinois, Urbana-Champaign) and S. Gillespie (Illinois,
Urbana-Champaign) on Preclassic Mexico; S. Kowalewski (Georgia), G.
Feinman (Wisconsin, Madison), and L. Finsten (McMaster) on the Valley
of Oaxaca; W. Sanders (Pennsylvania State) on the Aztec *pochteca*; and T.
Charlton (Iowa) and D. Nichols (Dartmouth) on the Aztec of Otumba.
George Marcus (Rice), the discussant, was present for all papers and later
submitted his summary paper written from a non-Mesoamericanist's per-
spective.

When the dust had cleared after the session, it was deemed necessary to
broaden our coverage of elites for the volume. To this end, papers were
solicited from: G. Cowgill (Arizona State) to discuss central Mexico's Teotihuacan; D. Webster (Pennsylvania State) to discuss the southeastern Maya
site of Copan; D. Pendergast (Royal Ontario Museum) to discuss the eastern Maya sites of Altun Ha and Lamanai; J. Fox (Baylor), D. Wallace
(SUNY, Albany), and K. Brown (Houston) to discuss the Quiche of highland Guatemala; and J. Marcus (Michigan, Ann Arbor) to compare the
Oaxaca and the Maya areas. All of these papers provide a needed dimension to the topic under consideration and round out the coverage of
Mesoamerica as a whole.

It is not our intent that *Mesoamerican Elites* be the definitive work on
this subject. Rather, we see this volume as accomplishing several things.
First, it presents unpublished archaeological information. Second, it offers
a current assessment of how Mesoamerican archaeologists view elites and,
by extension, how they perceive Precolumbian society in Mexico and northern Central America to have been organized. Third, the data provided and
the positions taken in the papers within this volume may stimulate both
present and future researchers in Mesoamerica to ask new questions and to
seek new ways to interpret their data. Finally, this volume may be of use to

archaeologists working in other parts of the world who are faced with similar problems of definitions and models.

As always, the completion of this volume required the assistance of others. In addition to the authors of the various chapters, a number of individuals were particularly helpful in the preparation of this volume. We wish to thank Edward Zaino for spurring us on with discussions of bourgeoisie, Rusty Okoniewsi for helping with stateside arrangements for the volume while we were in the field, Ella Tepper for compiling the index, Debby Carpenter for helping to correct the bibliography, Richard Spencer for photographic work, and Mildred Logan for the energies spent in editing.

Mesoamerican archaeology tends to be parochial; we hope that this volume can transcend its chosen boundaries.

Arlen F. Chase
Diane Z. Chase

Winter Springs, Florida

Mesoamerican Elites

1. Mesoamerican Elites: Assumptions, Definitions, and Models

Arlen F. Chase and Diane Z. Chase

MOST archaeologists are familiar with the term "elite," as much from colloquial use in contemporary situations as from descriptions of past cultures. From an archaeological standpoint, it is used not only in reference to people and artifacts, but also in relation to theoretical discussions of the organization and complexity of ancient societies. Despite all of its uses, however, the term "elite" is imprecisely defined in the general archaeological literature and no less so in relation to Mesoamerica.[1]

Most Mesoamericanists associate the use of the word "elite" with the "rich, powerful, and privileged in any society" (G. Marcus 1983d:3, 1983e:34) and correlate elites with a wide array of material remains. However, other definitions of the term would nearly preclude it from the material realm of archaeology, for elites may also be seen as *those who run society's institutions* (cf. G. Marcus 1983b:12-13; see also Mills 1956). Under this definition, elites are not necessarily characterized by luxury goods and other items found in the archaeological record; rather, the elite would be those who managed the political, economic, social, and religious institutions. A consideration of the elite, then, must by definition concern itself with the concepts of power and control; these are abstract notions that are difficult to identify concretely in the archaeological record.

This ambiguity in the definition and use of the term "elite" is not limited to the discipline of archaeology (cf. G. Marcus 1983b:7, 1983e:34) and the problems that archaeologists have are not unique (see G. Marcus 1983b:21-22). It is apparent that several issues require resolution with regard to elites in Mesoamerica (fig. 1.1). It is particularly important to attempt to define the ways in which elites can be identified archaeologically and to assess the relationships between elites and the overall social and political system(s) of a particular culture. While there are *a priori* models for Mesoamerican social organization, a brief review of contrasting opinions and strategies makes it evident that ground level identification of elites must be reevaluated as a prerequisite to the reconstruction of ancient Mesoamerican social order. Differences of opinion on the percentage of elites, on the amount of labor expenditure that is required to sustain them, and on their relationships to other social groups make for critical divergence in the analyses of the structure, function, and change of Mesoamerican society through time and over space.

Archaeological Identification of Elites

Although archaeological research has focused on major centers in Mesoamerica, we still do not fully comprehend their organization, much less how the elite or those who had access to elite goods were distributed in or about these centers. It is also unclear to what degree there is overlap among systems of sociopolitical organization throughout Mesoamerica.

The archaeological identification of elites exemplifies many of the problems found in the use of the term in Mesoamerica. In contrast to Fried's (1987:186) focus on limited acccess to basic resources as a primary condition for stratification, elites are generally defined in the archaeological record on the basis of their access to luxury goods (Rathje 1970; Tourtellot and Sabloff 1972; Pires-Ferreira 1975; Drennan 1976; see also Morley, Brainerd, and Sharer 1983:Table 9 for enumeration of these items), their presumed association with more elaborate architecture in their domiciles (Harrison 1969, 1970; Blanton 1978:67; Price 1978; Webster and Abrams 1983; Webster 1985a), and their supposedly sumptuous treatment in death (A. Smith 1950:90; M. Coe 1956, 1975:102, 1988; Rathje 1970). Just as the presence of certain items are used to attempt an identification of the elite, the absence of certain criteria are used in identifying those who are not elite. Furthermore, the presence of specific archaeological items is sometimes thought to indicate that particular buildings or constructions cannot have served an elite function. For instance, under the predominant interpretive paradigm for Mesoamerican studies, elites as consumers ideally should not be associated with flint tools that would indicate labor in agricultural fields (i.e., ones that are broken or used) and should not be directly associated with evidence of craft specialization (such as in the production of manos and metates or utilitarian lithics or pottery). However, the elite are often viewed as regulating the systems of production and distribution of all such items, whether luxury or utilitarian (Fried 1967; Sanders and Price 1968:161, 188-89; Rathje 1971, 1972; Grove 1984:71). Some members of elite groups also were involved in the painting of elaborate polychrome vessels (cf. Houston, Stuart, and Taube 1988).

The possession of luxury goods is viewed as having been a sign of wealth and prestige in Precolumbian society. C. C. Coggins (1975:5) has noted for Tikal that "it is reasonable to assume that most decorated objects were the possessions of the elite" and that "the possession of such objects has served to define an aristocratic class that is termed elite." The distribution, production, and ownership of these items is often conceived of as being entirely elite controlled (Adams 1970:492). Luxury goods include, among other things, jade (Leventhal, Demarest, and Willey 1987:187), pyrite mirrors (Flannery 1968), imported pottery (Coggins 1975:5; Leventhal, Demarest, and Willey 1987:187), sea shells (Andrews IV 1969:48, 60-61), and stingray spines (J. Marcus 1978:187). Such items are thought to be accessible to the

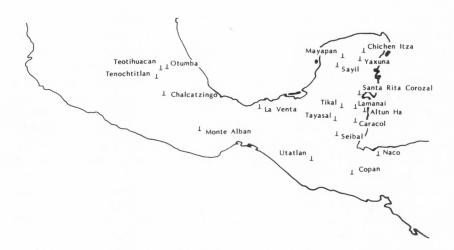

Fig. 1.1. Map of Mesoamerica with relevant sites noted (north is to the top of the page).

elite and perhaps a small group of close retainers, probably composing well under 10 percent of Maya society (Webster 1985b:388).

What is considered to be an elite or luxury item, however, often differs from site to site. At Preclassic Chalcatzingo, ceramic figurines and obsidian tools were both interpreted as elite-associated goods; they were either representative of the elite in and of themselves or were viewed as being "produced under elite direction" (Harlan 1979:472) as were the production and distribution of "greenstone" and "iron-ore" (Grove 1984:71). In the Maya area, elaborate polychrome pottery is often interpreted as representing an elite good (M. Coe 1975:95; Ashmore and Sharer 1978:17; Sharer 1978:63; see also L. Schele and M. Miller 1986) in spite of the fact that R. E. Fry (1979:496; see also Adams 1971:141) has pointed out that such vessels are often found in garbage dumps in Tikal's peripheral areas.

In death the elite are presumed to be more elaborately treated than nonelite members of society. The expenditure of effort that went into any one burial rite, as represented in the size of the associated grave or chamber and the rites associated with the interment, has been used as a worldwide indicator of status (Chapman, Kinnes, and Randsborg 1981; O'Shea 1984). Often the very location of the grave provides a clue as to the status of the individual (Sharer 1978:57; Flannery and Marcus 1983b:80; D. Chase 1986:359). Finally, the contents of the grave are used to provide data relevant to the status and role that the individual may have had in life. Some even argue that certain elaborately painted pottery vessels were produced only for elite burial and that their production served to bind together royal lineages from various sites (Adams 1963, 1971:75-78; see also Coggins 1975 for Tikal).

One other common assumption seen in Mesoamerica is that stone architecture is more likely to be associated with, or even representative of, the elite than wooden construction—partially because of its permanence, but also because of the presumed labor expenditure involved (Kurjack 1974:83-84, 94; Arnold and Ford 1980:720; Folan et al. 1982:431). Elites are viewed as being associated with architecture that has better stonework, a higher elevation, or more monumental construction (Kurjack 1974:8, 92; Price 1978; Willey and Leventhal 1979:82-83; Sanders and Webster 1983:28-29, table 6; Webster 1985a:40; Abrams 1987:495), and often specific plaza plans (Flannery 1983b:293; M. Coe 1984:92, but see Willey et al. 1965:572; Becker 1972, 1982; Millon 1976; Blanton 1978:30, 67; Blanton et al. 1981:95; and A. Chase 1985a:38 in relation to "Plaza Plan 2"). However, arguments are made that the elite, and particularly the "royal household," did not live in masonry constructions, but rather in perishable buildings (M. Coe 1987:93).

In some cases, biological evidence or skeletal modification has been utilized to identify elites. It is possible that the Maya elite were more likely to have practiced skull deformation (Haviland 1971). Dental modifications, particularly inlays, have also been interpreted as representing elite status among the Maya (Becker 1973:401; Sharer 1978:57). At Tikal, the elite were interpreted as being taller and better fed than the rest of society based on skeletal remains (Haviland 1967). At Teotihuacan, R. Storey (1985) has similarly argued that the upper echelons of that society enjoyed better health, which is reflected in their osteological remains.

Thus, it is evident that in practice the archaeological identification of elites is often based on the possession of specific artifact types or traits, the association with certain constructions and architectural groups, skeletal indicators of health and stature, and interment in certain locations and types of graves. Other classes of data, however, exist—reading/writing (Houston 1989; Schele and Freidel 1990; C. Brown 1991) and iconography (Thompson 1973; M. Coe 1975; L. Schele and M. Miller 1986; Leventhal, Demarest, and Willey 1987; Grove 1987c:425-26; Laporte and Fialko 1987:156). The various stone monuments in the Maya and other areas of Mesoamerica that show individuals on their surfaces are interpreted as presenting portraits of rulers or other elite(s) in that society. Unfortunately, it often proves impossible to associate monumental portraits directly with specific human skeletal or residential remains, and it is extremely difficult for an archaeologist to assess an individual's role in a past culture; in fact, only on the uppermost tier of society, when one is dealing with the royal lineage(s), is it possible archaeologically to identify members of a group who must have occupied positions of power and extremely high prestige. Even these individuals may elude identification by researchers where there are no hieroglyphs to aid interpretation.

When one assembles all of the postulated archaeological indicators of elite status or goods at any one or combination of sites, a gap appears between theory and practice. In theory, and with a definition of the elite as "those who run society's institutions," their numbers should be small. In practice, following all of the various archaeological indicators that are cited, a large segment of society may be and has been classified as elite merely because of the presence of so-called elite goods—at least during the Classic and Postclassic periods. This usage of the word "elite" does not fit the predominant Mesoamerican conception of a small consumer group; it does, however, suggest that there is much room for refining the process of identifying elites using archaeology.

Ethnohistory: Mexico and Maya

Interpretations based on ethnohistoric records are nearly uniform in their discussion of protohistoric Mesoamerican social groups as consisting of two basic categories of people: rulers and the ruled—more particularly, nobles and commoners, with the addition of slaves (Roys 1943:33; Spores 1965:969, 973, 982, 984, 1983:228; Blanton et al. 1981:226; Flannery 1983a:133; J. Marcus 1983:470; Hicks 1986:38, 46). Early historic descriptions are largely responsible for later categorizations of Mesoamerican society as a two-class system (see, for example, Thompson 1966[1954] for the Maya). Further analysis of early historic material, however, suggests that this division of nobles and commoners was more complex than the cut and dry two-division approach would indicate: commoners could amass wealth, and nobles might on occasion be left to till their own land (Hicks 1986:38); in addition, there evidently were in-between statuses (Roys 1965:662). It would seem, then, that there were two distinct principles operating in Precolumbian society— on one hand, status in society was determined by membership in a social group-based kinship and descent on both the maternal and paternal sides (Roys 1943:33; Carrasco 1982:30), at least among the nobility (Edmonson 1979:10); but, on the other hand, actual material well-being could be affected by other factors such as line of work and achievements.

A basic contradiction exists between the groupings easily identifiable in the archaeological record and the groupings of people recorded in ethnohistory. Ethnohistory records the existence of commoners and nobles. However, the distinction between these two groups of people is made on the basis of kinship and descent (Roys 1943:33; Carrasco 1982:30), something very difficult to recover in the archaeological record; there are no direct material correlates for these abstract concepts, particularly if a ranking principle was operative within descent groups. Archaeological investigations, however, do provide information on the material well-being associated with particular individuals in death and in life. Even if we could identify kinship and descent archaeologically (see Haviland 1985), we could not expect a one-to-one correlation, for other principles were also operating.

We know, for instance, that Mixtec priests could come from either the commoner or the noble group (Spores 1983:231) and it is likely that other professions could derive from either group. Pedro Carrasco (1982:28-29) has noted that, for the Aztec and Inca, "one also finds intermediate social strata whose estate position was less precisely defined. Members of such strata might belong to the lower levels of the noble estate, or they might be individuals or groups chosen from among the common people." Among the Maya there were also individuals who fit somewhere in between the nobles and commoners (Martínez Hernández 1929:69; Tozzer 1941:62-63; Roys 1943:33-34; Barrera Vásquez et al. 1980:18) and some professions, such as merchants, could be undertaken by noble and commoner alike (Roys 1943:33, 34, 51)—although perhaps at different levels. Among the Maya there may also have been strata between commoners and slaves and both nobles and "wealthy commoners" could own slaves (Roys 1943:34).

Thus, from an archaeological standpoint it could, and does, prove extremely problematical to discriminate between a noble and a commoner, for the status and roles available to each group cross-cut one another and it is probable that similar goods were also available to at least certain members of each group. While the elite of any society—by their very power over the various societal institutions—may well have had greater access to trade items or other luxury goods, the mere presence or absence of such items does not automatically prove that a particular building or burial belonged to a member of the elite. The reverse is also true. Likewise, an archaeological assessment of occupational specialization may or may not correlate with the distinct categories of noble or commoner. A strict two-part division of Mesoamerican society may not be appropriate and may be partially based on ethnocentrism supplied by the early European recorders.

While any given complex society may have a small group of elite people that run it, a larger group is necessary to ensure the maintenance of that society by undertaking a variety of administrative or other occupational tasks. While certain distinctions may be made between members of such a society based on kinship and descent, these are not necessarily reflected in the actual roles of individuals or in the archaeological record. Both archaeological and ethnohistoric data suggest that a simple model of a small number of elite and a much larger number of nonelite does not easily incorporate the complexity of Precolumbian Mesoamerican society. It is, however, one's perceptions about the nature of the relationship between elites and commoners that give rise to various ways of viewing the development and organization of the Precolumbian cultures of Mesoamerica.

Models of Mesoamerican Society

Traditionally, Mesoamerican society has been viewed as having been two-tiered, consisting of nobles, usually read as elites, and commoners, or nonelites (Haviland 1970; Blanton 1978:67; Becker 1979; Adams 1981:341;

Sanders 1981a:359; Flannery 1983a:133; Spores 1983:228; Webster 1985b). In this widely accepted and used model, the nobles governed society while the commoners constituted a large group of peasants or farmers. The elites (read "hereditary rulers") and what is usually referred to as an "upper class" (Adams 1970) or "hereditary noble" group (Spores 1983:228) resided in the center of sites within monumental architecture. The larger peasantry—also referred to as the "humble" or "plebeian class" (Spores 1983:228) or the "sustaining population" (Haviland 1970)—resided in the periphery. The latter group also included "landless tenant-servant tributaries," at least for the Oaxaca area (Spores 1983:228). Slaves are also mentioned, but were "not an identifiable social group" (Spores 1983:228). Importantly, this traditional model is used to portray a society that is either a highly developed chiefdom or an incipient state (cf. Adams 1981, Adams and Smith 1981, and Webster 1985b). Commercialization is not perceived as having played a major role in such a society.

A significant point within the two-tiered traditional model is that central architecture is associated with the elite and elite-related functions and residences. As noted, elites usually are seen as being intricately associated with the core of the site (Blanton et al. 1981:135, 138; Morley, Brainerd, and Sharer 1983:226). R. E. W. Adams and W. D. Smith (1981:341) have claimed that at least 90 percent of the formal architecture in Maya centers appears to have been for elite use and have explicitly noted "that there was thus a locational separation between Maya social classes and status groups." Site-center palaces were interpreted to be explicitly for elite residence (Adams 1974, 1981; Haviland 1982:427; Flannery 1983a:133; Flannery and Marcus 1983b:80). While Peter Harrison's (1969:172, 1969) early research at Tikal gave credence to the interpretation of palaces as being equated with elite residences (at least in the Maya area), his recent reanalysis of the data has shown that this was one of their lesser functions (Harrison 1986:53-54).

A variant of the two-class model of Mesoamerican social organization sees these societies as being much more complex than the above picture, but with the same "elite-equals-epicenter" focus (see Haviland 1970; Kurjack 1974:93). This greater complexity is based primarily on inferred occupational specialization (Adams 1970; Becker 1973; see also Haviland 1963, 1974; Blanton et al. 1981), although the existence of class structure in association with such specialization has been questioned by D. L. Webster (1985b:389). R. J. Sharer, however, has recently suggested that Maya society was "multiclass" and had an emerging nonelite "middle class" (Morley, Brainerd, and Sharer 1983:226, 249; but see J. Marcus 1983c:470). Sharer (Morley, Brainerd, and Sharer 1983:226), however, places his three groups—elite, middle class, and peasants—in a concentric arrangement around the archaeological site center, in conformance with the spatial dicta of the two-class model. In his analysis of Dzibilchaltun spatial dynamics, E. B. Kurjack (1974:93-94, 97) foreshadows Sharer's conclusions.

Two of the basic underpinnings of the Maya two-class model may be questioned: first, the association of all elite residences with the site epicenter (Ford and Arnold 1982:437; A. Chase and D. Chase 1987b:58) and, second, the projection of concentric rings of status-differentiated people about this epicenter (Arnold and Ford 1980; Ashmore 1981b, 1981c, 1988; D. Chase 1985b, 1986:364; D. Chase and A. Chase 1986a:23, 1986b, 1988:68-71). A contrasting model would view these cities as nonconcentric and the societies as more complex than either of the two-tier variants. Some elites and much of what has been referred to as an upper class may be seen as being distributed throughout a site. The central monumental architecture is viewed as combining both public and elite functions. While such interpretations are new and to some degree still contested in the Maya area (Folan et al. 1982; Haviland 1982), such a model has already been applied in the highland regions of Mesoamerica. The data that R. Millon (1976:220) has presented for Teotihuacan suggest that this site would fit this model: he notes that there was no "simple linear decrease in status from center to periphery," but rather that there was a "mosaic quality to the barrio structure of Teotihuacan." The apartment compounds that he has analyzed at Teotihuacan were replete with different status individuals and did not appear to co-vary in terms of status or elaboration with distance from the site core. Richard E. Blanton (1978:table 4-1, 97-98) seemingly describes a similar situation for Monte Alban. On a slightly different level, but consistent with such data, G. Tourtellot (1983:37) notes for the lowland Maya that "the average area of structures in Seibal dwelling classes seems not to change with distance from the site center."

This latter view of Mesoamerican social organization has been developed largely on the basis of recovered archaeological data. The discovery of luxury items and elaborate architecture and burials outside of the site epicenter is seen as indicating that the strict conception of "center-equals-elite" residence and "periphery-equals-peasant" occupation is incorrect. This does not mean that the site epicenters were not used by the elite, for clearly they were (see, for example, Blanton 1978:20-21, 64); however, not all elites were physically situated in the site epicenter. The archaeological recovery of luxury items in a large number of contexts throughout a site and its environs is also suggestive of a larger proportion of consumers (cf. A. Chase and D. Chase 1989) than some have suggested (Adams 1981; Webster 1985b), although some models of site organization deny a market function to a primate center (Blanton 1978:36). Market economy or not, the recorded distributions and patterns of luxury items and architecture within the Valley of Mexico, the Valley of Oaxaca, and the lowland Maya area during the Classic and Postclassic periods are indicative of a complexity conforming with Carol Smith's (1976) expectations of an extremely advanced economic system representing a high level of state organization.

Definitions and Assumptions

Based upon both archaeology and ethnohistory, it would seem that Classic and Postclassic Mesoamerican social organization was less clear-cut than a simple two-class system, for there appear to have been varying intermediate categories of individuals. Problems in the usage and theoretical definition of the term "elite" are also evident. If the archaeological data indicate that a large number of people had access to luxury goods, then it is perhaps inappropriate to use those goods alone to identify individuals as belonging to the elite. Rather, the ascription of an individual or architectural group to the elite requires careful consideration of a series of variables (see Haviland 1982:429; Sabloff 1983:419-20).

While it may be quite clear when one has found a royal burial based on its location, the associated objects, and perhaps even the hieroglyphic texts present, a large number of impressive remains are not so easily remanded to elite status. These remains have been ascribed to a "secondary elite" (Adams 1981:342) or an "upper class" (Adams 1970:493), often seen as being a minute segment of society. Yet the use of the word "class" (see Kurjack 1974:6 for a definition) may be inappropriate (see also Webster 1985b:385 for concordance on this point, but for a different reason), for we do not know whether Mesoamerican society was truly a class system. The hereditary nature of the nobility is stressed throughout Mesoamerica (Tozzer 1941; Haviland 1968:101; Thompson 1973; Spores 1983); one must therefore wonder if it was a simple matter to move from one status or role to another, as is indicated by the use of the word "class." The intermediate group of people defined archaeologically by their possession of luxury or high status material remains could be characterized—in keeping with the Western use of the term "elite"—by a similarly materialistic label such as "bourgeoisie." However, in order to avoid the other connotations of this term, perhaps a rough translation of the more neutral Maya term *azmen uinic* or "middle men" might better be employed. No matter which term is used, the important point is that this group existed.

While the elite may have controlled "political administration, formal religious activities, architectural planning and direction, and leadership in warfare" (Adams 1970:490), they were aided by a larger number of nonelite individuals who had various degrees of access to the trappings accorded the formal elite. It is these individuals—the "middle men" using the correlated Maya term—who appear to have constituted a sizable percentage of certain Mesoamerican societies. Whatever the term—"bourgeoisie" or "middle men"—such a distinction is directly reflective of an archaeologically based model that does not emphasize a simple two-group system in Mesoamerica.

A question also remains as to the relationships between the various groups in Mesoamerican society and the system(s) of production and distribution. Occupational specialization is generally assumed for all Mesoamerican civilizations (Adams 1970; Becker 1973; Blanton et al. 1981:36-39); explicit description of Aztec merchandise (Berdan 1986) suggests this specialization was extensive. Attempts have been made to reconstruct prehistoric economic systems (Isaac 1986a; McAnany and Isaac 1989). For the Maya, R. E. W. Adams (1970:490) has suggested that there must have been armorers, costume makers, sculptors, scribes, accountants, and musicians and entertainers, as well as stone-cutters and masons. M. Becker (1973) has suggested that there must have been dentists, woodcarvers, stucco-workers, and monument carvers. To this list we would add artists, priests, and architects as well as warriors, police, and adjudicators. Little evidence has actually been recovered that shows other than "potters" (Fry and Cox 1974) and "knappers" (Shafer and Hester 1983, 1986). Epigraphic work indicates specializations in vessel painting (Stuart 1988; Houston, Stuart, and Taube 1988) as well as monument carving and plaster working (N. Grube, personal communication, 1990). Such specialists also appeared to be mobile, traveling from site to site within a single political area (Stuart 1988; N. Grube, personal communication, 1990). Merchants along with many of these specialists probably were individuals of intermediate status or "middle men," individuals with varying degrees of access to elite items, even if lacking a noble birthright.

In spite of the widely known arguments for occupational specialization, there are those who would see Maya society, in particular, as composed of less than 10 percent consumers and at least 90 percent producers. But consumers and producers of what? Some suggest that the Maya were not commercialized, that there was little in the way of crop production for anything beyond the local area, and that there is little actual evidence of craft specialization, particularly as compared with the Mexican highland areas (Webster 1985b). While the identification of occupational specialization is in fact a problem, as noted above, there are sites that indicate the specialization of entire communities (such as lithics at Colha—Shafer and Hester 1983, 1986; or food items in the Hondo Valley and Candelaria Flood Plain—Siemens 1978:124, 1982:216-7; Turner 1978:181; Turner and Harrison 1983:252-3) as well as ethnohistoric indications of commerce, trade, and specialization (Roys 1943:46-56) demonstrating that production often did involve wider areas or markets. In addition, ethnohistoric notations of markets (Tozzer 1941:96), provisional monetary units (Tozzer 1941:94; Roys 1943:52), and terms for various specialized laborers (Martínez Hernández 1929:74-111; Roys 1943:46), imply that there probably were more complicated systems of production and distribution than can yet be reconstructed from archaeological evidence.

The actual identification of elites, "middle men," and commoners can be accommodated using traditional archaeological data, but with a bit more rigor than has sometimes been used in the past. Energy expenditure in burial preparation, house and platform construction, access to basic resources, and the movement of luxury goods can be used to help identify status distinctions. However, there must be realization that differences uncovered may reflect, but not solely equate with, elite status. Michael Smith (1987b) demonstrates the difficulty in making simple correlations between household wealth and status because of a large number of complicating factors such as family size, developmental cycle, and the occupation of household members. There is no universal agreement among researchers and data bases when it comes to such considerations (if they are recognized). Even a consideration of energy expenditure (cf. Sidrys 1976, Tourtellot 1988b) in relation to goods and constructions may not be indicative of elite use or restrictions. The elite themselves may represent the apex of labor investment in interments; alternatively, their burials may be identifiable by their placement in key locations at the site and written indications of relationships or positions of power. At the site of Tikal, H. Moholy-Nagy et al. (1984:116) notes that, although "obsidian from different sources was preferred for different types of artifacts," source distance was not a factor in utilitarian as opposed to ceremonial function, citing the fact that green obsidian (central Mexico) blades and points were commonly found in general excavations and utilitarian contexts while most eccentric obsidians found in ceremonial contexts were of gray obsidian from highland Guatemala sources. Indeed, the very association of obsidian with elite usage has been questioned for the end of the Late Classic period in the central Peten of Guatemala based on its ubiquitous appearance in most contexts (P. Rice et al. 1985:601). Greater effort must also be expended in identifying symbols of elite authority as opposed to luxury items.

One further series of relationships also needs to be taken into account: the connections among the peoples of the various sites and regions within Mesoamerica. There are obvious differences in material remains among sites (see, for example, Ashmore and Sharer 1978:17 for Quirigua). Sites are most often assumed to fit into hierarchies (Hammond 1975; Marcus 1976a; Adams 1981; Adams and Jones 1981; Blanton et al. 1981:30-32; Harrison 1981; but see also Haviland 1981) with "central places" filling the majority of administrative, economic, and religious functions and middle- or lower-order places serving subsidiary and sometimes specialized functions. The implications for elites are clear—it is expected that the ranking of nobility may exist not only at a single site, but among sites within a region. Presumably this should be indicated in distinctions in burial data as well as in the evidence of architecture (Price 1978) and ritual activity (D. Chase 1985b, 1986, 1988), with the apex representations of each data set being located in the highest-order center. Importantly, such a hierarchical model may reflect economic specialization, as borne out in both archaeological and ethnohistoric data. If specialization is likely to exist primarily at the subsidiary centers (see, for example, Shafer and Hester 1986:163), then one might not expect these workshops and activity areas in abundance within the central places themselves—thus, the potential problem in identifying division of labor and workshops in Classic period Maya archaeology.

Traditionally, highland Mesoamerica has always been viewed as having a more highly stratified social organization than that inferred for the lowland Maya area (Sanders 1981a:369); yet, it is debatable whether or not this is in fact the case. The elites in highland regions of Mesoamerica are seen as being easily identified, often associated with particular building forms (Blanton 1978:30); the topic of elites in the Maya area raises more discussion and little agreement. In part, much of the divergence of thought between the two areas may be due to differing research methods and techniques (D. Chase 1985c). Many of the highland syntheses (Blanton 1978; Sanders et al. 1979—but not all, see parts of Flannery and Marcus 1983a) are based on traditions of surface reconnaissance without associated large-scale excavation, a situation that more easily permits sweeping statements and generalizations—especially given the smaller body of potentially conflicting data provided when excavation is not undertaken. In the Maya area extensive excavation and mapping have almost always been conjoined; such a research design often leads to interpretational problems of grand schemes that have been suggested based on surface analysis alone (see, for instance, Haviland 1981). That general statements of cultural evolution, or agreements about such development, are rare in the Maya area is partially due to the extremely rich and varied data base that exists in the Maya lowlands. Others, however, would argue that the disagreement over an understanding of Maya society is due to archaeologists being overly concerned with the elite to the detriment of any investigation of the peasant lifestyle (Rathje 1983). We would note, however, that this criticism is misguided. Without firm knowledge of the Maya elite, the individuals responsible for setting the tenor of lifestyle and the belief systems found throughout the Maya social order, one has little chance of understanding the rest of Maya society; the same holds true for the rest of Mesoamerica (see Blanton et al. 1981:249-250). More studies identifying and indicating relationships among the various levels of Mesoamerican societies are needed.

Concluding Statements

From this discussion it should be apparent that a number of difficulties remain with regard to the archaeological identification of elites in Mesoamerica. There is a distinct divergence between the theoretical definition of elites and their archaeological identification. Identifying the skeletal or residential remains of the powerful in society is not an archaeological absolute—for power, while often associated with material wealth, is not automatically correlated with specific kinds and numbers of items or a particular house plan; these correlations are inferred and neither direct nor absolute. Even the identification of rulers is often a problematic and controversial task.

The relationships that exist within and between social organizations in the various parts of Mesoamerica are also somewhat unclear. The traditional interpretations based on ethnohistory point in all areas to the existence of two basic classes of people—nobles and commoners. Most archaeologists would see the ruling elite in both the lowlands and the highlands as being less than 5 percent of the population, but the ways in which such a percentage is derived vary dramatically from one site or researcher to another. Sometimes the distinction is made solely on the numbers of elaborate vs. nonelaborate residences; in other cases, the percentage is derived from available sleeping space in "palaces;" in some instances, figures are derived on the basis of the presence of specific burial goods. Yet, regardless of the part of Mesoamerica under examination, the reconstruction of its Precolumbian society is incomplete. If elite houses are posited as being identified, one generally lacks an elite burial sample; if rulers have been identified in a burial sample, it is often not known where they resided. The establishment of a percentage of elite in any society based solely on a single attribute, whether house size or burial items, is likely to be misleading (see also Haviland 1982:429 and Sabloff 1983:419-420)—unless those variables have been considered in broader contexts and carefully cross-checked with other data.

Settlement archaeology, as developed in the Maya area by G. R. Willey et al. (1965), was defined to include all of the inhabitants of a particular area regardless of their social status. As operationalized, however, settlement pattern studies often have focused on commoners to the exclusion of other members of society. Even from its earliest manifestation, settlement pattern archaeology in the Maya area was examining a complex network of social relationships without defining how this cacophony of people fit into an overall site or regional organization (see Willey 1956:779; W. Coe 1966). A study of any one group will be incomplete without the placement of that group in a wider social context. We would further argue that, if one wishes to investigate the lower segment of Maya society, extensive vacant terrain excavation must be undertaken in order to identify house pads that leave very little in the way of material remains (see Kurjack 1974:29; Folan et al. 1982:435; Tourtellot 1983:44; and D. Chase 1990). As in other areas of Mesoamerica (such as the Valley of Mexico and Oaxaca), Maya settlement archaeology has illustrated how a specific site epicenter, composed of monumental civic architecture, fits into a wider habitation pattern (Kurjack 1974 for Dzibilchaltun; Webster 1985a for Copan; Ashmore 1981b for Quirigua; Tourtellot 1982, 1988b for Seibal; Haviland 1963, 1970 and Puleston 1983 for Tikal; A. Chase and D. Chase 1987b for Caracol). Yet, by accomplishing this, new questions have appropriately been raised that point to problems in our older models. These questions relate directly to the role of elites in Maya society and, more importantly, to how their centers were organized and functioned within a larger context—problems of obvious interest to all Mesoamericanists.

There is a need to resolve the difference of opinion as to where the elite and "middle men" lived—in the center itself, elsewhere in the core, or distributed throughout the site. Such considerations are directly related to other aspects of the social, political, and economic institutions of a group as well as to the level of complexity achieved by a particular society. Archaeologists themselves also vary in their adherence to a strict two-class model of society; part of this internal disagreement may stem from distinctive research strategies. Some argue for the presence of a relatively large group of intermediate-status individuals; others apparently find enough distinction in the use of the terms "noble" and "commoner." Our own work suggests that a middle-ground group—perhaps even a "bourgeoisie"—is a material reality regardless of the political truth of the sixteenth century historians. Ancient Mesoamerica may have professed an ideal or even heuristic two-tier system; but, in most cases, there must have been other principles involved that affected the economic and material well-being of many members of its society.

Monumental architecture has been associated with elites, and centrally located monuments have been seen as representative of the ruling elite in their glorification of divine kings (J. Marcus 1974b; L. Schele and M. Miller 1986). While such a focus serves to reinforce the distinctiveness of the elite, it does little to reflect the actual mechanizations of Mesoamerican society. The elite may be seen as a "prime mover" in the development of society and also as an important force in the integration and organization of society. Regardless of how they are conceived, elites are difficult to identify archaeologically, and one is left with an array of questions. How does one view Mesoamerican society and how complex is it? Are there administrative buildings in the site core? Do palaces represent elite residences, administrative buildings, schools, storage facilities, or a combination of these functions? If there are markets (W. Coe 1967:73) and market economies (Fry 1979) at such sites as Tikal, what are the implications of this for the organization of a Mesoamerican site?

There is still a long way to go before archaeologists can adequately model ancient Mesoamerican society. We need more studies on who the elite were, where they lived, what they ate, and what they owned. And, just as importantly, we also need to know how these data relate to other contemporary social groups and how, or whether, the social system changed over time. Delineation of the complexity of Mesoamerican social organization is critical to our assessments of its political organization. Identification of the economic system is key not only for assessing the political order, but also for interpreting models of change. For how can one assess the impact of elite demands on the population if we can't ascertain who they were, where they lived, and how they and their imputed demands related to the rest of Mesoamerican society?

Notes

1. This paper is essentially the same version that was circulated to all volume participants in 1987. It has been left largely intact as a number of the volume's participants make reference to it. Even though little changed, we believe that the substantive message remains as valid now as it was then.

2. Interregional Exchange as Elite Behavior: An Evolutionary Perspective

Kenneth Hirth

ARCHAEOLOGISTS working in Mesoamerica have not been particularly successful in identifying the role of elites in the course of cultural development. The reasons for this are twofold. First, the diacritics used to identify elites are either all encompassing or too imprecise to do so in a consistent fashion. This makes it difficult to identify the behavior of elites in archaeological contexts and to interpret their role in implementing culture change. Second, and more importantly, archaeologists frequently do not have a good working model of elite behavior necessary to develop analytical concepts useful for studying and reconstructing elite interaction. These two problems fall comfortably within the standard dilemma of archaeological theory and method: until investigators have a comprehensive understanding of the type of behavior under investigation they will not be able to develop an appropriate methodology for studying it using archaeological data.

In this paper I do not focus on a particular group or region in Mesoamerica or on the methodological problems incumbent upon the study of elites in archaeological settings. Rather, I address a more fundamental concern: the development of an accurate conceptual understanding of elite behavior.

The recent work of George Marcus (1983a) has shown that elite behavior is multifaceted in content and difficult to characterize in terms of how it actualizes culture change. Scholars have long agreed, however, that elites can be defined in relative terms by their ability to control, produce, or mobilize large quantities of resources within their respective societies. While the *forms* of resource control are extremely diverse, the *basis* on which the elite maintain claims on resources is relatively simple and revolves around norms of resource ownership and access to labor within societies. A primary focus of elite behavior is to influence or mediate the flow of resources through the production and/or distribution networks. It is not surprising, therefore, to find elites involved in the movement of materials between regions and over long distances, since this is one facet of a more generalized concern with resource control.

This paper does not attempt to model elite behavior in a synthetic or comprehensive fashion. Rather, it focuses on a single but important aspect of elite behavior: the development of regional and interregional interaction networks involving the production and exchange of primitive valuables. In the process I hope to clarify several aspects of elite behavior and to foster the development of analytical concepts appropriate for studying and identifying elites from an archaeological perspective. In Mesoamerica regional and interregional exchange appears to have been a significant factor in structuring sociopolitical relations within ranked agrarian societies.[1] During the Formative period the intensification of interregional exchange was coincident with the appearance of permanent social elites and growing regional populations.

By "elites" I mean specifically individuals with ranked status who occupy positions of permanent authority within their corresponding communities or social units.[2] While I am not arguing that interregional exchange should be viewed as a "prime mover" explanation for the evolution of complex social stratification in Mesoamerica, I do believe that its role as an integrative mechanism during the Formative period has been largely overlooked in favor of production-oriented explanatory paradigms.[3] The archaeological record provides overwhelming documentation for the existence and importance of interregional exchange and elite interaction during the Formative period (Hirth 1984). It is perhaps paradoxical that it is the pervasiveness of interregional exchange during this period that has led archaeologists to underestimate its importance as an integrative mechanism shaping the formation of social hierarchies.

Interregional Exchange as Elite Behavior

Research has established that prestige and utilitarian goods were exchanged widely and in significant quantities throughout Mesoamerica by 1000 B.C. (Parsons and Price 1971). Obsidian was one of the earliest utilitarian commodities to circulate between regions. J. W. Pires-Ferreira (1975, 1978b) has documented four separate exchange networks that moved obsidian over distances up to 700 km from their source deposits. Prestige goods including marine shell and a variety of iron ore types were also exchanged throughout Mesoamerica during the Early Formative period (1500-900 B.C.; see Pires-Ferreira 1976, 1978a, 1978c; Coe and Diehl 1980:391; Winter 1984; Grove 1987a:376-80). Furthermore, jade and serpentine manufactured into ornaments and portable carvings were circulated widely as high prestige items after 1000 B.C. (Grove 1974). Long-distance trade continued to supply elites with exotic objects and prestige goods until the Spanish conquest; this trade, together with local subsistence support and the tribute collected from conquered provinces, provided the economic foundation for all the Late Horizon states (Berdan 1978).

Transportation costs limited the type and amount of commodities that moved through interregional exchange networks during all periods of Mesoamerican prehistory. For the most part, only high-value items such as jade, turquoise, cotton textiles, obsidian, marble, marine shell, cacao, and copper moved over large distances between regions. Except for obsidian, most of these goods fall within categories that archaeologists label primitive valuables, prestige goods, or sumptuary items. These goods are important because of their role in the regulation of social and economic relationships within societies lacking modern market mechanisms (Dalton 1981; D'Altroy and Earle 1985).

Staple commodities like maize and beans rarely moved far from their source of production even under tribute conditions. R. D. Drennan (1984) has suggested that transportation systems made it energetically inefficient to move staple commodities beyond 275 km from where they were produced. It is significant that the political power of elites in Mesoamerica did not reside in their custodial management of staple surpluses as it did in some ancient societies (Brumfiel and Earle 1987:6). In Mesoamerica staple commodities were stored at the household level and mobilized through periodic markets to meet fluctuating levels of resource demand. These markets were special places where individuals pursued their individual economic objectives without deference to differences in social or economic rank. Although the elite assumed supervisory responsibility for the operation of these marketplaces, they had only indirect control over the exchanges or the resources moving within them.

Mesoamerican elites were more directly involved with the control of prestige goods, which moved either through interregional exchange networks or within the broader context of elite interaction. Cross-cultural research has shown that interregional exchange was an important source of elite wealth, power, and prestige in many times and places in prehistory (Curtin 1984; Carol Smith 1976). Scholars working in Mesoamerica have traditionally interpreted the role of interregional exchange in one of two ways. First, as a means for controlling access to strategic utilitarian and/or consumable subsistence resources used by all members of the society. Approaches that emphasize control over subsistence commodities as the basis for elite power I refer to as resource procurement models of exchange. A second and more common perspective is to view interregional exchange as a means by which prestige goods were procured for use by elites to reinforce or modify existing social hierarchies. I refer to this approach as the status legitimation model of exchange, discussed in greater detail below.

Resource procurement models encompass a variety of analytical perspectives on the evolution of ranked societies in Mesoamerica. Examples include: (1) the symbiotic interaction model (Sanders 1956) for cultural interaction between adjacent but distinct environmental zones; (2) the utilitarian monopoly model (Rathje 1971, 1972) for control of salt and lithic resources in the Maya lowlands; (3) the resource-banking model where primitive valuables obtained through trade can be converted into food during periods of resource shortfall (Flannery and Schoenwetter 1970; Halstead and O'Shea 1989); and (4) the subsistence support model where exchange of primitive valuables guarantees and solidifies exchange networks through which utilitarian commodities and foodstuffs also move (Rappaport 1968:107; Pires-

Ferreira and Flannery 1976). The resource procurement model is also compatible with some recent discussions of state-level development in Mesoamerica. In central Mexico, for example, the emergence of Teotihuacan as a major political center has been discussed in terms of its monopolistic control over both the production (Millon 1973) and the distribution of obsidian (Sanders and Santley 1983).

Resource procurement models assert that the primary purpose of interregional exchange is to maintain access to the subsistence resources or utilitarian craft products necessary to exploit successfully the local environment. From an evolutionary perspective, these models argue that political power stems from a leader's ability to mobilize and control subsistence resources for survival. Vital resources not available from local sources must be acquired through forms of exchange from groups that have access to them. When this occurs, managing the procurement and distribution of scarce resources provides the elites with an opportunity to develop clientage dependencies within their respective groups. Maintaining exclusivity of sources of supply can become the basis for local authority, which is why interregional exchanges are sporadic, highly ritualized, or embedded within other forms of interelite interaction.

While survival depends upon maintaining access to adequate stocks of food and tools, it does not follow that the primary role of interregional exchange falls within the realm of subsistence provisioning. Examples exist throughout Mesoamerica where many utilitarian commodities were exchanged between regions even when local commodities such as chert, limestone, or andesite could perform many of the same cutting and grinding functions as imported obsidian and basalt. Available ethnographic literature indicates that a great amount of interregional exchange is focused *primarily* on obtaining primitive valuables that are unaccompanied by any corresponding utilitarian commodities (Dalton 1981). In fact, when we examine the nonstaple utilitarian commodities such as cutting and grinding tools circulating between ranked societies during the Formative, we find that their usage rates are so low that we may question whether households could have been controlled in such a direct and simple fashion. Clearly, there are important reasons leading to the establishment of interregional exchange networks other than direct resource procurement.

Interregional Exchange as Status Interaction

The status legitimation model takes a different approach. It assumes: (1) that interregional exchange of primitive valuables is important for its own sake and frequently involves the expenditure of considerable energy in stateless societies and (2) that the movement of these items is not dependent upon the concurrent exchange of staple or utilitarian goods. Perhaps the most influential piece of Mesoamerican research adopting the status legitimation model has been Kent Flannery's 1968 article on interregional exchange in the Valley of Oaxaca. In this work the procurement of Olmec style materials was the focus of extensive interelite exchange networks linking many areas of Mesoamerica during the Early and Middle Formative periods (Flannery 1968; Grove 1974a). The acquisition of these materials was a means by which local elites affiliated themselves with groups on the Gulf Coast. Demonstrating these affiliations strengthened the authority of elites within their respective societies, which was the primary goal of interregional interaction.

A common problem of the status legitimation model is that the investigation often focuses on the prestige goods rather than on how they were used by elites in the formation and validation of ranked statuses. One of the simplifying assumptions most frequently employed about the prestige goods moving through exchange networks is that their primary function was publicly to proclaim the rank and status of their owner. Here archaeologists have difficulty distinguishing badges of authority, which represent rank, from generalized wealth that elites control and use to suit their political and social purposes. This distinction is important because it clarifies a difference in how elites both perceive and use primitive wealth.

Unfortunately, archaeologists usually combine badges of authority and undifferentiated wealth under a single analytical category of prestige or status goods. While this practice may be useful methodologically to identify elites from archaeological materials, it obscures the fact that relatively few primitive valuables are actually intended to indicate rank in stateless societies. Primitive valuables are correlated with elites because of their scarcity and because elites control and make use of these and other available resources in mediating social relationships with neighboring groups. Badges of office frequently have precious value and should be perceived as a subset of the larger universe of primitive valuables. The functions of badges of authority and generalized wealth, however, are very different. Badges of authority characterize the rank of specific individuals or offices and are not highly mobile, while primitive valuables are produced and procured for the purpose of being used and distributed in a number of socially prescribed ways. This difference needs to be made explicit because it has important implications for the way archaeologists perceive, identify, and interpret elite behavior from material remains.

Another prevalent assumption found in the archaeological literature is that interregional exchange was a mechanism by which individuals acquired the status goods that defined and reinforced positions of social rank. The problem with this approach is twofold. First, it fosters an orientation that narrowly perceives primitive wealth as a status symbol rather than a dynamic currency for building social relationships. Second, and more importantly, it fosters the belief that rank is created by amassing private wealth. Rank is *not* acquired by obtaining badges of authority through interregional exchange. While exchange provides a mechanism to acquire private property within systems where usufruct rights rather than ownership define access to resources, it does not by itself provide an independent avenue for social advancement. Resource inventories acquired through exchange are useful only when they are used or reinvested in forging social alliances (Befu 1977). Archaeologists must discard the notion that the circulation of primitive valuables through interregional exchange networks was stimulated by a desire to obtain status markers (i.e., badges of authority) and begin to examine the more specific ways in which primitive valuables are used in the formation of social hierarchy.

Interregional Exchange and Alliance Formation

Although archaeologists have recognized the importance of interregional exchange in structuring social relationships, no unifying perspective has emerged that accounts for why it is so ubiquitous throughout Mesoamerica from 1000 B.C. onward. The perspective suggested here is that regional and interregional exchange is an important component of all subsistence systems and provides a network through which *social* relationships between nonkin can be established and expanded. Exchange relationships become important in building rank when community leaders use this framework to establish local alliance dependencies between one another that create a sphere of social interaction not replicated within their respective communities and to attract and build clientage relationships with less influential leaders at the regional level. Before discussing how elites utilize exchange relationships in building social hierarchy, it is useful to review why local exchange networks are a common feature of agrarian societies around the world.

The economies of stateless agricultural societies are characterized by two dominant features: (1) subsistence production is focused on and organized at the community level, and (2) producers strive for a balance between specialized and diversified production strategies.[4] These two characteristics are obviously interrelated. The community-based mode of production is a feature of both short and long fallow agricultural systems, and most forms of intercommunity cooperation in production do not appear until after the appearance of state-level institutions. Agricultural communities in nonmarket societies must engage in production strategies that minimize the risk of resource shortfall throughout the year. In these societies it is necessary to balance increases in production achieved through agricultural specialization with diversification strategies that minimize subsistence risk due to environmental fluctuation. W. T. Sanders and D. Webster (1978) have argued that the initial choices societies make to minimize subsistence risk play a major role in their long-term evolutionary trajectory. Diversification strategies designed to minimize risk may also inhibit the intensification of production within the subsistence system. Some common diversification strategies include intercropping, sequence planting, combining agriculture with a variety of alternative subsistence activities (e.g., hunting, fishing, wild resource collection, or arboriculture), or distributing agricultural plots in space to maximize ecotonal production differences (Murra 1975) or minimize the risk of harvest failure (Schneider 1981).

Extending kinship networks and developing reciprocal exchange relationships are also important ways in which societies offset periodic resource shortfall. This diversification strategy is based on expanding the means of distribution rather than the means of production (Carol Smith 1976, 1983). Diversification through distribution and diversification through production are different approaches for minimizing subsistence risk that may be implemented independently of one another. What is important for evolutionary development is that groups intensifying their production systems may still be able to maintain relatively low levels of subsistence risk if they intensify exchange relationships as a means to avoid resource shortfalls. As a result, exchange networks connecting autonomous village communities provide the framework within which interelite exchange networks are established. These networks precede and provide the foundation for subsequent regional political integration.

Under what conditions does interregional exchange become an important elite behavior? Research by George Dalton (1977, 1981) provides a framework for understanding the function of exchange relationships in ranked societies. Dalton has argued that all stateless societies are constrained by their inability to produce and mobilize large amounts of material goods. These constraints are a result of: (1) their small-scale and limited technology, which inhibits their ability to take advantage of economies of scale and achieve high levels of resource production, (2) the continual threat of famine exaggerated by the absence of regional markets or other distribution networks to offset periodic shortfalls in agricultural production, and (3) the absence of a jural-political body to maintain and regulate regional peace (Dalton 1981:22-23). In Dalton's model these constraints are mediated through elite behavior. These problems are regulated through ceremonial exchange, which allows kin-based societies to establish reliable systems of material provisioning. Evidence for interregional exchange identified in the archaeological record is a direct reflection of this ceremonial behavior. Since ceremonial exchange is a response to natural economic conditions, it will be a widespread occurrence throughout all stateless societies. Moreover, it will be predictable socioeconomic elite behavior.

The ethnographic record suggests that, within stateless societies, interelite ceremonial exchanges help to alleviate provisioning problems in two ways: (1) by providing a means of controlling or influencing labor, which represents the productive capacity of these societies, and (2) by developing mutual dependency relationships that can mobilize resources during emergency periods. In ranked societies leaders rarely have strong exclusionary control over the prime productive resources of land, flora, or fauna. Resources are not controlled directly through forms of private ownership; rather, access to resources is through hereditary usufruct claims and resources are produced by mobilizing labor within corporate groups. This distinction is important because it emphasizes that in ranked societies resources are produced and controlled *through the social relations of labor.* Resources can be accessed and exploited only as long as households, lineage heads, or community headmen have the labor to do so (Harner 1975). For this reason, mechanisms of social integration and clientage formation play a prime role in the evolution of social systems.

The social linkages of production may follow several distinct evolutionary trajectories depending on how elites attempt to control resource production. Leaders may, for instance, take on the direct responsibility of guaranteeing resource provisioning by expanding the level of subsistence production or storage capacities within their respective households. This "entrepreneurial approach" results in elites having larger and diversified households. These households include greater numbers of clients, wives, and affines whose production is used to support the leader's household, sponsor periodic feasts, and provide emergency provisioning to the rest of the community during periods of scarcity.

Elites also expand their households in a figurative sense by affiliating within them headmen from lineages and other social groups. This expands the elite household's access to resource areas and increases the amount of affiliated labor that can be called upon for subsistence support. The basis for the social rank, power, and prestige of a leader resides in the amount of labor he or she is able to influence or control. In stateless societies labor is not controlled directly; instead it is controlled through the leaders of respective corporate associations, membership in which may be defined in terms of kinship, mutual aid, ceremonial ties, or other obligations. This is important because it reduces the focus of labor control to a relatively small number of lineage or association leaders. Social hierarchies may appear without having to replace local kin-based social relationships with more centralized forms of governance. Instead social hierarchies are formed by building alliance relationships between regional elites through which local populations may be influenced or directed.

Relations of social dependence between lineage heads are established through marriage and the creation of clientage relationships. An important way in which these elite networks are reinforced is through the exchange and circulation of primitive valuables as gifts, bride wealth, exchange items, or special payments. Primitive valuables, and the promise of acquiring these and other forms of support, act as powerful stimuli for attracting lineage heads into alliance relationships (Blanton and Feinman 1984). I believe that it is through this process that large village centers made their initial appearance throughout Mesoamerica during the Formative period. Large community size would have been favored by village headmen because it provided more labor by which wealth could be created (Drennan 1987). Social control within these communities was probably mediated through co-resident lineage headmen who were linked to a community leader by both kinship and clientage relationships. Primitive valuables produced locally or acquired through interregional exchange were a currency for attracting, building, and solidifying social clientage within this setting.

A consistent problem of ranked societies is that regional distribution networks are never sufficiently large or internally developed to allow individual households to mediate extended periods of resource shortfall. Emergency provisioning is one of the roles that elites play for their respective groups, activated through interregional exchange networks. While individual households may also mobilize provisioning networks through their affines and any existing trading partners, elites can access more resources through mutual dependency relationships established with headmen in neighboring villages.

Emergency provisioning is an obligation that leaders have to their respective communities. Since elites control resources, they are the individuals to whom the community turns in times of resource shortfall. Local elites recognize this responsibility as an important condition of their authority and ally themselves with individuals who will assist them to fulfill these and other social obligations. Interregional alliances help reduce subsistence risk by accessing resources from unaffected areas or from different environmental zones. Although the ability of headmen to mobilize resources within these alliances may be limited, they are usually the *only* means available to sedentary groups of accessing emergency material support without having to resort to theft or outmigration. Local elites control wealth to the extent they are able to direct local labor. When a request for emergency support is activated through interelite networks, local leaders access resources, just as they mobilize support for periodic feasts. It is within interelite dependency networks that primitive valuables may be converted into consumable resources, as suggested by K. V. Flannery and J. Schoenwetter (1970). These conversions, however, are subject to the general availability of subsistence resources.

Since authority of leadership is validated from within their respective communities, elites emphasize their ability to provide emergency material support even though it may never be evoked. This is accomplished in the cycle of sponsoring and attending public ceremonies for neighboring groups where interelite participation and interaction play a prominent role in relation to food displays and feasting behavior. These sumptuary events reinforce the idea that leaders have the ability to mobilize resources through elite interaction with neighboring groups (Kobishchanow 1987). It is within this context that primitive valuables are very important and may be prominently displayed, not as status symbols, but as indicators of wealth and the ability to mobilize resources at both the local and regional levels.

Finally, it should not be forgotten that interregional interaction and alliance networks provide the primary political framework in which peaceful relationships can be negotiated at the regional level. The absence of a centralized jural-political structure means that the best way to regulate disputes between ranked societies is to maintain peace. Elites mediate disputes as they arise and before they result in open conflict. Ceremonial exchanges between headmen structure the relationships between their respective groups. They reduce the possibility of regional conflict and reinforce the peaceful relations that exist between local groups. Just as primitive valuables are prominent in interelite interaction, they also are employed as special payments required to end hostilities when they do break out (Dalton 1981:23).

Conclusions

The foregoing discussion has several important implications for understanding and identifying elite behavior in archaeological contexts. The first of these is that regional and interregional interaction networks are important components of the subsistence strategy that help reduce subsistence risk by expanding the distribution system in stateless societies. Furthermore, interregional exchange can be expected to be present in all sedentary agricultural societies that are subject to periodic or fluctuating subsistence risk. Emerging elites are involved in mediating these problems and make use of interregional exchange to form social networks and dependency relationships within their societies. Interelite exchange networks provide three important functions. First, they provide the elite with an opportunity to broaden control over resource production through control of the social relations of labor. This takes its most prominent form in the formation of interelite clientages as lineage heads of smaller groups are recruited by or rely upon the support of prominent elites from larger or more influential groups. Second, interelite networks provide emergency provisioning in times of resource shortfall. In the absence of regional market systems or alternative forms of economic integration, these networks represent the broadest system through which resources may be mobilized to alleviate local shortfalls. Finally, interelite alliance networks provide the jural-political framework within which leaders mediate disputes and maintain peace between their respective groups. They establish the social and political relationships that are expected to be replicated between communities at the regional level.

The mechanisms involved in forming social hierarchies through interelite alliances duplicate those operating in household and lineage maintenance networks. The pattern and frequency of interregional elite exchange replicate the reciprocal relationships that distribute food and other resources between households both within and between communities throughout the region. An important component of interelite interaction is the procurement and exchange of primitive valuables. These valuables are used in the ceremonial exchanges that cement alliances between the leaders of different groups. Interregional exchange provides the elite with a means of amassing large stocks of primitive valuables that can be used to structure social relationships. They are used most frequently by elites to attract and establish personal clientage relationships with headmen of smaller or lesser-ranked groups. These clientage relationships provide the foundation for social hierarchies at the regional level.

From an evolutionary perspective, societies increase in complexity as they are able to produce and mobilize larger quantities of resources. In ranked societies, control over resource production is always *indirect* and mediated through the social relations of labor. Social alliances are the means of mediating the social relations of labor, and interregional exchange plays an important role in establishing and maintaining these alliances. It provides a structure to regularize interelite social and political relations at the regional level. Interregional exchange also provides a means of obtaining primitive valuables used to structure social relationships within respective groups. Clientage and alliance relationships provide the means by which elites control resources and operationalize subsistence production. Until the appearance of class society, private property, and the emergence of the state, interelite networks remain the means through which forms of economic work are organized and social and political needs are mediated.[5]

Archaeologists will be inhibited in their investigation of these evolutionary processes as long as they view primitive valuables solely as prestige goods whose purpose is simply to mark social status. Primitive valuables are better viewed as generalized wealth used to create and reinforce relationships within the society. The distribution of these goods reflects patterns of interelite alliance and interaction more than it defines social status. Archaeologists need to broaden their understanding of elite behavior and how it contributes to the formation of social hierarchies. This paper has attempted to clarify why I consider interregional exchange to have been an important elite activity. The data indicate that the development of complex regional and interregional exchange networks was integrally related to the emergence of ranked societies throughout Mesoamerica during the Formative period. Conversely, however, the data do *not* support the claim that intensive interregional exchange alone was sufficient to bring about the appearance of the Mesoamerican state. Future research will need to determine how social hierarchies based on interelite alliances and relative rank were transformed into permanently centralized and stratified forms of social control.

Notes

1. The traditional definition of a ranked society is one where the positions of valued and ranked status are limited so that there are fewer positions of leadership than there are individuals capable of leading (Fried 1967:109). This includes groups organized as both tribes and

chiefdoms in E. Service's (1962) classification of primitive social organization. Because this paper focuses on the relationship between interregional exchange and the role of elites, many of my comments refer specifically to those ranked societies in which forms of centralized leadership appear and become a feature of internal sociopolitical relations. While interregional exchange may also be present among acephalous societies based on segmentary lineage systems (Evans-Pritchard 1940) or age grading (Schneider 1979), it has different social implications than when permanent leadership is present and superordinate to lineage affiliation.

2. Inherent in my use of the term "elite" is the principle that they also maintain some privileged claim to strategic resources within their respective societies. In Africa differential access to resources appears to be a common feature and the basis of power in *all* sociopolitical systems where there is centralized leadership (Schneider 1981:143-66). For a discussion of the problems associated with defining elites in behavioral terms, see G. Marcus (1983a).

3. Many of the discussions concerning cultural evolution in Mesoamerica have favored processes that emphasize continuity in cultural development from the formation of chiefdom societies to the emergence of the early states. The two most common causes advocated for culture change have been population growth and agricultural intensification (Sanders and Price 1968; Carneiro 1970; Sanders 1972; Adams 1977a, 1977b). I believe that the specific factors leading to the appearance and elaboration of ranked societies were probably different from those resulting in the emergence of class society and the state. My position here is that inter-elite exchange resulting in the local and interregional movement of resources is at least as important as population growth and agricultural intensification for the growth of regional chiefdoms throughout Mesoamerica during the Formative period.

4. These same characteristics are found in economies in contemporary and historic state-level societies where market integration is low, transportation networks are poor, and production for consumption dominates production decisions.

5. It can be argued that these relationships continue to be important long after state forms of governance are present. For a discussion of how interregional elite alliances provided access to resources among the Late Postclassic Aztecs, see Michael Smith (1986).

3. Elites and the Changing Organization of Classic Maya Society

Arlen F. Chase

MUCH of what we know about the organization of Classic period Maya society derives from remains that are deemed elite. In spite of substantial "settlement pattern" work in the last three decades, it is the Maya elite that still provide the primary standard by which aspects of Classic society are judged. Epigraphic texts and iconographic scenes found on numerous carved stones and painted vessels provide data concerning the leading families—and, by extension, the elite—of the time. Large, well-built architecture is generally ascribed to this group of individuals, as are most items perceived to be of value. Yet not all aspects of Maya elites or the organization that they provided for their society are easily seen in the archaeological record; thus, the majority of our fleshed-out interpretations about the upper tier of the Classic Maya come from models that are taken from a variety of nonarchaeological sources. In fact, much of what we believe about Maya society does not come from data about the Maya at all, but rather from suppositions premised on the models being used. Thus, in order to understand the organization of Maya society and its elite, one first needs to identify the diverse models that are used to structure the archaeological remains. When this is done, it becomes clear that the archaeological data offer distinctive clues as to how such models should be structured or, rather, restructured.

Views of Classic Maya Social Organization

Models offered for the interpretation of Classic Maya society rely heavily on the social distinctions inferred by the use of the words "commoner" and "noble/elite." Yet, these two classes of people are not clearly seen in the archaeological record (Chase and Chase, introductory paper in this volume). In general, three different models of Classic Maya society have been offered. These versions of Maya society may be termed (1) egalitarian, (2) two-class, and (3) complex.

Based on modern-day ethnographic work, E. Z. Vogt (1961, 1969, 1983; Vogt and Cancian 1970) suggested that Classic Maya society was basically egalitarian, with rotating civic or ceremonial offices. Classic Maya were viewed as having dispersed populations and vacant ceremonial centers; important offices would have rotated among the different lineages much like the modern-day cargo system found in Zinacantan and other contemporary Maya communities. Associated research (Willey 1956; Bullard 1960, 1964) in the Southern lowlands initially tended to suggest a potential archaeological fit with such a model. It is likely, however, that the modern system of rotating offices is largely the result of Spanish contact and influence on modern Maya community structure (Price 1974:461). With more recent archaeological work and the discovery of large populations in and around Classic period Maya centers (Haviland 1970; Rice and Puleston 1981:144-45), this model has been generally discredited. It should be noted, however, that D. A. Freidel (1981; see also Vogt 1983:105) has attempted a bond between some elements of the egalitarian and feudal models with the use of a "pilgrimage-fair" approach to Maya centers.

J. Eric Thompson (1942 [1927], 1966 [1954]) is largely responsible for the two-class model of Maya society that dominates present-day conceptions of Classic period Maya social structure. Thompson's (1931, 1942 [1927], 1966 [1954]; see also Becker 1979:11) dichotomy between "priest" and "peasant" to some degree has been directly replaced in modern parlance by "elite" and "commoner." His model presented a Maya site as being less than a city, something he first termed a "ceremonial center" (1931:334) and then equated with vacant "religious centers" (1942 [1927]:12-13); this conception of a Maya center has recently been revived by Gair Tourtellot (n.d.). Ethnohistory was utilized with Thompson's model to further develop a two-class society comprised of nobles and commoners with scant reference being also made to the existence of slaves. Ethnohistorical data are often called upon (Roys 1943, 1965; Folan et al. 1982; J. Marcus, this volume) to support this model despite the fact that the same ethnohistorical material can also be used to support a more complex model (D. Chase 1986:364, this volume) and despite the fact that much of this ethnohistory was recorded by people who did not understand Maya culture and may have had an ethnocentric bias. Thompson's "ceremonial center" and his conception of it proved an easy fit to Bishop Landa's proposed "concentric model" of a Maya center where the temples occupied the node of the town and were surrounded by the residences of important people or elites, with the commoners living on the peripheries (Tozzer 1941:62-64). Serious questions have been raised as to whether Landa's model of a Maya town was even based on the Maya, for he freely helped himself to data provided by other contact period writers who dealt with cultures further south in Central America (D. Chase 1986:362-63). Furthermore, Classic (Ashmore 1981c, 1988:160-61; A. Chase and D. Chase 1987b:57-58) and Late Postclassic (D. Chase 1986:366; D. Chase and A. Chase 1986a, 1986b:25, 1988:68-71) archaeological data do not tend to support this spatial conception of a Maya community.

More recently, the imputed two-class model has been utilized in projections of Maya society as being either nonstate or prestatelike and relatively noncomplex. Support for this position is largely derived from analogies to societies outside of the New World. Under a feudal model, Classic period Maya elites are believed to have occupied the central architecture of a given site, surrounded by a huge mass of farming peasants (Adams and Smith 1981; but also see Webster 1985b). These small number of elites are also seen as having rotated among several sites and palaces (Adams and Smith 1981:343). Ethnographic analogy to African societies has also been used in conjunction with the two-class model to attempt to see the Maya as either a developed chiefdom or a "patron-client state" (Sanders 1981a:369). Joyce Marcus (1983c:472-73) has properly pointed to the problems involved with such approaches, noting that "one can find closer analogies to other Mesoamerican states than to . . . any model we could borrow from another hemisphere." Other models currently in vogue and based on the two-class construction of Maya society include the "segmentary state" model (Fox 1987, 1989; see conclusion, this volume) and the related concept of the Maya as having had "regal-ritual" cities (Sanders and Webster 1988).

The third model that has been applied to Classic Maya society was partly developed on the basis of the archaeological data, rather than from ethnography or ethnohistory; this model views the Maya as an urban and highly complex civilization (Haviland 1967, 1970, 1981; Adams 1970; Becker 1973; Folan et al. 1983; D. Chase, A. Chase and W. Haviland 1990). Based on archaeological assessments of wealth, some have also postulated the existence of an emerging middle class (Willey et al. 1965:5; Sabloff 1975a; Morley, Brainerd, and Sharer 1983:226) and additionally point to inferences of occupational specialization, often within a regional frame of reference. The nature of this third model, however, is hotly contested by others who emphatically state that "there was no Maya 'middle class'" (J. Marcus 1983c:470; see also Webster 1985b) and who subsume any specialization within a rigidly structured two-class system; while some complexity is recognized, it is deemed the exclusive purview of the nobles—seen as the elite— and their retainers—seen as the specialists—who are believed to have made up a maximum of 10 percent of Maya society, as compared to simpler commoners, who constituted the other 90 percent (Webster 1985b:385). Contrary to this view, the Caracol data—portions of which are presented below—fully support the complexity implied in the third model; these data point to the existence of more than two components of Maya society and effectively negate the use of any dualistic division of Maya society into a very small group of nobility-elite consumers and a very large group of commoner-peasantry nonconsumers.

A large part of the problem in modeling Classic period Maya society lies squarely in the archaeological realm and in the way that Maya sites and regions are researched. Either the archaeological data are difficult to interpret or, more likely, insufficient data are recovered that are pertinent to problems concerning social and political organization. Most Maya sites are huge sprawling metropolises. While many of their structures are visible as mounded buildings, many others were not mounded and lie under the level jungle floor; they are difficult to see archaeologically because of the nature of their perishable construction. Thus, the lowest segment of Maya society is likely to go largely undetected (cf. D. Chase 1990 and A. Chase 1990). Even if all mounded structures are recorded for a specific site, such information is difficult to interpret when extensive excavations are lacking, as William Haviland (1982:428-29) has repeatedly pointed out. Because archaeology in such Maya centers takes a lot of time and is also a costly enterprise, only a small number of visible constructions are ever sampled. Often such sampling involves only a small excavation to determine temporal information; data based on such probes are not conducive to being used for social interpretations (cf. A. Chase and D. Chase 1990). Even if a large number of years are spent working on any one site, the recovered sample is often still minuscule and plagued by unknowns. Often our models are neither confirmed nor disproved by the archaeological data themselves. It is, in fact, unusual when archaeological data may be used even to point to problems in the existing models, much less to derive models of prehistoric social organization. Thus, many of our models actually have little, if any, basis in archaeologically derived information.

Rather than decry the nature of Maya archaeological data, however, attempts can be made to use archaeologically recovered information to make some statements concerning social differentiation in Classic period society. In particular, it is possible to place certain archaeologically recovered interments at the upper end of the social spectrum. When such burials and their included items are compared with other interments from the same sites and throughout the Southern Maya lowlands, other differences and similarities can be discerned in a given burial population. When the distribution of luxury items and the distribution of burial types with architectural groups are examined, it is possible to gain some idea of how Maya sites and regions were organized and integrated over space and particularly of the ways in which segments of Maya populations were spatially located.

The following discussion utilizes interments from the site of Caracol (A. Chase and D. Chase 1987a, 1987b, 1989, in press; S. Jaeger 1991) as the primary data base and supplements this information with Classic period data from Tayasal (A. Chase 1979, 1983, 1985a, 1985b, 1990) and Santa Rita Corozal (D. Chase 1986, 1988, 1990, 1991; D. Chase and A. Chase 1981, 1986b, 1988, 1989). While none of these sites have been utilized in traditional arguments over the nature of Classic Maya society, each of them provides data relevant to our view of its organization. This analysis suggests a complicated social division and spatial distribution of the Classic Maya and demonstrates the utility of investigating single sites and their associated regions in an intensive way. The great diversity in the kinds of remains that may be recovered over the span of a long-term project also permits more control over the social variables of a given Maya society both for a single site and for other sites within its region. This, in turn, allows comparative statements to be made that can facilitate either the rejection or the refinement of the previously defined models.

The Identification of the Maya Elite: The Ruler

The imputed rulers of Classic Maya society are fairly easy to recognize in death because their tombs often contain many of the symbols that are associated with the named and titled individuals found on carved stone monuments. Although rulers alone did not represent the totality of the Maya elite, it is often difficult to ascribe many others to such a category. L. Schele and M. E. Miller (1986:67) have reviewed the costumes and imagery that are associated with personages appearing on Classic stone monuments. They conclude that the rulers could be clothed in three costumes. One of these was for daily wear; concerning this set of clothes, Schele and Miller (1986:67) note that "surprisingly, the king's hipcloth was often simpler than those worn by people of lesser rank . . . often made simply of white cotton." However, two other costumes are in evidence for the rulers; these are termed their "ritual" and "war" costumes, which "used exotic materials from distant regions" and included "ornate and weighty headdresses, masks, capes of complex design, large belts, ornate loincloths, skirts of jaguar pelt, ornamented backracks, high-backed sandals, leg straps, and jade and shell jewelry" (Schele and Miller 1986:67).

While the histories of Maya dynasties are well known from stelae and altars, few interments of rulers have ever been archaeologically recovered (cf. M. Coe 1988). The excavated sample of these elite includes: two rulers from Palenque (Chacaal I [Schele 1986]; Pacal [Ruz 1954b, 1973, 1977]), possibly ten rulers from Tikal (Jones and Satterthwaite 1982:124-31, table 6; Laporte and Fialko 1987; W. Coe 1990), and perhaps several from Altun Ha (Pendergast 1979, 1982a). While all of the potential rulers from this sample are known for some degree of opulence in their interment, most of their burials have not yet seen full publication or discussion. Thus, the associated markers of rulership that have been recovered archaeologically with the burials of known rulers are difficult to cull from the literature.

During the final 1985 season at Santa Rita Corozal, the Early Classic burial of a ruler (fig. 3.1) was recovered on axis to Structure 7—the largest and presumably the most important Classic period building at the site (D. Chase and A. Chase 1986b:11-12, 1988:31-35). This interment provides an excellent starting point for a discussion of the ruling elite. The skeletal remains of a male were placed in a huge tomb; the chamber measured 4.25 m by 1.5 m by just over 2 m in height. The objects that were recovered with this individual make it clear that he was of the highest status. As with most rulers, he was buried with textual material. Although no carved stone monuments occur at Santa Rita Corozal that might contain his name, a

Fig. 3.1. An Early Classic interment from Santa Rita Corozal Structure 7-3rd.

cache above his tomb provides hieroglyphs that we have loosely translated as "Great Scrolled Skull [*Yax Toh Pol*]"; this same text associates this name with other titles including *Mah-kin-ah*, a title usually indicative of rulership. A very decomposed codex was placed above his head and parts of him were covered with cinnabar. He was buried with eight ceramic vessels, including two cylinder tripods and one stone bowl. While I do not attribute magical abilities or underworld connotations to the nine vessels in the chamber, it is significant that stone vessels tend to occur only with burials of elite individuals, although not necessarily of ruling status (witness Chikin Tikal—Orrego n.d.; see also A. Chase in preparation). The limestone vessel that accompanied Great Scrolled Skull was carved with glyphic material (identifying it as a cacao vessel) and two portraits of God N, suggesting the theme of rebirth.

Great Scrolled Skull was also accompanied by a sizable amount of jade ornamentation, including a set of shell-backed pyrite and jadeite mosaic earflares and a jadeite pendant, as well as several hundred perforated flamingo-tongue shells, and a *Spondylus* shell that had been partially plastered and inlaid with cut shell. A large cowrie shell, which was an important status marker at Santa Rita Corozal during the Early Classic period, was placed inside the limestone bowl. A large composite blue-jadeite pendant resembling a bird was in his right chest area. Three large perforated jadeite tinklers of the kind usually seen on belt ornamentations of individuals on stone monuments were to his west. A 3/4 lifesize jadeite mask was set over the limestone bowl. A mosaic hematite mirror was also placed in the tomb along with three large *Turbinella marginata* shells, the body of a bird, two turtleshells (possibly representative of his bacab status), and three wooden disks covered with stucco and painted with figures in Teotihuacan style. Three cinnabar-tipped spearpoints rested in his pelvis area and covered a stingray spine; such spines are often found in important Maya burials of the Classic period (D. Chase 1991). Even more impressive was the huge chert bar placed over his right side; this was at one time presumably the middle element of a ceremonial bar and, when used, was partially wrapped in matting that ended in elaborately styled serpent heads similar to those so often portrayed in stone monuments.

Thus, this one burial included almost every conceivable marker of rulership (see below), far more than would have been found in the burials of interior rulers such as that of Burial 116 at Tikal, the burial of Ruler A or Ah Cacao (W. Coe 1990:604-09). The number of elite markers in this chamber may have been due to the wish of the ruler to publicize his esteemed status, perhaps because he occupied one of the edges of the Maya area. Santa Rita Corozal's positioning at a crucial trade node (D. Chase and A. Chase 1989) may have also meant that he had his choice of whichever foreign items he wished before they were sent into the interior.

The uppermost elite are fairly easy to identify—in spite of the fact that it is rather unusual that a match can be made between a burial and textual information contained in carved stone monuments; their remains tend to be distinctive because of both location and contents. Rulers can be identified primarily by the markers associated with their interments in conjunction with the special locations of such interments. Significantly, however, no one marker identifies a ruler; a combination of markers must exist for the appropriate identification to be made. Such markers include codex remains, cinnabar, mirrors, stone vessels, jadeite jewelry, jadeite earflares, jadeite masks, jadeite pendants, jadeite or stone tinklers, ceremonial bars, certain rare shells, textual materials, and perhaps stingray spines. However, as discussed below, interment in a tomb, in and of itself, does not necessarily identify one as being of the highest elite status.

The Elite and the "Middle Men" of Caracol

In their *Lexicon for Maya Architecture*, meant to be applicable to the whole Maya area, H. S. Loten and D. M. Pendergast (1984:9) have defined a "tomb" as "an elite interment." While once considered fairly easy to determine who was and was not elite based solely on the presence of this one characteristic, archaeological work at Caracol has shown that tombs are not the sole province of the elite (A. Chase and D. Chase 1987b:56-57, 75). Should such chambers be representative solely of elite burials, then an estimated 60 to 80 percent of the architectural groups at Caracol—based on patterns established for the site settlement area—would have been used by those accorded elite status; obviously, this one-to-one correspondence does not hold. Partially because of the general association of tombs with those of elite status elsewhere in the Maya area and partially because of the distribution of certain other material items at Caracol, we have been concerned with identifying markers of rulership and/or status and have ultimately postulated the existence—based on the archaeological record—of a segment of the Classic period Maya population that is neither elite nor commoner and may be equivalent to the ethnohistorically recorded Maya term *azmen uinic* or "middle man" (D. Chase and A. Chase 1988:75; D. Chase, this volume; see also A. Chase, N. Grube, and D. Chase 1991 and Jaeger 1991).

Thus far, more than 1600 structures have been mapped at Caracol, representing perhaps 25 percent of the total to be mapped in the core area (cf. A. Chase and D. Chase 1987b:72-73). Reconnaissance of unmapped areas has demonstrated (cf. Healy et al. 1983:408-09) that the density of Late Classic occupation at Caracol (Chase, Chase and Haviland 1990:502) was greater than that postulated for Tikal (Culbert et al. 1990). The causeway system at Caracol served to integrate this large population with both agricultural systems that abut the epicenter of the site and causeway termini which, for the most part, were special function plaza areas (A. Chase and D. Chase 1987b:52-53). Tombs occur in plaza groups throughout the site of Caracol

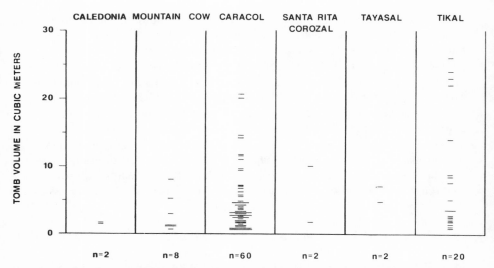

Fig. 3.2. Volumetric data for Caracol tombs relative to those within the region (Mountain Cow and Caledonia) and those at Santa Rita Corozal, Tayasal, and Tikal (cf. J. P. Laporte and V. Fialko 1987 and W. R.. Coe 1990:917, table 156).

and do not appear to be specifically correlated with the size or elaborateness of architecture; some of these are not associated with or on axis to raised constructions, but are rather directly set or built into the plaza itself. Likewise, the size of the tombs is not directly correlated with distance from the epicenter.

Data have been collected at Caracol relating to 60 tombs; the volumetric measurements of these are shown in figure 3.2. Other tombs are known (n=13), but have been neither measured nor excavated. Further work at the site will no doubt increase this sample substantially. Figure 3.3 demonstrates that the distribution of these tombs (n=73) is not limited to the site epicenter or the causeway termini. The Caracol tombs contain a diverse array of occupants and objects (cf. A. Chase and D. Chase in press). Elaborate goods are frequently found in small tombs far from the site epicenter while multiple individuals are found in tombs within both the epicenter and the core. The number of individuals present in any tomb ranges from 1 to 24. Higher-status individuals found in the epicenter are usually the sole occupants of a tomb; yet, multiple individuals also occupy large epicentral tombs, and single individuals occupy large and small tombs outside the epicenter. However, epicentral as opposed to core location for a tomb does not immediately indicate status. With the possible exception of written texts, the mere presence or absence of tombs or specific objects does not appear to provide a simple correlation with status at Caracol.

Glyphic texts accompany five tombs that have been documented at Caracol. While four of these texts occur in the epicenter, one of the texts occurs

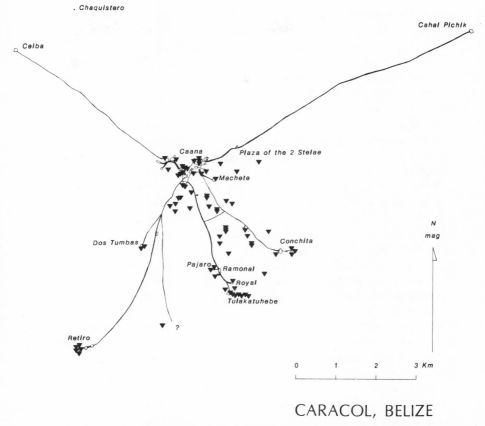

CARACOL, BELIZE

Fig. 3.3. The site of Caracol and its road system; each inverted triangle represents a known tomb.

in a smaller tomb occupied by a single individual in an eastern building at the end of one of Caracol's nine causeways. Interestingly, none of the deciphered dates or names of the individuals in the five tombs with painted texts are recorded on any of the stone monuments—and the most important interment in terms of size and location thus far recovered at Caracol is the tomb of a woman. One of these tombs with texts, however, contains an individual who is accompanied by a Caracol Glyph—indicating that the use of emblem glyphs is not restricted to rulers during the Late Classic era. None of the tombs contain clear markers of rulership, such as those seen at Santa Rita Corozal, Palenque, or Tikal. Based on the associated items within the five tombs and the content of the hieroglyphic inscriptions themselves, it is doubtful that any of Caracol's rulers have thus far been archaeologically recovered. Without doubt, however, all of the tombs associated with hieroglyphic texts may be assigned to Caracol's elite. Besides their direct association with Maya writing systems—usually the purview of the upper echelons of Maya society (Adams 1970)—the very location of such interments in spatially important constructions at the site lends support to such an interpretation, as do certain of the accompanying objects.

The other fifty-five investigated tombs are not dealt with so easily. Location and simple discussions of contents provide no clear correlations. The volume of some outlying tombs in the core of Caracol rivals the epicentral tombs; interestingly, some of these are in no way directly linked to or associated with Caracol's causeways. Similarly, some high status, or at least wealthy, chamber interments—as defined by the inclusion of luxury items—clearly occur outside of the site's epicenter and in groups of little architectural distinction. However, tomb volume itself may serve as the best single indicator of status—especially when considered in conjunction with provenience and material associations. A review of tomb sizes in conjunction with associated features and objects suggests that, while the elite may have clustered in the epicenter and in the areas about the causeway termini, they were also located in other areas of the core. The presumedly common households at the lowest end of the spectrum are residential groups of relatively small size with no tombs. By far the largest number of tombs occur in outlying groups in the core of Caracaol; tomb sizes within this group vary extensively. Given the large number of tombs, they cannot all be elite; yet some special status seems denoted. Thus, it would appear that the existence of a middle group is suggested by the data, with tomb use being limited to these elite and middle groups. Certain outlying elite or middle groups are located in close proximity to agricultural terraces—suggesting that the individuals occupying such groups were overseers of the fields. Irrespective of other considerations or associations, however, a tomb volume of over 7 sq m per person probably indicates elite status at Caracol.

Not all individuals within a residential group were interred equally. The majority of intensively excavated groups have uncovered differences in burial types (tomb, crypt, cist). These treatments may reflect a variety of differences. Some are separated chronologically and may reflect the fates of family members over time. Contemporary diversity, however, may suggest social variability due to age, sex, office, or achievements—and may include accumulation of wealth. The use of these indicators reflects social position not only at Caracol proper, but also within its greater polity. In general, the internal spatial volume of the tombs in Caracol proper is larger than that found in other sites within the Caracol region (cf. fig. 3.2), suggesting that tomb volume may also be used to measure social position within the overall Caracol polity.

The variability in the archaeological patterns recovered at Caracol does not accord well with models of Maya social organization that adhere to a two-class system. Clearly the elites were not restricted to the site epicenter, nor were the commoners the only ones living in the site core and, presumably, the site mantle (see A. Chase and D. Chase 1987b:51-54 for a definition of settlement terms for Caracol). The complexity of the recovered remains also suggests the existence not only of a central dynasty, but also of administrative bureaucrats who were necessary to keep the extensive terraced fields of Caracol operational and presumably may have occupied the fields that they managed. The site layout and the distribution of the archaeological remains also argue against the occurrence of any egalitarian society. When the Caracol data are combined with those for outlying settlements, the complexity of the situation becomes clear and tiers within the administrative and social system are clearly evident.

The Late Classic Maya Polity: Elites over Space

Caracol is one of several "primate sites" in the Southern lowlands; because of this, certain of the archaeological distributions seen at the site may be expected. For instance, given its primate status, one could easily predict that it would have been occupied by a high percentage of high status individuals. However, neither the actual number of well-to-do individuals at Caracol nor the existence of what appears to be a middle level of society was expected. The other unexpected item was the distribution of these elite and middle level groups at the site, for they are not limited to the site epicenter. It is clear from spatial distributions of plaza groups and terraced fields at Caracol that many of these people were located in areas that suggest an immediate relationship with the agricultural fields. The simplistic model of a nonfarming elite and a farming peasantry is contradicted by the Caracol data.

The question that must be asked is: how representative is the Caracol realm of other Maya polities? Is it in the mainstream or on one end of a coninuum of cultural variation? Archaeology in the Maya area has tended to be site-specific in interpreting Maya social and political relationships; to some extent, this focus has been fostered by the stress placed on the epigraphy of each site because the hieroglyphic texts are often very site-specific. The organizational models that have been used in the Maya area have also tended to ignore variability among sites or to adhere to preformulated models. Such models often homogenize the distinctions and variability among sites and their regions, usually being premised on the analysis of equal units. Thus, Maya sites and regions theoretically begin to resemble each other, leading to incorrect conclusions about the nature of Maya polities and their trajectories.

Examples of such problems are seen at several scalar levels. At a higher synthetic level, the problem is evident in the presentation of Maya political units as geographical areas based solely on the possession of an emblem glyph. P. Mathews' (1985) division of the central Maya area into territorial realms is premised only on one class of data and does not even take into account epigraphic interpretations of political relationships such as the domination of one named emblem site by another (cf. Yaxchilan and

Bonampak or Piedras Negras). Yet Mathews' heuristic divisions of Southern lowland Maya space have been provided with a reality all their own through interpretations concerning a supposed "balkanization" of Maya political units over time (Dunham 1988, based on Willey 1974). The use of such a balkanization model implies the early existence and subsequent breakup of a single large polity or a series of large polities; such a supposition does not reflect what we know about the archaeological record of most Classic period sites. Proponents of the balkanization or fragmentation model ignore the fact that over time empty space is largely being occupied and filled in by a burgeoning Maya population; no societal breakup is required (see also Escobedo A. 1991:72-74 for a critique of this model). S. D. Houston (1987:97) has in fact demonstrated that Maya polity size remains rather constant over time and "provides little evidence of progressive political compaction or of great differences in the size of Classic polities."

It should also not be surprising that there may be variability in the organization of Maya sites either by region or by polity. Thus, at Caracol and Tikal—another primate center—there might be a mixing of social statuses within the core of the site even though this pattern cannot be projected for certain other lowland sites (see Arnold and Ford 1980 and Ford and Arnold 1982:437, but see Folan et al. 1982 and Haviland 1982). The situation at Caracol does not easily accommodate a model that calls for Maya society to be composed only of elites and commoners. If one insists on the use of a two-class model, then one could argue, at least from Caracol's standpoint, that Maya society contained an almost even balance of commoners and elites—something that is inconsistent with the general usage of the term "elite" and that is unlikely even as an extreme end of a continuum. Alternatively (following Folan et al. 1982), one could argue that the entire core of the site was largely composed of elites and that nonelites lived further out in the mantle; however, again, the number of people that would have to be classified as elite, conservatively estimated at greater than 40,000 people for the immediate Caracol core, is inconsistent with the definition of the term.

Based on the archaeological distribution of both architectural groups and tombs at Caracol, we infer that the archaeology dictates the existence of a sizeable group of people in between the hereditary elite and the true commoners or peasants. These individuals may be similar to the *azmen uinic* or "middle men" described for the historic Maya. While at some sites such a group may have been small or perhaps even nonexistent, at others—such as Caracol—the group was quite large. It seems likely that such "middle men" would be concentrated at primate centers, for at second-level Classic period sites such as Tayasal or Classic period Santa Rita Corozal, the dichotomy between the rulers and the ruled is much easier to see.

If we tend to conceptualize the Maya as a series of city-state-like polities, it is important to conceptualize their associated sites within an interrelated and potentially varied framework. Classic period polities did exist, but sites erecting stone monuments and carving glyphic records were not all of the same level of independence. Caracol dominated other sites within its sphere of influence. This can be seen epigraphically, ceramically, and architecturally. Within the Caracol sphere other sites—such as La Rejolla and those in the Mountain Cow area—were loci of stelae erection. The La Rejolla and the Mountain Cow sites are located from 8.5 to 11 km from Caracol's epicenter, on the edge of that site's mantle (A. Chase and D. Chase 1987b:53). The dependence of the La Rejolla center on Caracol is recorded in its hieroglyphic record (Houston 1987:92, 98). These dependent relationships are defined in other ways as well. At least one of the Mountain Cow sites—Cahal Pichik—is joined with Caracol by a causeway. The hierarchy among sites may also be seen in the recovered remains. Excavations by J. Eric Thompson (1931) in the Mountain Cow region revealed a large number of high-status burials in this region, as seen in the size and number of tombs recovered in his early excavations and also to some degree in the contents of these chambers. The size (fig. 3.3) and contents of the eight chambers excavated by Thompson are consistent with a distribution of similar tombs in the Caracol core, as is the size of the associated architectural groups. The Mountain Cow tombs, however, are not as large as those at the end of the upper Caracol spectrum, and none is associated with painted texts. One smaller tomb contained a red-painted dot on its central capstone (Thompson 1931:290), a feature sometimes associated with elite burials at Tikal (Trik 1963:8) and similar to a high-status burial at Tayasal that had a specially imported red-sandstone slab used as a capstone (A. Chase 1983:402). These data suggest the existence of a structured status hierarchy that can also be seen even further afield within the Caracol polity. Some 16 km away from the Caracol epicenter—within the Caracol sphere— is the site of Caledonia (Awe 1985). While the site is small, it contains impressive architecture and even a ballcourt. Ceramically, it possesses a straightforward Caracol assemblage. Interestingly, from the standpoint of this consideration, the interments associated with Caledonia's more impressive architecture (fig. 3.3) fall on the lower end of the tomb volumes recorded for the Caracol core. Thus, given a concern with reviewing variation, it is possible not only to see some differences among sites within a single polity, but also to identify—based on architecture, burials, and texts—the probable tiers in the social and administrative system within a given region.

Classic Maya Elites Over Time: Changing Relationships

That the nature and role of the elite changed over time within the polities of the Southern Maya lowlands is likewise to be expected. During the Early Classic period, it would appear that a sizeable gulf existed between the elite and the rest of Maya society. Most elaborate burials and residences were likely to be found in central locales. Besides being reflected in the settlement data, this dichotomy can be seen in Early Classic burial data at such sites as Uaxactun, Tikal, Tayasal, Caracol, and Santa Rita Corozal. The Early Classic elite tended to be buried in chambers in prominent locations and to have been accompanied in death with far more luxury items and embellishment than in other contemporary interments. At Santa Rita Corozal, such burial patterning is clearly in evidence. The Early Classic high-status interments were all associated with central architecture and were accompanied by several elaborately painted or unusual vessels as well as with jadeite jewelry and special shells; other interments that can be assigned to this same era were fairly simple and were generally accompanied by a single vessel and/or, perhaps, a single jadeite bead. The gradations and blurring of labor investment in burials that is seen during the Late Classic period is not present. The "middle men" must not have been as prominent a factor during the Early Classic as they were during the Late Classic period. While the status of men would appear to have been higher than that of women—presumably because of the offices that they occupied and, perhaps, because of warfare—women were nonetheless interred in tombs placed in prominent locations during the Early Classic period at Santa Rita Corozal (D. Chase and A. Chase 1986:8-12), Uaxactun (A. Smith 1950:88), Tikal (Laporte and Fialko 1987:141-46; Orrego n.d. for Chikin Tikal), and Rio Azul (F. Saul and J. Saul, personal communication, 1989). Women continued to maintain their prominent political status during the Late Classic, as may be seen at both Altar de Sacrificios (Adams 1963, 1970) and Caracol (A. Chase and D. Chase 1987b:27, 60). At Caracol, it is clear that women also played a major role in problems of succession relating to rule at the onset of the Late Classic period.

Based on the spatial distribution of the Maya elite—as seen in their burials—and the larger number of small Early Classic sites that have yielded elaborate interments, the Early Classic polities may have been both smaller in total area and more numerous than the polities of the Late Classic. More local dynastic lines were probably directly competing for power during the Early Classic, not all of them using permanent epigraphic records. During the Late Classic, it would appear that the number of these competitive dynasties became smaller as polities grew in overall size and subsumed once independent elites within the frameworks of larger systems.

The Late Classic period witnessed the consolidation of power among a few select sites. Tikal and Caracol were two of these centers. Within the Tikal region, sites such as El Encanto, Navahuelal, Uolantun, and Chikin Tikal were probably subsumed within Greater Tikal and their once powerful and semi-independent elites became directly subservient to the elites of Tikal proper. In the Caracol region, Hatzcap Ceel and Cahal Pichik in the Mountain Cow area, both important and presumably independent centers during the Late Preclassic and Early Classic eras, were subsumed within the Caracol sphere by the onset of the Late Classic. Cahal Pichik was directly linked to the Caracol epicenter by a long causeway, implying its inclusion into the site proper. To the southwest of Caracol, a similar fate can be documented for the Retiro terminus (fig. 3.2). Sites to the northwest of Caracol were similarly included in Greater Caracol. While Caracol proper encompassed an area at least 6 km distant to the northwest of the epicenter, the site's dominance can also be seen in sites 11 km distant; Caballo exhibits a single Giant Ahau altar—a Caracol hallmark—and the monuments of La Rejolla explicitly document a subservient relationship of its lords to the Caracol ruler around 9.12.0.0.0 (A.D. 672).

Warfare also apparently increased dramatically in scale during the Late Classic period, and its nature began to change (D. Chase and A. Chase n.d.). While records of warfare are understandably spotty during the Early Classic given the paucity of texts, the picture that one gains of that era is of a single site striving to gain dominion over sites in its immediate region. During the Late Classic, these larger and more powerful survivors went after each other. Caracol Altar 21 records the defeat of Tikal by Caracol in 9.6.8.4.2 (A.D. 562), an event that had extremely traumatic effects at the latter site for over a century (A. Chase 1991). Caracol also records its conquest of Naranjo in 9.9.18.16.3 (A.D. 631)—both at Naranjo and on its own Stela 3—perhaps the reason for Naranjo's need to establish a new dynasty through a Dos Pilas female in 9.12.10.5.12 (A.D. 682). The lintels of Temple IV at Tikal record the conquests by Tikal Ruler B of Yaxha in 9.15.12.2.3 (A.D. 743) and of an unknown site (perhaps Motul de San José) in rapid succession 172 days later in 9.15.12.11.13 (A.D. 744). At Caracol, the rulers of three sites are simultaneously shown as being taken in 9.18.10.0.0 (A.D. 800) by the Caracol ruler and his sublords (A. Chase, N. Grube, and D. Chase 1991).

Thus, it can be documented that major Late Classic Maya centers were adding to or consolidating their polities, possibly attempting to gain control of larger and larger regions, either directly or through alliances. Presumably associated with such activities was the growth of a group of Maya with increased access to what had been previously thought of as solely elite items. By the end of the Late Classic, this middle level of society adopted many of the trappings once only associated with the elite. At Caracol, this is seen not only in the widespread adoption of tombs as places of burial, but also in the widespread use of special ceremonial ceramic cache vessels in many of the outlying living groups during Late Classic times (cf. A. Chase and D. Chase in press). Such specialized vessels were generally restricted to site epicenters elsewhere in the Maya area; their use in most Caracol households may have been a result of the widespread prosperity seen at the site—most likely due to its successes in warfare during the Late Classic era. At least by Terminal Classic times, several of these nonepicentral household groups were even erecting their own stone monuments, some of them carved and naming people other than the current ruler (cf. A. Chase, N. Grube, and D. Chase 1991).

For archaeological reasons noted above, it is highly unlikely that we are only witnessing the increasing size of the Maya elite "class" at Caracol—as some have argued for other sites (Lowe 1985:188). At Caracol Early Classic tombs only occur in the site epicenter or in important architectural groups some distance (2 to 6 km) from the epicenter. During the Late Classic, tombs occur in the majority of the mapped plaza groups and are not restricted to the site epicenter or other important architectural loci, as they were during the Early Classic era. Luxury items are also found with greater frequency in outlying tombs of the Late Classic. There may also be a tendency for Caracol's epicentral Late Classic elite not to be buried with the elaborately fashioned and polychrome pottery vessels that are found in outlying chambers. When the tomb data are combined with the widespread caching of specially-made ceramic vessels throughout the outlying settlement area of Caracol, it becomes clear that a sizable number of individuals and families at the site had access to items that are typically found in restricted distributions at other sites.

If Caracol can be used as any kind of guide, what appears to happen to Maya elites over the span of the Classic era is a decrease in their overall distance from the rest of the Maya community. Rulers may still be spectacularly buried in huge chambers and with the appropriate markers, but the rest of the Maya elite become blurred with individuals who formed an increasingly large Maya middle group.

The tendency for the elites to become less distinct from the rest of Maya society over time can ultimately be seen at the site of Tikal. It has been suggested that Tikal Burial 77 contains the remains of the latest known Tikal ruler documented on Stela 11 (Jones and Satterthwaite 1982:130), in spite of the fact that its occupant may have been female (Coggins 1975:586). Whether or not the individual in Burial 77 was female, it is an elite and possibly royal interment based on the accompanying jadeite objects, *Spondylus* shell, cinnabar covering, and overburden of flint and obsidian chips. Importantly, C. C. Coggins (1975:586, 591) has noted that the pottery from this burial falls squarely into the typical Late Classic burial assemblage found at Tikal and has also noted that "none of the Imix-related burials from residential groups is very different from Burial 77 in ceramic form or style." While she places Burial 77 as between 9.17.0.0.0 (A.D. 771) and 9.17.10.0.0 (A.D. 780) rather than the post-10.2.0.0.0 (post-A.D. 869) placement needed if Burial 77 did indeed contain the remains of Tikal's last ruler, other Terminal Classic elite interments at Tikal were also notable for their "poverty" (Coggins 1975:591). Rather than arguing, as Coggins (1975:591) does, for a population decrease at Tikal associated with fewer elite burials and the manufacture of fewer elite ceramics after 9.18.0.0.0 (A.D. 790), it is possible to view the social dynamics of the Terminal Classic as the outcome of a long-term process that occurred during the course of the Late Classic era. Through this process, not only did the gulf between elites and the rest of Maya society substantially lessen over time, but Maya society was also characterized by the accompanying growth of a middle level of individuals and families, as can be seen through analysis of settlement patterns (Arnold and Ford 1980; Ford and Arnold 1982). William Haviland's (1967:322, this volume, fig. 4.1) data on skeletal stature at Tikal can similarly be used to argue for a reduction in the dissimilarity between the elite and the less elite during the Late Classic.

Implications for the Maya Collapse

The model for Maya society that has been offered in this paper is one that is directly at odds with much of the traditional literature on the subject. Yet there is a growing body of archaeological data that support this reconstruction. In particular, the existence of a distinct Maya mid-level group is evident in the archaeological record of Caracol. And, while it may be easier to discern such a pattern at Caracol because of its fallen and open tombs in combination with the easily visible agricultural field system, it is unlikely that Caracol was a completely isolated case among the Classic polities of the Southern lowlands.

This reconstruction also affects our general understanding of the evolution of Classic Maya society in the Southern lowlands, particularly in relation to the development and change of its social and political systems. To some extent, it may be argued that the increasing amount of warfare seen in the Late Classic Southern lowlands may be directly linked to the rise of a Maya middle level of society, possibly similar to the historic *azmen uinic*. As warfare was extended to larger and larger arenas during the final era of the Classic (A. Chase and D. Chase 1992), this middle level of society could have gained considerable influence. Individuals other than rulers are named with regard to taking captives in the carved monuments of this time. The possibilities for changing relationships in Maya society could only have been heightened by warfare that may have expanded during the Terminal Classic era beyond neighboring polities and even have been carried on far outside of the Maya area at sites such as Cacaxtla and Xochicalco in the Mexican highlands. Such postulated events and relationships also have implications for interpretations relating to the Maya collapse.

The most generally accepted model for the Maya collapse in the Southern lowlands is premised on a two-class society. The model, as articulated by J. Eric Thompson (1966 [1954], 1970) and paraphrased by J. W. Lowe (1985:70), saw the collapse as "caused by (1) a growing gulf between the commoners and the aristocratic elite, (2) the increased demands of a growing elite class, and (3) perhaps ideological invasion of religious ideas from outside the Maya lowlands undermining the position of the elite." Such a model has to some degree been embraced not only by Lowe (1985), but also by R. J. Sharer (1977) and G. R. Willey and D. B. Shimkin (1973). Yet, with the possible exception of the last tenet (see A. Chase 1985c and D. Chase and A. Chase n.d.), there is little to recommend such a model in the archaeological record.

Recently, D. L. Webster (1985b) and E. M. Abrams (1987) have been able to demonstrate that there would have been little stress on Maya society from elite demands during the Late Classic period at Copan. Their data may probably be extended to other parts of the Maya realm. Given the data presented here, I would argue that there is also little to suggest that there was an increasing gulf between the elite and the rest of Maya society during the Late Classic; rather, the elite and the rest of Maya society in the Southern lowlands, at least at Caracol, and probably at Tikal, were growing more similar over time. If this picture accurately describes the situation during the Late Classic in the Southern lowlands, then the way in which the Maya collapse has been cast is in need of serious revision. The postulated ideological changes relating to the Maya collapse loom large, for by the Terminal Classic era a large and semiwealthy group of people would have existed within the Southern Maya lowlands who were not members of the formal elite establishment, but who were key to the functioning of that establishment. An examination of the nature, composition, and changes within this middle group may provide clues to the events that caused not only the Maya collapse but also overall evolution and cultural shifts in Maya civilization.

Conclusion

Identifying elites below the level of the ruler is extremely difficult archaeologically. However, the archaeological data can provide us with information concerning social divisions that are present in any given society. For the Maya site of Caracol, Belize, a minimum of three social groups can be inferred. The mechanisms for the way such groups came into being can also be derived from the warfare that is documented in the site's hieroglyphic texts. Successful warfare—especially over important neighbors such as Tikal—creates prosperity. Indeed, such prosperity can be seen in the widespread nature of tombs and ritual complexes at Caracol—to which many of the site's inhabitants had access. The large numbers of people who had access to high-status items at Caracol indicates that a simple two-class dichotomy of nobles and commoners cannot explain the archaeological situation there.

The detailed information from Caracol has also yielded an objective means for measuring status—tomb volume—both within Caracol proper and for the Caracol region in general. These data further suggest that, in order to model the social and political organization of Classic Maya society over time and space, we need to look intensively at regions, variability, and change. A single-site focus may not be able to identify regional diversity, but—on the other hand—this diversity may also be missed if the central site for a given region is not extensively investigated. To understand the structure of Classic Maya society, a comparative approach is needed that looks at a series of sites in any one polity. For, while one site may appear to have two social groups in a cursory analysis, placement of the same data into a more regional perspective may show that it has only two of three or more groups that are differentially distributed throughout a given polity. Each region or polity should also not be expected to exhibit the same structural patterns. The archaeological definition of these structures will be difficult. And, although research in the Maya area is hard-pressed to address such problems, we should expect to uncover great complexity and even greater diversity in the case of the Maya.

Acknowledgments

The research reported here was supported by a variety of sources. The Santa Rita Corozal tomb described above was recovered in 1985 with the aid of a grant from the National Science Foundation (BNS-8318531). The work at Caracol, Belize, has been supported by the University of Central Florida, private donations, the Institute of Maya Studies in Miami, the Harry Frank Guggenheim Foundation, the United States Agency for International Development, and the Government of Belize. The Belizean Departments of Archaeology and Forestry have also greatly aided the project. Diane Z. Chase is responsible for some of the clarity that I hope is evident in this paper.

4. Distinguishing the High and Mighty from The Hoi Polloi at Tikal, Guatemala

William A. Haviland and
Hattula Moholy-Nagy

ALTHOUGH the existence of a ruling elite among the Maya of the Classic period (A.D. 250-900) is now accepted by virtually everyone (e.g., L. Schele and M. Miller 1986), it has not always been so. Back in the late 1950s, when archaeological work was just getting underway at Tikal, the idea that ancient Maya society was essentially classless claimed considerable support (Haviland 1966:38-40). In this view, ably championed by Evon Vogt and others at Harvard University, positions of leadership were filled on a rotating basis by people who had accumulated the resources necessary to take up residence in a major center and discharge the duties of various civic and ceremonial offices. Once in office, their funds were soon exhausted, whereupon these individuals returned to normal lives in their home communities. Being somewhat skeptical of all this, those of us engaged in the investigation of residential structures at Tikal began early on to look for the kinds of evidence that might indicate the presence of a full-time ruling class at the site. Such evidence was indeed forthcoming, allowing us to answer the question: what was the archaeological signature of Tikal's ruling class?

The presence of social elites in human societies is manifest in a number of ways: what people have to say about others in their society (verbal evaluation); who associates with whom and how; and observable differences in lifestyles and life chances. Archaeologically, data on the latter two are usually easiest to come by, but, for a variety of reasons, these are cruder indicators of class standing that the other two (see Kowalewski, Feinman, and Finsten, this volume, for a discussion of perturbing factors). Although perhaps less evident, information on patterns of association still may be retrievable. Most difficult to deal with is verbal evaluation, although decipherment of the glyphs is shedding light on how the elite were regarded (at least by themselves) in ancient Maya society. However, since the papers in this volume deal with an archaeological assessment of Mesoamerican elites, we shall concentrate on what archaeology has to tell us about the high and mighty of Tikal's society. Even so, some reference to other sources of information cannot (and should not) be avoided, and a definitive understanding of this center's aristocracy will require input from epigraphers and art historians, as well as archaeologists.

Class and Housing

In the category of lifestyles, the high and mighty in stratified societies usually live in more imposing houses than do the hoi polloi (Chase and Chase, introduction, this volume). At Tikal, there was considerable variation in residential architecture, as has been noted in numerous publications (e.g., Haviland 1965:17, 1966:31, 1970:190, 1978:180). Houses themselves show an unbroken range of variation all the way from simple pole-and-thatch buildings without supporting platforms, through structures of varying complexity, to massive, all masonry range-type structures or "palaces." Similarly, associated buildings such as family shrines vary widely in floor area and quality of construction (e.g., Haviland 1982:428; Becker 1986:81, 83). Though not all palaces built entirely of masonry were houses (e.g., Jones 1969; Harrison 1986:55), some clearly were (Haviland 1981:93), and it is reasonable to assume that those who inhabited such imposing edifices were of considerably higher standing than those who lived in smaller houses built partially or wholly of perishable materials. Although palace groups differ considerably in the number of buildings included and the complexity of their arrangement—compare, for example, the Central Acropolis (Harrison 1986:fig. 9) with Group 7F-1 (Haviland 1985:fig. 5)—they do tend to command more space per living unit than do lower class household groups (cf. Haviland 1981, 1988). They also tend to protect the privacy of their occupants to a greater degree; for instance, various stairs, stairblocks, screens, and gateways seem to have been added to the Central Acropolis for no other purpose than to preserve the privacy of those who lived there (Harrison 1970:186-94). Finally, palace groups also have more outbuildings, probably including storehouses, kitchens, and servants' quarters as well as private shrines (e.g., Haviland 1981; Harrison 1986:fig. 17). While separate kitchens, storehouses, or shrines may sometimes be found in nonelite settings (e.g., Haviland 1965:21; Becker 1986:83), servants' quarters never are.

   Although major palaces are not confined to epicentral Tikal, they are far more prominent there than elsewhere (Puleston 1983:24). At the very heart of the city is the Central Acropolis, in which the ruling family probably lived. Consistent with this, Peter Harrison (1970:270, 1986:55) has noted the suitability of Str. 5D-46, one of the earliest Central Acropolis palaces, for "family residence." This edifice resembles Str. 7F-32, for which a residential function is firmly established (Haviland 1981, in press). Found beneath the west stairway of 5D-46, on its axis, was Cache 198, contained within a carved vessel with fitted lid bearing the name, with emblem glyph, of one of Tikal's Early Classic kings (Coggins 1975:208; C. Jones and L. Satterthwaite 1982:126). The rest of this inscription is now known to refer to the dedication of this man's house (Linda Schele, personal communication, 1990). The burial of Early Classic kings in and beneath nearby temples on the North Acropolis parallels the interment of men who once lived in Str. 7F-32 beneath the nearby temple Str. 7F-30 (Haviland 1985:39, in press).

Whether or not Str. 5D-46 was the only royal residence on the Central Acropolis is so far not settled. Although a number of other probable residential palaces are present, Harrison (1970:table 15, 1986:55) is inclined to interpret them as places where priests and boys in training lived. On the other hand, the early establishment of Str. 5D-46 and the manner in which the acropolis subsequently grew through addition and accretion is suggestive of an expanding extended family of great wealth and power. Overall, the pattern duplicates on a larger scale the same developmental cycle that has been described for smaller household units (Haviland 1988). Given the proximity of the royal living quarters to what C. Jones argues was Tikal's marketplace (W. Coe 1967:73; Jones, Coe, and Haviland 1981:307), one wonders if the residents of the Central Acropolis didn't control what went on there; certainly they were strategically located to do so.

In addition to the Central Acropolis, epicentral Tikal includes a ring of palaces—many (perhaps even most) of which were probably elite residences—that stretch in an arc from Str. 4D-14 south and east through the South Acropolis, thence north and east to Strs. 5E-1 and 4E-44 through 48 (Puleston 1983:24-25). There is no concentration of palaces elsewhere at Tikal remotely like this, suggesting that the bulk of the nobility resided at the civic and ceremonial heart of the ancient city. Some (if not all) of the few widely separated palaces that occur at some distance from Tikal's center also housed people of high rank, one of the better known being Group 7F-1, the "Dower House" group on which two preliminary articles have appeared (Haviland 1981, 1985). This was established by the family of a deceased noble who was probably of the ruling lineage, perhaps a ruler himself (perhaps the eighteenth successor of Yax Moch Xoc, anchoring ancestor of the Tikal dynasty; Haviland in press). Apparently banished from the center of power, his survivors nonetheless retained their upper class standing. They were even able to evict and tear down the houses of people who were obsidian workers—a relatively low-status occupation at Tikal (Haviland et al. 1985)—in order to build new living quarters for themselves (Haviland in press). Other such palace groups, unlike Group 7F-1, may have been occupied by nobles who were responsible for the administrative affairs of their localities, but who were answerable to the lords of Tikal (Haviland 1981:117).

Class and Burial

Heads of elite households, when they died, were regularly placed in tombs or graves reminiscent of tombs, usually beneath a temple. The most spectacular examples are, of course, those of the North Acropolis and vicinity, which contained the bodies of men who in life were probably housed on the Central Acropolis. On the basis of glyphic evidence, two of these tombs have been identified as those of the rulers Animal Skull and Ah Cacao ("Ruler A"), and the others are almost certainly those of earlier and later kings (C. Jones and L. Satterthwaite 1982:124-30). Unlike the burials of lower-class individuals (e.g., Haviland et al. 1985:141-53), these royal graves are far larger than required to contain the body of the deceased as well as all the other objects that were placed with it. In death, as in life, the high and mighty were able to command more space than the hoi polloi. In addition, tombs were engineered in such a way as to prevent earth or other fill from entering (lower-class people, by contrast, were almost always buried with dirt in the face). Some idea of the planning, time, and effort that went into constructing the last resting places of kings is illustrated by Burial 195—that of the ruler Animal Skull—and Burial 23—possibly that of Shield Skull. The former, a truly cavernous, vaulted chamber, required removal of the entire face of Str. 5D-32-2nd and its replacement by 32-1st (W. Coe 1990:565). Similarly, extensive destruction of Str. 5D-33-2nd's midline preceded construction of Burial 23's commodious vaulted chamber, which had to be placed so as to avoid impinging on the earlier Burial 48 (W. Coe 1990:537, 540). Following the tomb's completion, Str. 5D-33-1st was built above it, over what remained of the earlier temple.

Royal tombs were not only expensive to build, but were expensive to stock as well. Unlike lower-class burials, which rarely include more than three pottery vessels (often used or damaged ones at that), accompanied by one or two other items such as spindle whorls or other mundane household belongings, those of kings usually include large quantities of fine pottery vessels, as well as other items never found in lower-class graves. Some of the vessels appear to have been treasured heirlooms (e.g., Coggins 1975:153), while others were specially commissioned for the burial (Coggins 1975:515). Other objects invariably present in North Acropolis tombs are beads of jade and *Spondylus* shell, stingray spines, and red pigment dusted or painted over the body as well as associated objects. Specific to the earliest tombs, although they appear sporadically in later ones, are small anthropomorphic stone sculptures, greenstone and shell face masks, imitation pearl pendants carved from nacreous shell, and other worked marine shells. Added in Early Classic times (A.D. 250-550) were large ear-plugs of stone or shell, pyrite mosaic mirrors, sets of scraped out and perforated *Spondylus* valves, carved jade beads and pendants, vases of alabaster and calcite, true pearl pendants, unmodified marine shells and other marine invertebrates (including corals, sponges, bryozoans, and gorgonians), and painted wooden sculptures, trays, and bowls. After A.D. 550, other types of durable items accompanied elite corpses: jade mosaic vases, headbands made of small jade flares, bracelets and anklets of jade cylinder beads, bone, and/or shell objects interpreted as handles for fans, sets of bones inscribed with hieroglyphs, and jaguar pelts (identified from the groups of toe bones left in the skins, which either cushioned or covered the deceased). Two other hall-marks of elite burial were placement of masses of chert and obsidian debi-tage over the tomb and (until ca. A.D. 524) placement of human sacrificial victims within.

Other examples of elite-class burials are those beneath Strs. 7F-30 and 31 in Group 7F-1 (Coggins 1975:215-32, 233-36, 312-29, 420-28; Haviland in press). The earliest of these, Burial 160, is fully comparable in its construc-tion and contents to the North Acropolis tombs and contains the body of a man who may have been one of Tikal's rulers (Haviland in press). Sub-sequent burials are probably those of this man's descendants and thus col-lateral relatives of Tikal's later rulers (Haviland 1985:38). Although their graves are not as large and elaborate or as richly stocked as Burial 160, they are still tomblike in their construction, contain items reminiscent of those in royal tombs, and outclass all other Tikal burials save those at the site center. As usual with high-status burials of men, those of Group 7F-1 were placed in funerary shrines (often beneath them). While the heads of lower-class households were also interred in such shrines on occasion, this was not regularly done—nor were the overlying edifices as imposing as those of the aristocracy. Thus, inhumation in or beneath a temple by itself does not connote elite-class standing; what counts is the grave's size and quality of construction, the quantity and quality of objects placed within it, and the impressiveness of the structure built above it.

Class and Belongings

As one would expect, artifacts recovered from excavations in and around residential palaces reflect the high standing of those who lived in them, although not so obviously as do the objects recovered from elite burials. For one thing, highly valued items of the sort found in tombs were rarely discarded with the detritus of day-to-day living. For another, the presence of live-in servants of lower class than those they served (e.g., Haviland 1981, in press) more or less ensures that their trash has mixed with that of their elite masters. Differences between upper-class and lower-class litter may be further obscured by the occasional presence in and around relatively hum-ble dwellings of objects made for elite consumption by commoner craft spe-cialists; the presence of so much shell debris in Group 4F-1 (Haviland et al. 1985), for example, is a case in point. Marine shell is usually quite scarce in refuse associated with simple houses of pole and thatch at Tikal, but be-cause people who lived in Group 4F-1 were professional shell workers, evi-dently a low-status occupation, bits and objects of marine shell are well represented in their trash. A final complication is that living debris is rarely found that has not been contaminated to one degree or another by con-struction fill. The problem here is that trash was constantly being recycled in new construction, so that artifacts used at one location might ultimately wind up somewhere else. While it is probably safe to assume that much of the fill in residential groups was originally discarded by occupants of those same groups, our experience at Tikal is that the larger the construction, the less likely it is that there was sufficient debris available locally to use as fill. Thus, to build large palaces, the high and mighty probably found it necessary to commandeer the trash of the hoi polloi.

Allowing for these difficulties, objects from houses of whatever size and construction within the confines of Tikal may be separated into three categories: basic domestic items invariably present in living debris (including manos, metates, cores, ovate and elongate bifaces, irregular retouched, used and unused flakes, prismatic blades, and—except for Early Classic deposits—figurines); items commonly but not invariably present (censers, centrally perforated sherds, bifacial blades, pointed retouched flakes, hammerstones, and rubbing stones); and items rarely present (all other classifiable artifacts). In palace groups, more of the common types are present, and in greater numbers, than in smaller domestic groups. Conversely, such basic items as figurines, prismatic blades, debitage, and in fact any kind of workshop debris are usually more abundant in and around small structures. Outside of workshop situations, finds of rare artifacts are few and far between in small domestic groups, but occur in greater numbers and diversity around palaces. The same is true of those basic or common types most easily made from locally available raw materials that were instead made of imported luxury materials (obsidian or imported chert, for example, rather than local chert; the only basic or common type of chipped stone artifact almost always made of obsidian was the prismatic blade).

One especially noteworthy difference in refuse from the Central Acropolis, compared to smaller domestic groups, is its relatively high content of artifacts of bone, as well as unworked bone. For example, though present in Groups 4F-1 and 4F-2 (Haviland et al. 1985:176-77), unworked animal bones were proportionately more common in the Central Acropolis, suggesting that the elite ate more meat than did less exalted members of society. The highest proportion of unburied, unworked human remains found at Tikal was also from the Central Acropolis. Their presence here, as elsewhere in Mesoamerica (e.g., Storey 1985), poses an interesting problem for analysis.

In ceramics, our impression is that there is a higher frequency of decorated, mostly polychrome pottery from palace groups than from smaller domestic groups; unfortunately, the Tikal Project did not record the relative frequency of such pottery for each residential situation (data for a few lower-class groups may be found, however, in Haviland 1963). C. C. Coggins (1975:203) suggests that the many Manik polychrome and fine blackware sherds found in Central Acropolis fills relate to the royal residence, Str. 5D-46. Similarly, in Group 7F-1, pieces of carved cache bowl lids in living debris clearly discarded by occupants of the palace (Str. 7F-32) are not the sorts of things normally found around lower-class houses (Haviland in press), suggesting that some pottery in elite households consisted of specially commissioned, one-of-a-kind pieces.

In sum, the kinds of objects necessary for day-to-day living found their way into the refuse generated by those who lived in imposing palaces, as well as those who lived in far humbler dwellings. Although objects most obviously indicative of wealth and power are not often found in such trash, qualitative and quantitative differences suggestive of richness can nonetheless be seen when artifact inventories from palace groups are compared with those from smaller domestic groups.

Class and Osteology

Further insights into the lifestyles of the high and mighty come from analysis of human skeletons. For this, the Tikal burials have been divided into three categories: those from major palace groups (including the tombs of the North Acropolis and vicinity); those from small domestic groups; and those from intermediate structure groups that fall between these two extremes (reflected by this arrangement is the fact that the hoi polloi did not constitute a single nonelite class, but were themselves stratified). As one might expect, there is evidence that people of noble rank had customs and performed tasks unique to themselves. The lower limb bones of the aristocrats are platymeric and mesocnemic, those of people who lived in small domestic groups are mesocnemic but only moderately platymeric, and those of the occupants of intermediate domestic groups are platycnemic and moderately platymeric, reflecting functional differences. These varied shapes represent a response on the part of the bones to differences in ways that people were using their leg muscles. In the same vein, a supratrochlear foramen is found much more often among the elite than among any other segment of the population. The particular activities that these differences reflect are, unfortunately, unknown.

Skewed skulls, known only from the Central Acropolis, may indicate some cradling practice unique to the members of the aristocracy. Moreover, deliberate alteration of normal head shape, though not restricted to aristocrats, was adopted by high-ranking women before it was taken up by others of their sex. Similarly, among men, the custom was adopted first by those of high social position. Evidently, the hoi polloi were following a fashion trend set by the high and mighty. The same may be indicated by the social and temporal distribution of squatting, as opposed to sitting on raised seats. Squatting facets disappear first on the bones of the elite, followed by those on the bones of people who lived in intermediate domestic groups. The occupants of smaller domestic groups continued to the end to squat sufficiently to leave marks on their bones.

In the category of life chances, data on stature indicate a more favorable nutritional environment for the people of higher rank than for the rest of

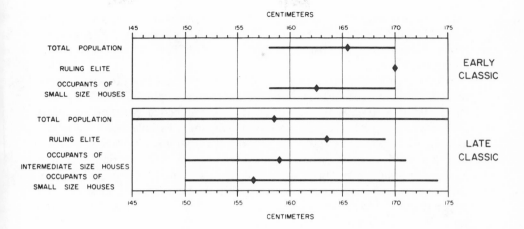

Fig. 4.1 Stature ranges for the recovered burial population of Tikal by broad societal segments and periods.

the population. Because of their favored circumstances (including among other things greater access to animal protein, as already noted), aristocrats were best able to realize their full growth potential. Those who were least able lived in small domestic groups, while the stature of residents of intermediate domestic groups falls in between. Contrary to first impression (Haviland 1967), in Early as well as Late Classic times, people buried in tombs were usually taller than those from intermediate domestic groups, who in turn were generally taller than those from small domestic groups (see fig. 4.1). Degrees of robustness seem to have been unevenly distributed in the population in like manner. To reinforce all this, there are hints from the skeletons that life expectancy was somewhat better for the elite than for other members of society. Here is one example of how Tikal's inscriptions can help us; unless the Maya were lying (always a possibility in records written for political purposes), at least two rulers of Tikal (Ruler A and Ruler B), if not more, lived to ages in excess of sixty years (C. Jones 1977:39, 53). By contrast, highest mortality for nonelite men seems to have been in the forties.

Origins of the Tikal Elite

At Tikal, the high and mighty became easily distinguishable from the hoi polloi in the last hundred years B.C. Although large scale public architecture, in the form of a solar observatory (Str. 5C-54) made its appearance a few centuries earlier (Laporte and Fialko 1990), this by itself does not signify the presence of a discrete elite segment of society (see Henderson, this volume). Nor is the facade text of Temple VI, which apparently projects dynastic rule at Tikal back several centuries before Christ (C. Jones and L.

Satterthwaite 1982:117), to be trusted; this more likely reflects an official Late Classic "party line" than reality. On the other hand, P. Mathews' (1985:31) proposed date for the beginning of the Tikal dynasty, A.D. 238, is undoubtedly too late.

An emerging elite at Tikal is probably best revealed by the sequence of burials. Not until ca. 100 B.C. do we have what might be called a proto-tomb (W. Coe 1965:8-9). Although this was preceded perhaps 100 years earlier by the burial of a young adult accompanied by jade and shell beads, as well as stingray spines (W. Coe 1965:8), this individual's grave was other-wise not at all tomblike. Not until 50 B.C. do the first full-fledged tombs appear, in which individuals were laid to rest with their elite belongings, *without* earth covering their bodies or dirt in their faces, in chambers far larger than needed for mere containment of the corpse and associated mate-rials (W. Coe 1965:figs. 6, 10). Paintings on the wall of the earliest sepul-cher, and on the exterior of the shrine built above the second one, depict individuals with the trappings of royalty (W. Coe 1965:figs. 9, 12). Worth noting, too, is evidence for the existence of monumental stone carving at this same time (C. Jones and L. Satterthwaite 1982:117), a favorite medium in the Classic period for aggrandizement of the elite. That these people held considerable authority as early as 50 B.C. is suggested by the placement of extra bodies with them in their earliest tombs.

In the earliest tomb, the two skeletons display artificial alterations of head shape. Twenty-five years later, it shows up in a woman from a small domestic group. By the very beginning of the first century A.D., the marked differences in physical stature and robustness between social classes had developed. Although the beginnings of the Central Acropolis go back to the time of the earliest North Acropolis tombs, we don't know what kind of houses the new elite occupied, but by A.D. 379 at the very latest they were living in palatial residences built entirely of masonry.

As Haviland (1972:13) suggested some years ago, Tikal's elite may have emerged as certain lineages, able to monopolize important civic and cere-monial positions, were ranked above other lineages, to form the basis of an upper class. An apparent link between the early ruling Jaguar Paw lineage and the architectural complex of which the solar observatory was a part (Laporte and Fialko 1990) suggests that control of important astronomical ritual may have played a key role in their rise to power.

If members of the important lineages tended to intermarry, then they would have constituted an endogamous caste. Hints to this effect are af-forded by the presence of a dwarf in a North Acropolis tomb, the fact that certain vertebral anomalies as presently known were confined to the elite, and the fact that wormian bones—for which a genetically set potential may be involved—appear more often in these people than in others. Taken together, these might suggest congenital anomalies showing up in a family line through time. Here again, the glyphs help us out, by indicating that this kind of intermarriage between royal lineages did in fact take place. For example, C. C. Coggins (1975:576) has argued that a daughter of Tikal's Ruler A married a lord at Piedras Negras. Ruler A himself seems to have married a woman, "Lady Yellowbird," whose sister is depicted on a stela from El Peru (W. Coe 1990:855). She seems not to have been his sole wife, however, for the mother of his son, Ruler B, has a different name (C. Jones and L. Satterthwaite 1982:129). On the lintels of Temple IV, Ruler B is noted as being in his fourth katun of life (i.e., between sixty and eighty years old) in 9.15.10.0.0 or A.D. 741 (C. Jones and L. Satterthwaite 1982:103). Therefore, he was born no later than A.D. 681, earlier than the time of Lady Yellowbird's death (W. Coe 1990:855). If the practice of polygyny was a royal prerogative, as this implies, we have found no archaeological evidence at Tikal to confirm it.

The Mexican Connection

At Tikal, the authority of the elite may have rested in part on a connection with the central Mexican site of Teotihuacan. This is reflected in the architecture of certain buildings and burials at Tikal, the presence of Mexican motifs in some of the monumental and ceramic art found in elite contexts (royal tombs and dynastic monuments, for example), and the presence of limited amounts of green obsidian from sources near Teotihuacan. C. C. Coggins (1980:734-36) has noted that the reign of Curl Nose, who came to power at Tikal in A.D. 379, is associated with a number of traits, practices, and symbols of central Mexican origin. Under his successor, a fusion of these foreign and indigenous Mayan elements took place, a phenomenon repeated later under the auspices of Ruler A (Coggins 1975:401-2, 444-45, 450, 452). More recently, some sort of connection between those who ruled at Tikal before Curl Nose and Teotihuacan has been described (Laporte and Fialko 1990). Thus, over the many centuries of Tikal's existence, there seem to have been periodic surges of influence emanating from central Mexico, which appear to have affected the local elite more than other segments of society.

Like the elite of Postclassic Yucatan, those in power at Tikal may have espoused some form of what D. Freidel (1985:303) has called a "cult of foreignness." In Yucatan, the nobility went so far as to proclaim their ethnic distinctness from everyone else and periodically quizzed one another on their own esoteric lore to prove that no others had infiltrated their ranks. Whether or not they went to such an extreme at Tikal is not known, but Coggins (1987) suggests that signs of a special ritual language, reminiscent of that used by later Yucatecans in their periodic interrogations of one another, can be detected in the inscriptions of the Classic period. At Tikal and elsewhere, being able to claim some sort of Mexican connection may have had the same aura that the claim of Toltec descent had for the ruling class of Late Postclassic Mexico.

Conclusions

What, then, do we know about Tikal's high and mighty? That they lived and acted the way members of a favored socioeconomic class usually do: they seem to have eaten better, lived longer, and wielded more power than the hoi polloi. Their housing was more substantial, permitted them to command more in the way of personal space for themselves (as their tombs did in death), and was arranged in such a way as to minimize their contact with people of lower standing in society. Consistent with this, marriage seems to have been with others of their own kind. Their needs were catered to by live-in servants, and they were able to afford more belongings, and of better quality, than less exalted members of society. Finally, they engaged in different activities than did people of lower standing.

Symbolic of their position in society were certain of their belongings, their housing, where they lived, their physical appearance, how they were treated in death as well as in life, and undoubtedly much more. This is where analysis of the entire corpus of Tikal art—nonelite as well as elite— will help us enormously to understand the full range of symbolic indicators (class differences in clothing, to cite just one example) and the meanings behind much of the symbolism. Here iconographic analysis of tomb contents, now being pursued by C. C. Coggins, shows promise of revealing much about elite worldviews. These sorts of analysis, however, have yet to be completed and we can all look forward to them.

5. Noblesse Oblige: The Elites of Altun Ha and Lamanai, Belize

David M. Pendergast

THE phrase that heads the title of this paper is an apposite one for ancient Maya society, as it is for any in which nobility or other elite rank or status separated a controlling group from the remainder of the populace. Such separation conferred upon the upper echelon a set of rights and privileges, but also established a reciprocal relationship of obligation to the nonelite community. The existence of that obligation renders any characterization of the elite incomplete unless it rests in part on an understanding of the people they controlled, from whom they drew their sustenance.

There is no question that the degree of separation from the masses can be assessed with reasonable accuracy in any Maya polity for the nobility, and with varying but lesser accuracy for other elements of the elite, on the basis of a variety of archaeological evidence. Information on aspects of the reciprocal relationship between elite and commoner may also be extracted from artifacts and from site plan, but the data base for commoners' material culture is never very likely to approach the solidity of that for the Maya upper crust itself. It is evident, however, that the most profitable approach to the elucidation of the obligations borne by the elite should rest equally on an examination of the richness of upper-class life and an attempt to discern the benefits that accrued to the community at large in return for services rendered.

The internal coherence that derives from extensive excavation may at least assist in setting the data in a solid framework. In this respect, both Altun Ha and Lamanai provide conspicuously fertile ground for examination of ancient Maya elites and their socioeconomic roles. Several significant questions can be addressed by close scrutiny of the archaeological record at the two sites. First, what criteria of elite status are discernible in the archaeological remains, and what is the degree of their reliability? Second, what can the evidence tell us about the histories of the elites within the historical frameworks of their two communities? Finally, can one proceed from the characterization of an elite to a real elucidation of the relationships between the group and the other segments of the society? In the following discussion, these matters are examined in as orderly a progression as possible for data from two comparatively proximate but often sharply different sites.

Architecture as an Identifier of Elite Status

At the highest level of size and complexity, the buildings of Altun Ha and Lamanai (and indeed of all Maya sites) leave no doubts as to their use by nobles and perhaps by other elements of the elite. By their very nature they reflect, in fact, the essentially reciprocal relationship between noble and commoner, the former in the role of guide and intercessor and the latter in the role of hewer of stone and drawer of water. In this respect, the principal structures of any site's central precinct tell us nothing that is not apparent in other sources of information. They also embody, however, a considerable quantity of secondary information regarding the composition of the upper class exclusive of the nobles themselves.

The complexity of Maya large-scale civic buildings is in itself evidence that extensive construction experience was requisite to the architectural work. Furthermore, thorough dissection of civic structures has shown that highly sophisticated construction staging was employed, with numerous widely separated units of a building in simultaneous independent production. This obviously required the application of a very high level of management skills if buildings were not to end up as nonfunctional, unstable jumbles. It follows from this that Maya civic buildings had to be brought into being with the aid of detailed plans and specifications. Such materials must have been created by a cadre of architects, who surely functioned both as designers and as supervisors. These functions are in themselves sufficient to have established the architect as a member of the elite; what is uncertain is whether such status was related to or separate from noble rank.

Monumental architecture may also provide us with a moderately specific measure of the breadth of the gulf that separated noble from commoner. The existence of the gulf is readily apparent in the form and scale of the structures, but the expression of its measure in mortar and stone is not a necessary element in Maya architecture. It is, in fact, far more often absent than present. At Altun Ha, however, there are two cases of what I see as architectural reification of social condition as well as process. To a limited extent in Structure A-1 (Pendergast 1979:40-91) and a far greater one in Structure B-4 (Pendergast 1982a:132-36), architectural development appears to mirror social development and to give us a normally intangible part of the community's history in truly concrete form.

It is not necessary to set forth the full construction histories of the two structures here, because it is the process they embody that is at issue. In both A-1 and B-4, what began in the Early Classic as moderate-size temples with comparatively open frontal plans evolved in Late Classic times into structures quite different from the originals. The change in A-1 created a side access route that was more tortuous, and in part more concealed, than the antecedent frontal one. The lower frontal stair was left open, but the development of the new side stair appears to have usurped its role as access.

Its condition indicates that it was not fully maintained and may have been allowed to fall completely into ruin while the upper part of the structure remained intact and in use.

The effect of the modifications of A-1 was to increase the claustral atmosphere of processions up the face of the structure, though the laity's line of sight from the plaza to the doorway of the building remained unobstructed. The link between the viewers and the performers in religious drama was therefore only partially altered, but the alteration may well have conveyed a message. The viewers could scarcely have avoided the impression that the gulf between themselves and the main participants in the drama, never narrow, had been widened.

In B-4, the erection of an increasingly formidable barrier between those assembled in the plaza and those engaged in ritual acts on the temple dominated most of the structure's Late Classic history. The earliest form of the structure offered onlookers an unrestricted view of ceremonies, presumably with a corresponding sense of direct linkage to such events. The first major reconstruction began the severing of that linkage through creation of a Lamanai building type structure with a building set athwart the stair; later alterations and additions sundered the linkage fully and ultimately created floor surfaces unusable for ceremonial or any other purpose. The conclusion is inescapable that B-4, always a monument to the power of a deity and his representatives, grew into an expression in stone of an ever widening gulf between rulers and ruled.

The second category of architectural evidence that bears on the elite is, of course, residential. At Altun Ha, far more than at Lamanai, evidence available in quantity allows identification of classes of elite domestic buildings as well as the tracing of the histories of a good many such structures. Residential structures offer the additional advantage of association with refuse, a link that embodies specific meaning in itself and also yields a variety of evidence that complements and amplifies the architectural information.

There are three architectural criteria on which identification of a structure as an elite residence can rest: location, form (and occasionally specific elements of plan), and construction type. A building may meet all three standards, but may quite easily omit the first of the three. It is self-evident that the criteria are applicable only in a context of reasonable social stability; in circumstances of sociopolitical disintegration it is entirely possible, as we shall see, that none of the three will serve to distinguish an elite residence. I have placed location at the head of the list simply because it is very often the first basis on which elite residences can be identified and the only one that can serve as a guide prior to excavation in conditions of major structural decay. It would be comforting to think that excavation thus guided yields confirmatory evidence in the form of the other two criteria, but it is intriguing that it sometimes does not.

It is axiomatic that residences within the central precinct will be identifiable as those of the elite—indeed, generally those of the nobility—throughout the period in which the central precinct retains its original function. Within this axiom it is a reasonable premise that structures closest to the main civic edifices were occupied by those of highest rank and that grading of rank and status is reflected in fairly direct fashion by distance from such edifices. It is obvious that this scheme will work only in areas immediately peripheral to the central precinct; no mechanical approach to linear distance can elicit information on social distance beyond a fairly restricted limit. Once outside that border, identification must rest on the remaining two criteria. Even inside it, the application of the principle of proximity to the community's nerve center as a measure of status produces some seeming anomalies that are interesting and possibly instructive.

Structure A-8 at Altun Ha (Pendergast 1979:100-42) exemplifies the palace class most clearly of the three central precinct residential buildings. It meets all three criteria for identification as the dwelling-place of nobility and is associated with a very large quantity of elaborately decorated pottery that underscores the identification. Yet there are twists in its history that distinguish it from its counterparts in the community's heart and also leave a good many questions regarding form and pattern of use unanswered. Most of these are relevant only to the structure or to Altun Ha, but one in particular bears on the relationship of noble to lower-elite echelons and to commoners as it is expressed in architecture.

In its earlier form, A-8 had a fairly standard plan in which four transverse rooms were ranged back from a single entrance on the east side, facing Plaza A. By virtue of its size and its separation in level from the three rear rooms, the outermost chamber appears likely to have served as a hall of audience, a function made quite appropriate by the relationship of structure to plaza. In a radical transformation, the later version of A-8 shifted to a southern orientation and an increased number of rooms that were smaller than those of the antecedent building, but perhaps still included a hall of audience as the front chamber. The shift in orientation was augmented by construction of a large platform between A-8 and the plaza, part of the set of events that brought the south access to A-1 into being. Here again the increase in the cloistered atmosphere of noble life may reflect a Late Classic widening of the social gap between ruler and ruled.

Across Plaza A from A-8, a glance beyond the eastern border of the plaza shows us the potential limitations in the use of proximity to major civic ceremonial structures as an accurate measure of elite status. The distance between Structure D-2 (Pendergast 1990a:4-14) and Structure A-5 is no greater than that between A-8 and A-3, the temple with which A-8 may have been linked in its early form. The small overall size and largely nonmasonry construction of D-2 suggest, however, that the building's occupants were not members of the nobility, though they may well have enjoyed some level of elite status. The difference between D-2 and the palaces as regards linear distance is not great; the critical element is the location of D-2 at the back of A-5, perhaps on a subsidary unit of the Plaza A platform. In this circumstance it is tempting to see the location of D-2 as equivalent to "The Backs" in later communities: a statement of status by association with the community's heart, but encompassing a distance far greater than a simple measure of distance would suggest.

Within the neighborhoods that surround Altun Ha's two central plazas there are numerous structures, such as C-6 and C-10 (Pendergast 1982a:151-69), that exceed D-2 in architectural quality and permit at least a rough ordering of elite families within the central precinct periphery. Such an ordering obviously rests on the assumption that building size and masonry content are closely correlated with status, an assumption that is entirely logical but not entirely unassailable. Unfortunately, none of the structures yielded cultural material that might reinforce or allow refinement of this sort of house-pride ranking.

Of the several neighborhoods that border directly on the central precinct, none appears to exemplify an elite residential district more fully than Zone E (Pendergast 1990a:19-246). Virtually all structures investigated, as well as a very considerable number left unexcavated, are marked by elaborate masonry-faced platforms and masonry or part-masonry buildings. The percentage of such structures is so high that upper level elite presence appears to have characterized virtually all of the northern half of the zone, the area closer to the central precinct, and a considerable portion of the southern half as well. Location relative to the community's center presumably dictated choice of the area for elite residence, but neither the particulars of this factor nor the bases for choice of building site within the densely packed zone can be extracted from the archaeological evidence.

Once one moves farther from the site center, the location criterion obviously breaks down completely. This is not to say that site selection for elite residences was a random matter in outlying zones; it is simply that relationship to the central precinct did not direct selection, and intrazonal factors in such choices are absolutely unapparent. Structure H-1, a building of sufficient size and complexity to qualify as a palace were it situated on one of the central plazas (Pendergast 1990a:figs. 127, 131), seems to sit virtually isolated, facing a scattered lot of small structures of clearly greater simplicity and possibly nonelite quality. Its hall of audience, though very small, bespeaks the building's mixed public and residential function, but the public served cannot be identified on the basis of proximity to H-1 or any other grounds. H-1's features deny isolation in the operational sense; hence the reasons for choice of the building's location remain enigmatic.

At an even greater remove from the site center, the plazuela group K-29 through 35 (Pendergast 1990a:333-88) provides an example of an elite residential compound identifiable as such partly on the basis of structure form and construction type and partly on nonarchitectural grounds. Such groups are widely dispersed at Altun Ha, and it is reasonable to assume that most, if not all, are extended family residential units that, like K-29 through 35, were of comparatively simple form and small scale initially and developed over time into moderately complex assemblages.

Although the status of the occupants cannot be assessed over the full span of development of plazuela assemblages, it is quite likely that most or all such groups represent the elite from beginning to end. A considerable amount of elite family history can be read from the Zone K group, as it can from H-1 and other more central residences; the most outstanding example is in Structures E-14 and E-54 (Pendergast 1990a:123-66), which appear to represent a family's step up from a modest home to a far more pretentious one erected in the backyard. The details of this sort of individual family history are not of consequence here; what is of importance is the time of many positive events in such histories, a matter to which we shall return shortly.

At Lamanai, divergence from the standard plaza plan makes identification of residential structures a very tricky matter in the absence of excavation data and sometimes almost equally perplexing when the data are available. The large courtyard complex (Plaza N10/3) at the north border of the plaza associated with Structure N10-9 (Pendergast 1986b:231-33) is identifiable as a multifaceted, multipurpose assemblage in which all buildings had some domestic use. It appears to have served as a residential center for the community's rulers for an exceedingly long period, but surely cannot have been the only noble domestic architecture in the central precinct. On architectural grounds, however, no other excavated structures in the precinct are unequivocally identifiable as palaces.

Although the pinpointing of possible noble dwellings in much of Lamanai poses formidable problems, it is possible to identify a considerable number of residences within or very close to the central precinct. In most cases, it is location rather than any other criterion that raises the possibility that these were the homes of Lamanai's elite. Contemporaneity with neighboring ceremonial structures is clear-cut in many instances; hence it may be that the somewhat more diffuse community plan allowed for greater fluidity in elite residence location than at sites more formally laid out. It also appears quite likely that the degree of such fluidity increased in the ninth or early tenth century, especially in the more northerly portions of the central precinct, where abandonment of some ceremonial structures may have been underway.

The Lamanai data, fraught with difficulties though they are, suggest strongly that the criteria applicable to elite residence identification at Altun Ha are of limited utility at the more westerly site. Either some noble residences were meaner dwellings than those in the N10/3 complex or the complex was in fact the principal home of Lamanai's nobility for a very great part of the site's long occupation span. There is no question that palaces, as they would be definable elsewhere, were not widely distributed at Lamanai. Though this fact is open to many interpretations, I am inclined to conclude from this that the community's rulers were fewer in number than their confreres at other centers, a matter to which we shall return when we consider the different fates of the ruling groups at Lamanai and Altun Ha.

Mortuary Evidence of Elite Status

Fortunately, none of the architectural evidence of elite status at Altun Ha and Lamanai exists in isolation. Both sites are replete with burial and refuse-heap data that augment the architectural record very substantially and shed light on aspects of elite life that are not illuminated by the buildings alone. Some of the identification of elite material culture, of course, proceeds from the categorization of the buildings themselves, but it is largely in the area of criteria independent of architecture that the more significant questions arise regarding the elite as a cultural stratum.

If one allows for the flawed perception that arises from loss of evidence on perishable materials, it is possible to rank burials on the basis of grave goods and to segment the ranking in a manner that at least has the potential of reflecting some ancient social realities. It is equally possible to apply this approach to grave type and, with considerably less success, to burial position. Because each of these variables presumably reflects, first, status differentiation within the elite and, second, distinction between elite and nonelite, there should be reasonable correspondence among the three rankings. In fact, there is not—and when the fourth and highly important variable of context is introduced, the waters are muddied even further.

Although the means of measuring quality of grave form and contents are inadequate to the task of sorting out gradations in status, at Altun Ha both burial locations and the amounts and kinds of accompanying artifacts generally indicate very strongly that individuals encountered in an elite structure were members of the elite. No great problem is posed by this identification when a single interment, or even a small group of burials, constitutes the entire sample from a residential structure. This is especially true when many of the burials are encased in secondary elements, generally benches, as in Structure E-14 (Pendergast 1990a:fig. 62). A very considerable problem does arise, however, when the number of burials in the core of a major residential modification greatly exceeds the possible total for deaths in a family immediately prior to and during construction. The matter is given a slight additional twist when the structure involved is civic rather than residential.

The general status of numerous individuals interred in a residential or civic construction unit is not subject to doubt; context surely provides the answer on this point. Nonetheless, the existence of marked disparities in grave goods and types among such immediately contemporaneous burials raises serious questions regarding the bases for identifying elite status even at the most general level. Of equal importance, though presumably not in the area of rank or status classification, is the nature of the relationship between the individuals and their final resting-place.

Structure C-13 (Pendergast 1982a:170-204) provides an early example of multiple burials in a civic building, whereas Structure E-7 (Pendergast 1990a:72-122) is an even more striking example of numerous burials in various modifications of a structure that probably combined residential and administrative-ceremonial functions. The very large numbers of burials in various levels of modification indicate that the relationships of the individuals to the structures must have been essentially the same in both instances. Rather than being residents in or users of the buildings, the dead are very likely to have been those whose rank or status was high enough to assure them a place of honor at death. The choice of place could have rested on some sort of functional tie between the individual and the structure, such as residence in a specific administrative unit, but it may well have been dictated by nothing more than coincidence between the schedules of the builder and the grim reaper.

An additional factor that affects interment-based perception of the elite is sampling error induced by the very obvious fact that nonstructure-associated burial must have been a common practice among the elite, as it was in the remainder of the population. Both Altun Ha's and Lamanai's burial yields per elite structure are higher than those for many sites, but neither approaches a plausible total for deaths in a given period. The same is true of what are surely elite family burials in the family's residence, such as those in Structures E-14 and H-1 at Altun Ha (Pendergast 1990a:123-43, 279-308). The inescapable conclusion is that cemeteries or some other form of site-peripheral or off-site disposal of the dead characterized Maya communities from beginning to end. Hence there is no question that in treating an elite burial sample, no matter what its size, we are not dealing with a population in any sense.

Because no identifying features of nonstructural interment sites can be distinguished, we are not now able to go beyond the recognition that such places exist. As a result, we can only examine the effects of their use on the assessment of elite population physical characteristics in the most general terms. Furthermore, there is considerable likelihood that the sample is a structured one, given shape by the factors, probably numerous, that determined whether a deceased member of the elite was accorded structural or nonstructural burial.

Dietary and Midden Evidence of Elite Status

Just as ranking of burials offers the possibility of evaluating some aspects of elite life, comparison of structure-associated middens sheds considerable light on elite lifestyle. Altun Ha is virtually a textbook example of the correlation between architectural complexity and midden richness, and as such it permits judgments regarding dietary distinctions within the community's elite. Lamanai provides less information on this facet of elite existence, but the reasons for the absence of data are, in a way, as instructive as the data themselves would be.

At Altun Ha the mass of refuse alongside the platform of the palace-type Structure A-8 (Pendergast 1979:127-38) gives us what is often lacking in the midden sample: the top end of the spectrum. From this top downward, the site's refuse deposits can be graded with regard to both cultural and faunal content, and the grading very closely parallels diminishing complexity in architecture. We can focus here only on the broad pattern that emerges: nobility brought with it in the Maya city-state more or less the same degree of culinary privilege recorded in other heavily stratified societies and such privilege diminished as status distance from the top stratum increased.

Privilege meant, as elsewhere, both quantity and quality. The preponderant portion of the bone that represents the legs and other major cuts of meat comes from the A-8 midden and from others associated with structures, such as H-1, that unquestionably housed upper-level elite families. The A-8 midden yielded, along with fair quantities of deer and other bone, the entire site sample of the largest and finest turtle, *Dermatemys mawii*; non-noble families seem not to have enjoyed a scrap of this excellent creature. I suspect that for the occupants of A-8 privilege extended to special preparation of food as well, which may have involved cooking away from the palace and bearing dishes to the dining area at mealtime. The absence of an identifiable kitchen in the intensively examined vicinity of A-8, the basis for the foregoing suggestion, is unfortunately characteristic of all other elite residences except for Structure E-14 (Pendergast 1990a:128-29). Hence we have only the food remains themselves—and only the meat, at that—as a mirror of the difference between an elite repast and a lower-class meal.

All of our attempts to wrest social stratification from data on dietary difference obviously can deal only with the two phenomena exemplified in Altun Ha's A-8 midden: differential distribution of cuts of meat from the larger species and wholly class-specific foodstuffs. Both of these necessarily involve resources available in limited supply; hence the particulars are quite likely to vary with significant environmental differences. For example, striking variation exists between comparatively turtle-poor Altun Ha and turtle-rich lakeside Lamanai, where *Dermatemys* made as frequent an appearance on the tables of the low as it did on those of the mighty.

Coupled with the impossibility of segmenting the faunal data along absolute social lines is a major problem regarding the nature of the association between middens and the structures they abut. We have long portrayed Maya residential areas as malodorous because of the great heaps of refuse that were allowed to accumulate around houses—and part of this portrait envisioned the middens as mirrors of life over very considerable periods.

The Altun Ha data made it reasonably clear, and those from Lamanai make it unquestionable, that the middens we encounter were in fact precursors of structure abandonment. This means that in virtually all sites what we investigate is the product of social breakdown and hence does not necessarily reflect patterns of life prior to the beginnings of distintegration. Of course, it does not follow that middens never accumulated until Terminal Classic times; there is ample evidence that they did, but equally ample evidence that they were periodically cleared away and very often incorporated in construction. We cannot know whether the clearing away was organized at the single-family, neighborhood, or citywide level, but we do know that only when the organizing force died, along with others in the community, did garbage round the doorstep become commonplace in Maya life.

The importance of assessing midden data as a reflection of Terminal Classic rather than earlier life, with the exception of such anomalies as the early Late Classic Altun Ha A-8 midden itself and the dumping of refuse in abandoned rooms of B-5 (Pendergast 1982a:27-30), lies in the fact that the road to collapse may have led to changes in dietary patterns. The possibility clearly exists as well that the supply was more limited in Terminal Classic times than it had been earlier. The limitation is less likely to have resulted from excessive exploitation of the environment than from less effective distribution of the hunting yield. There are two predictable results of distribution breakdown: the quantity, especially of larger game, will be less per household, and the cutoff point below which such game disappears from the menu will be higher than in times of plenty. The first may not alter our perception of the size of the elite community as defined by diet, but the second surely will. We should therefore recognize that the midden data on which we are forced to rely are very likely to show us an elite less well fed than in the Classic and smaller than it was even in Terminal Classic times.

The Lamanai data raise a final question in our assessment of elites on dietary grounds—the importance of nutritional difference as an issue in relations between upper and lower social strata. We are accustomed to depicting the lower classes of Maya society as impassive and willing to accept rule that offered many organizational advantages but exacted a heavy toll in labor tax in return. A further toll surely existed in the requirement that game, or major portions thereof, be provided for elite consumption. There is no evidence for the prehistoric period as to whether such a requirement was given legal codification buttressed by reverence for nobility and respect for others in power or was simply a matter of economics. It is highly probable, however, that in any form the need to pass high-protein foodstuffs up the social ladder would have added to other burdens in times of hardship.

It may follow from this that Terminal Classic distribution of elite victuals was reduced by retention of game lower down the ladder. If this was the case, it is clear that the elite of Lamanai would have enjoyed a singular advantage in the availability of an abundance of protein foodstuffs in the form of lake-dwelling fish and turtles. The existence of high-quality nutritional resources may have heightened the burden-bearing ability of the lower echelon of Lamanai society and hence may have been one of many factors that contributed to the community's survival in the face of disintegration on all sides, including nearby Altun Ha.

The Fate of Elites at Altun Ha and Lamanai

Surely no sharper contrast exists in the Maya lowlands than that between Altun Ha and Lamanai from the ninth century onward. Separated by only 40 km, the two communities diverged so markedly in the Late Classic that the gulf between them seems to have been ten times as wide. In fact, physical evidence of communication between the two is not extensive. The existence of Lamanai-type Structure B-4 at Altun Ha (Pendergast 1982a:43-141) bespeaks exchange of architectural ideas, if not of architects, but the presence at Lamanai of only a minuscule amount of pottery probably manufactured at Altun Ha suggests that exchange of goods between the two centers was not of economic significance. Finally, there is the absolutely amazing occurrence of one shell ornament or clothing fastener at Lamanai and the remaining three from the set at Altun Ha (Pendergast 1982b:4, fig. 2); this could be combined with the architectural data as evidence of elite contact, but it scarcely documents elite links on a grand scale. Transmission of information from one site to the other nevertheless surely occurred on a larger scale than the evidence suggests; despite the unpleasant nature of some of the terrain, 40 km can hardly have been an effective barrier to interchange as long as Altun Ha continued as a functioning community. Yet when Altun Ha descended into the dust, Lamanai held fast.

The decline of Altun Ha has already been partly traced (Pendergast 1982a:134-36, 139; 1990a:302-07, 331-32, 388), though not examined in full site context. Among the many classes of data relevant to the phenomenon there are three salient features of central precinct and nearby neighborhood evidence that reveal part of the effect of the decline on the community's elite. The first of these (Pendergast 1982a:134-36) documents a protracted period of diminishing control over the labor force, with concomitant reduction in the quality and scale of architectural modification. The second (Pendergast 1979:183-84, 1982a:139) argues fairly persuasively in favor of a final stroke in the collapse that was at least tinged with violence. The third (Pendergast 1990a:246, 388) shows us that events in the central precinct were not an accurate gauge of life throughout the site in Terminal Classic times. Together with other lines of evidence, the three permit some fairly educated guesses regarding the fate of Altun Ha's elite.

The diminishing ability of Altun Ha's ninth-century rulers and their administrators to marshal labor forces for temple renewal was almost unquestionably mirrored in other areas of community life. It is possible that maintenance of water reservoirs and other similarly critical facilities declined in concert with work on central precinct structures, but evidence on this point is highly unlikely to be recoverable. Garbage removal, at whatever level it was managed, was clearly a casualty of social decay. As we have seen, it is probable that a declining standard of living as regards food consumption attended the dissolution of power in the community. If these and other forces persuaded some elite families to decamp in the ninth century, their departure is not documented in the archaeological record.

In most cases, if not in all, the histories of plazuela groups and individual upper-class structures mirror the rising fortunes of elite families through at least middle Late Classic times. In a good many, the rise may have peaked in the eighth century, but subsequent events do not necessarily indicate decline. In the following century, as the center of their world was fragmenting, a number of elite families gave concrete evidence of positive attitude by continuing to modify their homes, often in quite substantial ways. Examples of this activity are provided by Structures C-16 (Pendergast 1982a:217-20), C-22 (Pendergast 1982a:240-45), E-7, and E-50 (Pendergast 1990a:72-122, 216-28), among others. It is clear that at least part of Altun Ha's elite refused, as conservative elements of societies very often do, to admit that the handwriting was on the wall. Though imprecision in dating does not permit certainty on the matter, it is quite likely that a kind of determined optimism in the face of incontrovertible evidence of societal failure continued in some households for half a century or more after all higher government functions had come to an end. What kept the spark alive is something that we cannot hope to know on the basis of the archaeological data.

Because Altun Ha rulers whose tombs were accessible appear to have suffered a Cromwellian fate, it is quite likely that the community's living leader, and perhaps his immediate retinue, fared rather badly in the last stages of the collapse. The most interesting question regarding this period and the years that followed is: what became of the remainder of the elite? What use was there now for architects, jade carvers, feather workers, and the like? The answer to the second question is self-evident; without noble and near-noble consumers, the market for the talents of such specialists was gone. This answer provides a response of a sort to the first query. Most of the elite who remained in the community—and the evidence suggests that many did so—must have undergone painfully quick job retraining.

The image of the soft hand forcibly hardened by manual labor is, I think, a very fitting one. We know from the amount of Terminal Classic material remains that depopulation is not likely to have been either sudden or massive; we know that no slaughter of the elite attended the collapse, unless we wish to posit careful interment of the dead following the carnage; we know from the cessation of communal construction that sustainment of the family rather than the community must have become life's main motive force; hence we must also know that many a craft specialist's, and perhaps even a great merchant's, hand was turned by the collapse to agriculture and other homely pursuits.

How does the foregoing suggestion relate to new construction in elite residences, especially in Structure E-7, where the architecture bespeaks combined administrative and residential use? Beyond simple refusal to admit that the apocalypse was upon them, some elite families may have genuinely attempted to snatch victory from the jaws of defeat by keeping up appearances—by continuing, in fact, leadership roles their ancestors had enjoyed for centuries. This suggestion holds particularly in the neighborhoods around the central precinct, where the atmosphere of decay must soon have become oppressive and the hopelessness of resurrecting the old way of life absolutely apparent. In outlying zones, death at the heart may have left a fair amount of blood flowing in peripheral veins and rebuilding may, for a time at least, have been less bravado than a reflection of the fact that removal of the head does not necessarily destroy the body.

At Lamanai, the collapse never came. Somehow, as organization raveled at centers nearby and distant, the people of this lakeside community made the positive attitude of some Altun Ha families into workable reality. I have elsewhere suggested a number of causes for Lamanai's strength, among them its location, which not only provided the protein advantage to which I have already alluded but also gave the inhabitants a major river avenue to the outside world. Furthermore, the labor tax imposed on Lamanai's working class may have been less than at some other centers, owing to a focus on limited frontal modification rather than complete transformation of major civic structures. Hence the burden borne may have been lighter while at the same time the strength to bear it was greater. The concept of a sort of adaptive advantage is attractive as at least a partial explanation, but it is weakened by the fact that neither at Altun Ha and Lamanai nor anywhere else do we have the kind of data required for real quantification of differential loading imposed on communities.

Together with the other factors, qualities of leadership may well have been a force in Lamanai's survival (Pendergast 1986b:247-48). This is not because there is evidence of particularly forceful leaders—what evidence could there be?—but rather because all of the socially and environmentally based explanations are too pat and monochromatic to serve in circumstances that must have been of the utmost complexity and difficulty. In making this suggestion I am not simply subscribing to the so-called Great Man view of history; rather, I think it self-evident that a special strength had to lie in the elite as a whole if survival was to be made possible.

Guided by the elite, Lamanai began in the ninth century a program that, on the one hand, had the appearance of retrenchment, but, on the other, involved major restatements of the community's continued well-being. Despite abandonment of the northern part of the central precinct in the ninth century and afterward, that same time saw the beginning of what was probably the largest single construction effort in the site's history, in an elite residential and administrative complex near the precinct's south end (Pendergast 1986b:231-33). This was clearly far more than failure to recognize defeat; such major public works seem an almost proud refusal to admit the possibility of defeat. The aura of pride stems not from the nature of the works themselves, but rather from the fact that the efforts were commenced at a time when Lamanai's people cannot have failed to be acutely aware that the vital force was being sapped from their neighbors, who were barely able to keep up the pretense of public architectural renewal.

The Fortunes of the Postclassic Elite at Lamanai

As the full enormity and scale of collapse events in the Southern lowlands became apparent to the rulers and the elite of Lamanai, a vast range of serious problems must surely have come to the fore. Primary among them was the fact that, although theirs was not the only center operating in the area in the Postclassic years, Lamanai's inhabitants were very largely cast in the role of the lone bulwark against chaos in their immediate region. By about A.D. 1100-1150, Lamanai may in fact have been the sole large community still functioning in Belize, but even before that time the site was effectively an island of calm in a very rough sea. As individuals and perhaps as a group under noble leadership, Lamanai's elite must have had to labor mightily to develop constructive strategies to deal both with the external world and with the pressures that world exerted on the community's internal stability.

An intriguing aspect of external pressure, but one on which no evidence is forthcoming, is the relationship between Lamanai's elite and whatever remained of an elite in neighboring communities. Surely, where close ties had earlier existed there must have been feelings of compassion, and perhaps of responsibility, that could have been translated into action. Lamanai was no soup kitchen for the unemployed specialists from Altun Ha or elsewhere, but knowledge of the community's survival must have fueled hungers of various kinds in former members of those elites. Were Lamanai's elite families pressured to accept refugees from among their compeers at other sites? We shall never know, but the nature of human interaction suggests that they were and raises the question of how the community held out against these and other pressures from what were now depressed areas in every sense.

That Lamanai itself escaped depression may have been due in large part to the "Dzuluinicob," that great water avenue that had served the city for all of its years. With its economic ties in the Southern lowlands severed, Lamanai must have begun to turn its eyes to the north more than it had ever done before the Postclassic, and the river made that turning feasible. The evidence indicates that reorientation of the community's economy northward involved production as well as consumption; the flow of goods in both directions was surely essential to the maintenance of status, as well as a truly viable way of life, throughout the Postclassic.

Meanwhile, although the formal management of trade networks within the Southern lowlands and beyond to the highlands had been sheared away by the collapse, there is ample evidence that materials formerly transmitted via such networks still made their way to Lamanai. The most solid element in the evidence is obsidian, which was used in the area well into the sixteenth century (Graham and Pendergast 1988). What we cannot determine from the evidence is how much of the on-ground structure of the Classic system survived despite loss of the organizing bureaucracy. This is because many of the same individuals very probably made their way over the same trading trails, carrying obsidian and other materials from the same sources, as in precollapse days; what better example could we have of the failure of material remains to reflect momentous sociopolitical events?

The flow of goods into and out of Lamanai occurred within a framework of maintenance of religious practice (Pendergast 1986b:234-35), and surely social organization as well, that must have given the elite essentially the same intrasite role as in Classic times, and very largely the same extrasite role as well. At the head of the elite remained a nobility whose graves, though somewhat less elaborate than those of Classic times, were still marked by the concentration of wealth that proclaims the concentration of power.

Structures that formed the heart of the Middle Postclassic community have the same aura as Structure E-7 at Altun Ha; they are packed with burials that on grounds of location and associated goods clearly represent Lamanai's twelfth- and thirteenth-century elite. Chief among the burials in Structure N10-2 is that of an unquestioned noble, Burial N10-2/9 (Pendergast 1981b:44, figs. 19, 20), whose gold-adorned wooden staff and other objects combine with a copper bell and elaborate censers to declare his rank quite unmistakably. A similar level of wealth is discernible in the multiple fifteenth-century Burial N10-4/46 (Pendergast 1981a, 1981b:47, figs. 21, 22), intruded among elite interments of earlier times in Structure N10-4. It is impossible, however, to be sure that the young person who was the grave's principal occupant was in fact the community's ruler. As in the case of his twelfth/early-thirteenth-century predecessor, the N10-4 individual bore with him to the grave both imported and locally made items of wealth, so that both power and the economic strength over which it held sway are in evidence.

At the end of Lamanai's prehistoric period, a few years at most before the Spanish put in their appearance at the site, the last identifiable ruler of Lamanai was laid in his grave (Pendergast 1984). His gravesite, though beside a Classic residence rather than in a major civic structure, was presumably no less honorific than those chosen in preceding centuries and his wealth, as documented by grave goods, was approximately the same as that of earlier Postclassic rulers. Yet the community that was his domain was architecturally not even a shadow of its Classic forebear and had shifted away in both location and form from its middle Postclassic antecedents. Whether the shift involved a population diminished from the levels of mid-Postclassic times unfortunately remains unclear. Nevertheless, a body of elite continued to form part of the social structure, and wealth was still there to be controlled. The tomb itself gives evidence of Lamanai's overall continuing strength and richness, as do ceramics from refuse pits. Sadly, no other burial of an elite individual of the period was recovered in excavation; architecture and other material culture remains tell us all we know about the community's upper stratum after 1500.

With the arrival of Spaniards at Lamanai, which probably occurred in 1544 (G. Jones 1984:31-32), came the end of noble rule as it had existed for three millennia or more. European presence also brought about the destruction, or at least the submersion, of the precontact criteria for definition of elite status. Community leaders were obviously identifiable throughout the period of Spanish presence, but the validation of their power was, on the surface at least, provided by Europeans rather than by ancient considerations. They went to their graves unaccompanied by the wealth that surrounded their predecessors and probably having professed no ties to those individuals. When circumstances permitted, however, their interments may well have been attended by as much Maya ritual as Christian, for when Spanish influence evaporated the old practices and their material manifestations quickly emerged once more (Pendergast 1985a:101-2, 1986b:5-6, 1990b).

As for the remainder of the elite, they, too, drew much of their status from Spanish-dominated economic pursuits and from their adherence to Christian doctrine; many of the same families may have occupied positions of dominance, but behind them now stood, however distantly, European power.

Unlike the early Postclassic, the opening century of the historic era is a time in which elite status seems very likely to be reflected by material culture items that we can identify without difficulty, because they are of European origin. Such objects, especially glass beads, form one of the principal bases for identification of Structure N11-18 (Pendergast 1985b:3-4, 1990b) as an elite residence. The truth is, however, that we have no specific knowledge of the significance of European goods in the sixteenth- and seventeenth-century Maya material culture inventory. We likewise know painfully little about the mechanisms of introduction and distribution of such goods, apart from the ethnohistorical identification of priests as principal importers of certain classes of objects.

It is reasonable to assume that the foreign products were highly valued because of their novelty and, in some cases, their utility. Such valuation would, of course, have made the objects very suitable markers of status, but they might equally well have been dispensed for religious reasons largely or wholly unrelated to rank or status within the community. In circumstances in which the precontact criteria for definition of elite status were blended with, altered by, and perhaps extensively supplanted by criteria introduced by the Spaniards, we can be reasonably sure that possession of European goods was some sort of mark of distinction, but far from certain as to how such distinction fit into Lamanai's social hierarchy.

The Spanish hold on Lamanai was never tight, and in 1641 it was permanently shaken by Maya rebellion (López de Cogolludo 1971:bk. 11, ch. 13). Whatever remained of an elite at the community in the seventeenth century appeared to the Spaniards to have decamped together with the rest of the populace, but in fact a number of families probably left only for the brief time of the Spanish stop at the site and then returned to reestablish some of the patterns of precontact life. The old religion, probably never really suppressed, came to the fore again in a combination of precontact and new material manifestations, and it is very likely that something of the life of the period before 1544 was revived as well. Evidence of the presence of people at Lamanai after 1641 exists (Pendergast 1985a:101-2, 1986a:5-6, 1986b:243-44), but nowhere is it plentiful and nowhere does it give us more than an indirect glimpse of the existence of an elite within a community of unspecifiable size and equally unspecifiable lifespan. By 1700, Lamanai had very probably ended its existence as a settlement; a few families may have continued to inhabit the site after that date, but there was surely no longer a basis for application of the term "elite" to any portion of the remnant population.

Reciprocity between Classes: The Nature of the Evidence

If we accept that reciprocal relationships in Maya communities extended beyond the link between noble and commoner to encompass the entire elite as a body with both privileges and concomitant obligations, it should follow that archaeology will yield evidence of such reciprocity. It is my view that, whereas direct archaeological evidence is rarely if ever forthcoming on this matter, a considerable range of indirect evidence exists that allows us to perceive part of the bond between the elite and those on lower rungs of the social ladder.

It is self-evident that the rulers of both Altun Ha and Lamanai, and their respective cadres of nobles, had several very specific things to offer to the rest of the population, including the remainder of the elite. Effective rule provides stability through long-term and short-term direction and organization. It also offers intercession with the gods and with any other external forces in defense of the community and a principal channel for communication of a wide range of information that, at least in its applied form, is vital to the community's continued existence. None of these things leaves behind concrete evidence, but every one is reified in the architecture and the other components of the material culture inventory. Much of what I have discussed above is, in fact, as close as we can come to direct evidence of the essentials provided for the commoners by the leaders of the two Belize communities, as they were provided by the rulers of all Maya centers.

In return for their essential services, leaders and their retinues received the material and philosophical support necessary both to their daily existence and to their ability to provide continuity in such services. Such support obviously came not only from commoners but also from all elements of the elite below the nobles themselves. Much of this is manifested physically in the nature of noble residences, the wealth items that were the trappings of nobility, and the massive efforts dedicated to providing suitable settings for religious activities directed by nobles. At the level of the bidirectional flow of services, and the accompanying monodirectional flow of goods, between rulers and ruled, the data from Altun Ha and Lamanai are as clear and as extensive as those at any center. They do not reveal attitudes, but they do give us the translation of those attitudes into action.

It is in the area of relationships between the non-noble elite and the lower echelons of the population that the picture becomes, predictably, quite a bit cloudier. We cannot know, for example, whether craft specialists whose products were destined for noble use derived from that upward link sufficient power to marshal peasant labor for the construction and maintenance of their homes. We can be fairly sure that jadeworkers did not extend their abilities with stone to the level of cutting masonry; but who can say whether the mason worked on command or for payment? Throughout the range of elite residences, the mason's skills are consistently evident; but because we cannot know how widely such skills were developed in the community, we cannot separate tradesman from handyman. Hence we cannot know whether a mandated or an economic relationship linked an elite homeowner to the builder or in how many cases the two roles were embodied in a single individual.

If we cannot specify the nature, or even the existence, of a relationship between merchant or artisan and mason or peasant laborer, surely we cannot hope to express in concrete terms the type of reciprocity that linked upper and lower segments of the society. One such link, the economic arrangement between purchaser and purveyor of service, is indisputably reciprocal and would need no discussion if we could confirm its existence. It involves, however, none of the sense of mutual obligation that I have suggested is very likely to have been of central importance in Maya life.

Reciprocity surely existed in any arrangement that was state-established, even though the apparent obligation flowed only from the lower element of the community to the upper. The sense of obligation in such circumstances is in fact as imposed on the elite individual as on the commoner by definition of role through prescription and proscription. An example arises if we assume state control over import and export and see it, as we surely must, as effected equally through administrators' decision making and merchant-traders' huckstering. In this context we can understand the entrepreneurial skills of the merchant as offered within the framework of state dictates, in return for state-established rewards provided ultimately by the masses. The difficulty here is that the degree, and indeed even the existence, of state control remains entirely within the realm of assumption.

It is the scale of exchange and the distances involved that conjure up the picture of major government intervention in the economy; we have no import control documents or excise stamps to verify our suspicions in the matter. There are, to date, not even very many emblem glyphs on communities' portable products, whether found at home or far from their source. Where they exist, no one can be sure what kind of political relationship or what amount, if any, of state economic control they document.

The contribution of the elite to the shape and richness—the quality—of life can be seen as having involved a type of reciprocity that lay beyond the reach of diktat and may never have been given verbal or tangible expression. Though impossible to resurrect from the archaeological record in any specific sense, elite-generated quality pervades all site centers in countless forms. It is this aspect that one would most like to grasp: community pride based on artisans' special skills, on architects' superior design abilities, on merchants' outstanding successes on the trading trail, or even on such mundane but important things as neighborhood atmosphere.

As in many other societies, the elite of Maya communities such as Altun Ha and Lamanai surely perceived their obligation to maintain a certain level of quality in their existence, to keep up appearances both individually and for the community as a whole. In return, they received both material and psychological support from those below them; the relationship enriched each group and sustained the polity in a viable setting. In the ninth century it may have been this, as much as any other relationship or force, that kept Lamanai on a level road while Altun Ha toppled off the cliff of Classic collapse.

6. "Will the Real Elites Please Stand Up?": An Archaeological Assessment of Maya Elite Behavior in the Terminal Classic Period

Gair Tourtellot, Jeremy A. Sabloff, and Kelli Carmean

THE term "elite" must refer, by definition, to a small number of people in a society or there is no point in using it. If the criteria by which we identify an elite recur frequently, then, clearly, either more than an elite group is being identified, or one is dealing with a substantially egalitarian society. However, no one thinks Mesoamerican civilizations were egalitarian; nor do any of the documents suggest they were.

To the extent these small elites or nobles are organized by "upper-class" kin and connections (E. Hansen and T. Parrish 1983), it may be easier for archaeologists to identify them as a group than to identify the real movers and shakers in a society individually. Epigraphers seem to be making much better progress in identifying powerful Maya individuals and some of their interconnections, although hieroglyphic texts seem to be mute concerning everybody else. However, these identified rulers must have resided and ruled somewhere and were embedded in households as well as in dynastic kinship relations. Additionally, even elites operate through retainers and administrators of various sorts, perhaps constituting a lesser nobility or lower level of the elite; archaeologists have a better chance of recovering these people (among whom the real decision makers may be hidden). Indeed, some critics might say that elites in this broad sense (including those who oversee the carrying out of decisions) are just about the only Maya people archaeologists have been finding for years, due to our usual research focus on major sites, easily visible (large) remains, and especially the centers of sites.

Although one might say that we need a return to examining elites as a counterpart to recent emphasis on ordinary people in settlement archaeology, we protest that there has never yet been a major or complete shift away from elites and central places. We maintain that the study of ordinary Maya commoners and the economic infrastructure remains underdeveloped (also see Sabloff 1983; Webster and Gonlin 1988). How many extended studies, not just test pitting, of complete households are there: Mayapan, Tikal,

Seibal, Copan, and several smaller studies? And what proportion of these actually deal with the simplest remains or the positive identification of actual farmers? Or with early periods? From another perspective, how many complete settlement maps do we have or even extensive transects? How many intersite or regional surveys and how many different Maya subregions are represented? In each case there is at most a handful, compared with the dozens of sites for which relatively complete records of monuments and texts are now available. It is not the case that settlement remains will always be there in contrast to the valuable and vulnerable sculptures, for looters are now trenching and taking apart hundreds of humble house mounds in their search for polychrome pots to satisfy the demands of collectors, and hundreds more fall to agricultural colonization schemes.

The foregoing is a preface to the major focus of this paper—the use of Maya architecture to identify a proportion of the population of ancient communities as elite (either rulers or lesser nobility). We suggest that elite behavior can be productively viewed through a window of interelite competition and social control of subordinate strata and that these elite and their goals can be partially identified and evaluated through architecture. In the following discussion, we shall examine certain architectural works as possible indicators of social status or ethnic interconnections between elites.

We take as our principal case studies the archaeology of two contemporary lowland Maya sites occupied during the heightened competition of the Terminal Classic period: Sayil in the Puuc region of Yucatan, Mexico, and Seibal in Peten, Guatemala. Our pretext for this exploratory study is the publication of *Maya Postclassic State Formation* by John W. Fox (1987), which attempts to explain much of the Postclassic period in southern Mesoamerica as derived from, or developed in response to, warrior and elite lineage migrations from the lower Gulf Coast.

The comparisons and contrasts between Sayil and Seibal are limited primarily to architecture here. One reason for this focus is that architecture is relatively permanent, functional and not merely symbolic, and, furthermore, not subject to the vagaries of gift, offering, payment, loan, accident, and disposal that conceivably explain the recovered distributions of portable items. Another practical reason is that we have completed the mapping phase of our work at Sayil, featuring an incredibly detailed map of architectural remains, but have only begun to analyze the excavations. Consequently, little use is made here of artifacts, ceramics, or burials, all potentially revealing indicators of elite behavior.

Architectural Construction

In Maya archaeology elite places have often been identified by means of standing architecture: stone-walled and/or corbel-vaulted buildings. These structures reveal a high investment of labor and skill that exceeds that of any other type of building (superstructure) and are usually the only type of building with ornamental sculpture (e.g., A. Smith 1950, 1962, 1982; Kur-jack 1974; Arnold and Ford 1980; Pollock 1980; Webster and Abrams 1983).

Sayil

At Sayil we can readily count the number and distribution of stone buildings as a measure of the elite and then compare their frequencies with other types of building remains to assess the reasonableness of the identification. Such enumeration is possible not only because of the visibility of structures on the thin soils at Sayil, but because of the uniquely thorough mapping achieved for this Puuc region site, with numerous long transects mapped completely across the clearly delimited site. Significantly, Sayil is a one-period site and very little architecture is buried beneath later constructions (Sabloff et al. 1984, 1985; Tourtellot et al. 1988, 1989; Sabloff and Tourtellot 1991). What we see on the surface—and what we have mapped—are relatively contemporaneous structures and synchronic activities.

Table 6.1 lists the counts and percentages of various types of buildings (features that may have contained rooms) on the 2.5 sq km fully mapped at Sayil. (The building counts in table 6.1 can be further multiplied by 1.8 to obtain roughly accurate projected counts for the entire 4.5 sq km that constituted ancient central Sayil; however, we believe that additional multistory stone buildings do not exist outside the mapped site-core. The percentages remain similar to those here, except the percentage of rooms in multistory stone buildings drops to 4.4 percent.)

If we make the usual assumption that stone architecture belonged to the elite because of its great expense, we see from table 6.1 that 19.3 percent of all structures at Sayil belong to the elite. Assuming that all or a similar proportion of rooms in each of the four principal types of building were used as dwellings—which is probably not a wholly reasonable assumption since some rooms must have been used for public, administrative, storage, and other mixed activities—then 35.9 percent of all rooms would have been elite dwellings. This percentage seems grossly excessive. An implied population ratio of 1:2 between the elite (rulers, administrators, and executives, even with their families and domestics) and the rest of society (commoners) is patently unbelievable. Consider the limited evidence for occupational specialization (specifically, the presumably small numbers of artisans) and the fact that much of the work to be supervised was traditional, repetitive, and labor-intensive—hardly the sorts of tasks that required the overbearingly tight supervision suggested by the ratio of 1:2. Although a matter of controversy, it seems unlikely that the proportion of elite or even noble people would exceed 2 to 10 percent of the total population (Adams 1974; Webster 1985b).

But the architecture of Sayil is more diverse than a simple elite versus commoner model of social structure would necessitate, with up to six different types of construction in evidence. As listed in table 6.1, stone buildings

Table 6.1: Mapped Buildings at Sayil

	Number of Structures	Percent of Structures	Number of Rooms	Percent of Rooms
Stone		19.3		35.9
Multistory	5	0.5	149	7.7
Other	209	18.8	548	28.2
Wall braces	362	32.6	597	30.7
Bare platforms	177	15.9	292*	15.0
Chich mounds	357	32.2	357*	18.4
Total	1,110		1,943.0	

* The room count for small bare platforms is calculated using the average room number for the foundation wall brace buildings, 1.65, although it is certainly possible that they were single-room structures only. Chich mounds probably supported only a single room apiece.

are divisible into at least two subtypes, according to whether they consist of multiple ("pyramidal") or single terraces of rooms (Sayil lacks courtyard quadrangles or acropolises of the Uxmal Monjas and Las Palomas types). There are also a few examples of a third subtype of stone-walled buildings that were never vaulted (and therefore much cheaper to erect than the other single-story stone buildings that bore massive vaults). Furthermore, cheaper still are three other types of probably domestic buildings with perishable superstructures, listed in order of decreasing architectural elaboration (expense) in table 6.1: braces are freestanding wall bases 1-5 courses high, while bare platforms have retaining walls and chich (small rubble) mounds do not (see Carmean 1990a, 1990b for discussions of architectural labor investment estimates for these structures).

The counts of structures in table 6.1 clearly do not exhibit the expected pyramidal frequency distribution (i.e., great numbers of simple buildings and few costly ones). Surprisingly, there are also far more of the vaulted than nonvaulted stone building subtypes. Even less of a pyramidal distribution is obtained when rooms are counted instead; at best, there is a truncated pyramid with a very broad top. Neither the absolute numbers nor their percentages accord with our standard expectation that the places of the elite should be few.

Of course, if the stone buildings were indeed for the elite, some or many rooms within them may have functioned for broadly administrative rather than dwelling purposes (e.g., as antechambers, audience halls, shrines, offices, visitors' quarters, dressing rooms, artisans' workshops, and storage rooms). Nonresidential uses seem particularly likely in view of the scarcity at Sayil of interior benches or storage niches, hallmarks of palace residences (Adams 1974; but see Harrison 1970). It will be very difficult and expensive to establish the use of individual rooms in stone buildings through excavation, because so little is usually left on their floors—and what little there is may instead be later or secondary precisely because the stone construction is so permanent. At Sayil we are approaching the question of use more indirectly, by surface collecting putative refuse areas associated with each type of structure, in the hope of efficiently picking up at least the gross variations in building use, including any signs of domestic occupation. But even if a certain percentage of the stone rooms is factored out as nonresidential, the number of rooms still seems excessive.

Another refinement is to consider only the multistory stone buildings (or palaces) at Sayil to be elite locales. Table 6.1 then shows that 7.7 percent of all rooms were occupied by elite people. This more reasonable percentage also accords with two other observations on multistory buildings: they are found in the site-core (narrowly defined as the features occurring along the central causeway on the Sayil Valley floor) and they possess almost all the "apartments" (two to four interconnected rooms with a single outside entrance, contrasting with numerous plans where all rooms have an outside entrance). Apartments certainly indicate a more specialized use of interior spaces (see also Freidel and Sabloff 1984) and may indicate occupation by larger co-residential groups that only an elite could sustain or a combination of elite family quarters and servants' rooms.

Nevertheless, another 28.2 percent of Sayil rooms are in buildings with similar construction. This proportion of the total still seems very large for a sustainable second-level nobility, even if intellectual and craft specialists were included. If the figure was lowered to take into account nonresidential rooms, it would still remain relatively large. While many of these stone buildings are found in or on the edge of the site-core, other examples are widely distributed throughout the peripheries of Sayil. The frequent location of peripheral examples on higher elevations accords with a superior status for their occupants, but their broad spatial distribution and generally few rooms call into question their identification as housing for the same sort of elite as in the larger or multistory stone buildings in the center.

In sum, the use of different floor plans, location, and architectural elaboration at Sayil produces some very equivocal results regarding the identification of an elite. Clearly, the use of stone buildings as a measure of the size of the upper class leaves something to be desired, simply because there are several subtypes, which are surprisingly numerous at Sayil. Four to six levels of architectural construction types and labor investment are in evidence, and further distinctions in status are suggested by the contrasts in number of rooms and geographic locations within the stone building subtypes (see Carmean 1990b, which uses vault area per platform as one means of differentiating elite levels).

Coincidentally, it may be worth recalling here that N. Hammond has suggested (1982:189-97) that logically there must have been some seven social levels in ancient Maya society. Even if the social system is broadly divided into two classes—an upper and a lower—each class would have had several levels within it (see Joyce Marcus, this volume).

Finally, it should be noted that we have not even considered the real possibility that some of the elite may have lived in the more elaborate perishable structures—such as ones with wattle-and-daub walls—mapped at Sayil. Clearly, such a consideration would further complicate the picture just outlined. The multiplicity of building construction techniques at Sayil points up the difficulty of sharply contrasting a unitary elite or noble group with a unitary class of commoners.

Seibal

For Seibal we again focus on architecture for comparison with Sayil, but we can supplement this with analysis of excavated artifacts associated with some building types. Both sites are roughly similar in population, with estimated populations of around 10,000 people apiece, although the settlement density of Seibal is much lower than at Sayil. Unlike Sayil, Seibal is not a single period site, but here we shall look only at the buildings and platforms constructed in the late Late Classic or Terminal Classic.

Stone buildings at Seibal are divisible into those with vaults and those without. These buildings in turn contrast with those having the skimpiest of wall braces and those that were entirely perishable above their platform floors (table 6.2). Comparison of the stone buildings at Seibal and Sayil reveals striking differences. Only four structures excavated or tested at Seibal were vaulted buildings, while another three had tall stone walls with perishable roofs. Three of the four vaulted buildings are temples (on pyramids). The other four buildings have only one story with three to six rooms apiece. All seven of these are confined to the central civic/plaza groups linked by causeways at the heart of Seibal (A. Smith 1982); although there might be nine more examples of stone buildings among the unexcavated structures elsewhere in the same major groups (A and D), we are confident that none exist further out. In all these respects, the Seibal stone buildings differ from their counterparts at Sayil.

Room counts have not been employed in these comparisons. At Seibal virtually no conclusive evidence for interior partitions is preserved in either wall brace or wholly perishable buildings. Yet these single perishable rooms, judging from their commodious floor areas, are often vastly larger than individual rooms in stone buildings. Thus, interior spaces at Seibal seem far less commensurate with building construction types than those at Sayil and are therefore an unreliable guide to calculating the number of elite versus commoner rooms or people.

Overall, the percentage of stone buildings at Seibal must be very low. Omitting the three stone buildings that are temples, the remaining four stone buildings constitute only 2.7 percent of all the 148 excavated building loci (table 6.2). When compared with all the 326 potential dwelling structures, excavated or not, just in the central 1.9 sq km of Seibal (the area of

Table 6.2: Excavated Buildings at Seibal

	Number of Structures		Percent of Structures
Stone	7		4.7
Vaulted		4	2.7
Nonvaulted		3	2.0
Wall braces	6		4.1
Platforms			
In major groups		12	8.1
Peripheral 3-levels		34	23.0
Peripheral 2-levels		70	47.3
Peripheral 1-levels		19	12.8
Total	148		

Data from A. Smith 1982 and Tourtellot 1982:table 14.

map 2 in Willey et al. 1975), the four excavated nontemple stone buildings represent no more than 1.2 percent (the number of potential dwelling structures in the central area is calculated from an average of 109 ordinary residential units in the Late/Terminal Classic phases, plus at least 11 [maximum 19] probable residential units within the central civic groups, multiplied by an average of 2.72 dwelling-type structures apiece [Tourtellot 1982:1035, 1061, table 45]). Stone buildings must represent a vanishingly small percentage when the calculation is expanded to the ancient community as a whole (only 15.25 sq km of which was even sampled during mapping, without finding all site limits).

These low percentages at Seibal are exactly what we should expect for elite buildings in a community and might very well be the habitations of the rulers themselves (omitting the temples, of course). The overall distribution of stone buildings, foundation walls, and entirely perishable houses of increasingly simple floor plan in table 6.2 also forms a very squat version of the expected frequency pyramid. However, the overall percentage of stone structures (4.7) is vastly lower than at Sayil.

Where, too, are the administrators, specialists, and retainers who might constitute the lesser nobility at Seibal? If they occupied the maximum 19 units of residential appearance in the central civic groups, then an estimated total of some 52 buildings (including the 4 stone ones) were occupied by the elite. These represent only 14.9 percent of an estimated maximum of 348 dwellings in just the central area. When much reduced to represent the whole Seibal community, the adjusted percentage of elite so calculated must be a far cry from the 19.3 percent obtained above for elite stone buildings from the entire Sayil community. The reader will note that the architectural criterion for identifying the elite has changed here somewhat, shifting from stone buildings to the locational criterion of central location adjacent to the major civic plazas and temple pyramids. In other words, the attempt to apply a uniform architectural criterion (stone buildings) to two contemporaneous Maya sites produces wholly incommensurate results. Either the social organizations of Sayil and Seibal were amazingly different or stone architecture per se is a poorly understood and misleading marker for the elite when applied indiscriminately.

At Seibal, as at Sayil, it was possible to extend the architectural analysis of social ranking far below the elite, assisted by excavated artifacts. It was found that two sets of architecturally based distinctions could be applied to the inhabitants of Seibal perishable dwellings. First, among the perishable buildings listed in table 6.2, it was clear that three-level structures were outstanding by reason of their unusual terraces, stairways, height, volume, floor area, early dates, numbers and qualities of artifacts, preferred position, and association with kitchens and oriented altar/shrines (Tourtellot 1982:700-7). It seems clear that these were the dwellings of higher-status commoners specifically identified with the founders or headmen of families and having the widest distribution across different units (Tourtellot 1988b).

Secondly, entire units of perishable dwellings could be rank-ordered along the positively correlated dimensions of area, height of tallest platform, volume, and their ratios, employed as surrogate measures for population, prestige, and expenditure (Tourtellot 1982:822-45). The resulting distribution of units again produced a frequency pyramid, with two deluxe units (appropriately located among the ten to nineteen centrally located elite units above), seven first class units, fifteen average units, and twenty-four economy units (the latter often lacking the three-level structures that appear to mark dwellings of independent headmen).

Consequently, as was the case at Sayil, there appears to have been complex status and wealth ranking within the basic elite and commoner classes, although expressed within a simpler framework of architectural construction techniques. Despite recovery of over forty-five burials at Seibal (versus five at Sayil), they are of little assistance in further identifying elite personages. None are truly elite in grave goods or grave structure, not only because most burials were from ordinary house contexts, but because construction fills consisting of forbiddingly loose boulders prevented excavation in the likely elite places around the major plazas.

Clearly, the preceding analyses reveal a serious problem, since highly disparate proportions of elites are identified at two sites where at least the temporal sources of variability are minimized. There are three other general problems with using architecture, specifically vaulted buildings, as a guide to the identification of elites. First, stone-walled, let alone vaulted, buildings simply were not equally common in all regions of the Maya lowlands (leaving aside the highlands in general). In this regard the Pasión region that includes Seibal stands in particularly sharp contrast to the Puuc region with its myriad stone buildings (Pollock 1965). Consequently, the architectural comparison above is instructive for the situations at Sayil and Seibal, but is basically ill-founded as a universal means for identifying elites. Moreover, the availability of limestone construction material in the natural environment must also be viewed as a factor. Thus, discrepancies in local resources further complicate site-to-site comparisons of elite when identifications of the elite are made on only an architectural basis.

Conceptually, too, there is no ever-present connection between vaults and elites, because numerous alternative "substitutions" that had the same meaning but different means of accomplishment conceivably existed. This phenomenon is already clearly visible in the notorious troping practiced in Maya languages and hieroglyphic signs. It is believed to be one of the reasons for the discordance among the multiple scales used to rank the perishable Seibal houses (Tourtellot 1982:822-45). The disparity between the Pasión and Puuc regions in their interest in erecting stone buildings must be another example, for it seems unlikely there was as great a discrepancy in the size and proportion of elites between the two communities as this architectural indicator alone would suggest.

Finally, there is the matter of distinguishing between public use and private—exclusively elite—use of particular artifacts, rooms, buildings, or building types (this problem is allied to the perennial questions concerning the form and function of palaces versus temples). For instance, in the absence of other data, does the rarity of major temple pyramids or grand palaces indicate they were major elite structures (in a sense, grandiose versions of ordinary household components), or do they represent buildings that served special central functions accessible to the public at large? Are we dealing with governors' palaces or city halls? From some of the recent epigraphic work at Palenque, Tikal, or Copan, one might think the elaborate structures were the private preserve of the elites, but, then again, how many texts and carvings acknowledge ordinary Maya at all?

Architectural Patterns

A different approach to architecture is suggested by the historical period during which these two sites were occupied—the Terminal Classic. It has long been recognized that one of the features of this transitional period was the intrusion of non-Classic Maya "foreigners" into the Maya lowlands (e.g., Sabloff and Willey 1967). Cases of conquest with the introduction of foreign elites may be the simplest situations for identifying elites on the ground and thus may provide an instructive contrast to the quandaries revealed by the foregoing analysis of stone architecture.

With the fall of many Southern lowland Classic Maya cities in the ninth century A.D., a new economic and political force began to have a significant impact on the Maya in the Terminal Classic. One possible model envisions the Chontal Maya as this new force. They were advantageously situated on the Gulf Coast as intermediaries between the Classic Maya inland and

Mexican civilizations to the west. Through trading activities, Chontal acculturation produced what J. E. S. Thompson (1970) has labeled "the Mexicanized Maya."

Whatever their own role in facilitating the decline of Classic Maya society, the Chontal were in a good position to insert themselves opportunistically into the leadership gap left by the fallen native elite. There may have been many separate Chontal expeditions, entering the lowlands along many routes, but we are concerned with early "pincer movements" (cf. D. Chase and A. Chase 1982:610) when they settled at Chichen Itza, on Cozumel Island, and in the Puuc, venturing upriver to Altar de Sacrificios and Seibal on their eventual way into the highlands (Thompson 1970; Sabloff and Rathje 1975; Sabloff 1977; A. Chase 1985c, among others).

John Fox (1987) has detailed the diaspora of Chontal "pioneer warriors" followed by their elite lineages, arguing that it was powered by the fierce dynamics of segmentary lineage organization. If his scenario is valid, it may be possible to identify specific lineages of Chontal extraction in Terminal Classic Maya sites, especially ones like Sayil and Seibal that experienced florescence at that time. This recognition may be a key for understanding the transformation from Classic into Postclassic Maya society as a consequence of the replacement of the elite superstratum by a new elite.

It should be possible to detect a foreign (Chontal) presence through diachronic analysis of architecture and community patterns at Seibal and Sayil. We would hope to see a shift from traditional Maya architectural styles and community patterns reflecting traditional sociopolitical organization to a pattern where we can recognize a foreign organizational overlay. Numerous sources indicate that the new lords were never fully accepted and remained something of a distinct minority right up to the Spanish conquest (Tozzer 1941; Thompson 1970). In addition, invaders may have left evidence of social control due to their tenuous position as somewhat unwelcome foreigners in traditional Maya society. One form of social control is the imposition of a new political and religious ideological system on a subjugated population.

As background to the new elite social control we propose to identify at Seibal and Sayil, let us mention that the still little known native communities of Acalan, part of the proposed Chontal homeland, appear to have contained irregularly shaped orthogonal plazas enclosed by long, low structures with a single temple pyramid at the plaza head (J. Fox 1987:38). To these were added alleged Mexican innovations like round or oval temples, radial temples dedicated to the Feathered Serpent, pyramids with few rather than many tiers, and I-shaped enclosed ballcourts, often forming a characteristic temple-long structure-altar assemblage familiar from Mayapan (J. Fox 1987:19, 39, 60, 83).

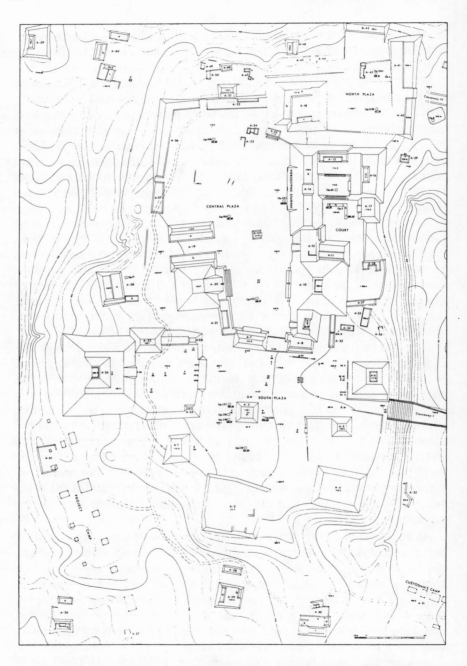

Fig. 6.1. Group A, Seibal (from A. Smith 1982; copyright 1982 by the President and Fellows of Harvard College).

Seibal

The Terminal Classic Bayal phase at Seibal is defined by the sudden appearance of many non-Classic Maya settlement, architectural, and artifactual features, whose ultimate origins appear to have been the western borderlands including the Chontalpa (Sabloff 1975b; Willey et al. 1975; Sabloff et al. 1982; A. Smith 1982; Tourtellot 1982; see also Sisson 1976). Changes from the traditional style on the carved stelae are likewise very clear, and at least one of probably two separate migrations came directly from the Gulf Coast (J. Graham 1973; Sabloff 1973; A. Chase 1985c). Although wholesale replacement of the ceramic industry occurred at Altar de Sacrificios in the slightly later Jimba phase (Adams 1971, 1973), at Seibal only the elite ceramic types switch from polychromes to imported fine paste ware, leaving the local domestic wares to continue mostly unchanged (Sabloff 1975b).

Plausible Chontal settlement features at Seibal are as follows (see A. Smith 1982 for maps and illustrations).

1. Seibal sits atop a long, high ridge. The choice of the more defensible Group D as the Late Classic site center may have been a response to the endemic warfare along the Pasión River (see J. Marcus 1976a; Houston and Matthews 1985) or even to early encroachments of the Chontal. By the beginning of the Terminal Classic period, Group D was abandoned in favor of new construction in the more accessible Group A.

2. Thus, elite or public activities shifted from the agglutinated Late Classic Group D to a newly spacious Group A, the focus for the non-Classic features. The South Plaza of Group A is one of those Chontal orthogonal plazas, with massive temple-pyramid A-24 at its head and several large platforms defining its edges as possible palace substructures (J. Fox 1987:83).

3. Temple A-3 was erected in the center of the South Plaza in Group A (fig. 6.1). Its central location, four-sided design with a stairway on each side, three tiers, veneer masonry, and the bearded Maya personages on the stucco frieze and Stela 10 point to its Chontal origin. No tomb was found within (A. Smith 1982). Its radically new central position, as for theater in the round, may reflect greatly increased public participation in state ceremonies with lessened emphasis on the traditional royal ancestor worship (Tourtellot 1982:1054).

4. Another radial structure, A-13, was erected in the middle of the reused Central Plaza of Group A, just off the axis of large ballcourt A-19. It contained the disarticulated skeletons of a possible ballgame team (A. Smith 1982:62). Its plan resembles Terminal Classic and Postclassic "dance platforms" (at sites such as Uxmal and Chichen Itza).

5. Ballcourts A-19 and C-9 were built, or at least their end zones were enclosed, during the Bayal phase, forming I-shaped courts that are characteristic of Chontal ballcourts (J. Fox 1987:83).

6. A large open-air marketplace may have been added to the Central Plaza at this time to enhance commerce, or the numerous little structures might have housed the garrison—this is highly speculative.

7. The cruciform sacbe system connecting the three core groups also dates to the Bayal phase (A. Smith 1982:236) and includes a stela platform reminiscent of those in the Puuc.

8. At the south terminus of the sacbe is Structure 79, a round pyramid with three tiers. Perhaps this shape corresponds to the imagery of a coiled serpent. In front of it is a jaguar altar supported by Atlantean figures (A. Smith 1982:165).

9. Bayal ceramics and construction are apparently highly centralized compared to the preceding Late Classic phase (Tourtellot 1982:1040-57). These Bayal materials either belonged to the elite, many hundreds strong, residing in a sea of traditional Maya or reflect a massive intervention and relocation of people into a more nucleated settlement with 60 percent greater density than hitherto existed.

10. House plans at Seibal throughout the Late Classic are distinct from those outside the Pasión region, featuring broad bench floors, frequently C-shaped. Possibly these are forerunners of the Early Postclassic style of C-shaped wall braces or narrow benches with open front sides, assigned to Early Postclassic Itza or Chontal migrants (D. Rice 1986; J. Fox 1987:84).

11. The final abandonment of outlying temples at this time probably indicates a centralization of religion, perhaps in an attempt to gain more control over the Maya populace through the suppression of traditional religion. Also, shrines or altars appear for the first time in a few households, placed over burials containing imported or imitation fine paste ceramics. A change from the traditional deity effigy incensarios to new spiked censers, along with a marked change in burial ritual, can be related to the religious changes plausibly introduced by the foreigners (Sabloff 1975b; Tourtellot 1982, 1990).

Clearly, there were massive changes in the archaeological assemblages in the center of Seibal, largely restricted to public, elite, or ritual structures or locations, whereas the distinctive ordinary house plans continued as before. Most of the enumerated changes can be paralleled by examples either in the Puuc region or at Chichen Itza, additionally including such telling details as the presence of engaged colonnettes, three-member moldings, patolli game boards, and sculptures of a prowling jaguar or a human head emerging from the jaws of a feathered serpent (A. Smith 1982:239-40). Chichen Itza and the Puuc are more or less contemporary regions known from ethnohistory to have been occupied by the Xiu and Itza people; John Fox (1987) strenuously argues that these were migratory lineages of Chontal origin. In any case, there is a fair amount of well-known Puuc-style architecture in "Old Chichen" (Andrews V 1979).

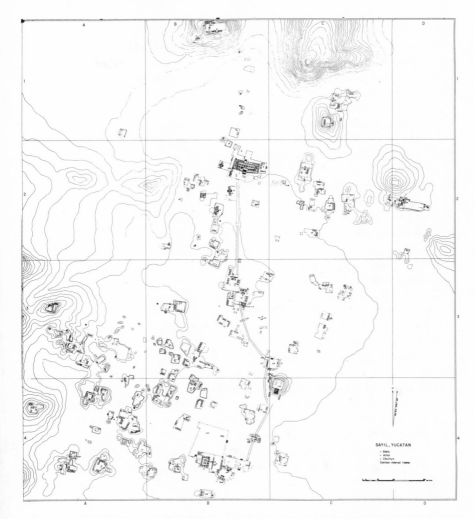

Fig. 6.2. Some of the large architectural complexes of the central core of Sayil (map by E. Shook; from H.E.D. Pollock 1980; copyright 1980 by the President and Fellows of Harvard College).

Sayil

Although the architectural and settlement data for Chontal influence and presence at Seibal has been developed in some detail, a full assessment cannot yet be given for Sayil because the excavation materials have not yet been fully analyzed. Nevertheless, a fair amount of information can be derived from our new maps and preliminary analyses because all evidence so far indicates that all of the construction is datable to the Terminal Classic Cehpech horizon alone (Pollock 1980; Sabloff et al. 1984, 1985; Tourtellot et al. 1988, 1989). Enough can be said to point up the linkages, but also to indicate that the Chontal presence at Sayil was probably quite different from that at Seibal. Most of the centrally located features to be mentioned are illustrated in H. E. D. Pollock (1980).

1. The plan of central Sayil is open, flat, and spacious. The major architectural complexes of the center are connected by an intrasite sacbe (fig. 6.2).

2. A stela platform is located astride the causeway.

3. The single ballcourt is enclosed on at least one end. Like one of the ballcourts at Seibal, it is attached to a causeway.

4. A small "dance platform" like A-13 at Seibal is located off one end of the ballcourt, in the middle of a plaza.

5. Again there is a small round pyramid outside the major groups, although this one is not connected to the core by a causeway.

6. A potential marketplace is located near the center of Sayil, filled with small platforms near several large building complexes and a stela. This description could apply to Seibal's Central Plaza as well. We'll have more to say on this functional identification below.

On present evidence, however, Sayil diverges strongly from the Seibal and Chontal pattern in several important respects.

1. Although it has fairly distinct boundaries, Sayil, like many other Puuc sites, sits defenseless in the middle of an open valley. Unlike Uxmal and some other northern sites, there is not even a wall around the central precinct.

2. For all its spacious layout and numerous large building assemblages, there are few definable plazas. Part of the problem may be the difficulty in identifying temples among the many range-type buildings, since no pyramidal substructure exceeds 3 m in height.

3. The candidates for the allegedly Chontal-derived temple-long structure-altar complex are weak. One is the plaza including the "dance platform" off the ballcourt, where, however, the temple faces the wrong way. Another might be the long structures associated with a platform in front of the Great Palace, but only if this famous three-story structure itself is considered the pyramid.

4. The organization of the Sayil site-core along the sacbe is like beads on a string rather than the radial arrangement of Seibal or the orthogonal plazas of the Chontalpa.

5. Sayil lacks a radial temple, as do Puuc sites generally.

In most respects, then, Sayil is a typical Puuc site. Therefore, whether the Chontal are the elite ethnic group responsible for the undoubted architectural parallels between Yucatan (Chichen Itza and the Puuc) and the Southern lowlands (e.g., Seibal) at the end of the Classic period or not (see A. Chase 1985c; A. Chase and D. Chase, in press b) depends on arguing both that the Xiu and Itza were already present in Yucatan in the Terminal Classic and that they were elite lineages of Chontal origin. These complex and detailed arguments have already been forcefully presented in detail (see Ball 1986; J. Fox 1987).

The theory of segmentary lineages and the dynamics of their fission applied by John Fox (1987) to Quiche and Chontal materials may be applicable to the Puuc as well. It has been suggested that the major Puuc sites were largely independent of each other, reflecting "dispersed factions at every level of organization" that formed "the powerful blocks from which larger scaled social entities were constituted" (Kurjack, Garza, and Lucas 1979:41). Fox proposes (1987:33, passim) that political loci are more or less direct transforms of the number and relatedness of the resident lineages ("space reflects genealogy"). Elsewhere we have suggested that the multiple nodes of architecture along the Sayil sacbe may include just such a series or sequence of elite residential groups, notably the multistory or courtyard groups (Tourtellot et al. 1988). Or again, given the propensity of segmentary organization to arise under pressure in broad areas of simple agriculture, like the eastern frontier of the Chontalpa (J. Fox 1987:71-79), it is significant that almost no evidence of intensive agriculture has been found at Sayil or in the Puuc. The Puuc may have been the northern flank of the Chontal world, reacting to the progressive encroachment of Classic Maya culture in tandem with the Acalan and other Chontal peoples to the south (i.e., the geographic and possibly temporal northward progression of architectural styles from Rio Bec to Chenes to Puuc and the westward spread of stela carving and Maya architecture from the Early into the Late Classic).

Although Seibal clearly exhibits the architectural markers of Chontal expansion, as codified by Fox, the evidence from Sayil is not so conclusive, as detailed above. Therefore, we would speculate that the Chontal presence in the Puuc, and perhaps other parts of the Yucatan, was of a different nature than the relatively quick and complete takeover exhibited at Seibal and other sites of the Southern lowlands. Perhaps the Puuc region, with its lower and more dispersed earlier Classic population, had been in contact with the adjacent Chontalpa for several centuries prior to the Terminal Classic onset of successful major expansions. Some authors have suggested this long-standing relationship, often naming the Itza as participants (Proskouriakoff 1970; Ball 1979). If they are correct, then the shocking expansionary migrations of the Chontal warriors and elites in the Terminal Classic may have been relatively uneventful in the Puuc and did not produce a particularly notable new suite of architecturally expressed organizational features.

However, there is the intriguing possibility of an alternative interpretation for the putative Sayil marketplace that might suggest direct foreign intervention and control. This place—called the Mirador Flat—is a paved open area about one hectare in extent between the Mirador roof-comb temple(?) building (Pollock's Structure 3B2 [1980]) and two large residential basal platforms. New mapping revealed an incredibly dense mass of over

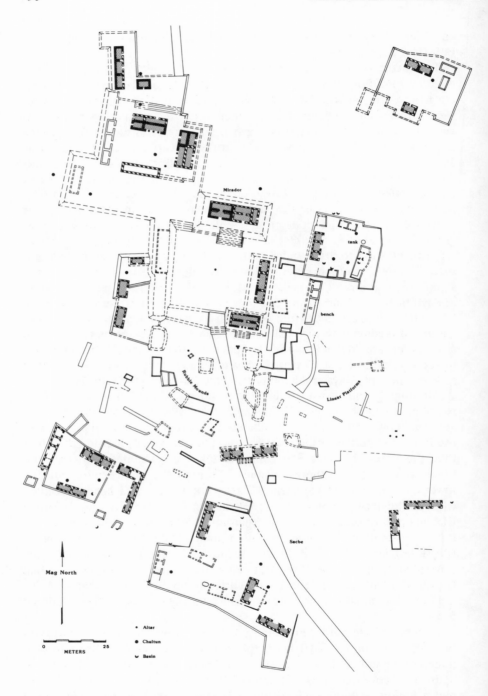

Fig. 6.3. The Mirador Flat zone of Sayil (drawing courtesy of the Sayil Archaeological Project).

forty-three aligned platforms, many so low as to be nearly invisible (fig. 6.3). The architecture exposed by excavation consists of rubble mounds and low platforms, with vertical slab wall foundations for perishable, open-fronted buildings that had narrow benches along the back walls. These characteristics coincide with our expectation for a permanent marketplace at the heart of the community and differ from anything else at Sayil. More interesting in the present context, however, is the close resemblance of these foundations to the Early Postclassic house style with C-shaped wall plan defined by P. M. Rice and D. S. Rice in the central Peten (Rice and Rice 1979; D. Rice 1986).

Is this architectural complex the remains of what Fox elsewhere identifies as pioneer garrisons established by Chontal warrior lineages? At Sayil these buildings represent a very compact area of occupation near the site center and astride the sacbe. The buildings, however, may be late and, therefore, presumably could not be part of a pioneering settlement. In addition, next to one building was an example of an Early Postclassic type of side-notched arrowhead similar to those seen at Seibal (Willey 1978:127) and also associated with the similar Early Postclassic houses reviewed by D. S. Rice (1986:340) as Chontal-related.

Intriguingly, and possibly conclusively if validated by ongoing analyses, the Mirador Flat area may exhibit an impoverished example of the allegedly quintessential Chontal temple-long structure-altar plaza, or pioneer garrison, plan (cf. J. Fox 1987:24-26, fig. 2.2). Here on the Mirador Flat the candidates consist of a 1.5 m tall rubble (dry-laid stone wall temple?) mound, a low altar platform, and a perpendicular open-fronted, colonnaded(?) long structure. These are located at the inner focus of the semicircular Mirador Flat area (Tourtellot et al. 1988). These findings and their possible significance are certainly provocative, and if validated could indicate that Chontal relationships with the Puuc were not pacific at all.

Typically, however, garrison sites occur on defensible hilltops, and certainly these were more readily available outside of flat Sayil. Here on the exposed Mirador Flat there is not even a visible perimeter wall around the buildings; nor were water cisterns or grinding stones found within the Mirador Flat "garrison" area, although these were absolutely essential items for permanent occupation of Sayil and the Puuc region. We look to ongoing analyses of the small finds from this area to help settle this fascinating question.

One aspect of Seibal archaeology is also relevant to this matter of Chontal garrison sites. Although Seibal may have been initially conquered by a leapfrog migration of a Chontal warrior vanguard (J. Fox 1987:82-83), it is curious that there was virtually no Terminal Classic construction, and only light occupation, inside the marvelously defensible Late Classic Group D hilltop following the conquest (A. Smith 1982). It may be that the light occupation represents the conquering Chontal warrior lineages who arrived first, and that attention was switched to the spacious ridge of Group A when aristocratic and elite Chontal lineages arrived to displace them and to construct their architectural matrix of social control, a pattern of succession evidently oft repeated during the centuries of Chontal expansion (J. Fox 1987).

Summary

After starting out by looking for Maya elites through examination of the disquieting frequencies of the stone architecture commonly attributed to them, then considering conquest situations as providing a sharper focus for identifying elites, we have ended by perhaps identifying the locus of a group of warriors who merely served them. We have three conclusions: (1) architectural construction per se is not necessarily a sensitive indicator of status (even among structures restricted to the same use); (2) we must examine still finer discriminations within construction types at similar levels of apparent expenditure (preferably employing a whole battery of additional contextual data); and (3) we must continue searching for the right perspective to isolate elites (more specifically, the aspects of architecture that held status meaning for the ancient Maya).

Acknowledgments

The Seibal field research was undertaken between 1964 and 1968 under the direction of Gordon R. Willey and A. Ledyard Smith of the Peabody Museum, Harvard University. The recently completed Sayil field research was undertaken between 1983 and 1988 with the support of the National Science Foundation (Grants BNS-8302016 and BNS-8616080), to which we are most grateful. Kelli Carmean was supported in the field in 1987 and 1988 in part by funds from the Tinker Foundation (administered by the Center for Latin American Studies, University of Pittsburgh). We deeply appreciate the assistance and support of our many collaborators and friends in the United States and Mexico. Finally, we thank Joyce Marcus for her extremely helpful comments on an earlier draft of this paper.

7. Children of the First Father's Skull: Terminal Classic Warfare in the Northern Maya Lowlands and the Transformation of Kingship and Elite Hierarchies

David A. Freidel

THE lowland Maya defined elitism in a specific and identifiable concept in Precolumbian texts: *ahau*. Although *ahau* simply means noble lord, this ancient Maya word refers principally to kingship (L. Schele and M. Miller 1986). As is the case in all such primary and encompassing political concepts (Cohen 1979:87), the word *ahau* is both ambiguous in its institutional referents and dynamic through time.

The elite institution defined by *ahau* emerged in the Late Preclassic period (300 B.C.-A.D. 100) as manifested in the ritual buildings and diagnostic implements employed by kings to access the supernatural on behalf of domains (Freidel and Schele 1988a). Initially, the institution appears to focus on the charismatic power of the ruler through shamanistic access to the supernatural as well as upon the direct lineage connections he claims to the mythical progenitors of the Maya (Freidel and Schele 1988b). Other elite statuses remain undefined in the present epigraphic record of this period, but, by inference from subsequent developments in the Classic, the elite were defined as those people closely related to the king and those with obligations to provide the labor, materials, and skills necessary to create and maintain the facilities and implements the royal *ahau* used to manifest power in his realm.

During the Early Classic period (A.D. 200-600), the principle of dynasty emerges as families with traditions of *ku'l ahau* (holy lord)[1] establish themselves (Mathews 1985). The major innovation of this period is the focus upon the person of the king and explicit presentation of the ritual actions he must perform to attain and sustain this status through written language and stelae portrayals (Schele 1985).[2] This innovation, in turn, must have clarified the specific qualifications surrounding the transmission of the status of *ku'l ahau*, not only in terms of genealogy but also in terms of the actions—principally successful warfare and sacrifice—that candidates performed to acquire that status. The number of prospective candidates was undoubtedly greater than the number of offices.

The Early Classic period also sees the proliferation of titles that high-born individuals could attain. For the most part, texts displaying these titles refer to kings of the status of *ahau*, but there is the prospect that a number of statuses other than that of high king (such as *cahal*; L. Schele and M. Miller 1986) were developing in response to the increasing size of the elite that sustained this central institution. By the Late Classic period (A.D. 600-800), Maya polities ruled by kings of the *ku'l ahau* status had greatly increased (Mathews 1986), and so had the internal complexity of the elite below the king (L. Schele and M. Miller 1986; Stuart n.d.). M. E. Miller's (1986b) analysis of the texts associated with the Bonampak murals indicates several individuals simultaneously holding the title of *ahau* in that polity. The polity-level dynamics of the Late Classic elite hold many clues to the great collapse of the Southern lowland kingdoms. W. L. Fash (1983a) and his colleagues (Schele, Stuart, and Grube 1986-1988) have been tracking the fragmentation of the Copan state in light of struggles between the *ku'l ahau* and his immediate subordinates in the community.

A key feature in the dynamics of the Late Classic Maya institution of kingship, and of elitism in this civilization generally, is warfare between polities. The dynastic transmission of the high kingship was dependent upon successful capture of suitable sacrificial victims for dedication rituals (Schele 1983; Freidel 1986a; L. Schele and M. Miller 1986). The proliferation of kingdoms ruled by individuals of the status *ku'l ahau* can thus be identified with an increase in communities capable of success in warfare against established neighbors.[3] The designation of kings of secondary rank, *cahal* (D. Stuart n.d.), was likewise closely tied to success in war and alliance with high kings (L. Schele and M. Miller 1986:plate 86). This particular title is found primarily in the Usumacinta drainage subregion, but also occurs in the Northern lowlands, as discussed below.

The politics and theology of Maya warfare thus constitute promising avenues for the investigation of the manner in which the elite institution of *ahau* evolved or failed to evolve (Freidel 1986a, 1986b) in the course of the civilization. An essential issue here is the role of militarism in the consolidation and elaboration of elite power (Webster 1977). The formation of large, stable conquest states, which often follows a period of war among small states (Cowgill 1979; Renfrew and Cherry 1986), was not the sole outcome of Maya military activity. Instead, there was both an increase in the number of new states during the Late Classic and ultimately the collapse of the civilization in the Southern lowlands in Terminal Classic times (Culbert 1973).

Elsewhere, I (Freidel 1986a) have proposed that the Classic Maya of the Southern lowlands suffered a severe conceptual constraint, a structural impasse (Freidel and Schele 1988), in their definition of central power, such that the status of *ahau* was a collective category of divine being to which new human members could be added, but which defined its membership as equivalents. Among other things, this equivalency allowed the substitution of victim and executioner necessary to display the mystery of rebirth out of decapitation sacrifice that I suggest was the focus of accession and heir designation rituals. At the same time, this principle effectively impeded attempts to create internal divisions of the status of *ahau*, beyond such qualifications as *ku'l ahau* (holy lord) and *y'ahau* (a lord possessed by another lord), which would legitimate the permanent consolidation of smaller states into larger ones under successful conquerors.

I think that this hypothesis concerning Maya political ideology still has merit and is commensurate with the epigraphic and iconographic data on the Classic Maya. However, the institutional corollary presented in that paper (Freidel 1986a) was that the thrust of Classic Maya warfare was territorial boundary maintenance aimed at the internal cohesion of kingdoms. In that context, the documented adventures in wars of conquest were identified as the exceptions, not the rule. This position is no longer viable in the face of recent interpretive developments in the textual and artistic representation of Maya war. Prior to the conquest of Uaxactun by Great Jaguar Paw of Tikal in the late fourth century A.D. (Mathews 1985; Schele and Freidel 1990), warfare aimed primarily at taking noble captives may have been a general practice. Certainly after Tikal's successful incorporation of Uaxactun—a major kingdom—into its state, the Southern lowland Maya lords generally prosecuted wars aimed at conquest and subjugation of their enemies. The fact remains, however, that while the Southern lowland kingdoms fought drawn-out wars of conquest with each other over a period of some four hundred years (ca. A.D. 380-780), these resulted in relatively small (perhaps 2,500-3,000 sq km at the maximum or about 12 percent of the overall territory of the lowland civilization) and unstable (roughly a century at the maximum) multikingdom hegemonies.[4] The question remains as to why the Southern lowland Maya failed to establish enduring empires and instead watched their civilization crumble.

The fate of the Northern lowlands in the Terminal Classic period (A.D. 800-1000) is different from that of the Southern lowlands (Freidel 1986b). There are at least two large-scale states in the Northern lowlands emerging in the same period that witnesses the collapse of the Southern lowland kingdoms: Chichen Itza and Coba (A. Andrews and F. Robles 1985; F. Robles and A. Andrews 1986). Yaxuna is the boundary between these large-scale states and holds information concerning the conduct of their wars contesting supremacy in the north. The Puuc polities are clearly a factor in these wars, but their role in the contest at Yaxuna is not so clear at present, nor is it clear how their political organization functioned at the supracommunity level, although the number of large centers implies an organization closer to that of the southern kingdoms than of the large-scale states under review.

As detailed in the following discussion, there are reasons to believe that the wars between Chichen Itza and Coba were conducted in the guise of a dispute between small-scale neighboring states sharing a common boundary and that the theological and political precepts of the wars were those traditional to Maya warfare as found in the Southern lowlands. At the same time, there are clues to a new political solution to the problem of consolidating losers and their polities and also to a new organization of *ahauob* at Chichen Itza, facilitating and legitimating permanent large-scale state organization.

Maya Warfare and Territorial Scale

Peter Mathews (1986) suggests that there may have been as many as sixty independent states in the lowlands during the Late Classic period (A.D. 600-900). The territorial organization of the Maya as a mosaic of small independent states is in sharp contrast to the organization of such contemporary large-scale states in highland Mexico as focused on the city of Teotihuacan (Millon 1981; Sanders 1981b) in the Basin of Mexico and Monte Alban (Blanton 1978) in the Valley of Oaxaca.

While there are a number of geographical and environmental factors that would have made large-scale state formation logistically difficult—the paucity of natural internal boundaries, the equal paucity of natural internal transport routes—for the most part the lowland Maya enjoyed the same level of technology that fostered such states elsewhere in Mesoamerica. Under the circumstances, the political, economic, and military institutions of the lowland Maya represent equally likely sources of difficulty in moving to large-scale states.

The history of Classic Maya warfare left to us in images and hieroglyphic texts from Southern lowland kingdoms generally shows a pattern of local consolidation of high kingdoms and the establishment of relatively small and unstable multikingdom hegemonies. Early Classic Tikal conquered neighboring Uaxactun under Jaguar Paw and placed that state under the aegis of Smoking-Frog, a Tikal lord (Mathews 1985; Schele and Freidel 1990). In turn, the Middle Classic polity of Caracol carried out successful war against Tikal (A. Chase and D. Chase 1989; A. Chase 1990a) and Naranjo (Mathews 1986), but was eventually eclipsed by these states later in the Classic period. The Late Classic kingdom of Dos Pilas carried out wars of conquest against its neighbors and incorporated such states as Seibal into its own dominion (Houston and Mathews 1985). Again, this attempt at territorial expansion ended in the collapse of the Dos Pilas dynasty and resurgence of the conquered polities. The absence of the stable consolidation of large states in the Southern lowlands cannot be attributed to the lack of attempts and hence must be attributed to an absence of effective means.

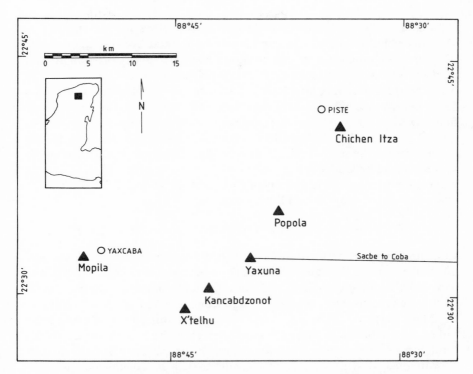

Fig. 7.1. Map of Yaxuna, Chichen Itza, and the satellite sites of the region.

In the Northern lowlands, warfare is likewise widespread during the Terminal Classic, as witnessed in the painted and carved scenes of battle, subordination of captives, and tribute processions (Freidel 1987:section 6). In settlement patterns, there is the Terminal Classic construction of fortifications around some six known centers (Kurjack and Andrews 1976; Webster 1979; Kurjack and Garza T. 1981). Although such increased evidence for military action is attributed by some scholars to the stress generated by high population density (F. Robles and A. Andrews 1986:83), the emphasis on the fortification of central architectural groups suggests that their capture is increasingly a focus of warfare. The hypothesis that fortification evinces warfare aimed at large-scale state formation has been posed by D. L. Webster (1979:169) based upon his work at the fortified sites of Cuca, Chacchob, and Dzonot Ake. As discussed below, the northern group at Yaxuna may have been a fortified acropolis in the Terminal Classic.

In contrast to the Southern lowlands, the north witnesses the Terminal Classic establishment of at least one large-scale territorial state that endures for more than a century: Chichen Itza (Sabloff and Andrews 1986). Coba also develops a large-scale state in the Terminal Classic, as demonstrated principally by the masonry causeway link to Yaxuna (fig. 7.1). The duration of the Coba state at the unprecedented territorial scale expressed in this sacbe is a matter to be resolved through further investigation at Yaxuna. The issue is important because, on the one hand, there are several examples of temporary expansion in the Southern lowlands that Coba might well parallel. On the other hand, Coba may have successfully established a stable large-scale state that lasted several centuries (F. Robles and A. Andrews 1986) before succumbing to Chichen Itza. The evidence of two seasons of field survey at Yaxuna shows that the major architectural groups were hastily and superficially refurbished in Terminal Classic times to focus on the Coba sacbe; at the same time, the extent of the Terminal Classic community is at least 3 sq km and shows a pattern of dense habitation. Clearly, while a modest town compared to the city of Chichen Itza, Terminal Classic Yaxuna was more than a temporary military camp.

The Politics of Large-Scale Maya States: Textual Evidence

Concomitant with the matter of the relative endurance of the Chichen Itza and Coba states is the equally vital issue of their political organizations and why these fostered expansion and consolidation on a large scale. A relatively recent focus on the epigraphic and iconographic records of warfare in the Maya lowlands opens significant new opportunities to investigate these political organizations from a historical perspective. First of all, in the Southern lowlands, where the textual records are particularly rich, successful attempts at large-scale state formation, such as documented for Dos Pilas (Houston and Mathews 1985), display the same highly ritualized battle, capture, and sacrifice sequences generally characteristic of Maya warfare (Freidel 1986a; M. Miller 1986b; L. Schele and M. Miller 1986; Schele n.d.b). At the same time, there are some clues as to distinctive institutions of statecraft devised by such Southern lowland conquerors. First and principally, during the period of expansion the conquerors raised monuments as rulers in the centers of their victims, as in the case of Late Classic Dos Pilas (Houston and Mathews 1985:18). Second, S. D. Houston and P. Mathews (1985:19-20) infer from epigraphic evidence from the end of the Dos Pilas dynasty that "there are two lords from the Dos Pilas dynasty who are ruling at different sites at the same time." Even earlier, the Early Classic conquest of the center of Uaxactun by Tikal resulted in the installation of a Tikal lord as ruler there (Mathews 1985; Schele and Freidel 1990). The present evidence indicates that one major strategy of Southern lowland territorial expansion was the expansion of the ruling dynasty to usurp the position of other dynasties at conquered centers.

A second Southern lowland strategy of political consolidation is found in the Usumacinta drainage. Here, in the course of the Late Classic, a category of second-rank nobility and rulers, tentatively deciphered as *cahal*, or personage of the community (D. Stuart n.d.; see also L. Schele and M. Miller 1986:chap. 3), appears to register the establishment of formal relationships between rulers of the first rank, *ahau*, and their subordinates in

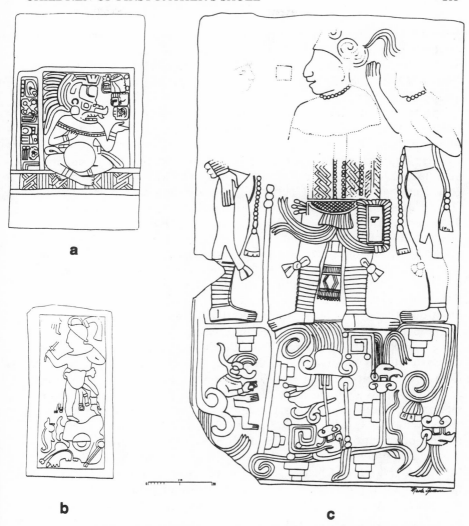

Fig. 7.2. Monuments from Yaxuna and satellite sites: a. Mopila Monument 1; b. Yaxuna Monument 1; c. X'telhu Panel A (after M.G. Robertson 1986).

secondary centers. Evidence of military conflict is sufficient to suggest that although some *ahau-cahal* relationships may have been joined peacefully, others resulted from successful subjugation through war.

In the north, textual materials from the Puuc sites (Kowalski 1985) and from Coba (Thompson, Pollock, and Charlot 1932; G. E. Stuart and G. S. Stuart 1976) show that these sites were ruled by kings of the status of *ku'l ahau*. Analysis of the text on one of the reliefs from the Yaxuna area, Mopila monument 1 (fig. 7.2a), shows that it celebrates the accession of a lord to the status of *cah*, a known variant of the *cahal* title. The presence of this action suggests that local lords were being integrated into a polity headed by an *ahau*, in a manner paralleling states in the Usumacinta region of the Southern lowlands. A second partially preserved text from the nearby site of Kancabdzonot is an almost identical accession statement (Freidel 1987:section 8, fig. 11). Unfortunately, the title to which the lord is acceding is destroyed.

The texts from Chichen Itza are particularly difficult to decipher (Davoust 1977; Kelley 1982; Krochock 1988), and interpretations of the dynastic history of this center are presently quite fluid. Certainly some lords of Chichen Itza carried the *ku'l ahau* title; in particular, there is an important historical lord named Kak u Pacal, Fire Shield, who participated in the government in the critical period of consolidation there. M. Davoust (1977) identifies a number of personal names in texts on lintels used to dedicate major buildings at Chichen Itza as rulers of the center, commemorated by Kak u Pacal, who commissioned their construction. R. J. Krochock (1988, 1991), on the other hand, demonstrates that some of these named individuals were contemporaries of that famous lord who were privileged to dedicate lintels in these buildings. In sum, there are promising investigations underway by several scholars suggesting the outlines of a political order that employed some traditional lowland Maya official titles.

There are preliminary indications in texts, however, that the political order at Chichen Itza is different from that found in the Yaxuna area and other traditional kingdoms. For example, the *cahal* title is not reported from the texts at Chichen Itza. Furthermore, Krochock's (1988, 1991) analysis suggests multiple lords carrying out the dedication rituals associated in the Southern lowlands principally with kings and their spouses at major centers. Finally, David Stuart (1988) has identified a deciphered reading of a relationship glyph found at Chichen Itza that suggests that Kak u Pacal and others dedicating monuments there were siblings. The notion that the high lords of Chichen Itza regarded themselves as sodalities of kin might suggest a precursor to the contact era Maya political institution of *mul tepal* (joint rule), attributed to the last great capital of Mayapan (Roys 1962:54).

The Iconography and Facilities of the Chichen Itza Wars

Chichen Itza is famous for its iconographic ties to the central Mexican center of Tula and for the presence of foreign influence generally. Current interpretation of the significance of such foreign influence emphasizes its syncretism with existing lowland Maya symbolism (Freidel 1986b; Lincoln 1986; Kowalski 1989; Wren n.d.). The role of foreign intrusion in the innovative political and religious organization of Chichen Itza and other Terminal Classic states of the Northern lowlands remains hotly contested. This discussion addresses this issue both from the perspective of what is revolutionary in the establishment of the Chichen Itza state (Wren n.d.) and from the perspective of what the common ground rules of war and politics might have been that allowed Chichen Itza successfully to carry out its conquests and to consolidate the vanquished into a single state.

There is an emerging corpus of interpretation of the rituals of Maya warfare and sacrifice that focuses on the ballcourt and the ballgame (Freidel 1986a; M. Miller 1986a; L. Schele and M. Miller 1986; M. Miller and S. Houston 1987). In a major breakthrough, M. E. Miller and S. D. Houston (1987) identify scenes of ballgame ritual and sacrifice in which the victim is trussed up as the ball and thrown down a stairway before decapitation at the site of Yaxchilan on the Usumacinta River. Identification of ritual sacrifice occurring on stairways in association with a pseudo-ballgame has allowed Miller (1986a) to interpret the function of grand stairways in the Late Classic center of Copan and further to tie such stairways to the ritual and iconographic program of the one explicit war, capture, and sacrifice sequence depicted in the murals of Bonampak in the Usumacinta drainage (M. Miller 1986b). The Bonampak sequence shows that suitable victims for such sacrifice were obtained through warfare involving alliances between rulers. The Yaxchilan and Bonampak examples indicate that war and sacrifice were central to ceremonies of heir designation and accession of rulers.

These decorated facilities link Late Classic Maya warfare and its ballgame sacrifice to the theology of the Ancestral Hero Twins, the Sun Jaguar, and Venus in his guise as *chac xib chac*, the axe-wielding executioner. The Popol Vuh, a contact era version of the Maya genesis myth, describes the manner in which the Ancestral Twins of the Maya people sacrifice each other and bring each other back to life in the place of death, Xibalba, and through this magic overcome the Lords of Death. An example of this stairway-ballcourt complex containing reference to this iconographic program occurs at the Late Preclassic (300 B.C.-A.D. 200) Southern lowland center of Cerros in Belize (Freidel 1986a), indicating great time depth for this ritual complex.

The Popol Vuh myth (Tedlock 1985) further ties these events to the father of the Ancestral Twins, who was earlier sacrificed by decapitation after a ballgame with the lords of Xibalba and had his head hung on a tree. This head inseminated the mother of the twins by spitting upon her hand. I think this skull is found in Southern lowland iconography in two sacred symbols of royal power: a skeletal form depicted at the base of the World Tree termed the Quadripartite Monster, as in the Temple of the Cross at Palenque (Robertson 1974; Freidel and Schele in press);[5] and a growing form that is the seed from which a corn plant containing the Ancestors grows, termed the Waterlily Monster,[6] as in the Temple of the Foliated Cross at Palenque (Schele 1976, n.d.a). This head is intimately associated with the white heron, called *zac bac*—often depicted in headdresses with a waterlily attached and a fish nibbling this plant.[7] This term also can mean "white, resplendent, or human-made bone." The large seed of fruiting trees is termed *bac* (Freidel and Schele in press), which also means "skull" and "captive" (D. Stuart 1985).

Severed heads, which I identify with First Father, *hun ahpu*, are clearly the central icons in the accession rituals of Chan Bahlum of Palenque, dedicator of the Temples of the Sun, Cross, and Foliated Cross. The association of the Waterlily Monster variant of this head with decapitation sacrifice is displayed at Palenque in stucco reliefs on piers b and f of House D of the North Palace (Schele 1983), where both the axe-wielding executioner and the victim are placed upon images of this head. The means of obtaining suitable victims for such sacrifice is warfare, as depicted at Bonampak (M. Miller 1986b).

The Waterlily Monster is a thematic symbol linking the iconography of Chichen Itza to that of the Yaxuna area and tying both to the ballgame and the ballcourt as the place of sacrifice following success in war. The Waterlily Monster occurs in the Lower Temple of the Jaguars of the Great Ballcourt at Chichen Itza in a number of contexts, including the baseline of piers (Tozzer 1957:fig. 345), the top of piers with a corn-tasseled individual emerging from the head as in the case of the Temple of the Foliated Cross at Palenque (Tozzer 1957:fig. 346), and the border along the west wall (Tozzer 1957:fig. 162).

It is likely that the head with a tree growing from it depicted on the balustrades of the North Temple of the Great Ballcourt is also this basic icon (Tozzer 1957:fig. 184) by analogy with the World Tree depicted in the Temple of the Cross at Palenque. This same "cosmic tree" is found in the reliefs within the North Temple (Wren n.d.). At Palenque, the World Tree of the Temple of the Cross is symbolic of the accession of Chan Bahlum to the status of ruler. L. Wren (n.d.), in a recent iconographic and epigraphic study of the North Temple of the Great Ballcourt, makes an interesting case that this facility commemorates the accession of Kak u Pacal to the status of ruler at Chichen Itza.

Finally, the reliefs decorating the ballcourt itself display a decapitation sacrifice following a ballgame. From the severed neck of the victim emerges vegetation with attached blossoms that can be interpreted as waterlilies; the ball before him carries a skull.

The bas-reliefs from sites in the Yaxuna area occur as frontal facades on low, rectangular structures of a kind termed "palaces" or "range structures" in the Maya area. These structures are central to their communities and probably constitute the foci for such political activities as the courts of rulers and lineage houses by analogy with epigraphically documented functions in the Southern lowlands (Freidel 1986b). Reliefs from one of the satellite sites near Yaxuna, X'telhu (Robertson 1986), show a comparable thematic emphasis on the Waterlily Monster. These reliefs depict a processional scene focused upon a principal figure who is probably the local ruler (fig. 7.2c). This individual stands directly upon the head of the Waterlily Monster. In this local style, the Waterlily Monster carries the diagnostic features of a square eye, a very large brow scroll, long nose beads, and a bifurcate tongue. As in the case of the Waterlily Monsters depicted in the base lines of the piers of the Lower Temple of the Jaguars at Chichen Itza, the waterlily stalks emerge from the eye sockets of the monster. Only one blossom is shown in the X'telhu scene, and three smaller heads are attached to these scrolls. The "stacked dot" water motif, often associated with the Waterlily Monster (Schele n.d.a), further decorates these scrolls. Finally, the smaller heads emerging on these scrolls replicate the square eye and large brow element of the main head and are further decorated with square scrolls emanating from the snout or the ear-plug.

This same variant of the Waterlily Monster forms one of the most diagnostic features of the local style found in reliefs from the Yaxuna area when worn as a headdress. At X'telhu (Robertson 1986:fig. 11), several processing individuals dominating captives wear this monster; these helmets differ from the monster found in the baseline described above only by the addition of feather panaches: the square eye, large brow element, bifurcate tongue, and long nose beads are all present. Additionally, these masks characteristically have square scrolls emanating from the ear-plugs. These variants of the Waterlily Monster are found not only at X'telhu, but also at the site of Popola (Robertson 1986:fig. 16), to the north of Yaxuna, between that center and Chichen Itza.

Finally, the association between the Waterlily Monster iconography and the ballcourt is found in Monument 1 from Yaxuna (fig. 7.2b; Freidel 1987:section 10). This architectonic relief was originally built onto the side of a small structure directly to the north of the ballcourt and within the same architectural complex at this site. Monument 1 at Yaxuna shows an individual dancing upon the head of a Waterlily Monster. This particular variant of the Waterlily Monster has a waterlily directly attached to the head with a fish nibbling at the flower. While the monster carries the large brow element of the other examples in the local style, and the long nose beads, the eye is round and segmented rather than square. In this respect, the Yaxuna example resembles the other major polymorphic entity in the local style, which M. G. Robertson (1986) has identified as being a boa constrictor. Despite this difference, there is clearly a thematic connection between this use of the Waterlily Monster and that seen at X'telhu in the panel standing upon the Waterlily Monster.

The thematic interest in the head of First Father as an icon of political power links the iconography of warfare found in the Yaxuna area with that of Chichen Itza. The further association of this icon with ballcourts at Chichen Itza, where the Great Ballcourt may be the accession monument of lord Kak u Pacal (Wren n.d.), and at Yaxuna, where the ballcourt is part of an architectural complex that constitutes the only original primary construction datable by surface indications to the Terminal Classic (Freidel

1987:section 3.7), indicates that the wars between Chichen Itza and the Yaxuna-based polity were carried out in the context of a shared political and theological framework.

The focus on the ballcourt and ballgame ritual proposed here provides a further link to the site of Coba. As detailed in Freidel (1987:sections 3 and 4), preliminary research by the project at Yaxuna indicates that the Terminal Classic occupation of this site constitutes a hasty refurbishment of existing earlier architectural groups, including a focal pyramid of substantial size (Freidel 1987:section 3.6), in conjunction with the construction of the great sacbe from Coba to Yaxuna. The exception to this pattern of reuse is the ballcourt group at Yaxuna, linked to the terminus of the great sacbe by a raised concourse. The Coba terminus of the great sacbe similarly contains a massive pyramid and a ballcourt complex. The Coba ballcourt complex contains reliefs depicting rulers, ballplayers, and bound captive figures (Navarette, Uribe, and Martínez 1979).

The significance of the ballcourt as a focus of the Chichen Itza wars with Yaxuna—and through Yaxuna with Coba and the Puuc sites (Uxmal has a central ballcourt)—is underscored by the rarity of these facilities in the Northern Maya lowlands and the high concentration of those known in the Terminal Classic period (Robertson, Kurjack, and Maldonado C. n.d.) the notable exception is Chichen Itza, which has thirteen known ballcourts including the Great Ballcourt. Indeed, in light of the relative lack of ballcourts in the Northern Maya lowlands prior to the Terminal Classic, and the pervasive presence of such courts in the Late Classic Southern lowlands, there is reason to suspect that the focus on the ballcourt in the Chichen Itza wars draws on an orthodoxy in warfare with roots in the south rather than the north.

As detailed in the Yaxuna Project first season report (Freidel 1987:section 6.4), the processing figures in the Lower Temple of the Jaguars (part of the Great Ballcourt at Chichen Itza) include several wearing regalia generally diagnostic of rulers and warriors of the Terminal Classic lowlands. One individual in particular (Row A7) shows a strong resemblance to the principal figure in the reliefs from X'telhu. There is the prospect that further iconographic investigation will show that this procession marks the successful conquest of the Yaxuna polity, among others. That the action displayed is not simple domination of captives but rather procession with tribute bearers corresponds to the presentation of jaguar pelts in the X'telhu reliefs and registers an institutional interest more focused upon concordance and consolidation than on sacrifice.

A similar prospect of diplomacy exists for Popola. Panel 2 from Popola (fig. 7.2) depicts a larger individual wearing the First Father helmet of the Yaxuna area processing with a smaller individual in front of him. The smaller individual wears a round helmet of segmented plaques surmounted by short or chopped feathers. This helmet carries a feather panache and strikingly resembles a helmet form that is peculiar to Chichen Itza (with a full-figure bird attached rather than a simple panache) and diagnostic of its iconography. The smaller figure is not a simple captive, for both of these individuals have smaller captive figures at their feet. The implication of this scene is concordance between members of the Yaxuna and Chichen Itza polities, but with the domination of the Yaxuna polity. If the conduct of these wars was revised toward the objective of consolidation of losers into the realm of the victors, the victory statement at Popola was clearly premature.

On the other hand, this line of investigation indicates that the Great Ballcourt complex at Chichen Itza was a monument to the final victory of that state in these wars. Despite the implied political innovation of the consolidation of some losing rulers into the state in addition to sacrifice of others, the other feature of this monument is clearly traditional: the accession iconography in the North Temple, attributed by L. Wren (n.d.) to Kak u Pacal, is an expectable Maya adjunct to success in war.

Summary of the Iconographic and Epigraphic Evidence

Preliminary research at Yaxuna and at the satellite sites surrounding this center suggests that the decorated reliefs and their associated facilities in small palaces and a ballcourt reflect the rules pertaining to the conduct of war with Chichen Itza and its political ramifications. The premise underlying this approach to the evidence is that war as an instrument of statecraft is much more than physical combat and that antagonists must share not only rules of conduct on the battlefield, but also rules relating conqueror to vanquished in the aftermath of battle. The arguments given in this discussion are as follows:

1. The lowland Maya had a pervasive and enduring theological and political framework for warfare anchored in rites of passage for their rulers through the reenactment of primordial events of sacrifice and rebirth in the context of the ballgames in Xibalba.

2. This framework is adhered to by the contestants in the Chichen Itza wars, with particular emphasis on the original sacrifice by decapitation of First Father followed by the germination of his skull as a great seed, progenitor of the Maya people. There are a number of scholars working on the general importance of First Father in the theology of the Northern lowlands. C. C. Coggins (1983), for example, identifies the iconography of the Waterlily Monster as the main theme on the Late Classic stuccoed Structure 1-sub at Dzibilchaltun, a major Northern lowland center. M. Pickens (1979) has investigated the theology of First Father in the northern ethnohistorical accounts and tied it to codex presentation of "black gods," which are captive figures identified with deer. Deer antler tines are featured in the iconography from X'telhu, where processing dominant figures carry these as

weapons or batons (Robertson 1986:figs. 8, 11). A small full figure in the baseline of X'telhu panel A may be such a "black god" (fig. 7.2c).

In a recent article (Freidel 1986b), I have proposed that the Northern lowland Maya generally appealed more to this progenitor god than to the Ancestral Hero Twins as part of a political order that emphasized community over lineage. Finally, this progenitor god, possibly Cauac/Chac, has clear agricultural associations (Schele n.d.a) and specifically is reborn as the maize lord (Taube 1985), probably the first human being. The focus, then, is on the creation of the Maya people and affinity with the original Maya lord.

3. Classic Maya warfare was aimed at obtaining suitable victims for such rituals, with the political ramification of temporary subordination of the vanquished. Recent breakthroughs in epigraphic and iconographic interpretation show the presence of a political and theological rationale for conquest warfare under the aegis of the Mosaic Monster and Tlaloc. Attempts at consolidation of multikingdom states did not generate an enduring and acceptable form of imperial government in the Southern lowlands.

4. The Chichen Itza wars were aimed primarily at conquest, territorial consolidation, and defense of large-scale states. This political objective is innovatively displayed in the emphasis on processional scenes involving antagonists in the reliefs from the Yaxuna area and in the Great Ballcourt complex at Chichen Itza (among many other examples at that site).

5. Epigraphic evidence suggests that the political tactics of state consolidation employed by the peoples of the Yaxuna area are indigenous, involving the establishment of *ahau-cahal* relationships. The *cahal* title in the Northern lowlands has been elsewhere identified only at the Puuc site of Xcalumkin (Freidel 1987:section 7.5); the *ahau* title is used in the Puuc sites and at Coba.

6. Epigraphic evidence suggests that the political tactics of state consolidation at Chichen Itza are innovative, involving use of the *yitah* (kin or sibling) relationship (D. Stuart 1988) linking *ahaoub* into sodalities sharing power in "joint government." Building dedication rituals sequentially link individuals who are contemporaries and who hold the *ahau* title (Krochock 1988). This is evidently the glyphic analog to processional scenes. L. Wren (n.d.) argues from the iconography of the North Temple at Chichen Itza that the accession of Kak u Pacal employs syncretic theological and political principles from Mexico, a further and intriguing source of innovation. This is commensurate with the generally held view that Chichen Itza displays an "international" symbol system (Freidel 1986b; Kowalski 1989).

The Archaeological Evidence for Yaxuna as the Battlefield

As detailed in Freidel 1987 (sections 3-5), the 1986 season of survey and reconnaissance at Yaxuna shows clear surface evidence that the major architectural construction at the center was carried out in Late Preclassic through early Late Classic times. The Terminal Classic occupation of the center constitutes superficial refurbishment of these architectural groups to orient them to the terminus of the great sacbe from Coba. Terminal Classic architecture of the Puuc style, as found at Yaxuna, is distinctive from earlier styles and techniques of architectural construction in a number of readily identifiable diagnostics. The Terminal Classic construction employs veneer masonry blocks tailed into concrete hearting, specialized "boot-shaped" beveled masonry blocks in corbel vaulting, freestanding columns in doorways— often decorated with three-part binding elements, and architectonic relief sculpture decorating jambs and walls.

Because ruins in the Northern lowlands have relatively sparse vegetation on them, soil buildup on major ruins is very thin and the building complexes have the appearance of islands of rock in a sea of bush and farmland. The architectural diagnostics described above are easily and confidently observable on the surface. Systematic observations on such surface indications taken in the course of the survey provide an initial estimate of the extent of Terminal Classic construction in the center. These surface indications show the Terminal Classic construction to be limited; it is confined to buildings that focus on the terminus of the great sacbe and on the northern group that contains the ballcourt complex.

Accurate survey of the major groups carried out in 1986 further shows that Terminal Classic reuse of architecture involved significant modifications of original design to suit the purposes of the new inhabitants. The most dramatic refurbishment involves the reorientation of the largest acropolis at the center of the site (Freidel 1987:section 3.6) from the south to the east in order to face the terminus of the sacbe. A southern group of architecture (Freidel 1987:section 3.4) was reoriented from the west to the north, where it borders the incoming sacbe. A number of small new buildings were constructed in the plaza area surrounding the terminus of the sacbe using Early Classic or Late Preclassic monolithic blocks quarried from the southern face of the main acropolis. Finally, the northern group (Freidel 1987:section 3.3) was refurbished by the reorientation of one of its pyramids from west to south, facing the ballcourt group, and by the addition of a substantial masonry wall along the southern margin of its plaza area, cutting off normal access on the original primary axis of this acropolis. This last modification, taken with other evidence of walls along the margins, suggests that this group was fortified in Terminal Classic times.

Much of the Terminal Classic refurbishment of Yaxuna involved the reuse of monolithic blocks quarried from the Late Preclassic or Early Classic construction in the main central acropolis. Scatterings of such huge blocks were discovered by the project along the eastern and southern margins of the southern group, clearly indicating that activity was halted in the middle of construction.

The only original major construction showing surface indications of being initiated in Terminal Classic times at Yaxuna is the ballcourt group (Freidel 1987:section 3.7). In addition to the ballcourt, this group contains sculptured columns with figures wearing "goggle" eyes, an iconographic motif characteristic of the Terminal Classic in the north, a partly standing masonry superstructure in typical Puuc style, and the building containing Monument 1, described above. The importance of the ballcourt is emphasized by the initiation of its construction in the Terminal Classic reoccupation of Yaxuna.

In sum, preliminary investigation at Yaxuna supports the view that this site was reoccupied and reestablished as a center specifically in conjunction with the construction of the sacbe from Coba. This evidence, in turn, indicates that the motivation for the construction of the sacbe was not to link existing centers and to consolidate an existing polity into the Coba realm, but rather to establish a new center as a border to territory claimed by Coba. In light of the extraordinary effort put into the construction of the sacbe—some 750,000 cubic m of stone construction fill stretched over 100 km—the logistics necessary to carry out such work suggest that Coba was in fact consolidating on this large territorial scale as it constructed the sacbe. The normal motivations for political consolidation on a large scale—the uniting of existing polities—would probably apply to inhabitants along the traverse of the sacbe, but would not apply to Yaxuna at the terminus. Rather, Yaxuna would express Coba's interest in establishing its territorial and political boundary there.

There are two plausible reasons why Coba would terminate the sacbe at Yaxuna. First, Yaxuna provided an existing architectural mass suitable for rapid refurbishment into a large center. Second, Yaxuna was in proximity to Chichen Itza in a fashion typical of bordering polities of small scale in the Maya lowlands—polities of the kind that traditionally participated in boundary maintenance warfare. This strategy would be sensible if Coba wanted to engage Chichen Itza in war in the context of traditional spatial parameters, despite the actual scale of the contest.

The satellite sites surrounding Yaxuna on three sides (by present reconnaissance, the eastern perimeter has not been explored but contains a possible satellite site of Chichen Itza; Charles Lincoln, personal communication) show surface indications of construction and occupation in the Terminal Classic. These are small sites and small centers showing no evidence of earlier construction, but they nevertheless contain elaborate relief sculpture, which ties them stylistically, theologically, and politically to each other. Yaxuna is their spatial center and, in terms of settlement hierarchy, is clearly at the apex of the local community organization. These sites show indications, then, of expressing the perimeter of the Terminal Classic polity centered on Yaxuna. In light of the evidence that Coba deliberately established Yaxuna as a center, the surrounding sites appear to have been established for the same general purpose, as a territorial polity to define and sustain the boundary of Coba's political authority. Furthermore, these satellite sites show evidence of having been abandoned, along with Yaxuna, in the Terminal Classic. There is no construction in them that can be related to later periods.

Fernando Robles and Anthony Andrews (1986; see also Andrews and Robles 1985), specialists in the territorial dynamics of the Terminal Classic Northern lowlands, have summarized the evidence showing that the rise of Chichen Itza was accompanied by the eclipse and collapse of Coba, probably the largest single community in the Northern lowlands. They hypothesize on the basis of ethnohistorical descriptions of the Itza incursion, the archaeological distribution of diagnostic ceramic assemblages associated with Chichen Itza and Coba, and the settlement pattern evidence of the great sacbe (Freidel 1987:section 1.2) that Yaxuna was the scene of the ultimate confrontation between Chichen Itza and Coba. Investigations and analysis carried out by the present project support the general hypothesis that Yaxuna was a major battlefield in the Chichen Itza wars.

Archaeology, Art, and History of the Yaxuna Polity

The archaeologically testable proposition that the sites housing the Yaxuna area reliefs date to a brief span of the Terminal Classic is critical to their proper interpretation. M. G. Robertson (1986) suggests that these reliefs probably predate the art at Chichen Itza because they are stylistically distinctive. The arguments made for contemporaneity are iconographic rather than stylistic, but clearly the independent evidence of archaeological context is critical to further interpretation of the relationship between Chichen Itza and other Maya polities through art and textual history.

On the other hand, the art and texts of the Yaxuna area are central to any useful interpretation of the settlement history, construction activities, and economic practices of this polity viewed through archaeological remains. Yaxuna is materially linked to a vast community at Coba through the sacbe. This is an archaeological fact and an expression of political power impinging on a very substantial portion of the Maya lowland region in a particularly critical period in its social evolution. This phenomenon is being investigated through a combined inquiry into the archaeological record and the record left by art and texts at Yaxuna.

Concluding Remarks

The hypothesis being pursued here, then, is that the state of Chichen Itza succeeded in consolidating a conquest state by transforming the institution of dynastic kingship based on *ahau* into that of *mul tepal* still based on that rank. This institution resembles the Mexican rule by a "first speaker" in an assembly of rulers, and Mexicanized Maya may have syncretized the existing

Classic Maya kingship in such a fashion that conquered Maya kings could acknowledge that the Chichen Itza ruler was indeed an *ahau* and also a first among equals. The syncretism proposed here underscored the continuity of the ritual means the Chichen Itza ruler employed to achieve that status, through war and enactment of the primordial ballgame decapitation sacrifice that resulted in rebirth of the ruler as the direct progeny of First Father. At the same time, the result of war was principally incorporation of the conquered rulers into the state, and the Chichen Itza *ahau* ruled by dint of performance in addition to lineage, as in traditional Maya states.

In this interpretation, the institution of *ahau* came full circle, in appropriate Maya fashion, from a Late Preclassic institution that emphasized the ruler's charismatic ability to access the supernatural (Freidel and Schele 1988a, 1988b) through the long Southern lowland Classic definition of the ruler, which emphasized lineage, to the Terminal Classic Chichen Itza *ahauob*, which again emphasized charismatic performance more than lineage. The ruler at Chichen Itza claimed a relationship of legitimate superiority to subordinate rulers because his relationship to them was not defined by principles of lineage, which operated to structure not only dynasty but also subordinate elite in the Southern lowland kingdoms—an institution that made each *ahau* equally the pinnacle of descent as the living incarnation of mythical ancestors. Instead, a ruler's authority was defined primarily by personal charismatic success in war, either his own or that of the assembly that chose him.

The details of the theological and political syncretism of accession through warfare remain to be explored, especially from the perspective of the Mexican component (Kelley 1982) but also from the perspective of the Maya. Beyond that, there is the prospect that Chichen Itza really was a "New Empire" as traditionally proposed by Maya scholars. The timing of the ascendancy of Chichen Itza is well within range of persisting Southern lowland Maya kingdoms; Jeff Kowalski (1989), among many others, is in hot pursuit of the interconnections between Chichen Itza and kingdoms to the south. Perhaps one factor in the great collapse of the southern kingdoms was the failure of those Maya to accept *mul tepal* and the vision of an international Mesoamerican Maya culture (Freidel 1986b).

Notes

1. *Ku'l ahau* is David Stuart's (1988) phonetic decipherment of the "watergroup prefix" of J. E. S. Thompson. This is a component of the emblem glyphs used in Classic period kingdoms of the highest status to denote membership in the dynasty and affiliation with the polity.

2. Richard Hansen (1987) reports the presence of Late Preclassic style carved stone stelae at the sites of Nakbe and El Mirador. I agree with his hypothesis that the individuals portrayed on these monuments represent kings. I also agree with the stylistic dating to the Late Preclassic. Nevertheless, the explicit quality of the royal ritual actions of the king found on Classic stelae remains to be documented in the Late Preclassic. Further, Late Preclassic stelae with

glyphic texts likewise remain to be discovered. Pending such discoveries, I stand by this current statement of development.

3. Perhaps the most dramatic documented rise of a new major dynasty through military effort in the Classic period is the case of Dos Pilas (see Houston and Mathews 1985).

4. Putting time brackets on expanding dynastic power is simpler than putting spatial parameters on such temporary hegemonies. The longest-lasting hegemony known at the moment appears to be Caracol (A. Chase 1990a; A. Chase and D. Chase 1989). Caracol conducts "axe-war" against Tikal on 9.6.2.1.11, A.D. 556, and Tikal does not emerge again historically until Ah Cacaw dedicates Temple 33-1st on 9.13.3.9.18, A.D. 695 (Schele and Freidel 1990). The nature of such hegemonies during the Classic period is variable. Tikal apparently maintained a continuous line of divine lords through the period of its subjugation by Caracol. Dos Pilas (Houston and Mathews 1985), as noted in the discussion, attempted to install its own lords in conquered capitals. Under the circumstances, the territorial extent of such domains must remain an open question.

5. The Quadripartite Badge consists of a partially fleshed skull surmounted by a bucket containing the *kin* glyph and three elements. Usually these three elements are a central stingray spine or other bloodletter flanked by a crossed-bands motif and a shell. The central element can be replaced by a square-nosed jeweled polymorph, which David Stuart has identified as a glyph for lineage. A bird I would identify with the white heron, *zac bac*, can replace the flanking elements. The Quadripartite Badge is usually regarded as an avatar of the Sun because of the *kin* glyph (Schele 1976). John Justeson, however, argues that the sun-in-a-bucket motif is designed to be read in Yucatac as *lac* (bucket) *kin*, meaning *lakin* (east or dawn). D. Tedlock (1985) suggests that dawn in the Popol Vuh is used as a metaphor for ascent. I read this as a determinative of the skull as ascendant. The skull of First Father, after the triumph of his sons, is brought to partial life and is left hanging in the dusty court of Xibalba halfway between life and death—the metaphor of the seed—hence the Quadripartite Badge is the ascendant skull, the skull of First Father as a seed.

6. As noted by Karl Taube (1985), the corn god that emerges from the Waterlily Monster head in the Temple of the Cross is also found emerging from skeletal forms of the head as seen in painted ceramics illustrated by F. Robicsek and D. M. Hales (1981) in what they term resurrection scenes.

7. J. Quirarte (n.d.) notes that ballplayers on ceramic vessels are often depicted wearing a large bird head that might be identified as this white heron, an association with *zac bac* that is sensible in light of arguments given in this paper. Further, such ballplayers often wear a waterlily blossom.

8. Postclassic Maya Elites: Ethnohistory and Archaeology

Diane Z. Chase

OUR views of prehistoric Maya society are colored largely by ethnohistoric descriptions of activities witnessed during the century following European contact in Central America. Spanish accounts, especially published materials (Relaciones de Yucatán 1898-1900; Tozzer 1941) and compilations of historic works (Roys 1943), are used to fill in gaps in Maya archaeology and to offer an interpretation of ancient culture and day-to-day life. This is true not only for the epoch immediately preceding the conquest—the Postclassic—but also for the even earlier Classic period. Ethnohistoric information is used for a variety of interpretations, ranging from the identification of structure function (Wauchope 1934; D. Chase 1982:573-78; Freidel and Sabloff 1984) to the organization of sites and polities (Roys 1957; Folan et al. 1983; D. Chase 1986).

While there is no doubt that ethnohistoric resources are an invaluable source of information about the Maya, the use of these written materials without critical evaluation can lead to misleading or inappropriate interpretations. There are numerous reasons why this might be the case. The early chroniclers were unfamiliar with the ways of the native inhabitants of the New World and, thus, frequently did not understand what they were witnessing—making misinterpretation of native culture quite possible. Often, European-based models—specifically those pertaining to a society such as existed in medieval Europe of the time—were applied to New World societies and indigenous forms of organization were ignored or contorted to fit a Western mindframe. Some recorders may have been more thorough or reliable—less ethnocentric—than others, but even the best of these historical resources have flaws and all require critical evaluation (cf. Nicholson 1975:490). This is true of both the Spanish and the later native Maya chroniclers. Bishop Diego de Landa, perhaps the premier source of data for the contact period Maya, was noted as a plagiarist (Genet 1934), and native chroniclers such as Gaspar Antonio Chi were sometimes more likely to "sway" history in favor of their own family's importance (Tozzer 1941:44-45, note 219). Ethnohistoric accounts are also generally transcribed, translated, and published before they are accessible to archaeological researchers; these activities can sometimes lead to nearly imperceptible changes—such as in wording—that nevertheless can greatly alter documentary interpretation. Beyond these factors, the Maya society described in Spanish documents was not the same as had existed in precontact times; it was altered due both to Spanish influence and to depopulation caused by disease. On a further note, the descriptions of the lowland Maya in the early European documents tended to refer to the Yucatec Maya, and it is not always evident to what degree they were representative of the various other parts of the Maya realm. Finally, as is always the case in recounted information, the degree to which historic accounts have embodied ideal as opposed to real distinctions in the social order can be questioned.

The truly unanswered issue, however, is the amount of change in Maya culture that took place somewhat earlier following the Classic Maya collapse (ca. A.D. 900). Even should ethnohistory be reliable with regard to the Late Postclassic Maya, it does not provide us with any consensus on the relationships between the Classic and Postclassic periods, much less on whether or not historic events in the Northern Maya lowlands have any direct bearing on Classic period events in the Southern Maya lowlands. Most scholars describe the Classic Maya collapse as having had dire effects on the population of the Southern lowlands (Willey and Shimkin 1973; Sharer 1977); Postclassic peoples have been described as decadent in contrast to their ancestors (cf. Proskouriakoff 1955). I have disagreed with these ethnocentric statements about Postclassic Maya culture (D. Chase 1981, 1982, 1985b, 1986; D. Chase and A. Chase 1988, n.d.), nevertheless, I wish to restate here that direct transferal of ethnohistoric statements to describe and interpret a civilization that existed over 600 years earlier is clearly problematic.

This presentation reviews some of the more commonly used ethnohistoric descriptions of Maya society with respect to the Maya elite and their spatial organization within sites. These descriptions are examined with regard to information gleaned from Maya archaeology. The primary data used here are investigations at the archaeological sites of Santa Rita Corozal (D. Chase 1982; D. Chase and A. Chase 1986b, 1988) and Mayapan (Pollock et al. 1962; R. Smith 1971). Both of these are well-documented Late Postclassic sites that flourished after A.D. 1350. Santa Rita Corozal, located in northern Belize, was probably the capital of the province of Chetumal and, as such, was abandoned in A.D. 1531; it has already been demonstrated that analogy to the Yucatec Maya is appropriate for this site (D. Chase 1982, 1986:349). Mayapan, situated in northern Yucatan, was the capital of a much larger confederacy, the "league of Mayapan," and is believed to have been largely depopulated following A.D. 1450; it is particularly appropriate to compare the archaeology of this site with ethnohistoric statements because it is specifically described by early chroniclers. After comparing the data from these late Maya sites to interpretations that have been and can be made based on ethnohistory, the discussion moves back in time to analyze the Classic period. The results of such combined study suggest that a number of frequent assumptions concerning Maya elites are not applicable to the Postclassic period, much less to earlier eras. A more critical use of ethnohistorical data—in conjunction with archaeological data—also suggests that a more varied social and political organization existed than has often been proffered.

Maya Elites: Ethnohistory

Maya society at the time of first European contact is generally described as either a two- or three-group system composed of nobles and commoners with the addition of slaves (Tozzer 1941:26, 62; Roys 1965). Elites have been previously defined as "those who run society's institutions" (Chase and Chase, introduction, in this volume). Such a definition would appear to accord well with ethnohistoric descriptions of Maya nobles as administrators, adjudicators, and ritual leaders (Tozzer 1941:87, 98; Roys 1943:33, 59-64). Nobles or *al mehenob* had a status determined by descent through both the male and female lines (Roys 1943:33). Descent alone, however, may have been insufficient for positioning in certain political offices, and individuals were also questioned as to their esoteric knowledge so as to preclude inappropriate pretenders to power. This is indicated in the interrogation of the "chiefs" in the Chilam Balam of Chumayel (Roys 1933:192). Offices held by nobles are defined to a certain degree in entries and passages found in the Motul dictionary (Martínez Hernández 1929) and the *Relaciones de Yucatán* (1898-1900), including Landa (see also Tozzer 1941). These offices are summarized by Roys (1943:59-64) and included the *halach uinic* or territorial ruler, the *batab* or town ruler and hereditary war captain, the *ah cuch cab* or leader of a particular segment of town, the *ah kulel* who assisted the *batab*, and the *holpop*, who may have either been the governor of a smaller town or possibly the head of an important lineage. Priests were also members of the elite, and the *ah kin* was perhaps the most important religious leader within a community (Tozzer 1941:27). There were two very different personages who bore the title *nacom*—one often served as the officiator for human sacrifice, and the other was elected to serve for three years as a war chief. Of the two, Landa (Tozzer 1941:112-13) notes that the war chief was accorded high status, while the *nacom* who undertook the role of executioner in human sacrifices was not. This latter point, however, has been questioned, based on some of the better-known individuals documented to have served as *nacom*s in Yucatan (Roys 1943:79).

According to the ethnohistory, Maya of different social statuses lived in distinct locales at any given site and were also accorded varying degrees of material wealth. The ethnohistoric model called for nobles to have lived at the center of towns, often in elaborately painted and permanently constructed residences (Tozzer 1941:26, 62). At least certain of these elite also bedecked themselves with necklaces of shell or jade beads (Tozzer 1941:95-96). At death, those of the highest status were reported to have been cremated and their ashes placed in idols (Tozzer 1941:130-31), although certain of the elite—such as priests—may well have been buried without cremation below their houses (Tozzer 1941:129-30). Following an interment in a house, the structure was supposedly abandoned and, in certain cases, temples were erected over the former house site (Tozzer 1941:130).

But what of the rest of Maya society? What ethnohistoric data relate to the nonelite segment of Maya society shortly following contact? The commoners were reportedly the largest segment of Maya society. In the most frequently used ethnohistoric model, these people lived at the outskirts of town and provided subsistence items for the elite, as well as service required for such things as house repairs (Tozzer 1941:26, 62, 86, 87). They lived in buildings that resembled those of the nobles but were entirely constructed of perishable materials (Tozzer 1941:85, 86)—reinforcing the idea that noble houses were made of stone. We are told that commoners were buried below or to the rear of their houses; maize or valuable stones were placed in their mouths to provide for them in death (Tozzer 1941:129-30). Lower in status than the commoners were slaves captured in war and used either as sacrificial victims or as servants (Tozzer 1941:54, 123).

Indications exist in the ethnohistory, however, that stratification of individuals in Maya society was not quite as simple as the "noble-commoner" and, sometimes "slave" terminology might indicate. While this basic dualistic or tripartite division *may* have been the *ideal* social situation described to the Spaniards, it is unclear how inviolate these categories were in reality or whether they always related directly to material well-being. The *holcans*, for example, were mercenaries of unclear status who were paid only in times of war (Tozzer 1941:123). Merchants might derive from either the nobles or the commoners (Roys 1943:33, 34, 51). Both nobles and commoners could own slaves (Roys 1943:34). There was also a term for a group of individuals who by their designation as *azmen uinic*—"middle" or "medium men"—were neither commoners nor nobles, but had "middling status" (Roys 1943:34; see also Martinez Hernandez 1929:69; Barrera Vasquez et al. 1980:18). These individuals may well have been those of "high esteem," described by Landa (Tozzer 1941:62, 130-31) as living closest to the houses of the nobles and priests and as sharing similar burial patterns with these two groups. Thus, while the general description of Maya social organization used widely by ethnohistorians and archaeologists traditionally consists solely of nobles, commoners, and slaves, there is evidence even within the early historic materials that there were at least certain "in-between" individuals, who in many ways must have mimicked the nobles. Given statements about the burial rites of these individuals being similar to those of the nobles, one might also expect that they could be particularly difficult to define in the archaeological record.

Ethnohistoric description of the plans of Maya towns are largely based on what the Spaniards were told about the then already abandoned Mayapan; such accounts are fairly rigid in their descriptions: "Their dwelling place was as follows: —in the middle of the town were their temples with beautiful plazas, and all around the temples stood the houses of the lords and the priests, and then (those of) the most important people. Thus came the houses of the richest and of those who were held in the highest estimation nearest to these, and at the outskirts of the town were the houses of the lower class" (Tozzer 1941:62). Because of this ethnohistoric depiction, Maya communities were believed to have been concentrically organized. This concentric view of Maya site organization has been often uncritically applied to archaeological settlements of both the Classic and Postclassic periods (Haviland 1982; Folan et al., 1983; but see also Arnold and Ford 1980; Ashmore 1981b:461-62, 1988:160-61; Ford and Arnold 1982; A. Chase and D. Chase 1987b:58).

Elites and Archaeology

An archaeological testing of the generalized ethnohistoric statements concerning Maya social, political, and spatial organization requires the identification of particular material remains, or combinations of remains, as likely to be elite associated. Notwithstanding the problems in distinguishing status archaeologically (see Chase and Chase, introduction, in this volume), certain kinds of data have been useful in this regard. Architectural mass, building techniques, and structural elaboration have all been used to derive differences in status, based on the assumption that increased effort expenditure in architectural remains was/is an indicator of increased status. Such assumptions are bolstered by historic documentation, as indicated previously. However, consideration must be given to the possibility that a greater number of rooms or an enlarged overall area might also represent either a larger number of activities and/or more residents, rather than simply the increased status of the occupants. Thus, information on architecture must be cross-checked with other material classes.

Refuse and primary activity areas have obvious utility in assessing the function of specific areas. Maya elites were reported to have been involved in administration, ritual, and—to some extent—warfare (Tozzer 1941:87, 98, 122; Roys 1943:33, 59-64). While warfare and ritual may provide indicators in the material realm, administrative activities are more difficult to assess. Maya interments also vary greatly in the effort expended in the creation of a final resting place, the treatment of the body, and the manufacture or accumulation of objects placed with the individual; presumably these factors are reflective of differential status. In addition, written materials or symbols of power and authority may sometimes accompany an individual in death. Trade items, while not always limited to the elite, may sometimes provide an indication of status—especially when encountered in primary context in residences or in burials. Rarity and/or distance from the point of origin of a trade object may prove particularly useful in status assessments.

By assessing the relationships among these variables, it is theoretically possible to define the basic status groups present at a site. These definitions can then be used to assess spatial organization. Strict conformity to the concentric model of site or town organization calls for the location of all elite houses in the central area of a site surrounding the central ceremonial constructions. Residences of other individuals would be located at greater distances from the site center in direct proportion to their decreased social status. Commoners would be located in the furthest extremes of any given town. Therefore, concentricity, or lack thereof, may be assessed by viewing the occurrence and variability of the above-mentioned material indicators in conjunction with specific building types and groups in comparison to their distance from a given site center.

Archaeology and Elites: Santa Rita Corozal

Research undertaken by the Corozal Postclassic Project (D. Chase and A. Chase 1988) from 1979 through 1985 focused on a large number of structures dating to the fifteenth century just prior to Spanish contact (A.D. 1300-1530). In all, intensive excavations were carried out in forty-three structures, of which thirty-five produced construction or significant occupation dating to the Late Postclassic period (cf. D. Chase 1990). These investigations can be further amplified by using the earlier work of Thomas Gann (1900, 1918).

If one views the distribution of presumed elite-associated items and activities at Santa Rita Corozal, some surprising information surfaces about the nature of status distinctions and site organization as well as about the excavations necessary to answer these questions. Santa Rita Corozal serves as an excellent reminder of the problems in making interpretations in archaeological sites based solely on surface remains. Both elaborate residences and constructions in which elaborate burials have been encountered were often not visible based on surface inspection or survey. The most impressive Postclassic burial encountered at Santa Rita Corozal came from a building that was not perceptible without extensive excavation. Such findings have clear negative implications for the *a priori* association of presumed nonelaborate dwellings with commoners. Attempts to assess status at the site have led to the definition of three categories of residential groups (fig. 8.1). The most easily identified were the areas in which the highest-status individuals are presumed to have resided. These locales tended to contain at least one elaborate residence, consisting of a multiple-room construction, generally with an enclosed shrine. Residential groups in this category also were distinctive in their artifactual associations. Nearly the entire archaeological spectrum of Postclassic artifactual categories may be found in association with these high-status architectural groupings. Even more significantly, all high-status groups also have ritual associations in the form of either effigy caches (fig. 8.2) or paired incense burners (fig. 8.3). There is also a strong correlation between high-status residence and items associated with warfare—chert and obsidian arrowpoints occur with great frequency in these structures. Interestingly, evidence of weapons in the form of chert and obsidian arrowpoints is more common at Santa Rita Corozal than at

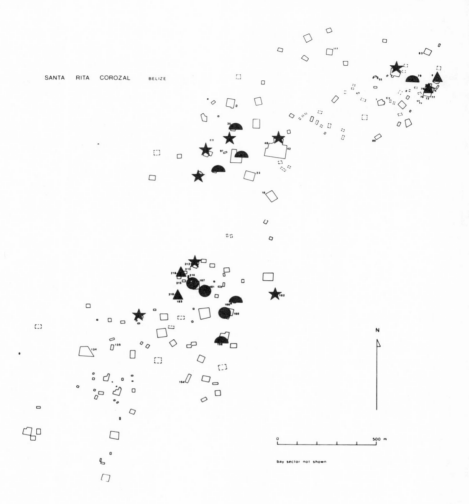

Fig. 8.1. Distribution of Postclassic buildings and/or groups excavated by the Corozal Postclassic Project at Santa Rita Corozal, Belize: triangle = high status residence; circle = middle status residence; semi-circle = low status residence; star = ritual and non-residential.

Mayapan—eight times so for chert points and two times so for obsidian points. Perhaps this can be seen as affirming the notion of increased internal warfare within the lowlands following the deterioration of the league of Mayapan in the fifteenth century. Significantly, the presumed highest-status groups were not limited to the central portion of the site; there was generally more than one of these groups in each of the defined sectors of the site (cf. D. Chase 1982).

The lowest category of residential occupation uncovered at Santa Rita Corozal includes several locales, one of which has no definable base walls.

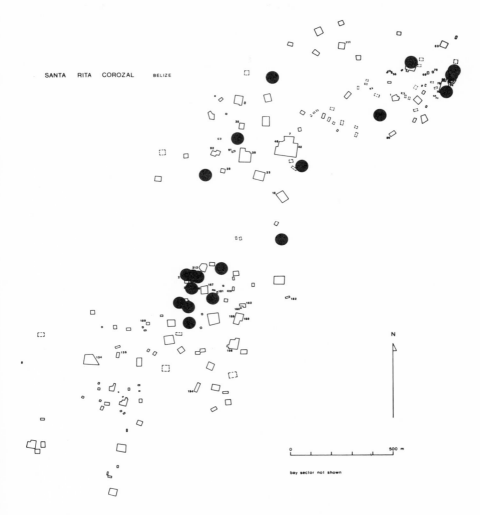

SANTA RITA COROZAL BELIZE

N

0   500 m

bay sector not shown

Fig. 8.2. Distribution of Postclassic caches at Santa Rita Corozal, Belize.

No group termed "low-status" contains elaborate multiple-room constructions. None of these constructions are built upon a contemporary platform.
When any of these constructions rests on a raised platform, the platform
was invariably constructed at a much earlier date and only subsequently
reused for Postclassic residence. Interestingly, none of the low-status constructions contains ritual items in the form of caches or paired incense
burners. Additionally, these groups lack not only the greater number of
other artifactual associations found in the high or middle categories, but
also complete categories of artifacts such as obsidian arrowpoints or pot-
lids. Presumed lower-status housing is distributed throughout the site and

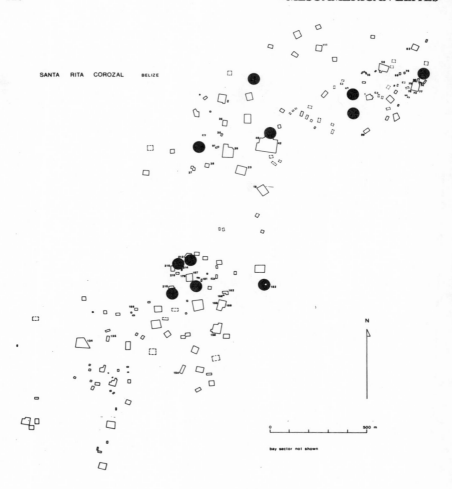

Fig. 8.3. Distribution of paired and reconstructible censers at Santa Rita Corozal, Belize.

not solely at its edges; it often exists directly adjacent to what are inferred to
have been nonresidential ritual structures.

Even though either extreme in housing is archaeologically evident, the
dividing line between the high- and low-status residential areas is sometimes quite hazy. Middle-range residential areas have been tentatively identified based on the distribution of artifacts and/or the labor investment in
architecture. Middle-status groups at Santa Rita Corozal did not have the
association with ritual materials seen in the highest-status residences. Importantly, however, middle-status residence groups did share certain artifactual types—such as obsidian points, pot-lids, and large numbers of ceramic
beads—with high-status groups. However, burials and architecture tended

to be less elaborate than those found in high-status groups, but more elaborate than in low-status groups. Presently, middle-status groups have been identified from one portion of the site only, in an area surrounded by both higher- and lower-status residence categories.

Elaborate Postclassic burials at Santa Rita Corozal were limited in their occurrences, but were found throughout the site. Contrary to statements by Landa (Tozzer 1941:130-31), there is no indication that elites were cremated. At Santa Rita Corozal, important individuals were generally buried in a flexed, seated-upright position. In partial confirmation of Landa's other suggestions, however, certain of these individuals had their grave sites marked by small stone shrines. High-status burials have been identified primarily on the basis of location, grave type, and associated items. An interesting consideration, however, is the fact that variation occurs in burial practices even within a single construction or group; if one can assume that contemporary burials from these contexts were likely to be of individuals related along kin lines, then this reinforces the concept that there can be no simple correlation of burial items with ascribed status. Imported objects, such as jadeite and metal, were also found in burials in different sectors of the site, often at some distance from the presumed epicenter of Santa Rita Corozal. The distribution of metal objects in particular may be significant, given their explicit association with the elite in their area of origin (Noguera 1971:260, 267; Pollard 1987:744). Presumed ritual symbols of power, such as stingray spines (cf. D. Chase 1991), were extremely limited in their distribution, but were found only in association with apparently high-status residences or nonresidential ritual structures. They were not found in any proximity to the presumed central area of the Postclassic occupation as defined by the muraled Structure 1 (Gann 1900).

The remains of Postclassic ritual activity are distributed throughout Santa Rita Corozal, albeit in a patterned way. Censers were deposited within structures in paired sets and may have played a part in katun ceremonies (D. Chase 1985c). Ceramic figure caches in particular have numbers and kinds of items that appear to be associated with specific areas of the site. I have previously suggested that these deposits are patterned in such a way as to indicate their function as integrative units within the site with regard to ceremonies pertaining to the completion of the ceremonial round during the unlucky five days of the Uayeb (D. Chase 1985b, 1988). The effigy caches and paired censers were found in both high-status residential groups and nonresidential ritual and/or administrative buildings. Based on such a distribution, it is evident that the high-status individuals at Santa Rita Corozal were intimately involved in both the religious and secular realms.

The archaeological investigations at Santa Rita Corozal have provided a body of interesting data with regard to Postclassic elites. While it is possible to identify either end of the social spectrum in terms of their living areas and burials, archaeological evidence does not provide the clear-cut divisions into groups that would be expected following the traditional two-group social model of nobles and commoners. Instead, the archaeology indicates the existence of gradations in status; certain residential groups at the site are intermediate in terms of architecture, artifacts, and burials. These may represent the ethnohistorically recorded "medium men," the *azmen uinic* mentioned by R. L. Roys (1943:34) and found in the Motul dictionary (Martínez Hernández 1929:69) or possibly those of "highest esteem" described by Landa (Tozzer 1941:62, 130-31).

Other common assumptions that have been made about the Postclassic Maya do not hold for Santa Rita Corozal. Ritual activity is not associated with all households; paired censers and caches occur only with the elite residential areas or in separate nonresidential ritual structures. These buildings and areas are distributed more or less evenly at the site, although there are spatial variations in the kinds of effigy figures included in caches. Thus, investigations support the idea of elite associations with religion (cf. Freidel and Sabloff 1984:184), but not the common assumption that ritual activity had become completely individualized (cf. Proskouriakoff 1962:428; Thompson 1970:187-91; Rathje 1975:427-30). Finally, distributions of residences and burials at Santa Rita Corozal do not support the existence of any form of concentric model of site organization. The presumed elite households and interments are located at the limits of the Late Postclassic occupation, and differing status households are instead spatially mixed.

Archaeology and Elites: Mayapan

The archaeological site of Mayapan provides further information on the Maya elite and their spatial distribution. Archaeological investigations at Mayapan have been taken directly to support ethnohistoric statements of Maya society (Pollock et al. 1962; Folan et al. 1983). However, a brief review of the documentation for Mayapan (Pollock et al. 1962; R. Smith 1971) suggests that alternative interpretations are both possible and appropriate. Specifically, even though the concentric model was described as characterizing Mayapan in the ethnohistory, the archaeology at Mayapan suggests a nonfit with such a model of site organization based on a number of criteria.

Robert E. Smith (1971:vol. 2, table 13) has defined a series of excavated structures as being "elaborate residences," most of which had multiple rooms and benches and a good number of which had beam and masonry construction. One assumption might be that these structures, by virtue of the extra effort that went into their construction, were elite residences. If one plots the distribution of Smith's elaborate residences on a map of Mayapan (fig. 8.4), it becomes quite evident that they were not located in any proximity to the central area. The majority were located midway between the central precinct and the outlying wall. Importantly, it must be noted that the Carnegie Institution focused its investigations predominantly on

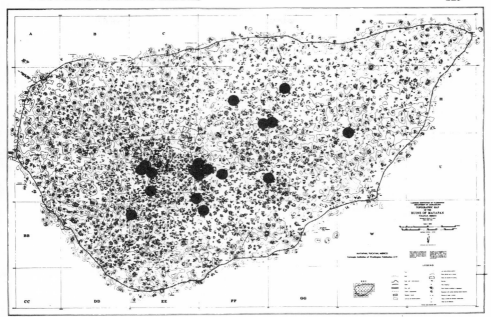

Fig. 8.4. Distribution of elaborate residences at Mayapan, Yucatan, Mexico.

the central area of the site; thus, while an increased number of elaborate residences would undoubtedly be defined with more excavation, any further archaeological work at Mayapan is unlikely to decrease the associations of these elaborate residences with noncentral locations. Even if one were to argue that the centrally located colonnaded halls were residences—a stance that could be difficult to sustain—Smith's elaborate residences would minimally represent living areas occupied by those of "high esteem," if not "noble," status and would *not* be located in a concentric fashion around Mayapan's central area.

Likewise, burial chambers and contents suggest other interesting facts. Crypts and burial vaults (empty crypts or tombs), both presumably indicative of relatively high status based upon the increased effort required to create them, were not limited to the site center or even to the area in immediate proximity to it, but were generally located at some distance away (fig. 8.5). High-status interments also occurred in outlying buildings and groups that were not associated with Smith's "elaborate residences." Luxury items within Mayapan's interments—specifically jadeite and metal—were limited neither to burials in the central area nor even to burials within the limits of Mayapan's wall. Metal objects that must have in some way been within the purview of the elite were, in fact, primarily found in areas away from the site center.

Ceremonial buildings and special activities that involved caching practices did appear to aggregate in the center of Mayapan. Even here, however, there is no exact correspondence. Although the majority of ceremo-

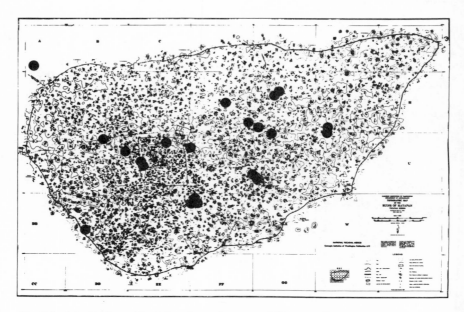

Fig. 8.5. Distribution of burial vaults and crypts at Mayapan, Yucatan, Mexico.

nial architecture at Mayapan was located within or relatively close to the central precinct, there were notable exceptions. Groups within the overall walled area with ritual constructions that were not centrally located specifically include the group containing Str. H13. Unlike the situation at Santa Rita Corozal—and contrary to assertions by W. L. Rathje (1975:429) about the nonconcentrated nature of Mayapan's Postclassic caches—caches at Mayapan were found clustered in proximity to the central area of the site (fig. 8.6). This distribution reinforces the idea of Mayapan's central area having been an administrative and ceremonial precinct. However, this distribution does not in any way prove the concentric model, for such a model is more correctly assessed based on the locations of residential areas of differing status—and, at Mayapan, these do *not* accord well with Landa's model.

Thus, the archaeological picture at Mayapan does not support a strict concentric model of spatial layout. Those that would argue concentricity by suggesting that the entire population within the site wall was elite are also clearly incorrect—for a number of reasons. The limited work undertaken outside the wall surrounding Mayapan shows indications of elaborate architecture and imported artifacts of the same kind found within the wall. Additionally, if one accepts Landa's depiction of Mayapan, the elite would have had to have been located in a smaller walled area encompassing one-eighth of a league (Tozzer 1941:24) rather than having been dispersed throughout the larger walled area of the site (cf. Relaciones de Yucatán 1898-1900:vol. 1, 254; Tozzer 1941:note 131). The distribution of constructions at Mayapan suggests that the heads of the various political units re-

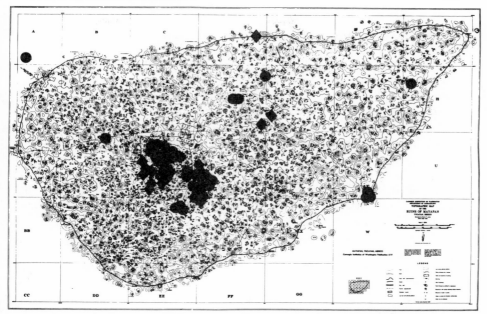

Fig. 8.6. Distribution of Postclassic caches at Mayapan, Yucatan, Mexico: diamond = effigy cache; circle = non-effigy cache.

ported to have lived at Mayapan as part of the *mul tepal* or joint government would have had residences well integrated within the overall population (while colonnaded halls may have served as their titular administrative/ritual buildings).

Maya Elites: Back to the Classic

A strict interpretation of the concentric model does not fit the Postclassic sites of Santa Rita Corozal or Mayapan. This does not mean that certain elite might not be located in central areas or that an administrative-ceremonial precinct might not have existed. It does, however, imply that residences and statuses are mixed beyond the central precinct. Should the discrepancy between ethnohistory and archaeology be surprising? Yes and no. There is a description of Mayapan in these historic materials, but it was made when the site was no longer occupied. The concentric description applied to this abandoned site also may have originated outside of the Maya area (D. Chase 1986:363). There is other ethnohistoric information, often overlooked, that would support an alternative to the concentric model, for Roys (1943:63, 1957:7; see also Tozzer 1941:note 292) noted the existence of site sectors or barrios—something inconsistent with the strict concentric model. These divisions of the town or *cuchteel* had a leader or *ah cuch cab*, and residence in each of these wards was not limited to a single lineage. While the sector or ward model is not as well described as Landa's concentric model, it clearly suggests a more mixed residential arrangement. It also accords well with models of site organization used in other areas of Mesoamerica (Calnek 1972, 1976; Michels 1977). What *is* surprising in all of this is not really that differences exist between archaeology and ethnohistory, but rather the general and uncritical archaeological acceptance of a single untested model for Maya spatial organization.

While this conclusion may be interpreted as contradictory to certain ethnohistoric information, it should not be surprising given the era and circumstances in which the information was recorded. Such a concentric town plan may have formed an ideal form of site layout, but it is not congruent with the complexity generally found in the archaeology of the ancient Maya. If the generally held views of Maya society that have been derived from ethnohistory do not fit the Postclassic period archaeological data, there is no reason to assume that these same models should apply to the earlier Classic period.

It has generally been assumed that the historically documented terms for specific individuals and different offices hold for the Postclassic. There is no internal mechanism for testing them, so it is the most elaborate burials or residences that are usually correlated with *halach uinic*s or *batab*s. Although we know many of the terms used for specific individuals and their offices during the contact era (see above), only limited attempts have been made to correlate these with titles found in hieroglyphic texts. There has as yet been little overlap noted between historic and Classic period texts with the exception of the word *ahau* or lord; most readings are composites from languages other than the most appropriate lowland choices—Yucatec or Chol (for example, Lounsbury 1973, who uses Quiche). The degree of continuity present in titles has clear implications for the nature of any change in sociopolitical organization and should form a basis for future work. At present, however, there is a recognized general lack of agreement between the contact era ethnohistory and the Classic period epigraphy, suggesting both that these historic sources should not be directly applied to earlier eras and that there may have been titular changes in Maya society between the Classic and Postclassic periods.

Interestingly, as shown above, the Postclassic archaeological distribution of ritual containers (incense burners and cache figures/figurines) demonstrates that they were controlled by the individuals of highest status at Santa Rita Corozal and presumably at Mayapan as well. Individuals of middle and lower status did not have access to cache vessels and incense burners in residential contexts in Postclassic society. The data, in fact, contradict ethnohistorically based assertions that all contact period Maya practiced idol worship in the privacy of their homes (cf. Thompson 1970:188).

These same data also shed some light on changes between Classic and Postclassic religion. For Postclassic Santa Rita Corozal, all ritual containers were restricted to high-status contexts and form a single analytic subassemblage. For Classic era Caracol, two distinct subassemblages of containers coexist and are generally found in two very different contexts. (A. Chase and D. Chase in press). One kind of cache vessel and one kind of incense burner are found in the epicentral administrative/ritual buildings of the site, while a different subassemblage is found in the residential settlement outside of the epicenter. While elements of the epicentral ritual container subassemblage may occassionally occur in the outlying area—presumably in elite contexts—the nonepicentral ritual container subassemblage generally does not occur in the site center during the Classic period. Thus, in contrast to the Postclassic era, it would appear that middle- and low-status groups at Classic Caracol had access to a ritual container subassemblage of their own. A further difference exists between Classic and Postclassic ritual items; the symbolic system used in Postclassic caches is far less abstract than that of Classic caches and would be more easily recognizable to the population at large (D. Chase 1988).

Looking at the archaeological differences between the Classic and Postclassic, it would appear that there was high-status or elite control of religion and religious ceremonies during the Postclassic era, but that religion was far more popularized than in the preceding Classic period (D. Chase 1988, 1991). Therefore, it would appear that the "Classic Maya collapse" marked a religious transformation of Maya society. During the Late Classic era, certain religious ceremonies were carried out in the hearts of Maya centers, but were presumably restricted to high-status or elite participation and were independent of the remainder of the population; members of the local nonelite populace carried out their own ceremonies with their own special containers in their own residential groups. During the Postclassic era, the nonelite apparently did not carry out similar personal ceremonies. Rather, they appear to have been integrated into a single religious complex characterized by more public ceremonies controlled and carried out by the Postclassic elite.

Concluding Statements

Ethnohistory is useful, but it must be critically compared and contrasted with other data—particularly archaeological—when dealing with such difficult topics as social or site organization. Archaeological evidence from Santa Rita Corozal and Mayapan indicates that the concentric model for site organization derived from Landa cannot be strictly applied to either of these Postclassic sites. Historic period information about the structure of Maya society also hits snags in archaeological verification. There are undoubtedly multiple problems at work here—particularly the difficulty of associating status with material remains and the possibility that the ideal social categories did not correlate with actual practice and real divisions. Regardless of what is ethnohistorically recorded, it is evident from the archaeological data that material associations do *not* reflect clear-cut divisions into two or three social groups—nobles, commoners, and slaves.

These findings have two concrete repercussions for earlier reconstructions of Maya society. First, given this much-changed perspective on the previously misunderstood Postclassic Maya, it is evident that elite distributions at Classic period sites must be reevaluated—as must the nature of the changes associated with the "Classic Maya collapse." Second, archaeology and ethnohistory must be critically conjoined to portray Maya society anew. Any attempt blindly to impose ethnohistoric categories on the archaeological data ignores the complexity seen in these data and reflects a naiveté about the use of contact era sources.

Acknowledgments

The Corozal Postclassic Project undertook excavations in northern Belize from 1979 through 1985. The research reported on here was supported by the National Science Foundation (Grants BNS-8318531 and BNS-8509304), the Explorers' Club, Sigma Xi, The University Museum, the University of Pennsylvania, and the University of Central Florida. The research was aided significantly by the Belize Department of Archaeology. I would also like to thank Arlen Chase both for his help in the field and for his intellectual input in this paper.

9. Maya Elites: The Perspective from Copan

David Webster

IT is fair to say that Maya archaeologists and other scholars have over-whelmingly concentrated their efforts on the elite manifestations of Maya society for the last century and a half. It is also symptomatic of the nature of this research that, even after such prolonged effort, there still remain fundamental unresolved issues concerning Maya elites, many of which are of broader interest for Mesoamerican prehistory as well. This paper identifies what I believe to be the most important of these issues and evaluates them, predominantly from the perspective of recent research carried out at Co-pan, Honduras, since 1975, by projects led by Gordon Willey, Claude Baudez, William T. Sanders, and me. Although data and ideas are drawn from all phases of research at Copan, most come from Phase II of the Copan Archaeological Project, which Sanders and I have co-directed since 1980. Much of the research carried out over the last thirteen years has been published (Willey, Leventhal, and Fash 1978; Baudez 1983; Fash 1983a, b; Webster and Abrams 1983; Abrams 1984a, b; Sanders 1986; Webster 1985a, 1989a; Freter 1988), but I also rely upon many data sets that are unpub-lished and/or still under study. Readers are directed to cited works for de-tails of data and interpretation that can only be briefly summarized in this paper.

The most basic issues concerning Classic Maya elites, of course, relate to the nature of Maya sociopolitical institutions and to the larger theoretical considerations of stratification and ranking. Since other papers in this vol-ume explore stratification and ranking, I shall defer my own brief remarks on these concepts, and Maya sociopolitical institutions at Copan, until more specific elite issues have been addressed. It is, nevertheless, necessary to define "elite"—a term both useful and frustrating because of its generality. On the one hand, in any preindustrial hierarchical society there exist indi-viduals or groups that are differentially and invidiously ranked—and here I use the word "rank" in its broadest sense (i.e., the assignment of differential value to things or people in a hierarchical system)—whether on the basis of ascription or achievement. Those individuals or groups occupying the lim-ited positions of highest value may be properly said to be elites. The advan-tages of this definition are that we presumably would all agree with it—a rare thing among anthropologists—and that it does identify an important principle of comparative social organization. On the other hand, the con-cept so defined is so general that it includes everything from the titled chiefs of tiny Northwest Coast societies to the occupants of the highest castes of the traditional Indian status system and the dominant classes of stratified preindustrial states. It implies nothing about the actual forms or principles of stratification and ranking (here used in their restricted anthropological senses), social mobility, gradations among elites themselves, or the prerogatives that accompany them, in terms of prestige, authority, power, or wealth. Perhaps, given current debates about the structure of Classic Maya society, this very vagueness is felicitous.

Since at least the early 1960s, Maya archaeologists have recognized what might be termed "titled elites"—individuals bearing titles denoting such statuses as king or ruler, royal consort or relative, priest, scribe, or perhaps head of a large corporate kinship group. While we do not know in any detail how these titles were acquired, or often even what they imply, it is reasonable to assign elite rank to people who possessed them, not only because of the impressiveness and obtrusiveness of the titles themselves, but because of their associations with other indicators of high status—public art, large and elaborate religious or residential edifices, elaborate tombs, and lesser status symbols such as dress and ornament.

There was undoubtedly considerable gradation among titled elites. Kingship was clearly extremely exalted and seems to have been largely ascribed, but quite possibly lesser titles, such as scribe, may have been achieved by talented individuals of modest social origins, as they were in ancient Sumer or Old Kingdom Egypt. For the purposes of this paper, I assume that those possessing titles occupied the positions of highest prestige in Maya society, dominated decision making in the spheres of politics, administration, war, religion, and the political economy, and controlled disproportionate wealth in terms of both status symbols and capital resources. These people I refer to as "primary elites."

There also undoubtedly existed many individuals or groups who occupied much more ambiguous (from the archaeological perspective) but still important elite statuses. It is difficult to generalize about such people, but perhaps a few specific examples will clarify what I mean. Assuming that Maya kings were polygynous, a king might have one or more titled royal wives who would clearly be members of the primary elite. But he might also have consorts or concubines of lower social origins in his household. Such "wives," while perhaps not formally titled themselves, would obviously be people of considerable status vis-à-vis women in the wider society. Similarly, a full-time royal architect or sculptor would occupy a privileged position, as would, say, an unusually successful warrior. Judging from ethnohistoric accounts, even "slaves" enjoyed considerable social mobility and could occupy privileged positions based on their proximity to primary elites and services to them. I refer to such people as "secondary elites." Whether their statuses were ascribed or achieved, all such elites were essentially clients or affiliates of the highest levels of primary elites. For all we know, many of them actually had minor titles that went unrecorded in books or monuments.

Secondary elites differ from primary elites in that their statuses, wealth, and decision-making prerogatives are derivative and much more limited. Nevertheless, such secondary elites, as will become clear, may have had certain important systemic functions and effects comparable to those of primary elites, and it is for this reason that I identify them. A corollary point is that the systemic functions or prerogatives of elites may not be commensurate with their formal status ranking. For example, in Tokugawa Japan artisans and farmers who possessed land were ranked above merchants in terms of social prestige, although the latter as a class enjoyed far more of the material perquisites that we normally associate with high status.

The categories of primary and secondary elites are commonsense ones and are useful precisely because they do not imply anything in detail about the degree of Maya political centralization, the presence of ranking, classes, or castes, or the specific correlates of elite status. The following discussion distinguishes where necessary between the two—otherwise the term "elite" refers to both forms.

Major Issues Concerning Maya Elites

The Origins and Nature of the Copan Dynastic Sequence

The principal primary elites at Copan—the royal dynasty—are currently undergoing renewed and intense scrutiny, especially through the work of William Fash and his colleagues at the Main Group. Much of the information on this project is summarized in the Copan Notes series, issued by the Instituto Hondureño de Antropología e Historia and Northern Illinois University, one source for many of the data reviewed here.

According to the succession glyphs on the monuments, there were at least sixteen Copan kings. These rulers are most comprehensively represented by the sequence shown on Altar Q, formerly thought to record a "conference of astronomers" but now recognized as a dynastic political monument erected by the sixteenth ruler, Rising Sun. We can identify ten of these kings by name, including the first, who reigned during the fifth century (G. E. Stuart 1989). The last five rulers can be placed in time with reasonable precision, given the dates and succession data (*hel* glyphs) on their monuments. These are: the twelfth ruler, Smoke Imix (A.D. 628-695); the thirteenth ruler, XVIII-Jog (ca. A.D. 695-737); his shadowy successor, Smoke Monkey, who appears to have reigned for only eleven years after XVIII-Jog's putative military defeat at the hands of Quirigua; the fifteenth ruler, Smoke Shell (ca. A.D. 749-763); and, finally, the sixteenth ruler, Yax Pac (A.D. 763-ca. 800). Although we can sort out this sequence, it is not known whether the rulers followed one another according to any specific rule of succession.

Rulers preceding or following these four kings are more difficult to place. There is a possible reference to a seventeenth ruler at Copan, U Cit Tok, on the unfinished Altar L at Copan, and an associated date of A.D. 822 (G. E. Stuart 1989:503-4). If this individual ever actually occupied the throne, his reign must have been a very weak and attenuated one. More important and well documented is the immediate predecessor of XVIII-Jog, Smoke Imix, who reigned throughout much of the seventh century and who may have attained the status of "four-katun lord." Smoke Imix is significant for more than his longevity. During his reign, effective political centralization focusing on the royal compound at the Main Group (fig. 9.1) seems to have become firmly established, major changes occur in the Copan ceramic sequence, and, as we shall see later, there was a dramatic population increase in the region. Smoke Imix also set up, in the middle of the seventh century, a series of seven stelae, all bearing identical or very close dates, whose distributions have been hypothesized to mark the boundaries of his domain (Spinden 1913, Baudez 1986).

The five Copan rulers from Smoke Imix to Yax Pac who may be reasonably well placed in terms of succession order and chronology thus bracket almost perfectly the two centuries A.D. 600-800, the period of major growth and complexity of the Classic Copan polity. We know virtually nothing about the first eleven rulers. Conceivably, some of them represent mythological ancestors of the royal line rather than real individuals. A sequence of sixteen successive rulers is not, however, unreasonable, given the date of the appearance of elite Maya markers in the region. A new stela found in 1989 bears a date in the fifth century (A.D. 435) and the title and name of the individual who may have been the first ruler—Mah K'ina Yax K'uk Mo' (G. E. Stuart 1989:498). Construction on the earliest stages of major elite structures, such as the ballcourt and what may be royal residences, begins at about the same time, but much of this construction is poorly known because it is deeply buried.

The abrupt appearance of such markers of Maya elite culture in a region that was on a linguistic frontier in the sixteenth century raises the possibility that a group of elite Maya and their retainers and followers established themselves, about A.D. 400, in a valley already occupied by non-Maya speakers. If such an incursion happened, it must have been on a very small scale. Our surveys and excavations have turned up very few signs of occupation from this period; an informed guess would place the population of the Honduran section of the valley at perhaps 2,000 people. It is clearly unnecessary to envision any kind of massive or aggressive intrusive process or to assume that the earliest Maya "rulers" referred to by the later monuments, if they existed at all, were more than petty chiefs.

Major Maya centers with long dynastic sequences such as Tikal exhibit marked fluctuations in the fortunes of royalty, especially as reflected by discontinuities in monument erection and building programs. This I take to

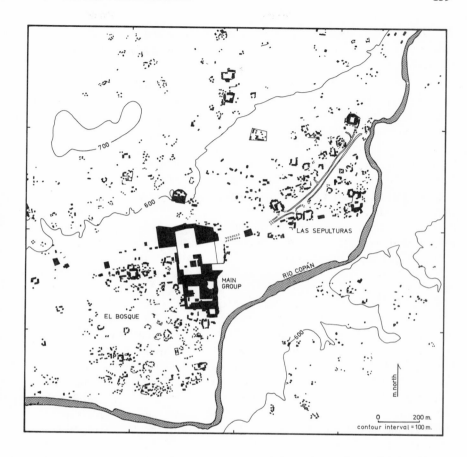

Fig. 9.1. The urban core at Copan (adapted from endpocket map in C. Baudez 1983).

be mainly symptomatic of the essential weakness of Maya political institutions. In the case of Copan, as noted, the achievements of any rulers up until Smoke Imix appear, on the basis of current evidence, to have been very modest. Smoke Imix, obviously long-lived and dynamic, seems to have laid the foundation for effective and large-scale political consolidation. XVIII-Jog respected and preserved his illustrious predecessor's monuments, possibly to augment his own prestige, and embarked on a program of ambitious monument erection (including stylistic shifts to a more sophisticated, in-the-round style) and building, only to have his career cut short by his losing confrontation with Quirigua. His own successor seems to have been very undistinguished, but was followed by Smoke Shell and Yax Pac, who in the last half of the ninth century presided over a Copan polity of unprecedented size. It has traditionally been assumed that the massive final construction levels at the Main Group—and particularly on the acropolis—were the products of Yax Pac's reign; possibly, though, Smoke Monkey, or even

XVIII-Jog, was responsible for more construction than we formerly thought, an idea currently being investigated by epigraphic and architectural research.

The Nature, Distribution, and Function of Elite Establishments

Although structures traditionally labeled "palaces" have long been identified at Maya centers, few have been excavated sufficiently to demonstrate with certainty that they were elite residences or what their range of functions was (see Harrison 1970 for a review). Part of the confusion derives from the old "ceremonial center" conception of major Maya sites. J. L. Stephens (1969:133) contributed to the origins of this confusion by asserting categorically that there were "no remains of palaces or private buildings" at Copan and that the acropolis should be thought of as a "temple." It is symptomatic of the nature of the intervening decades of research, which emphasized reconstruction of monuments and buildings rather than the recovery of features and artifact assemblages, that Richard Adams (1977:152) could maintain that "almost nothing can be designated as elite-class residences at Copan."

Ironically, even as Adams was penning this remark, Gordon Willey and his colleagues were developing a settlement model for Copan based on the hypothesis that most sites were the remains of residential compounds and that the variation among them reflected a status hierarchy of Maya households, with the most complex sites being elite establishments. Their heuristic model eventually identified five basic types, defined by both quantitative and qualitative criteria (Willey, Leventhal, and Fash 1978). Small isolated mounds and Type 1 sites are at the low end of the ranking, with Types 2, 3, and 4 of increasingly higher status. By extension, the Main Group constitutes a unique category—the royal household. The most sensitive indicators of rank are the height of buildings within groups (which roughly reflects mass, and thus energetic investment) and the presence of vaults, well-cut stone, and sculpture. We used basically this same model during our later surveys and excavations, which largely confirm the Willey hypothesis, as do the energetic construction estimates of E. M. Abrams (1984a, b).

We now know that there is a virtual continuum of site complexity at Copan and that most sites tested did have residential functions (Freter 1988; Webster and Freter 1990a). There does seem to be something of a break in this continuum, with single-mound Type 1 and Type 2 sites in a lower echelon than Type 3 and 4 sites. The latter, then, generally constitute the major elite residential establishments at Copan, although they themselves show considerable variation and in a few instances do seem to have ritual as opposed to residential functions. The break in the continuum is defined by a polythetic set of factors. Sites of Type 2 rank and lower are much more numerous and widely distributed than Type 3-4 sites, as well as being smaller and of inferior construction (although some structures in Type 2 sites may occasionally have vaulted roofs and even sculpture).

Our collective surveys have located a total of 1,425 sites of all ranks in the Honduran section of the drainage. Of these, only forty-nine fall into the elite Type 3 (thirty) and Type 4 (nineteen) categories. These elite sites are strikingly concentrated near the Main Group. Twenty-eight of them are in the urban core (fig. 9.1), within 1 km from the royal establishment. Fourteen others are outside the urban core, but still within 4-5 km of it. The remaining seven are in outlying parts of the valley, and at least two of these are nonresidential. There are probably two reasons for this concentration. First, the Copan pocket—the region of about 24 sq km immediately around the Main Group—has by far the largest zone of high-quality alluvial land in the entire drainage. It is in this pocket that we find evidence of the earliest occupations, the earliest and strongest evidence of a Maya presence, and the highest population densities. The agricultural potential of this zone clearly provided a centripetal attraction for people of all social levels during virtually all periods. It is also clear that, at least from the time of Smoke Jaguar, there were strong political incentives for elites to maintain residences near the royal court. Conversely, even though Copan had a large hinterland, there were few administrative, military, economic, or other incentives for elites to establish themselves at any considerable distance from the Copan pocket.

The Royal Establishment. Our current thinking envisions the Main Group as essentially a royal household of a kind common in preindustrial hierarchical societies—what Richard Fox (1977) has called the "regal-ritual center." Such centers are very common in Mesoamerica (Sanders and Webster 1988); their nuclei are royal residential complexes, but also include other facilities such as shrines, courtyards for public gatherings, political monuments, administrative and storage buildings, and all of the other necessary appurtenances of royal dominance. In many cases, these facilities are hypertrophied versions of household features found in residences of lower rank. Part of the confusion concerning the functions of Maya centers has resulted from the presence of structures that had highly impressive ritual or at least nonresidential functions. The value of Fox's model is that such features are seen as necessary components of the mode of governance emanating from regal-ritual centers and in many cases as modified versions of features occurring more widely in the settlement hierarchy.

Because the early work at Copan emphasized recovery and restoration of monuments, buildings, caches, and tombs (see Longyear 1952 for a review), little attention was paid to recovery and analysis of features and artifact assemblages from behavioral contexts that might have revealed residential functions, thus perpetuating J. L. Stephens' original "ceremonial center" misinterpretation. In all likelihood, sizable portions of the Main Group proper had primary residential functions, particularly the East Court, which probably was a private precinct of Rising Sun. Sanders and I have long felt that the "Temple of Meditation" (Trik 1939), which dominates this court, is really a royal residence, partly on the basis of its similarity to other undoubted elite residences we have excavated at Copan. Claude Baudez (1978:67) has recently expressed a similar conclusion, based on the iconography of this and nearby buildings. Fash and his colleagues now believe that the last phases of this structure may have been built during the reign of XVIII Jog, rather than Yax Pac, as originally proposed. Earlier palaces may be buried beneath the latest construction phases of the acropolis, and the imposing but largely unknown Group 1 on the northwest corner of the Main Group might be another. There are undoubted elite (but probably nonroyal) residences in the El Bosque zone to the east and south of the Main Group proper. Sanders believes (personal communication, 1986) that this zone housed elements of the secondary elite closely affiliated with the royal line and that many ancillary functions of the royal household (e.g., storage, cooking, burial) might have been carried out there. Both the early excavations conducted in this zone (Longyear 1952) and our own most recent test excavations in this area in 1988 turned up much evidence in support of the general residential function of El Bosque.

In 1980-81 we excavated half of Structure 223, an imposing range building on the northeast corner of the Main Group, thinking it might be a royal palace. Instead we uncovered huge undecorated rooms with enormous benches associated with a sweat bath. There were no burials—common in residences of all levels at Copan—but remains of eleven human skull masks were found. Domestic refuse was very sparse. Our current interpretation of this structure is that it was a dormitory/school for elite young men (Cheek and Spink 1986).

The Main Group and perhaps associated portions of El Bosque are thus seen as the residential core of the Copan primary royal elite. The obtrusive ritual themes and buildings (which in any case are intimately concerned with royal prestige and authority) are manifestations of royal rule expressed in the context of an expanded royal household.

Nonroyal Elite Establishments. By far the most abundant and convincing evidence concerning nonroyal elite residential establishments comes from the Las Sepulturas zone (fig. 9.1), where the Harvard project extensively tested a Type 3 group, and where Phase II research carried out virtually complete excavations of a Type 3 and Type 4 unit. I shall briefly review the data from the Type 4 group 9N-8, which have been extensively published elsewhere (Gerstle 1987b; Hendon 1987; Webster 1989b; Webster and Abrams 1983; Webster, Fash, and Abrams 1986).

Group 9N-8 (fig. 9.2) is the largest preserved elite establishment in the Copan Valley outside the Main Group, with the possible exception of La Canteada in the upper reaches of the valley. It consists of at least eleven conjoined courtyards (parts of the site have been destroyed by the river) and approximately fifty individual buildings. Virtually all of the group, including courtyards and peripheral spaces, has been excavated, and the evidence

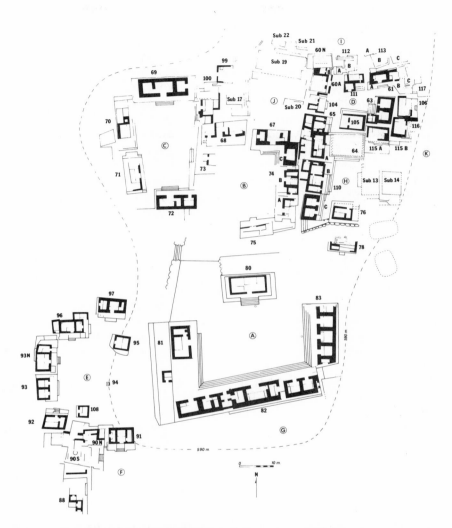

Fig. 9.2. Group 9N-8, Copan; circled letters designate courtyard groups.

that it functioned as a residence for both primary and secondary elites is overwhelming. Domestic refuse is abundantly associated with all court-yards, and, except possibly for Courtyard J, all possess what we interpret to be residential structures, most obviously marked by the presence of interior benches.

Special-purpose buildings occur in many courtyards, such as shrines and/or burial structures (e.g., Strs. 63, 64, 80) and kitchens (e.g., Strs. 78, 95). Some courtyards, particularly J, seem to have been almost entirely given over to specialized ancillary domestic functions such as cooking, stor-age, and refuse disposal. A. Gerstle (1987a, b) has argued that Courtyard D housed a residential foreign enclave, and Randolph Widmer has turned up impressive evidence of specialized craft production (production of shell ornaments and possibly specialized weaving) in Courtyard H.

In 1980, we predicted that if Group 9N-8 had largely residential functions it would yield numerous burials and that these would include people of all ages and sexes in a variety of burial contexts. Some 287 individuals of all ages and sexes were subsequently recovered from 9N-8 and most have been studied (Rebecca Storey, personal communication, 1987). The bulk of this burial sample is associated with the latest construction phases of the group as a whole. Burials range from those interred in substantial stone-built chambers to those informally jammed into construction fill or middens. Although all courtyards produced burials, there are some striking concentrations, with about 75 individuals from Courtyard D and 60 from Courtyard E.

There is striking variation among courtyards in number, arrangement, quality, and function of buildings, and the surface architecture of the group as a whole obviously grew by a constant process of accretion and renovation for at least a century, and probably considerably longer, beginning about A.D. 700. Size of buildings, quality of construction, and presence of sculpture are the best indicators of relative status; on this basis Courtyards A, B, and C are clearly of the highest rank, and the shoddily built Courtyards J and K the lowest. In other words, if specific courtyard groups were ranked individually, they would be assigned low rank in the Willey hierarchy. It cannot be stressed too strongly that, although 9N-8 as a whole is an elite enclave, people of many social ranks lived in it, judging by variation in artifacts, burials, and architecture.

Courtyard A dominated the whole compound. It included a ritual building with associated ballgame paraphernalia (Str. 81; this may have been another young men's house similar to the much grander Str. 223 in the Main Group), an apparent shrine (Str. 80), and typical range structures that we interpret as elite residences in the strict sense (Strs. 82 and 83). The latter are complexes of buildings that underwent periodic enlargement and renovation. Of special interest is Str. 82-center, an imposing vaulted building heavily ornamented with facade sculpture and a hieroglyphic bench (Webster 1989a). We believe that this building, apparently erected at about A.D. 787 (the date on the bench—see Riese 1989), was the palace of the dominant elite personage of 9N-8 as a whole. The bench inscription includes his name (as yet untranscribed), the title "Calendar Priest" or "Scribe," a glyph possibly identifying him as the second in succession to that title, and a reference to the contemporary king, Rising Sun. The facade sculpture and the bench include not only elements reflecting scribal attributes, but also the bacab imagery so important at Copan during the reign of Rising Sun (Baudez 1989). B. Riese (1989) has noted that Copan is unusual in that nonroyal elites have access to impressive displays of iconography and epigraphy glorifying their persons.

Group 9N-8 is clearly an elite establishment second only to the Main Group itself. While unusually complex, it is generally representative of the other elite residences that we have excavated in Las Sepulturas and, with a few exceptions, that we have tested in our outlying surveys, in the sense that unusually large and high-quality structures are associated with abundant domestic refuse. J. L. Stephens and Richard Adams notwithstanding, there are many impressive elite residences (palaces if one chooses) at Copan. Group 9N-8 is an expanded elite household of a rank second only to that of the ruler. At least one titled person—probably a member of Rising Sun's court and quite possibly a relative by descent or marriage—dominated the compound, which included many secondary elites and perhaps persons of lower social rank as well. His establishment may be seen as a smaller version of the king's, consistent with the model of ranked households proposed by Willey. The compound is eerily reminiscent of that described by Cortes (1971:31) in sixteenth-century Yucatan:

There are houses belonging to certain men of rank which are very cool and have many rooms, for we have seen as many as five courtyards in a single house, and the rooms around them very well laid out, each man having a private room. Inside there are also . . . rooms for slaves and servants of which they have very many. Each of these chieftains has in front of the entrance to his house a very large courtyard and some two or three or four of them and all are very well built.

Territorial and Demographic Size of Political Units Dominated by Elites

The territorial and demographic sizes of Maya polities are obviously key issues in understanding overall sociopolitical structure. The enormous variation in, and frequent modifications of, such estimates reflects three things: (1) overemphasis on centers as opposed to wider elements of settlement systems; (2) the paucity of widespread, comparable settlement system studies and methodological agreement on how to interpret them; and (3) the differential packing of centers in various regions of the Maya lowlands. We feel that the Copan settlement data currently in hand are very reliable (Webster 1985a, 1988; Freter 1988; Webster and Freter 1990a), and I shall briefly review them here.

One of the problems in delimiting territorial and settlement boundaries in some parts of the Maya lowlands (e.g., the northeast Peten) is the lack of strong physiographic compartmentalization. Copan, in a well-developed, fertile river valley surrounded by comparatively unproductive uplands, is an exception. Although the polity probably drew some minimal resources and political support from an area of 300-500 sq km (roughly the area of the drainage basin in Honduras and immediately adjacent Guatemala), the zone of basic settlement and agricultural exploitation is only about 200 sq km (i.e., the valley floors and adjacent foothills of the main and tributary streams). As we shall see below, the most intensively settled and utilized part of the valley was the 24 sq km Copan pocket. Copan thus had a comparatively large territory in the general sense, but its effective sustaining area for resources and political support was only slightly larger than the area delimited by *bajos* and embankments at Tikal. Sanders has calculated (personal communication, 1985) that there are about 70 sq km of high-quality land in the drainage as a whole.

Another problem is the dense packing of major centers in regions like the northeastern Peten, which makes it difficult definitely to ascribe territory or settlement elements with assurance to one or another center and also adds the possibility of complex, multicenter political hierarchies. Fortunately, at Copan there are no remotely comparable Maya centers closer than Quirigua, so all of our settlement components fall into Copan's domain. Our current estimate of the demographic size of the Copan polity at its largest, ca. A.D. 700-850, is 18,500 to 26,000 people. If our estimates are reliable, Copan emerges as a far smaller elite domain than we would have guessed in 1980.

If elite dominance as measured in terms of people was weaker than we previously thought, social and political centralization, measured in settlement and demographic terms, was very pronounced prior to A.D. 800. At least 85 percent of the total population of the mature Late Classic polity was concentrated in the 24 sq km Copan pocket, where, as already noted, most of the elite establishments are located. So extraordinary is this concentration that we should regard the Copan sociopolitical system as essentially one more adapted to the Copan pocket than to the larger Copan Valley. Whether this concentration reflects inherent strengths or weaknesses of the Copan sociopolitical system is another issue, which I shall address briefly later. It is, does, however, strikingly confirm that Smoke Imix's valley stelae were set up to mark the limits of a political domain, an idea proposed long before large-scale, systematic settlement surveys were ever done at Copan.

Size of Maya Elite Components

Essential to our understanding of Maya society is the question of how large, proportionately speaking, elite components were. This issue is important not only because of its structural implications, but because of its implications for the Classic Maya "collapse," which I have considered in detail elsewhere (Webster 1985b).

Using a complex model of room occupation estimates for sites recorded in the Copan surveys, we have calculated that approximately 74 percent of the people of Late Classic Copan lived in sites of Type 2 rank or lower (Webster and Freter 1990a). Since many of the Type 3 and 4 sites such as 9N-8 undoubtedly housed, as we have seen, people of comparatively low rank, this total percentage as measured by residential size and quality should probably be raised to something like 80-90 percent. Thus, a figure of 10-20 percent is suggested for combined primary and secondary elites. I am inclined to agree with Richard Adams and W. D. Smith (1977, 1981) that the primary or titled elite component was very small—say 2 percent of the whole population. Using these figures the Copan elite, collectively, would have maximally numbered 3,700-5,000 if the population range given above is accepted, with the titled or primary elite numbering only 370-500. My own feeling is that the collective elite total should be more conservatively estimated using the 10 percent figure—1,850 to 2,500. Whatever the number, most of these elites lived in the urban core near the Main Group, which Freter and I estimate had a population of ca. 5,800 to 9,500 people.

Another way of conceiving of elite identity is by ignoring the vagaries of social rank and distinguishing between consumers and producers in energetic terms. The notion here is that significant elite rank presupposes unbalanced reciprocity through the consumption of food energy produced by others (producers); various elites are thus collectively lumped as consumers, and variations in elite rank become irrelevant (see Webster 1985b for details of this argument). In preindustrial, agrarian, hierarchical societies, especially "low-energy" ones such as those in Mesoamerica, where energy sources apart from human muscle were limited and technological efficiency was low, ratios of consumers to producers were generally similar to those given above. Thus, data independently derived from settlement analysis provide an estimate that is extremely plausible in cross-cultural perspective.

Elites and the Political Economy

By "political economy" I mean the manipulation or control of significant components of the economy by elites, thus facilitating the acquisition, maintenance, or augmentation of high sociopolitical status, prestige, and authority. The issue of Maya political economy has been a leitmotif in virtually all comprehensive Maya studies, and a specific concern at least since W. L. Rathje (1971) published his trade hypothesis. In its simplest form, it asserts that Maya elites had access to surpluses of food and other commodities produced by commoners, as well as their labor, leaving the mechanisms of access unspecified.

The issue of political economy relates most closely to the behavior and prerogatives of the primary elite, and I would distinguish four levels of analysis. The first level, which I regard as by far the most important, involves the control by such elites of locally produced agricultural energy in the form of foodstuffs—what we might call the agrarian political economy. The second is their control of the production and exchange of essential or desirable raw or finished goods—the commercial political economy. The third is agricultural intensification. The final level—elite demands for labor—is discussed as part of the consideration of the Maya "collapse" (see below).

The Nature of the Agrarian Political Economy. The crucial issue here is the direct or indirect control of agricultural production by primary elites. It must be discussed against the distinctive backdrop of the regional landscape, which in many respects is unlike that of most of the rest of the Maya lowlands, particularly in terms of differential agricultural potential. The first distinction we must draw is that between uplands (foothills and mountains) and bottomlands (old river terraces and active floodplain). In general, the former are much less productive, in terms of maize/bean agriculture, than the latter. The second distinction involves variation within these categories. In upland areas (most of the region) long-term productivity varies enormously, depending upon altitude (which affects rainfall), slope (strongly related to erosion), and, most importantly, soil development on various kinds of bedrock (e.g., restricted zones of limestone-derived soils are much more fertile than those weathering from ancient volcanic bedrock). Bottomland variation includes susceptibility to flooding, poor drainage, variation in soil texture, and especially irrigability. In general, the Copan environment exhibits much more pronounced fine-grained variability in agricultural production because of these factors than elsewhere in the lowlands and hence greater scope for political manipulation. Although the largest and most important transactions in the agrarian political economy involved locally produced and consumed food energy products, I shall also say a few words about commercial crops.

Virtually all elite establishments are situated on, or immediately adjacent to, the area of greatest productivity and security, the bottomland of the Copan pocket. Although there is no present means of demonstrating that Maya elites therefore had privileged control over high-quality land, this is the settlement pattern we would expect if they did. Certainly it is the pattern today, when politically and economically influential families in the community dominate large tracts of the best land. Both the urban core and the Main Group are situated—as is the modern town—next to the largest extent of irrigable land in the pocket, which can produce two to three crops per year. Both the settlement history and the distribution suggest that there was unusual scope for Copan elites directly to dominate land of the highest quality and thus to form some prehistoric variant of the strong client-patron relationships found in the valley today.

Intensification and Commercial Cropping. I shall discuss intensification and commercial cropping briefly here because they relate closely to the issue of the control of agrarian production and elite dominance, although also to the commercial political economy, discussed next. Irrigation is the main concern. The most valuable lands in the entire drainage are those in the Copan pocket around the modern town, which can be irrigated in the dry season from the Sesesmil tributary. Not only are multiple crops possible on this land, but it is suitable for the production of commercially valuable native crops such as tobacco and cacao. The potential for elite leverage here is not managerial, but rather proprietorial, since the necessary irrigation works are minuscule. The owners of this land are today some of the most privileged and powerful in the valley, and they now irrigate, using pumps, most of the best bottomland elsewhere in the pocket as well. The problem with extensive prehistoric irrigation is insufficient water (lacking pumps), not insufficient land. There are a few other small permanent streams in the pocket, but their irrigation potential is very limited. Because of the steep gradient of the main Copan River at the east end of the pocket, it is conceivable that a major canal system, perhaps running where the modern highway is situated, might have been engineered to irrigate most of the bottomland north of the river. Such a system would have created considerable managerial demand, but there is absolutely no evidence for one. If irrigation existed anywhere prehistorically—which I think extremely likely—we have no direct evidence for it. I do not believe that the "Maya" dam reported by B. L. Turner II and W. Johnson (1979) is ancient. The issue of prehistoric irrigation and its relationship to the political economy is thus fascinating but currently moot.

The issue of elite-controlled production and trade of nonsubsistence commercial crops is much the same. Copan is famous for its tobacco, a major colonial export crop grown as early as the end of the eighteenth century (Larry Feldman, personal communication, 1985). Until recently the valley also produced large quantities of cacao, which would have benefited from irrigation. If either of these crops was significant aboriginally—and I would expect cacao to have been much more important—primary elites would presumably have been in control of them. Unfortunately, apart from effigy cacao pods, there is no evidence for the existence or trade of either crop.

While on the subject of intensification, it should be noted that our surveys have turned up only a few possible indications of intensive agricultural practices of any kind, and these have not been sufficiently well investigated to be sure they are prehistoric. Given the generally steep topography of the region, agricultural terracing would have been highly desirable. Such terracing is minimally used in the valley today, even though destructive erosion is rampant, and there are many indications that hillside erosion was destructive in the past as well.

Leaving aside the difficult issue of irrigation, there seem to have been few if any capital improvements in terms of landscape modification related to agricultural intensification, even though these would have been appropriate. Such improved segments of the landscape were often dominated by elites in Mesoamerica (e.g., the domination of the chinampa zones in the Basin of Mexico by Mexica and other lords), and were key components in the political economy. No such process is apparent in the Copan Valley.

The Commercial Political Economy. The hypothesis that control of production and exchange of basic consumer goods buttressed Maya elite authority is widespread. Copan is again distinctive from this perspective. Raw material for most essential utilitarian commodities can be locally had in the valley. For example, chert is available, as are various kinds of igneous rock (rhyolite and basalt) used for grinding stones and clay suitable for ceramics. Conceivably, there was internal control of the production and flow of some of these, but it is unlikely that elite monopoly (in any case logistically unnecessary) could have been effective enough, or demand high enough, to create significant economic leverage, as M. Spink (1983) has argued for grinding stones. In the latter case, as elsewhere, alternatives were available; many grinding stones at Copan are made from the soft but ubiquitous volcanic tuff.

The one exotic resource that shows up obtrusively is obsidian (Mallory 1984), which, despite the abundance of local chert, makes up by Late Classic times about 75 percent of the chipped stone inventory. Obsidian tools, especially prismatic blades and flakes, are found abundantly in all social contexts, including isolated low-rank groups and even field huts (Webster and Gonlin 1988), and most or all of the reduction process is associated with the areas of use or deposition of tools. J. K. Mallory (1984) has offered persuasive quantitative data suggesting that—despite its frequency and the probable participation of elites in its initial procurement (by Late Classic times virtually all comes from Ixtepeque)—the scale of obsidian use was low and that elites would not have derived important economic benefits by controlling either its production or its distribution. Since Mallory's study, we have discovered that even sites occupied long after the royal collapse and elite decline are well provided with obsidian, thus strengthening his argument.

If some goods such as obsidian flowed into Copan, something must have flowed out, however fitfully. The most abundant and widespread presumed product of the Copan Valley found elsewhere is Copador Polychrome ceramics, although Copador exhibits sufficient variety that there must have been multiple centers of production. Copador ceramics are found in varying quantities in central Honduras and El Salvador and are very sparse in other Maya sites (e.g., Wendy Ashmore and Robert Sharer inform me [1984] that there is very little at Quirigua, despite that center's ostensible close ties to Copan). We know of a few Copan sites that may have specialized in ceramic production of some kind (none seems very impressive), but none has been excavated. Evidence for specialized site production of any kind is comparatively rare, although we can identify locales where obsidian was consumed in great quantities (Mallory 1984), where rhyolite metates seem to have been made and stockpiled (Spink 1983), and where plaster was made.

Interregional Elite Interaction

Intermarriage, visitations for elite ritual (e.g., funerals), pilgrimage, and exchange of status items have all been emphasized as important in creating and maintaining elite Maya uniformity. Apart from the possibility that Yax Pac's mother was from Palenque, that Smoke Imix carried out ceremonies at Quirigua, that the Copan/Quirigua connection was violent (perhaps a dynastic squabble), and that Water-Lily Jaguar (an early Copan king) is mentioned at Caracol (Grube 1990), I know of no evidence for formal interactions between Copan and other specific lowland Maya centers. In fact, I have been struck by Copan's apparent isolation from the rest of the lowland Maya world, which seems to increase during the Classic period. The best evidence comes from elite imports.

Until overall artifact counts are available, the best that can be said is that the volume of imported elite items or raw materials seems minimal. We certainly find the general run-of-the-mill elite items such as shell, jade, stingray spines, and perhaps such finished objects as ritual ballgame paraphernalia, but these are few and far between. The best indicator of the curious isolation of Copan in terms of such imports may be exotic pottery. In the elite contexts my students and I have excavated, there are very few imported wares from the lowlands proper (e.g., northeastern Peten) even as represented by sherds, much less whole vessels. Far more abundant are polychromes imported from central Honduras, which seems to have far stronger connections with Copan, although I think Copan's political and economic influences on presumably non-Maya peoples to the east and southeast are greatly overrated. Even some elite items, such as raw jade, may have come from non-Maya regions (e.g., the Motagua Valley, reputedly a major jade source, may well have been only partly settled by ethnic Maya).

In terms of elite architecture, monuments, iconography, and epigraphy, Copan does seem soundly Maya, remembering, however, the regional variation present even in these quintessential Maya attributes. Presumably some sorts of interactions with the lowlands proper at least periodically reinforced this uniformity, but the nature of the relationships is unclear. Copan primary elites, as Maya elites did generally, used symbolic display and the ideology behind it both conservatively (to reaffirm traditional identity and values) and dynamically (to strengthen their positions in their local political arenas). The latter is what in part creates regional variability. Claude Baudez (1986, 1989) has discussed this dynamic use of ideology and imagery during the reigns of the various Copan kings. Of particular interest is the bacab imagery that becomes so apparent during the reign of Yax Pac, which he feels suggests strong ties to the northern rather than the central lowlands.

The Elite Maya Collapse

Mesoamericanists in general are broadly concerned with all of the elite issues so far discussed. The next is one of particular relevance to Maya archaeology—the so-called collapse of Classic Maya society in the central and southern parts of the region. This phenomenon was first recognized on the basis of cessation of important primary elite activity at large centers—especially the cessation of the erection of carved and dated monuments and large-scale civic construction. We know that there is considerable regional variation in chronological terms in these manifestations of the collapse

(Culbert 1973). We are just beginning to appreciate how much more prolonged and complex the collapse was within particular regions as other
kinds of powerful data accumulate, particularly settlement data (e.g., Ford
1986). Our recent work at Copan provides an example of such refinement,
and we now understand the processes of the collapse there very differently
than we did in 1980.

Copan research between 1975 and 1980 reinforced the traditional view
that major royal activity ceased rather abruptly at, or shortly after, A.D. 800.
It also provided detailed settlement information for the Copan pocket,
where the extremely dense visible architecture was well recorded and correctly seen to be overwhelmingly associated with Coner phase ceramic deposits. This phase was assumed to begin at about A.D. 700 and end at A.D.
850, or perhaps as late as A.D. 900 (Fash 1983b, Viel 1983). Our own
revisions of this scheme are based upon large-scale excavations in elite and
nonelite groups, an extensive program of rural settlement survey in outlying
parts of the valley, 701 test excavations in sites of all ranks, and 2,048 obsidian hydration dates processed by Ann Freter. Our excavations broadly confirm the Coner phase association, but the obsidian dates show that the duration of the phase was much longer than expected; although Coner begins at
about A.D. 700, it essentially continues into the thirteenth century (Webster and Freter 1990b).

The association of obsidian dates with architecture allows us to break
down post-A.D. 700 occupation in a much more fine-grained manner than
hitherto possible, and the Copan collapse is now seen as having several
distinct and protracted phases, with different processes defining each
(Freter 1988). Royal activity ceases abruptly at the end of Yax Pac's reign,
A.D. 800 or a little later (leaving aside the possibility of his shadowy successor). Establishments of other elites—including that of the titled elite at
Group 9N-8—exhibit continued occupation as late as ca. A.D. 1000. Population probably peaks in the valley at about A.D. 850, having overshot all of
our carrying capacity models for the Copan pocket about a century earlier.
Although the nonroyal elites maintain themselves after 850, overall population begins to sharply decline then and to disperse heavily for the first time
into rural zones outside the Copan pocket, where numerous sites of Type 2
rank and lower are founded. By A.D. 1000, the system is in general politically and spatially decentralized, and population decline continues. The one
exception to this generalization is found in the upper Copan Valley, where
the Type 3 center of Piedras Negras seems to have been founded shortly
after A.D. 1000 and to have functioned as the political center for a rural
population of about 1,000 people for perhaps a century. We have no evidence for substantial population at all after A.D. 1200. This sequence of
events is independently supported by David Rue's (1987) pollen core analysis for the Copan pocket.

There is no space available to discuss in detail the explanations for this process of collapse. I have elsewhere (Webster 1985b) argued, partly on the basis of E. M. Abrams's (1984a, b) energetic studies, that one factor in the political economy—elite demand for labor—played only a minor role. This argument was made even though the traditional assumption was that the last major king, Yax Pac, was responsible for an unprecedented spurt of building activity during the last half of the eighth century. Should Fash's current research confirm that much building formerly attributed to Rising Sun was actually done by Smoke Monkey, or even XVIII-Jog, the argument is strengthened.

Sanders and I believe that the pattern of the collapse—and especially the character of demographic decline—is much more consistent with an ecological explanation than the more abrupt declines previously projected for Copan and other sites. Sanders' unpublished data on modern subsistence agriculture in the valley indicate striking declines in maize yields on hillside lands over periods as short as a decade, and erosion is a widespread and serious problem today. There is considerable evidence for prehistoric environmental degradation in the valley, including massive sheet erosion. This erosion was so severe that it deeply buried even substantial structures on the northern fringe of Las Sepulturas, as shown during research by Baudez, and more recently by an excavation that I carried out in the summer of 1989. Storey has recently completed paleopathological studies on approximately 300 individual burials recovered from the elite Type 4 group 9N-8. Her data indicate that by A.D. 700-850 physical problems related to malnutrition were serious even among this relatively privileged subpopulation (personal communication, 1987).

Elites and Sociopolitical Structure at Copan

The last and most fundamental issue is the relationships of the Copan elite with the overall sociopolitical structure of their own polity. Specific issues concern the degree of stratification or ranking present, the strength of political centralization, and the mechanisms by which these were maintained. The following interpretations are still highly provisional and even speculative, but summarize the current perspectives of those of us involved in the Phase II research. They are based upon the archaeological record from Copan and also upon comparative ethnographic data—particularly from Africa. They are also in many respects Copan-specific and cannot be uncritically extended to other Maya polities.

Sanders and I believe that the mature Copan polity was characterized by a high degree of segmentation. By this we mean that, although the system was politically centralized around a group of preeminent titled elites (the royal lineage), kinship was still the dominant mechanism in overall social, political, and economic organization. Essentially, our argument is that there were multiple, effective political interest groups in the polity, which we conceive of as maximal lineages with their own internal ranking structures and, most importantly, their own corporate identities and resources (see Fash 1983a for a settlement analysis related to this model). The most important feature of this model is that the polity was characterized by what E. Durkheim called "mechanical solidarity" in economic and hence political terms. In such a society the effective power of rulers is to a high degree circumscribed by the presence of lesser magnates with their own power bases. Leaders of such corporate groups (inheriting their positions through some sort of intralineage structure) would be occupants of such impressive Type 3 or 4 groups as 9N-8, and their supporters/kin would consist not only of other occupants of the elite households, but of segments of the rural populations as well. These second-level elites at Copan, at least some of whom seem to have enjoyed the possession of court titles and ranks, were stewards of large corporate, kin-based land holdings. I cannot stress too strongly that, although this model emphasizes decentralization of political power, it is not a feudal model. Feudalism is a certain kind of political decentralization, based upon a hierarchy of landed proprietors whose holdings derive primarily from nonkin vassalage relationships, a very different system from that proposed here.

The system we envision was characterized by well-developed principles of ranking, but the degree to which it was socially stratified is a more difficult question. One possibility is that there was very little stratification, in the sense that whole groups of people were not ranked vis-à-vis one another. In this case the heads of a particular maximal lineage, roughly equal to the others, would monopolize royal titles and other prerogatives, with heads of other lineages collectively forming an effective check on royal power, as occurs in some Yoruba polities. A more stratified variant of this situation occurs when the royal lineage is conceptually ranked above all the others in terms of prestige, although its internal structure may be similar and most of its members may be denied access to effective political status positions by the king. The Yoruba kingdom of Ife had a structure of this sort (Bascom 1984). A third variant occurs where military expansion has allowed the ruler not only to augment his personal control of wealth and force, but to create a court and bureaucracy consisting of nonrelated clients responsible only to him, thus providing a dimension of power not available within the context of his original kin-based society. This is the Baganda analogue.

The first variant seems too egalitarian for Copan, while the last is inconsistent with the small demographic size of the polity, its highly concentrated settlement pattern, and the lack of evidence for military expansion. I think that the second model, which emphasizes the importance of kinship integration and ranking, but which allows for the presence of weak social stratification in the form of an elevated royal "class" (itself internally ranked), is the most plausible for Copan. This is basically the sort of system R. Carmack (1981) has proposed for the Quiche Maya.

Whether there was any marked degree of economic stratification remains arguable. The Copan royal line, at least in the eighth century, was certainly able to draw economic support—most obviously in the form of labor—from the population at large. By the mid-seventh century, some economic stratification must have appeared in the agrarian political economy, given the extraordinary growth of population in the Copan pocket from ca. A.D. 650 to 750. This certainly would have benefited some kinship groups, or some privileged members of them, at the expense of others, and it is at this time that the possibility of elite or royal dominance of high-quality land, and possibly commercial production on it, would have been most pronounced. As noted previously, manipulation of other commercial commodities, at least as far as we can perceive them archaeologically, seems to offer little scope for enhanced economic stratification. I suspect that among the Classic Maya elites gained some economic advantages, as they did in the Late Postclassic, from the possession of slaves, a source of labor and support independent of the traditional kinship organization. The possible ethnic mix of Maya and non-Maya speakers in the Copan Valley suggests another potential dimension of stratification. There is, however, no archaeological evidence for stratification along ethnic lines; by the eighth century, any small Maya intrusive group seems to have been effectively assimilated with the original inhabitants.

This hypothetical reconstruction of mature Copan society raises the question of the relationship between royal and lesser elites, who were potential competitors for power. Supremacy of the royal line may have been based upon elite intermarriage, as well as the integration of nonroyal elites into the structure of the royal court at the Main Group. For example, the elite Maya personage who dominated Group 9N-8, in addition to his personal power base, might have been a royal affine, with his title—"Calendar Priest"—conferred by the ruler and indicating court rank. I think that anything resembling a formal, centralized state bureaucracy was very weakly developed, with the royal court—people of all degrees of status around the king—forming the basic nexus of centralization. Many court titles were probably effectively devoid of significant administrative function, being rather prestigious honorifics reflecting royal favor. The point here is that complex societies require administration, but that this does not necessarily imply well-defined administrative specialists and complex bureaucratic structures.

That the nonroyal elites and the corporate groups they dominated ultimately proved more durable than the royal establishment is reflected archaeologically by the survival of some of them, even if in an attenuated form, long after the abrupt royal collapse.

Earlier I raised the question of whether the striking spatial centralization of elite residences and population in the Copan pocket around the Main Group indicated a correspondingly high development of political centralization, in the sense of effective royal power. Given the model discussed above, the answer is quite the contrary—royal power was weak. The centripetal forces that dictated this concentration were rather the attractions of the agricultural resources of the Copan pocket, the desirability of proximity to the royal court as a political arena, and possibly the reluctance of Copan kings to countenance the establishment of potentially competing elites at any distance from the Main Group.

Many scholars have interpreted the impressive ritual and political displays of Maya rulers as signs of great political strength. I would reverse the argument and regard intense royal display, at least at Copan, as indicative rather of the essential weakness of royal rule, all of the "blood of kings" hoopla notwithstanding.

The major concepts of the preceding discussion—stratification and ranking—are, as Sanders (this volume) has pointed out, principles of social ordering. Terms like "chiefdom" and "state," which I have so far consciously avoided, refer to specific political forms. Since the issue of Maya statehood has been much discussed (see Fash 1983b for a Copan version) I shall finish with a few words on the subject. If by "state" we mean, as M. Fried (1967) has defined it, a society with a set of effective institutions that specifically function to uphold a structure of social and economic stratification and in which kinship has seriously attenuated as an integrative institution, then Copan was not clearly a state. Such institutions were not obviously present, and neither were the necessary dimensions of stratification for them to reinforce, and I have argued that kinship was still very important. That some forms of stratification and political centralization intensified, during the reigns of Smoke Imix and his successors until the royal collapse, is equally clear. Copan is such a dynamic polity during the seventh and eighth centuries that it would probably be impossible to put a neat political label on it even if all the details of change were known. Ultimately, however, its political evolution was cut short by successive phases of a royal, elite, and demographic collapse, testifying to the weaknesses of its political and economic underpinnings.

10. Elites and Ethnicity along the Southeastern Fringe of Mesoamerica

J. S. Henderson

THE territory to the south and east of the Maya world represents a frontier zone in which Maya cultural patterns give way to others that are not typical of the Mesoamerican tradition (Henderson 1978, 1987a, 1987b; Schortman and Urban 1986). The Precolumbian societies of this southeast periphery of Mesoamerica—embracing what is now western and central Honduras and most or all of El Salvador—are usually considered to be differently, more simply, structured than those of the Maya world. The existence of elite groups is a critical issue for understanding the prehistory of the region, but the traits traditionally interpreted as elite markers in the Maya world—particularly hieroglyphic inscriptions and epigraphic monumental political art—are not applicable in the southeast periphery.

Traditional Approaches to Elites

Surprisingly, students of the prehistory of the southeast periphery have not devoted particular attention to operationalizing the concept of elites. On the contrary, both the abstract definition and the archaeological recognition of elites have typically been treated as nonproblematic. The evolutionary significance attached to the emergence of elite groups, the subsequent developmental roles attributed to them, and even the basic sociopolitical attributes of the societies in which they appear are topics of debate, but virtually all analysts associate elites with social stratification and the state (whether or not they equate the two). Elites are usually alleged to be central to the evolutionary transition from chiefdom to state as well.

The most recent consideration of rank, wealth, and power in the southeast periphery (Healy 1987) focuses on the emergence of chiefdoms, which are taken to be societies in which social, economic, and political ranking are key features, and which have at least incipient social stratification and political centralization. Chiefs and their close relatives and associates occupy the pinnacle of the hierarchy, maintaining and enhancing their status and power by controlling surpluses, redistributing resources, and managing community affairs. More specifically, they control long-distance exchange with other chiefs and access to the exotic goods such exchange typically serves to acquire; they use these and other sumptuary goods; and they organize public works projects. As in much of the general literature on the correlates of chiefdoms (e.g., Peebles and Kus 1977; Creamer and Haas 1985; Drennan and Uribe 1987; Earle 1987), the most serious drawback of this general approach is the inherent difficulty of identifying specific material correlates of the key features that are archaeologically detectable. Typically, chiefs and their close kin and associates are held to constitute an elite group, which, in turn, is supposedly recognizable not only in such relatively direct material correlates as status goods, but also indirectly in the archaeological markers of a chiefdom, which implies the existence of an elite.

These features are exceedingly difficult to operationalize in a specific fashion: often, virtually any indication of status differentiation—in domestic architecture, in craft goods, and especially in mortuary treatment—is considered to reflect the existence of an elite group. All these types of status goods are recognized subjectively, in terms of high-quality, valuable (especially exotic) materials and fine craftsmanship. Thus, in the southeast periphery, jade ornaments, particularly in mortuary contexts, are often said to reflect elite status, on the grounds that the raw material does not occur naturally in the region. "Monumental" structures—typically, vaguely defined or specified in terms of some arbitrary size threshold, since so little structural excavation has been carried out in the region—are frequently alleged to represent public construction projects that could only be undertaken by stratified societies, which by definition include elite groups. In the same way, settlement hierarchies are sometimes interpreted as exclusive features of chiefdoms (and/or states) and are therefore taken to imply the existence of elite groups.

In any case, archaeological signatures of elite groups in the southeast periphery have typically been considered to be self-evident; the task of recognizing elite groups has certainly not been thought to impose special sampling requirements or distributional studies. On the contrary, the notion that intuitively recognizable status goods necessarily reflect elite groups has encouraged inferences based solely on objects without archaeological context.

Defining Elites

Operationalizing the notion of elites more satisfactorily requires both a sharper conceptualization of the key issues and a more rigorous identification of their archaeological correlates. The Chases' (introduction, this volume) general consideration of defining elites and their structural roles in Precolumbian Mesoamerican societies provides a very useful starting point. From the perspective of the southeast periphery, their framework needs to be refined and expanded in two respects. Their focus on the notions of power and control of institutions is perfectly appropriate, but a much greater degree of specificity, even at the abstract conceptual level, is essential for identifying archaeological correlates. At the same time, clarifying the evolutionary significance of elites is a major concern of anthropological thought, and this places major constraints on approaches to defining and recognizing them.

The key issue—whether for developing models of Mesoamerican society at large, for characterizing societies sociopolitically, or for evolutionary interpretation—is the relationship of elites to particular forms of social, economic, and political organization. If elites really are associated with states (or chiefdoms, or some other sort of sociopolitical organization), then inference about them becomes much simpler: evidence for the state in the archaeological record would imply the existence of an elite, and (perhaps) vice versa. If, however, the possibility of a correlation between elites and the state is to be the subject of investigation—if it is to be demonstrated rather than assumed *a priori*—then the archaeological correlates of elites must be defined independently of those that mark the state.

In any case, it is important to specify the relationship that is posited between the archaeological markers and the elite. Irrespective of any inferences about the state, civic construction projects might very well indicate the existence of an elite if they are of sufficient scope to imply a permanent managerial group. Likewise, a hierarchy of settlements may imply the existence of a state and an associated elite group, but only if the levels of the classification actually correspond to differences in political function and in economic or social status (Wright 1986), a condition that is not often demonstrably fulfilled. Variability in the number, size, and elaboration of structures and sites is not necessarily an indication of such a hierarchy.

In order to preserve the independence of the concept of an elite from that of any particular type of sociopolitical organization, it is essential to specify separate sets of material correlates. Monumental architecture and other indicators of large-scale public works activity are more reasonable reflections of the state itself than of elite groups. The most direct material correlates of elites are those indicating status differentiation, whether in terms of residential architecture, domestic equipment, or mortuary treatment. These material correlates are secondary status markers in the sense that they themselves need not (and probably seldom do) directly represent the basis of the elevated status (special moral authority, unusual ritual expertise or qualification, wealth in land). In fact, status differentiation need not be reflected at all in the sorts of material goods that readily survive in the archaeological record (G. Clark 1986), but an extreme, formalized contrast in status—social stratification proper—usually is.

Central to the recognition of social stratification is the criterion of contrast, often alleged but rarely demonstrated. Rigorous identification of elites is necessarily contrastive; that is, status goods can *only* be identified by a detailed analysis of the contexts in which they occur. The distribution and associations of putative elite markers must be distinctive; ideally they should all occur in association with one another, in limited spatial distribution within and among communities. In fact, this will seldom (if ever) actually be the case, since any reasonably complex society will have not one but several elites in various social spheres. The importance for anthropological theory of the relationship between ruling political elites and the state lends additional significance to distributional considerations: the material correlates of these ruling elites should be associated in some specific way with the state. Moreover, the overall material contrast between elite and nonelite contexts should be very sharp, implying a distinct social group, not simply the upper end of a hierarchical continuum. Such a clear-cut material contrast would not, of course, imply an impermeable social barrier. Unlike traditional approaches to the recognition of elites, this approach not only imposes specific analytical requirements, but also presupposes very good archaeological samples drawn from the full range of social and functional contexts.

It is also important to develop frameworks for assessing the value of putative status goods that are more objective than the vague notion of "quality." M. P. Beaudry's (1987) approach to evaluating the relative cost of ceramic types in terms of the energy required for their manufacture and decoration (with an allowance for any special skills or esoteric knowledge required) and for transport of raw materials and/or finished products is exemplary, but requires considerable elaboration. Comparable approaches must be developed for other major artifact categories as well.

Current archaeological data from the southeast periphery cannot satisfy the stringent requirements of this sort of contrastive approach to recognizing elites, and serious revision of typical field research strategies will be required to bring about the requisite improvements in our data base. Eliminating subjectivity in identifying the material correlates of elites will require specific, explicitly justified archaeological signatures that are empirically determined for each region, period, and socioeconomic context. Different material markers may reflect membership in comparable elite groups in various places and times; conversely, the very same material objects may reflect elite status in one context, foreign cultural identity in another.

The Quiche Model

Judicious inference by analogy with ethnographic and ethnohistorical cases in which the nature and material correlates of elite groups can be thoroughly documented will provide a healthy dose of "social realism." The richness of available ethnohistorical, ethnographic, and archaeological data (Carmack 1973; Wallace and Carmack 1977) makes the Quiche elite by far the best-documented such group in eastern Mesoamerica. Combining the Quiche view of their own society, presented in considerable detail in the Popol Vuh, with recent archaeological studies of Utatlan, the Quiche capital, R. Carmack (1981) has developed a synthetic interpretation of the structure of Quiche society that focuses on a castelike distinction between two basic social strata:

lords, called *ajawab* (Saenz 1940), and their vassals, the *al c'ajol*. The lords were patrilineal descendants of the original warlords who came from the east and therefore claimed Toltec descent. Their forefathers were created by the majestic Toltec deities Tepew and K'ucumatz (Quetzalcoatl). The vassals, though not created separately, were perhaps more closely associated with the procreative deities, Alom and C'ajolom (Engenderors; Villacorta 1962, p. 20). They were said to be the "children" (*al c'ajol*) of the lords who were born outside the noble patrilinies. Some of them, in fact, were probably fathered by lords with secondary commoner and slave wives. Others, however, were conquered commoners who became subject to the Quiche lords, while still others were dissident peoples from neighboring towns who took refuge with the Quiches at Utatlan.

The social contrasts between the lords and the vassals were all-inclusive (Carmack 1976). The lords occupied the political, religious, and military offices of state, while the vassals performed the physical labor of building, providing food and offerings, and fighting for the lords. The lords were sacred, surrounded by royal emblems: feathers, gold ornaments, jade and other precious stone, and jaguar and lion claws. They were linked to the gods and temples through ritual participation. The vassals were secular, kept away from contact with the royal emblems and patron gods. The lords received tribute to support their subsistence and ostentatious living. The vassals paid tribute and also provided their own humble subsistence. The lords lived in elaborate palaces, within the walls of the town. The vassals lived in the rural zones, in simple mud-and-pole huts roofed with straw. The lords dressed in fine cloth woven from multicolored cotton threads. The vassals were expected to dress in henequen cloth (Estrada 1955, p. 73). Similarly, braided hair and the use of metal earplugs and quetzal feathers as adornments were restricted to the lords. Even the postmortal state of the two strata differed. There was a tendency to immortalize the lords, and some of the most important rulers were said to have disappeared without leaving notice whether or not they "tasted death." Las Casas (1909, p. 630) reported that high-ranked lords were burned and their bones gathered into bundles, which were kept in stone or wooden boxes to be worshiped like gods. The vassals were the servants of deity, fit only to make sacrificial offerings to the gods. We know from modern ethnographic studies (Carmack n.d.; Bunzel 1952) that no attempt was made to preserve the bodies or memories of deceased commoners. The body of the vassal was food for the earth, while the essence of the deceased was believed to enter the air and clouds, where it would coalesce with the other dead, to be carried to and fro with the winds. The individual lost his personal identity, returning to the earth and sky from which he had never been far removed.

The traditional caste features of economic complementarity, ideas of ritual contamination, and political domination characterized relations between lords and vassals at Utatlan. Also castelike was the endogamous marriage patterns of the two strata. While the lords could have secondary commoner wives, legitimate wives had to be "ladies" (*xok'ojaw*) (Las Casas 1909, pp. 624-25). Typically, ladies from outside Utatlan were preferred as wives, probably for political reasons. There are references in the documents to Utatlan rulers who took wives from the Tzutujils, Cakchiquels, Ilocabs, Tamubs, Quejnays, Mams, Mexicas, and possibly Itzas. The vassals, in contrast, married only other vassals who lived in the same community.

The respective caste statuses of the lords and vassals were firmly established in law (Las Casas 1909, pp. 616-17; Fuentes y Guzman 1932-33, 7:388-89). Some of the laws directly maintained the inequalities between the castes. For example, there were laws against fleeing from vassalage or influencing a vassal to disobey his lord. The tribute vassals were to pay their lords was fixed by law, both in amount and in frequency (probably every eighty days in most cases). Other laws, though not directly establishing the caste relationship, maintained it indirectly. Thus witchcraft was punished by death from burning, no doubt because it was a challenge to the priests of the lordly caste. (Carmack 1981:148-50)

Slaves formed in effect a third caste, at the base of the hierarchy. Class-like groups—warriors, merchants, artisans, and serfs—cut across the caste structure, as did a complex set of ranked segmentary lineages.

Even this very schematic summary suggests the richness of the Quiche case as a source of insights into the nature of elite groups in eastern Mesoamerica, particularly their material correlates. Two aspects of the Quiche elite are particularly important: their cultural distinctiveness and their relationship to the state. The lords' claim of descent from Toltec forefathers amounted to an assertion of a cultural identity different from that of the populace at large; their foreign connections and distinctiveness were reinforced by a variety of fairly obvious material emblems as well as by behavioral contrasts and aspects of the belief system that would be reflected materially in more subtle ways.

Political and kinship systems, state and lineage facilities and personnel, were inextricably intertwined, yet analytically separable. Lineage houses were basically administrative—particularly those of the royal lineage, in which much, perhaps most, state business was conducted—but they had some residential functions. Conversely, palaces were fundamentally residential complexes of the rulers and their close relatives, but special court-yards within them were devoted to administrative activities. The blending is obvious, but it is clear that the Quiche lords can be distinguished from the Quiche state both conceptually and in terms of material correlates. The major temples and administrative buildings would qualify as "monumental" by most definitions, but they are not particularly impressive in scale, especially in comparison with comparable structures in earlier Maya centers. A. W. Wonderley (in press) suggests that a lack of emphasis on massive civic construction projects was typical of Postclassic states in eastern Mesoamerica.

Maya archaeologists have not adequately exploited the Quiche case as a source of specific analogies or of general models for sociopolitical organiza-tion in the Maya world. A continuing "Peten-centrism," dictating an ex-tremely restricted focus on lowland Maya societies, especially those of the Southern lowlands, has in effect defined highland societies as beyond the bounds of Maya civilization (Brown 1987; Henderson 1987b). Highland polities that reached peaks of scale and complexity late in prehispanic times, like the Quiche state, have been considered (though rarely explicitly) so different in fundamental structure from earlier Maya societies as to be irrelevant to the task of reconstructing them.

Part of this perceived aberrance is apparently a reaction to the foreign connections of the Quiche elite. Actually, very similar internal cultural con-trasts characterize at least some earlier lowland Maya societies. At Chichen

Itza in the Early Postclassic (Tozzer 1941, 1957; Coggins 1986) and at Tikal in the Early Classic (Coggins 1979) elites celebrated foreign (Mexican) connections in much the same way as did the Quiche lords. It may be that early Maya elites claimed foreign cultural identity as commonly as did their Postclassic counterparts, who routinely attempted to glorify themselves by flaunting a Toltec heritage (whether real or fictive). Wonderley (in press) suggests that the pattern of mobile foreign elites establishing and maintaining dominance over culturally distinct populations was quite common in the Late Postclassic Maya world. As M. W. Helms (1979, 1987) has argued, distant links by their very nature confer status and supernatural power on those who enjoy them, so that elites would not necessarily limit their boasting about foreign connections to those with societies that were particularly wealthy, complex, or sophisticated. In any case, the cultural distinctiveness of elite groups is an important general issue.

Operationalizing the Concept of Elites in the Southeast Periphery

The absence of hieroglyphic inscriptions and political art at Utatlan makes the Quiche case especially relevant for the southeast periphery, where these features are also absent. Sculpture and especially hieroglyphic texts (L. Schele and M. Miller 1986) can be extremely useful in determining the material correlates of Maya elites, but actually to define them iconographically or epigraphically would exaggerate the structural contrasts between Maya societies and their neighbors. A proper perspective on the relationships among these societies requires archaeological signatures for key cultural features that are at least theoretically detectable in the frontier zone as well as in the Maya world proper.

The Mexican connections of the lords of Utatlan is another feature of the Quiche case that makes it especially useful for understanding elites in the southeast periphery. Extensive interaction networks kept the societies of this zone in continuous contact with Maya communities to the north and west. Frontier elites might very well emphasize foreign connections to enhance their own status, especially ties with their wealthier, more sophisticated Maya neighbors. Apart from monumental relief sculpture and hieroglyphic texts, the standard archaeological markers of Maya elites—carefully dressed stone architecture; elaborate mortuary treatment; imported jade ornaments, ceramics, and marine products; and even cosmetic skeletal alterations such as cranial deformation and dental inlay—bear a striking resemblance to the material items traditionally interpreted in the southeast periphery as indicators of interaction with the Maya (Henderson 1987b). These "Maya traits" may be the status symbols of frontier elites claiming Maya connections or even a Maya identity. On the other hand, they may reflect a truly foreign Maya presence, involving individuals quite outside the local social structure. To resolve these ambiguities will require, as the Chases (introduction, this volume) put it, an assessment of "the relationships between elites and the overall social and political system(s) of a particular culture." This in turn will require far more extensive excavated samples than we currently have for any part of the southeast periphery. The following examples should illustrate the limitations of current data for defining archaeological signatures of elite groups in the region.

Monumental architecture and aesthetically pleasing (high-quality) craft goods appear in the archaeological record of the southeast periphery in the Middle Preclassic period, but they do not provide clear-cut evidence for the emergence of elite groups. Olmec celts and figurines certainly represent high-quality goods by any reasonable standards of energy input or skill, and comparable objects certainly functioned as status goods on the Gulf Coast. Unfortunately, the few examples known from the southeast periphery are without archaeological context, so that their social significance remains unknown. Probably a bit later in the Middle Preclassic, burials with imported jade jewelry appeared at Los Naranjos (Baudez and Becquelin 1973) and Playa de los Muertos in the lower Ulua Valley (Popenoe 1934; Kennedy 1980, 1986), accompanied there by well-made ceramic vessels and figurines. These artifacts may reflect elite groups, but they cannot be shown to contrast with a nonelite style of grave goods, and their other associations are unknown.

Large-scale public building projects began at Los Naranjos in the Middle Preclassic, and then at many sites in the Late Preclassic (Henderson et al. 1979; Wonderley 1985a; Schortman et al. 1986; Benyo and Melchionne 1987; Joesinck-Mandeville 1987). Few of these structures have been excavated, and, apart from a burial and a cache of jade celts at Los Naranjos, none can be associated with any independent indication of the existence of an elite group, although it might be argued that as indicators of chiefdoms or states they imply the existence of elites. There are not even any good candidates for elite craft goods in Late Preclassic sites.

Classic period data are much fuller, but also do not include the kinds of contextual detail needed to present proper definitions of specific archaeological signatures. Monumental architecture continued to be produced, but demonstrable associations are few, and civic buildings are no more convincing as elite markers than in earlier periods. The range of craft products that might represent elite goods is broader: careful stonework in residential architecture, elaborately painted ceramics and carved marble vessels, and imported jade, ceramics, and shell. Data on the contexts in which these materials occur are sketchy, but very suggestive.

Ulua marble vessels (fig. 10.1) represent the quintessential intuitively recognized elite marker: a considerable investment of effort was obviously involved in their manufacture; they are quite rare; and apparently they have been found as mortuary offerings in association with other putative elite goods (jade and gold or tumbaga jewelry) at Travesia, a large civic center that numbered temples, ballcourts, and other public buildings among its

Fig. 10.1. Ulua marble vessel.

hundreds of structures. Unfortunately, these associations are not verifiable, since no Ulua marble has ever been found by an archaeologist in the lower Ulua Valley, where they are commonest and where a strong circumstantial case can be made for their manufacture. Without a great deal more excavation, it is impossible to be certain about the locations or contexts in which they were produced or subsequently used.

Gross distribution patterns suggest that Ulua polychrome pottery (fig. 10.2)—another expensive craft product in terms of the labor invested in producing the elaborate painted decoration (Beaudry 1987)—was likewise almost certainly manufactured mainly in the lower Ulua Valley. Contextual data are fairly spotty, but it is at least clear that Ulua polychrome occurs at sites of many types and sizes. It certainly occurs in some frequency at very large sites like Travesia, but specific contexts are unknown. The most likely examples of elite residential architecture—from a relatively small site at the fringe of Travesia and from Cerro Palenque (Joyce 1988)—do have associated Ulua polychrome, but the excavated contexts in which it occurs in highest frequency (roughly 5-10 percent) are garbage deposits associated with very small perishable structures in communities that can be best characterized as hamlets. It is, of course, possible that the residents of these tiny settlements had access to what was normally a sumptuary item of restricted distribution because they manufactured it; in fact, there is no direct evidence that they did so, although they certainly did make some kinds of ceramic vessels and figurines. What is certain is that our current understanding of the temporal and spatial distributions and associations of the many types of Ulua polychrome pottery within the lower Ulua Valley is by no means adequate. We are in no position to reconstruct the basic patterns of production and consumption, let alone demonstrate the sort of contrastive pattern that would clearly signal elite usage.

Outside the valley, Ulua polychrome pottery occurs in association with a substantial, apparently residential, building at La Sierra in the middle Chamelecón Valley; here it was evidently an import and is represented in modest frequencies. At Copan, Ulua polychromes have been found in caches and tombs near the civic core and in a large outlying elite residential complex that is demonstrably the residence of a family closely related to Copan's ruling line (Gerstle 1987a). Here the general pattern suggests costly imported goods consumed by members of an elite group. More detailed contextual data reveal that the Ulua polychromes actually occur, along with other imported goods, in poorly appointed structures in a small, relatively inaccessible plaza within the complex. It may very well have been used by rather low-status individuals, quite possibly foreigners from one of the areas where the Ulua polychromes were manufactured.

Postclassic data provide the closest approximation of a reasonable archaeological signature for an elite group—not because the data are fuller or the samples better, but because analysis of artifact distributions suggests

Fig. 10.2. Ulua polychrome vessel.

contrastive patterns that should typify elite markers. At Naco, a very prominent commercial center at the time of the conquest (Henderson 1977), Wonderley (1981, 1985b, 1986a, 1987) has delineated the civic core of the community: a central cluster of temples, a ballcourt, and other public buildings. The largest residential structures in the town, featuring stone wall foundations and painted plaster patios, are situated in close proximity to them. At least during the final facet of the Late Postclassic, a distinctive type of polychrome pottery (Wonderley 1986a:fig. 12), whose iconography and style suggest foreign connections, is associated with this central sector, in contrast with the decorated ceramics in use in smaller perishable dwellings farther from the civic core. "Downtown" residences are also distinctive in food preparation preferences (they contain almost all of the *comales*) and in lithic production techniques. An earlier substyle of ceramic decoration shows a similar distributional pattern at Naco, but identical vessels seem to have nonelite associations in the lower Ulua Valley—another illustration of the dangers inherent in assuming that the material correlates of elite groups in one region necessarily have the same significance wherever they occur. It remains to specify the distributions and additional associations of these artifact categories in sufficient detail to convert what are now plausible hypotheses about elite associations into reliably defined archaeological signatures of an elite group.

These examples highlight the limitations of traditional, intuitive approaches to the recognition of elite groups along the southeastern fringe of Mesoamerica. An improved understanding of this aspect of the social and political organization of these frontier societies will require research designs that produce far better documentation of basic patterns of distribution and association of critical artifact categories. The kinds of analytical strategies that underlie Wonderley's interpretation of elites at Naco, elaborated and extended to the much richer archaeological record of the Classic and Preclassic periods, can provide a solid empirical foundation for the definition of material signatures for elites and for other key social groups.

11. The Emergence of the Quiche Elite: The Putun-Palenque Connection

John W. Fox, Dwight T. Wallace, and Kenneth L. Brown

THE Postclassic Quiche of highland Guatemala furnish a clear case for the nature and development of an elite. Their rich ethnohistory permits correlation of specific patrilineages with specific sites and, at times, specific buildings. As migratory adventurers from the Maya lowlands during the Epiclassic (A.D. late 800s), the three Quiche allies—Nima Quiche, Tamub, and Ilocab—rose from humble beginnings to rule over the indigenous Vukamak of the Quiche basin. Here, marking the Late Postclassic period, they established a new fortified site, Utatlan, which then expanded until their three adjacent elite centers, one for each ally, plus a surrounding ring of outlying suburbs, eventually formed an urban center, with dense and elaborate structures for both ritual and habitation.

We are concerned here with the most powerful of the allies, the Nima Quiche, and their elite center Utatlan (Gumarcaaj). Their settlement layouts allow the tracing of changes in sociopolitical organization through their six-century history. The abundant symbolics of the Quiche mythical/historical origins and later history related in their famous book of state, the Popol Vuh, allow the detailed examination of one lineage, the priestly Ajaw, who first conjoined the Cawek and later were integrated into one moiety with the Nijaib (fig. 11.1). We also examine their palace complex, with murals and an heirloom cache (Cawek), illustrating the very rapid and expansive rise of elite lineages at Utatlan. Finally, a study of the economics of such elite habitation throws light on the system of production, distribution, and consumption underpinning the capital of a segmentary state.

Quiche History: Spatial Ordering, Cardinality, and Ranking

At their Early Postclassic center, Jacawitz, the two Nima Quiche major lineages, the Ajaw and Cawek—newly arrived from the lowlands (Carmack 1968)—built two adjoining civic plazas in a north-south orientation (fig. 11.2). The Ajaw (lords) and their patron god (also called Jacawitz) were associated with the southern cardinal direction. The Cawek, with their patron god Tojil (storm, rain, and sun), occupied the northern plaza. The ballcourt, symbolic of the underworld and of the duality of cooperation/competition, was attached to the Jacawitz temple. As we shall show,

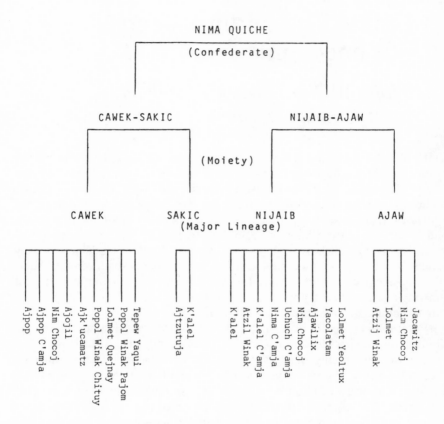

Fig. 11.1. Lineages of Utatlan (adapted from R. Carmack 1981:table 6.2).

the Ajaw were totemically linked to the Venus cycle, emblematic of the morning star. That both temples face southward, the cardinal direction of the Ajaw and Jacawitz, indicates the dominance of the Ajaw in the partnership at that time. East is where the morning star transformed into Junajpu, the early morning sun, as it emerged from the underworld (south, Xibalba; Fox 1987:131-33). Metaphorically, the two centuries during which the Quiche dwelt at Jacawitz are referred to in the Popol Vuh as "awaiting the dawn," that is, the time of Venus (or Jacawitz).

The tripartite Quiche at Jacawitz and at neighboring Amak Tam (Tamub) and Uquin Cat (Ilocab), along with the tripartite Rabinal at Tzameneb (Ichon et al. 1982), were essentially egalitarian. Lineage houses were undifferentiated in size, each about 30 m in length. In their wider social network, the Quiche acknowledged their august kin, the Lord Feathered Serpent lineage (Ajaw Canza Quetzal) of the radial-temple center of Tuja,

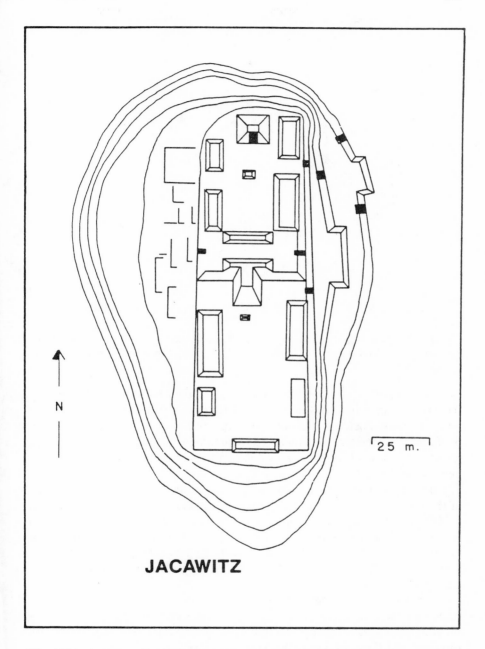

JACAWITZ

Fig. 11.2. Jacawitz, the Early Postclassic Ajaw and Cawek locus (from J. W. Fox 1978b).

20 km due north (Fox 1987, 1988b). The Tujalja, in turn, ritualistically recognized the authority of Chichen Itza on the northern cardinal point.

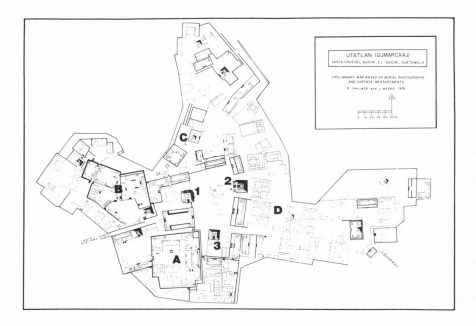

Fig. 11.3. Settlement plan of Utatlan showing the distribution of the major lineages and their temples (adapted from D. T. Wallace 1977b; J. W. Fox 1978b, 1989; and R. T. Carmack 1981).

Chichen was the seat of the tun (or katun) and the font of direct descent for the tutelary ancestor, in the persona of Kukulcan (Carlson 1981). There-fore, the Early Postclassic Quiche were one of the wider dispersed lineages of the solar calendar—or Amak Tun—in which ranking was premised on seniority in descent from the apical ancestor, said to be the Feathered Ser-pent of the Toltecs.

After the military defeat of the indigenous Maya (Vukamak) and creation of the Quiche state,[1] with the beginning of the Late Postclassic period (A.D. 1100s), the ranking of the lineages reversed when they relocated from Jacawitz to Utatlan, some 20 km to the south (after a brief sojourn in Mo-mostenango). Yet the north-south ritualistic positioning of the Ajaw and Cawek endured. The Ajaw's temple for their patron deity Jacawitz contin-ued to face south on a separate small southern plaza (fig. 11.3).

However, major changes occurred in the main (northern) plaza. Most important was the addition of a new warrior major lineage that comple-mented the Cawek, through their patron god, Awilix (the female moon), opposite the Cawek's Tojil (the male sun, storm, rain). Symbolizing this new relationship, the Cawek's new temple for Tojil primarily faced the ris-ing sun, in the east, while the Nijaib's Awilix, directly across the plaza, faced the setting sun in the west, which signaled the time of the moon.[2] To fill out the idealized social order, a small lineage, the Sakic, was adopted from

Tuja. Like Tuja, the Sakic were associated with the north, and their location on the north wing filled out the ideal quadripartite division of the four
cardinal points and completed the north-south and east-west *axes mundi*
(see Fox 1989:667-68, n.d.a), the intersection of which would occur at the
K'ucumatz (sun) shrine in the center of the main plaza (fig. 11.3). The
shrine's circular form recalls the shape of the tun and katun calendar stone,
the heart of the symbolic order (Taube 1988). Enhanced ranking between
the lineages is reflected in the length and height of the lineage houses,
which ranged from the original 30 m to 160 m for the Cawek lineage house
(see Fox 1981). There are twenty-odd lineage house complexes (with temples and shrines) throughout the site (Wallace 1977b:27), with size nega-
tively correlating with distance from the main plaza.

In this manner, the original Cawek-Ajaw dyad persisted as the ritual core
of Utatlan,[3] beneath the new Cawek-Nijaib east-west pairing of lineages
competing for temporal power. The lineages to the north and south were
the two "inward-focused" priestly lineages (Ajaw, Sakic); those to the east
and west were the two "outward-oriented" warrior lineages (Cawek, Nijaib)—another binary opposition.

The once top-ranked Ajaw now were in the shadow of the powerful and
enlarged Cawek major lineage. The Cawek split to include a new principal
lineage, the Ajpop C'amja, which provided the assistant king. The nine
principal Cawek lineages undoubtedly spread to various minor edifaces located on the north wing. The Ajaw remained relatively small, with only four
principal lineages. Their south and southwest areas manifest the most
crowded and compacted architecture in the elite center. Logically, then, the
top Ajaw official, the Atzij Winak, was housed in the impressive southwest
palace.

Symbolic of the new power alignments, the Cawek palace bordered on
the back (west) of the temple of their patron deity, Tojil, now the god of
state, and that of Quetzalcoatl, the Feathered Serpent (Popol Vuh
1971:183). The stairways of Tojil's new, modified radial temple faced the
north and south, as well as the main east cardinal point, symbolizing the
newly expanded function of the centerpoint of state. In architectural design
and in its placement in an unobstructed court with all sides free and open,
this Tojil temple radically differed from its antecedent one at Jacawitz,
which, like all other Quiche temples, had a single stairway facing a small
plaza. The new radial form recalls temples at the katun seats in Sacapulas
and at Chichen Itza. Thus, with the advent of the Quiche state during the
final settlement of Utatlan, the Temple of Tojil became the sacred nexus for
the dispersed lineages of the solar year, of the Putun descendants (Fox
1989:667). Perhaps through intermarriage with the Ajaw Canza Quetzal
lineage of Tuja, the Cawek now legitimately claimed pedigree from the
Feathered Serpent, which bestowed the charter for rulership in the "Toltec"
tradition.

Another notable change was the appearance and growth of the Nijaib major lineage, which rose rapidly in the tumultuous years of the formation of the Quiche state to rival the size and power of the Cawek themselves. Like the Cawek, the Nijaib grew to number nine principal lineages (fig. 11.1) by the time of the conquest, controlling vast estates both east and west of Utatlan (Carmack 1981:165). However, their lack of important ritual and political offices of state and relatively recent formation may account for their lack of a palace (fig. 11.3).

The last major lineage to take form, the Sakic, apparently never did expand, consisting merely of two principal lineages sharing one lineage house. A temple with dual habitation units, just north of the main plaza, apparently was Sakic (Wallace 1977b:38).

Palaces: Symbols of Elite Authority

The appearance of palaces marks the tendering of authority to a lineage, whose individuals now shared the sumptuary trappings and habitation with the revered ancestors and gods.[4] Palaces were large habitations with built-in, solid plastered benches, hearths, and round plastered cisterns (pilas, fig. 11.4c) arranged around two or more patios, all on a single basal platform (Wallace 1977b, see fig. 11.4). The interior patios, which were colonnaded like the Classic palaces at Palenque and Copan,[5] provided comparative privacy with limited access to the outside.

In the northeast corner of the southwest palace,[6] facing the main plaza, is a solid adobe base, 8 x 8 m, now standing 2 m above the level of the palace platform, apparently for a multistoried tower, as at Palenque. In this regard, the Título C'oyoi (Carmack 1981:194) shows a two-storied palace, with a sun figure accompanied by nineteen and possibly also twenty lines, plus a moon figure with twenty-nine lines. This suggests that the upper story was used for astronomical observations. Moreover, since the level of the floor of the palace was nearly 5 m above the main plaza, the report by F. Fuentes y Guzman (Carmack 1981:193) of a palace with five stories may not be so fanciful when the total height of the palace platform is considered.

The Palenque palace has a usable main platform surface of 3,800 sq m or total platform surface of 4,300 sq m, smaller than the 5,400 sq m of the southwest palace at Utatlan. Their respective courts are proportional; the palace court at Utatlan is 700-900 sq m, while the northeast court at the Palenque palace is some 350 sq m.

Murals in the Southwest Palace

Lineage ranking and function of the Ajaw may be inferred from three murals in the southwest palace: that of a "monkey," a "warrior," and a "bundle and gourd motif." Connections are drawn to the Ajaw as keepers of sacred traditions, including, quite possibly, interpreters of the Venus calendar.

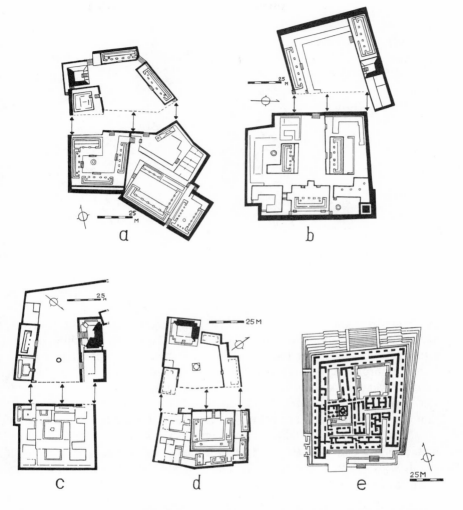

Fig. 11.4. Palaces and adjoining ritual plazas: a. West palace (Cawek), Utatlan; b. Southwest palace compound, Utatlan; c. Palace I - Plaza 1, Iximche; d. Palace II - Plaza 2, Iximche; e. Palace, Palenque.

The "monkey" fresco (fig. 11.5), from an outer wall overlooking the Jacawitz temple, depicts the lower half of a life-size anthropomorphic figure, in a bent-over, dancelike posture. The top half of the figure is missing. Simian imagery abounds for the Classic Maya, especially on Late Classic burial ceramics (e.g., M. Coe 1973; Robicsek and Hales 1981:127; L. Schele and M. Miller 1986:138-39), and for the Quiche, in the first saga of the Third Creation of the Popol Vuh.

In the Quiche myth, the Hero Twins Junajpu and Ixbalanque compete against and outwit their patrilineal half-brothers, Jun Baatz (1 Monkey) and

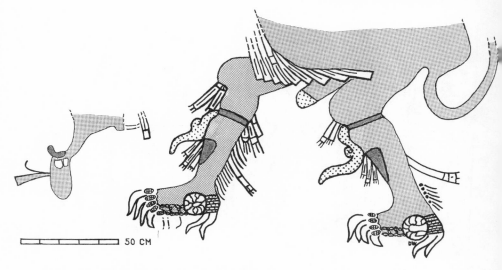

50 CM

Fig. 11.5. Monkey mural, Ajaw palace, Utatlan.

Jun Ch'oven (1 Howler), all four offspring of Jun Junajpu (Popol Vuh 1971:59). The plot involves the jealousies of the elder brothers, who prefer life in civilized surroundings as "flautists, singers, writers, carvers, jewelers, and silversmiths," directed at the younger Hero Twins, who are hunters and warriors. When hunting one day, the Hero Twins persuade their troublesome stepbrothers to climb a tree to retrieve birds shot by the Twins with their blowguns. As they climb, the tree suddenly and mysteriously grows. The Twins suggest that the tree-bound brothers retie their breechcloths so that the elongated ends are behind, whereupon the jealous siblings become monkeys. The juxtaposition of clawlike projections of the otherwise human feet, plus the tail, suggests this metamorphosis in process. The undoing of the breechcloth and reversal of the belt may also have involved uncovering the genitals, as in the mural, possibly an additional sign of humiliation.

The "warrior mural" (fig. 11.6) is from an interior mud-plastered wall of the palace. It depicts a "noble" warrior, with face painting, round shield and darts, rattle, nose-bone, and tobacco gourd pouch, rendered in an orthodox Mixteca-Puebla style. However, what might be Classic Maya hieroglyphs run along the base. In a nearby mural uncovered by R. Wauchope, R. Carmack (1981:296) interprets a blue lake with shells and a feathered serpent above as a narration of the migration epic of the forefathers from the Gulf lowlands. The warrior figure also seems to be walking over or by water, since the feet intersect a blue basal band.

Regarding the association of the Ajaw with Venus, only the blue face paint and shells might be attributed to the morning star (cf. L. Schele and M. Miller 1986:51). Perhaps the recounting of Quiche history was the purview of the Ajaw, so that these codexlike paintings could signify ethnic origins.

Fig. 11.6. Mixteca-Puebla styled "warrior," Ajaw palace, Utatlan.

A third mural, from the front of a bench in the main elongated room on the east side of the southwest palace (fig. 11.4b), is done in polychrome pigments on a clay plaster that was fired into ceramic state. It consists of a gourd alternating with a bundle of vertical rods (a scepterlike staff that is depicted at the Temple of the Cross at Palenque) and a fish with fingerlike projections, as if fins or feathers (fig. 11.7). Accordingly, the Ajaw would be keepers and bestowers of the sacred symbols of power, and the Cawek the temporal bearers. Moreover, in the origin epic, the Olmeca-Xicalango are referred to as the "Fish People." The gourdlike motifs could signify tobacco containers; J. E. S. Thompson (1970:173) notes that the Mexica regarded the tobacco gourd as a priestly insignia.

In the ballgame myth of the Popol Vuh, Junajpu and Ixbalanque vanquish the Lords of the Underworld, and Junajpu transforms (as Venus?) to rise as the morning sun. As such, the episode reflects the fraternal cooperation/competition between the Ajaw and Cawek, as does the positioning of the ballcourt between the Ajaw and Cawek ritual-palace complexes at Jacawitz and Utatlan (Fox n.d.b). Junajpu is the mediator—in descending to and ascending from the Underworld—between Venus (twilight) and the sun (day).

During the Classic period, *ajaw-* was a prefix ascribed to kingly lines at Palenque; for the Early Postclassic, to chiefly lines at Tuja. Yet the Popol Vuh states that the Ajaw were scribes and musicians, and performed other arts of courtly, urbane life. In contrast, the Cawek were initially relegated

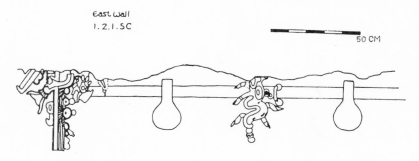

East Wall
I.2.1.SC

50 CM

Fig. 11.7. Conventionalized bundle-fish-gourd mural, Ajaw palace.

to warrior functions, like Junajpu and Ixbalanque. As in the myth and in political history, the Hero Twins reverse the original advantage of their fraternal rivals, the Ajaw, and lead their descendants into the patently historical Fourth Creation of the Popol Vuh. Remember, the Cawek chronicled the myth in the Popol Vuh. Junajpu continues as the mythological bridge between the *ancien régime* (Ajaw) and the new power brokers (Cawek).

Then the Ajaw, like Jun Baatz and Jun Ch'oven as patrons of writing, music, and the lapidary arts, may have retained some historiographic functions, although the Sakic would have also brought the written tradition from Tuja (Sacapulas 1968). The imagery of monkey-men as painters of codices is a frequent Late Classic motif (Robicsek and Hales 1981:fig. 28) and is associated with the divination (Braakhuis 1987:28, 35-36, 46). Since the Cawek were associated with the solar calendar, we propose that the Ajaw may have exercised prophetic authority of the Venus calendar (Fox 1988a) and served as the ritualistic companions of the Cawek, as Venus (GI) was the "right hand" of his sibling, the sun (G-II).

Since the honorific *ajaw* also linked the living incarnated with their hero ancestors during the Classic (cf. Freidel and Schele 1988a:548-49), it follows that the Ajaw major lineage continued the scholastic traditions of their lowland ancestors. In binary opposition, the Ajaw as Venus mediated the Cawek (sun, warrior king) and Nijaib (moon, warrior) factions. Likewise for the Palenque Triad, GII, the lastborn, mediated GI (Venus) and GIII (moon). While the Ajaw were not as visible in the ethnohistoric accounts of warfare and alliance as their Cawek and Nijaib counterparts, their former grandeur is reflected in the size of their patron temple and palaces, although they are set off from the main plaza.

Heirloom Vessels: Symbols of Rank

In a society where lineage ranking and access to office were premised on degrees of genealogical proximity to the deified ancestor, revered heirlooms from an ancestral homeland furnished tangible testimony of pedigree and

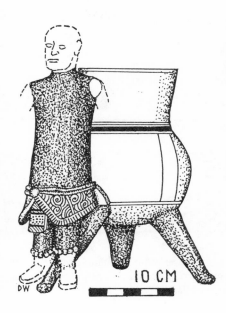

Fig. 11.8. *Mixteca-Puebla effigy vessel, from the Cawek antique cache.*

privileged status. In the west (Cawek) palace complex, Wallace uncovered sherds of nine vessels dating from the migratory period (Epiclassic or Early Postclassic).

Significantly, these antiques were in a long structure directly north of the lineage temple (figs. 11.3, 11.4a) within the largest of the three palace patios. The lineage house could well have housed the ajpop patrilineage, who provided the king. The vessels were strewn directly on the floor, evidently having been either stored in the building's rafters, as practiced in Quiche residences today, or pulled from a looted tomb under the center bench, a location reserved for high-status individuals. In either case, the breaking of the vessels might have occurred when the site fell to Pedro de Alvarado in 1524. The pots were antiques from a wide range of areas coincident with the Putun network. They could date as much as six centuries prior to the abandonment of Utatlan, and at least several centuries earlier than the site itself. One was, in fact, broken in antiquity and repaired by binding through drilled holes (fig. 11.8).

A Mixteca-Puebla style collared jar with tripod legs (fig. 11.8; Fox 1987:fig. 2.6) is decorated with black-on-orange Tlaloc heads (fig. 11.9b) on the body and Feathered Serpent and eagle heads(?) in postfired polychrome paint on the collar (fig. 11.9a). A fully modeled standing figure with fringed skirt and satchel (e.g., Webb 1975), both typical of the Gulf Coast (Anawalt 1981:843), is attached by its back to the vessel body. The jar is a common Mixteca form; another example with standing figure is from Oaxaca (Nicholson 1960:615, 1982:241ff; Ramsey 1982:fig. 15).

The collar has a seven-color painting on a thin stucco coating, depicting two heads (fig. 11.9a), one a Feathered Serpent with an elaborate feathered appendage on the snout and possible feathers on its head. The imagery recalls K'ucumatz/Quetzalcoatl, a Putun/Quiche deity, and the name of an early Cawek king. The second head, perhaps an eagle, also suggests the Toltec: the cropped feathered headdress recalls the Atlantean warriors on the Temple of Quetzalcoatl at Tula, and flowing feathers on the end with three G-symbols; the cardiumlike shell is costume elaboration in various codices.

Fig. 11.9. Designs on Mixteca-Puebla styled vessel: a. polychrome painting on stucco on neck of tripod jar with Feathered Serpent and eagle heads; b. black-on-orange false negative design on jar body showing four aspects of Tlaloc-Tojil.

The band around the globular body (fig. 11.9b) is painted in a black-on-orange false negative (i.e., the background is painted over the orange-brown slip color of the motifs) and has four poses of Tlaloc heads, distinguished by the goggle eyes and under-eye curved bands, with prominent upper teeth or fangs, minus a mandible.[7] Tlaloc effigies mark the Early Postclassic, as do Tlaloc masks on Putun-ascribed stelae at the site of Seibal (Green, Rands, and Graham 1972:pl. 103), in the battle murals at Cacaxtla (McVicker 1985:85, 92), and on Plumbate effigies from the highlands at Tajumulco, Asunción Mita, and Zaculeu. Both the Feathered Serpent and Tlaloc, represented on this vessel, signify aspects of Tojil—the Quiche deity of state.

Also in the heirloom cache, two effigy Tojil Plumbate vessels depict the head of a bearded Tlaloc (fig. 11.10a; Fox 1987:fig. 2.7) and an unidentified Mayoid deity (fig. 11.10b). The Tlaloc iconography includes the Classic Teotihuacanoid features of the ringed eye with half eyelids, the beard, the bifurcated tongue and the handle-bar moustache (Pasztory 1974:fig. 10). The second facial effigy (fig. 11.10b) is reminiscent of GIII of the Palenque Triad (a prototype of Ixbalanque, L. Schele and M. Miller 1986:50); Plumbate effigies with the same overlapping loop headdress and wide, raised eyebrows occur in the Gulf lowlands (Rands and Smith 1965:fig. 18g).

A subglobular jar that has incised/excised serpents (fig. 11.10c) also seems to be of Gulf Coast origin (Fox 1987:44, fig. 2.8). A black "wash," similar to that on this jar, occurs in the Pabellon modeled-carved type at Seibal (Sabloff 1970:365). The stylized serpent is like one from Champoton (Ruz 1969:fig. 37), and designs on the neck and lower body are known at Xicalango (Ruz 1969:24,25,71).

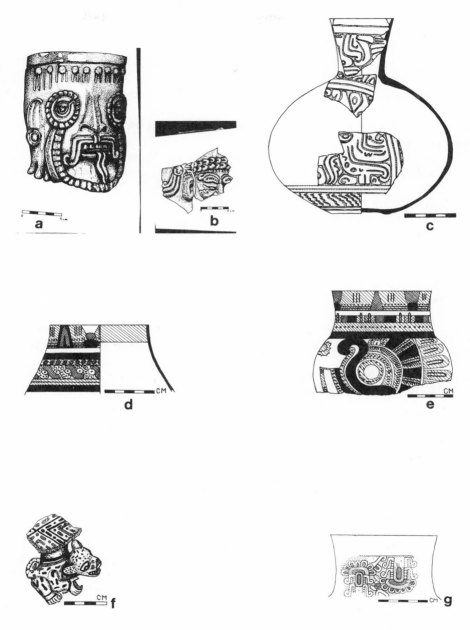

Fig. 11.10. *Other vessels from the Cawek cache: a. Tohil Effigy Plumbate, Tlaloc; b. Tohil Effigy Plumbate, unidentified Maya deity; c. fine paste vessel with serpent motif; d. possible Central American jar with red, black, and white-on-orange design under layer of stucco; e. possible Central American jar showing design on stucco with black, white, reds, and oranges; f. modeled jaguar foot from a bowl; g. other side of "e" showing design beneath stucco consisting of red and dark red on orange.*

Two rim sections (figs. 11.10d, e, g) of fine paste orange pyriform vases are perhaps variants of Fine Orange (e.g., DuSolier 1943; Ruz 1969) or Nicoya Polychrome (Woodbury and Trik 1953:265; Stone 1972:166, 171; Diehl 1983:89). Other vessels from the cache (fig. 11.10f) generally match ceramics from Tula (Diehl 1983:89) and the Campeche coast (R. Smith 1957b:fig. 51i, h).[8]

We offer three possible ways in which the Cawek may have obtained the heritage vessels.

1. They were carried into the highlands by the émigrés in the sacred bundle, the *pizom c'acal* (Popol Vuh 1971:212-13), when Jacawitz was first settled. However, Jacawitz had yet to attain status commensurate with the Putun "great tradition;" so far the site lacks exotic wares.

2. The vessels were acquired by the Cawek "prince" C'onache when he journeyed to the lowland Tulan to receive investiture of office. The "insignia of lordship" included royal canopy, throne, nose-bone, earrings, jade labrets, gold beads, panther and jaguar claws, owl skull, deer (skull?), armband of precious stones, snail shell bracelets, inlaid teeth, parrot feather crests, royal crane panache, and the codices (*u tz'ibal*) with which to make proper calendric prophecy. However, no mention is made of ceramics. The emblems of state were bestowed by the Feathered Serpent spokesman, Nacxit (Popol Vuh 1971:217-18), and some correspond to known grave goods from Utatlan.

3. These vessels were once kept at Tuja, Sacapulas, just 20 km north of Jacawitz. Cotuja-K'ucumatz, the first Quiche ajpop (ruler), apparently came from Tuja. The Quiche intermarried with Tuja lineages, probably with the Ajaw Canza Quetzal lineage (the Lord Feathered Serpent). The *Título de los señores de Sacapulas* (1968) specifically notes that the first Tujalja entered the highlands with painted books, thus boasting a literate tradition through the Early Postclassic and contrasting with back-country Jacawitz with its mundane material culture.

Economic Factors in the Development of an Elite

Segmentary states are characterized economically by kinship groups that produce their own food and acquire both utilitarian and prestige goods mainly through kinship networks (e.g., Fox 1987:279-80, table 6.1). W. T. Sanders and D. Webster (1988:534) define two categories of occupational specialization at Classic period segmentary Copan: "crafts people who produced elite goods (specifically lapidaries and weavers), who lived in elite compounds, and rural part-time producers who lived in the countryside . . . [who] produced most of their own food, but also manufactured mundane items as manos and metates . . ." This dichotomy characterizes Utatlan as well. Lineages of the conquerors of the Quiche Basin at Greater Utatlan were supplied with food by their vassals, the indigenous farming population. Two sets of data are presented here: the range of imported and/or scarce goods from burials found by Wallace and implications for redistributive economics from Brown's study of kinship-maintained workshops.

Within the northern long building attached to the southwest palace (fig. 11.4b) next to the temple, the following grave goods accompanied a seated, tightly flexed burial in the corner of the central bench (Carmack 1981:262):

1. A necklace of thirty-seven gold beads, shaped as split-base bell teardrops, nearly identical to a necklace from Iximche (Guillemín 1977:fig. 11.5).

2. Two hemispherical-shaped pieces of gold alloy with spun-cotton yarns partly encased in cupric oxide.

3. Jadeite carved as beads, as a univalve shell-form pendant, and as a plaque with a line design.

4. From a mosaic, numerous turquoise pieces, two bone eyes, and a series of flat shell and bone pieces.

5. Flat bone and shell beads, possibly sewn onto cloth.

6. Two amber beads and a solid cylindrical amber labret or lip-plug.

Additional luxury goods came from burials near the center of the bench of the Nijaib lineage house on the east side of the main plaza: some polychrome hemispherical food bowls, a large everted-lip serving bowl, gourd bowls with elaborate serpentine painted designs on stucco, and a chipped stone blade of honey-colored chert of the general shape and size of the Aztec sacrificial knives with mosaic handles.

These Ajaw and Nijaib grave goods illustrate a range of imported raw materials and/or manufactured objects. Gold and jade were available just beyond the Quiche state's eastern boundaries; jade from the middle Motagua River region, and gold from the eastern highlands and/or lower Central America. Amber originated in the mountains extending into Veracruz, as far as Tuxpan and Papantla, and in Chiapas near Soconusco and Azotlan (Caso and Bernal 1965:927). The turquoise evidently came from highland Mexico and the chert probably from the Maya lowlands.

What did the Quiche produce to obtain turquoise, amber, gold, and jade luxury goods? Brown's excavations at Utatlan reveal segmentary kin groups that each produced a wide variety of utilitarian goods, with just a few lineages specializing in elite-good production.

Brown sampled three of the major palace complexes, chosen for variation in size and complexity (Brown 1983; Majewski and Brown 1985; see also Freter 1982; Weeks 1983). These units were then compared with seven similar, although smaller, habitation units excavated in the residential area outside the elite center proper (fig. 11.11). Artifact frequencies from the outlying housing units for individual principal lineages were remarkably similar to those in the elite center area (see table 11.1).

With the problems of defining workshops in mind, eight distinctive zones of craft specialization, each coincident with a different patrilineage, were identified. The results are summarized as follows.

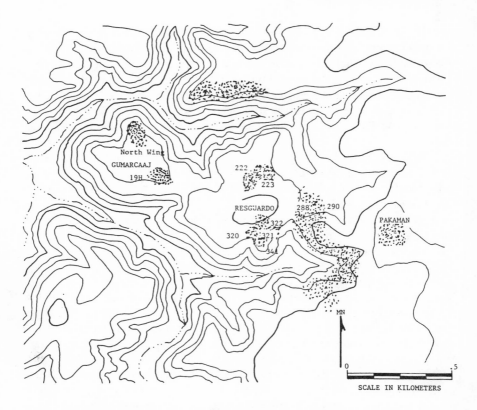

Fig. 11.11. Excavation locations directed by Brown at Utatlan (Gumarcaaj), El Resguardo, and Pakaman.

1. Workshops for the production of domestic ceramics, ritual ceramics, obsidian, and ground stone were isolated. At least two of these types were found in each of the ten habitation units.[9] Specifically, obsidian workshops were located in seven complexes, domestic ceramic workshops in six complexes, ground stone tool workshops in five complexes, and ceremonial ceramic workshops in four complexes (Table 11.1). These four activities also cover the expectable common industries except weaving, which would leave no remains. The ritual pottery consists mainly of ladle incensarios and large censers; both were used by all Quiche and found in even proportions across the site.

2. Workshops for two specialties, shell-bone working and cloth embroidery, were recovered only in the high-status complexes within the elite center proper, therefore defining them as elite goods. In the case of the cloth embroidery, identified by the presence of a large number of copper needles, spindle whorls, and minerals that could have been used as dyes, large quantities of embroidered items may have been produced in special workshop

Table 11.1: Domestic and elite craft workshops present in each of the defined structural complexes and the general types of elite items discovered.

Structural Complex	Domestic Craft Production Workshops					Elite Item Production Workshops			Status-Defining Objects						
	Obsidian tools	Domestic ceramics	Ceremonial ceramics	Ground stone tools	Textiles	Shell/bone carving	Weaving/embroidery	Metal ingots	Jade	Gold jewelry	Turquoise	Carved shell/bone	Copper jewelry	Green obsidian	Bright Chinautla Polychrome
North Wing	X	X	X	X		X			X	X	X	X	X	X	X
19H	X	X	X	X	X		X		X		X	X	X	X	X
47-41-320	X	X	X					X	X			X	X		X
47-41-290	X	?	X		X				X*	X*	X*		X*		X*
47-41-322	X	X													
47-41-321		X										X			X
47-41-288	X														X
47-41-222	X	X	X												X
47-41-341				X											
47-41-223		?	?	X					X						X

*Most of this material comes from a very high-status grave.

areas only among the elite. Thus, embroidery probably served as a status indicator.

A third specialty, metallurgy, was recognized by more than 200 molds for copper ingots in one architectural unit (Weeks 1977; Brown 1980). These molds refined a raw material just outside of Utatlan near the civic plaza of El Resguardo (fig. 11.11). Therefore, perhaps the final forms of the copper artifacts were produced in one or more of the residential units within the elite center. The quantity of copper ingots also suggests an export item: while copper artifacts occur in many contexts at Greater Utatlan, the quantity does not seem sufficient to account for the bulk of the raw copper produced at this workshop.[10] The ingots may thus have been used as a medium of exchange with Aztec traders in Soconusco or Chontalpa.

As an additional specialty, obsidian weaponry was produced by warrior lineages around the Pakaman plaza (fig. 11.11). Surveys (Weeks 1977; Fox 1978b; Freter 1982; Brown 1985) have all noted exceptionally high frequencies of obsidian cores, blades, and projectile points. These mercenaries are identified ethnohistorically as a garrison of Cakchiquel, closely allied with the Nima Quiche.

From the distribution of these domestic and specialty workshops, Brown draws the following inferences.

1. Full-time craft specialists were present across urban Utatlan, and separate activity areas existed for single crafts.

2. All Nima Quiche domestic units within both the elite center and the outlying El Resguardo fabricated most of their own utilitarian ceramics, obsidian, and ground stone. Since the patrilineages were also self-sufficient in food production (Carmack 1981:164), distribution was incongruent with a marketplace type; simple reciprocal exchange is a better fit. Distributions of pottery designs also underscore separate habitation and production/consumption units.

3. Workshops in central locations allow high-status artifacts to be distinguished, in contrast to the wider distribution of shell-bone and metal objects. The higher the status indicators, the greater the likelihood of an elite craft workshop in that complex. However, only one separate workshop (of copper ingots) has been uncovered.

Nevertheless, copper jewelry was widely distributed, and a cache of copper needles was found in a textile workshop in a high-status complex. As mentioned, ceremonial ceramics like incensarios were consumed in high frequency by all residential groupings.

4. There may have been surplus production in domestic ceramic workshops beyond local consumption. The principal clay source was probably near San Pedro Jocopilas, controlled by the Ilocab of Chisalin. Evidence from the basin survey suggests a sizable rural population during the Late Postclassic, also necessitating ceramics. The primary mechanism for distribution was probably redistribution along kin lines (Carmack 1981; Brown 1983, 1985; Fox 1987).

5. Findings by J. M. Weeks (1983) at Chisalin, the Ilocab elite center across a barranca north of Utatlan, suggest separate distributive systems between the confederates of Greater Utatlan. In contrast to Utatlan, Weeks recovered no obsidian workshops within Chisalin, few obsidian cores, and almost no nodules of the raw material. However, a relatively large number of fine-grained basalt artifacts were found, suggesting that basalt substituted for the obsidian. Therefore, the Nima Quiche of Utatlan controlled the importation of obsidian.

The only known obsidian sources lie outside the Quiche basin within the provenience of the Akajal Cakchiquel at Jilotepeque and at El Chayal. Accordingly, there were formal Cakchiquel garrisons at the sites of Jilotepeque Viejo and Chinautla Viejo (Mixcu), the two Late Postclassic sites for these two territories (Fox 1978a). Apparently, obsidian was obtained along kinship networks among political allies, notably between the Nima Quiche and Cakchiquel. In this regard, even the obsidian from the Early Postclassic center of Jacawitz is fingerprinted to the quarry at Jilotepeque, adjacent to the Akajal Cakchiquel at Ochal (Fox 1987:266). As noted earlier, the obsidian workshops at Pakaman, within Greater Utatlan, also linked the Cakchiquel and Nima Quiche. Also, if a true marketplace operated, the Ilocab would have purchased this highly desirable material; it seems unlikely that they would have been too impoverished to acquire it.

6. Turquoise, jade, and gold "long-distance" luxury goods, which occur in the Ajaw and Cawek complexes, were also respectively obtained by members of these kin groups, recalling the Cocom traders of Yucatan. The Quiche did not maintain a "middle class" of artisans and traders, like the *pochteca*; production, distribution, and consumption occurred along kinship cleavages. While the posthispanic Maya markets mostly traffic in food surpluses and some craft items from neighboring regions of sufficiently contrastive ecology (e.g., Tax 1953; Carmack 1981:109), we suggest that the weekly market only took root following the Spanish conquest.

Discussion and Conclusions

The rise of a Quiche elite is traced from fairly egalitarian alliances of small segmentary lineages, as early as the late A.D. 800s, to their formative segmentary state in post-A.D. 1100. Throughout this period, the various lineages changed in relative power and alliance. Like their namesakes at Palenque, adjacent to the Chontalpa, the priestly Ajaw ranked higher at Jacawitz. Later, after expansion and resulting elite status over the *indigenes* of the Quiche Basin, the militaristic Cawek lineage assumed the highest rank among the major lineages with their leader as a hereditary king. Their new settlement, shared by their Tamub and Ilocab allies, took the form of a large nucleated and densely populated "regal-ritual" center (Sanders and Webster 1988) or a Tulan (Fox 1989), replete with outlying estates.

It is also possible to trace the elaboration of symbolism of the lineage system. Proxemically, the structures around the main plaza can be seen as an overlay of bi-, tri-, and quadripartite arrangements. As at Jacawitz, the basic dualism of sacred and profane is maintained in the south-north plaza-temple units, with the ballcourt in between. But at Utatlan, the larger "main" plaza now contains an east-facing temple (the sun) opposite a west-facing one (the moon), symbols of the Cawek and newly adopted Nijaib major lineages, competing military specialists; these two temples and the similarly large temple (Jacawitz) on the Ajaw wing then formed the Sun-Moon-Venus Triad, previously known at Palenque. Finally, when the small Sakic major lineage was assigned to the north, the ideal quadripartite organization to the four cardinal directions resulted. In addition, the radial-temple for Tojil, the K'ucumatz (Quetzalcoatl) shrine, and the Cawek cache of exotic vessels legitimized the Nima Quiche and Utatlan as a tun center (Tulan); the widespread sources of the vessels represented the far-flung migrations of the Putun.

Murals in the Ajaw palace also paralleled symbols of the dynastic Ajaw at Palenque, and the Palenque Triad of Sun, Moon, and Venus is reflected in the triad of temples. These symbols bound the Quiche lineages to each other and made it difficult to draw distinctions between the leaders and the led. The crucial role of the Ajaw lineage and its sacerdotal authority escaped mention in the ethnohistory.

However, critical evidence for an elite is occupational specialization and control of production by other social segments. The internal distribution of raw materials by each lineage made everyday resources (except for obsidian) available to everyone. Only the Cawek and Ajaw (and presumably the Sakic) had access to rare imported sumptuary materials like jade, turquoise, and gold. But the indigenous population overseen by the four major lineages of Utatlan provided food and raw materials, thereby freeing the highly ranked lineages to produce the trappings of social stature.

That the Quiche lineages were each self-sufficient in almost all basic commodity production underscores their semi-independence. Theoretically at least, lineages could split off and create new alliances when advantageous (Wallace 1977a).

However, this situation does not fit the noble-commoner-slave societal divisions, where artisans were not within the upper class. Indigeneous Maya, who would have been farmers and part-time artisans before their domination, were promoted to warriors and artisans.

Thus, the term "elite" is inappropriate for the Quichean case. Not only do the documents consider the Nima Quiche (Tamub and Ilocab) as one community, albeit with ranked lineages and offices, but archaeology shows a fairly continuous gradation in size between the lineage complexes covering most of Utatlan (Wallace 1977b:31). The principal lineage officials listed in the documents—twenty-six for the Nima Quiche, fifty-seven for all the three allies at Greater Utatlan (Carmack 1981:162)—would, when combined with their immediate families, be a fairly sizable ruling "overstratum." Either "class" or "caste" (e.g., Carmack 1981:148) also applies to the Quiche-Vukamak distinction, although these two groups intermarried. Perhaps most Mesoamerican sociopolitical groups, like the Quiche, utilized kinship networks for political integration.

As at Palenque, palaces appear late in the development of the Quiche and Cakchiquel polities. However, a wide range of large and small elite habitations, all multipatio structures, are identified at Utatlan, each with its own attached courtyard with a temple or shrine and colonnaded lineage structures. The southwest palace (Ajaw) is somewhat larger than the palace at Palenque, although it also had a tower for astronomical sighting with possible emphasis on Venus (as at Palenque). Venus was an integral aspect of the Ajaw identity and apparently also for the regal dynasty at Palenque.

Moreover, the palace at Palenque was reoriented late to face the Northern Group, with its five shrines, Temple of the Count, and ballcourt. This might indicate political realignments or an attempt proxemically to link the palace with the cardinal point of the sun at zenith (god GII). In a parallel manner, the north wing at Utatlan was the last settled. There the Sakic lineage brought from Tuja to their Cawek moiety partners another genealogical tie to the "great tradition" (Tulan) of the lowlands. The Sakic and Ajaw, thereby, controlled the ritualistic north-south *axis mundi* at Utatlan (Fox n.d.a).

An ethos of kinship can be identified ethnohistorically for all those who could trace their lines to the Feathered Serpent. So dynastic kingship contradicts kin-related egalitarianism, but may have been accommodated by reorienting buildings north to the premier cardinal point. This was a basic difference in concentration of power—long established during the Late Preclassic-Classic continuum, but only tentatively approached by the Postclassic Quiche. Although both may well be based on a long-standing Maya ideal of shared power, at least the Classic elite required inscribed stone monuments to justify their claims to inherited status. Centralizing power in sacred authority contrasts with the Postclassic highlands, where shared power was more normative. Possibly only the Quiche attempted to mesh the inherent contradictions between idealized egalitarianism and the pragmatics of the dynastic rulership. Through all this, despite an elite asserting symbols of a Mexican pedigree, the Quiche remained fundamentally and distinctly Maya.

Notes

1. The authors agree that the Quiche maintained a segmentary-centristic polity (Wallace 1977a). Fox (1987, 1989) follows Carmack (1981) in considering the Quiche system a segmentary state. Brown (1983, 1985) considers the Quiche polity an advanced chiefdom.

2. One of the two largest palaces for the Cawek, the highest-ranked lineage, is immediately west of the Tojil temple (figs. 11.3, 11.4). Likewise, the large southern Temple of Jacawitz and the palace directly south are certainly Ajaw. There are various modest-sized palaces in the east wing, behind the Awilix Temple, for Nijaib lineages. The southwest palace, largest of all, borders the Temple of Jacawitz and south palace and is interpreted by Fox as Ajaw. This puts the Ajaw and Cawek, the two original lineages of the migration, on either side of a dividing passageway (sacbe) running from the western stairway, for access to the adjacent Tamub and Ilocab elite centers, east in a straight line through the ballcourt. Thus, the ballcourt bifurcated the Cawek and Ajaw, as earlier at Jacawitz.

3. Moieties are documented for the Tamub, Tujalja, and Quiche colony at Xoyabaj (Ichon et al. 1982). Wallace (1977b:35, 53) identifies two halves of Utatlan for moieties. The orthogonal-tending layout of the Ajaw and Nijaib buildings bespeak one moiety, and the lack of regular orientation of the Cawek and Sakic wings suggests another moiety. One each of the two main temples and two largest palaces belonged to the west-north and east-south groupings. In contrast, Carmack (1981) posits a "vertical" social and symbolic tiering of those original immigrants, with lowland pedigrees, versus the newcomers with indigenous origins, offering a Cawek-Ajaw moiety versus one for the Nijaib and Sakic.

4. If segmentary lineage organization was Preclassic Maya, the Classic florescence might, in part, have been due to the centralization of power in single lineages from once more egalitarian kin alliances (Freidel and Schele 1988a). The evidence of intermarriages and alliances between centers is borne out by the epigraphic texts and is compatible with the Postclassic triadic alliances proposed by Fox (1989; e.g., the Quiche-Cakchiquel-Rabinal triad).

5. Both the Palenque palace and the southwest palace (figs. 11.4b, e) had painted and sculptured decorations. The Palenque palace honored Pacal, the king at the apex of the site's

history. Its west side bordered the Temple of the Inscriptions, Pacal's famous burial structure, replicating the positioning of the Temple of Tojil at Utatlan.

6. In comparison, Iximche, inhabited by the Cakchiquel, also has twin palace complexes (figs. 11.4c, d), bespeaking moieties (Guillemín 1977).

7. The four panels portray Tlaloc, an omnipotent sky-rain deity, in quadruple aspects, each assigned a color and a cardinal direction (Nicholson 1971:414), as were the Maya chacs and the associated Gods B, D, and GII. Like the first panel of this vessel, God B was represented by a scroll below the eye, a volute as a pupil, a long pendulous nose, a projection above the nose ending in a curl, and a mouth that is usually toothless (Thompson 1970:252).

8. A seventh vessel, a Fine Orange tecomate, forms a bird with the bowl as its body and modeled head, triangular tail, and wings on its sides.

9. However, since not all ten units were fully excavated, it cannot be ruled out that all forms of specialties were practiced in all units.

10. J. M. Weeks' (1977) excavation near El Resguardo recovered molds and a small Fortress White-on-Red jar with a modeled monkey blowing into a long tube, probably as a draft for smelting or casting copper. The association of monkey symbolism and craft specialists has already been noted.

12. Archaeological Indicators of Formative Period Elites: A Perspective from Central Mexico

David C. Grove and Susan D. Gillespie

THE consensus among archaeologists today is that Early and Middle Formative period Mesoamerica (1200-500 B.C.) was characterized by chiefdom-level societies. These are "ranked" societies, and as William Sanders and Barbara Price (1968:42-43) have noted, "since commonly the entire society is believed to be descended from a single ancestor, and the occupant of the position of chief is chosen on the basis of descent from this original postulated ancestor, it follows that everyone else in the network is ranked according to his degree of relationship to the chief . . . the result is great variation in rank throughout the society but without sharply defined social classes." Three points follow from that characterization of chiefdoms and ranked societies: (1) kinship, not class, is used to organize society; (2) there are many different "ranks" based on perceived degree of relatedness to the chief; and (3) the lack of sharp distinction between social levels means that a continuum of possible traits marking those levels should be found archaeologically. Alternatively, if class distinctions were present, such traits should appear in tightly clustered co-occurrences.

Archaeologists, working solely with nonperishable material culture, have frequently had to assume that certain characteristics can be used to identify the presence of a ranked society or, more particularly, of the separation of society into elite and nonelite groups. Several archaeological criteria used to differentiate chiefdoms from egalitarian societies include "regional settlement hierarchies of two or three levels according to occupation size and also public architecture; pronounced differentiation among residential structures in terms of size, degree of elaboration, and relative quantity of 'high cost' items," and "marked differentiation in burial treatment among individuals of the same age and sex" (Spencer 1987:371-72). T. K. Earle (1987:290-91) has succinctly pointed out the problems associated with such assumptions and the difficulty in confirming them.

This chapter focuses on two sites in Mexico's central highlands and their evidence for an elite group, especially with regard to burial treatment. These are the Middle Formative period site of Chalcatzingo, Morelos, and the Early Formative site of Tlatilco in the Basin of Mexico. The data from those sites demonstrate that there is a continuum in the occurrence of the rank markers, as would be expected for a chiefdom level society. They somewhat call into question the markers of rank commonly used by archaeologists. These data also reveal an important change in the nature of the elite markers over time, specifically between the Early and Middle Formative periods. Finally, those observations are compared with the Gulf Coast Olmec data to ascertain if that culture is significantly different in terms of social evolution.

Chalcatzingo

The site of Chalcatzingo, in the Amatzinac Valley of eastern Morelos, is the most extensively excavated Middle Formative period site in central Mexico. It is also one of central Mexico's most famous archaeological sites due to the presence of monumental stone art there. The Formative and Classic period occupation areas at Chalcatzingo lie in a natural amphitheater created at the base of two rugged mountains, the Cerro Chalcatzingo and the Cerro Delgado. Excavations by the Chalcatzingo Archaeological Project in the 1970s (Grove 1984, 1987a) were particularly able to define and investigate the late Middle Formative (Cantera phase, 700-500 B.C.) settlement, which was spread out across the series of hillside terraces that characterize the site. Several of the uppermost terraces are distinguished by the presence of Cantera phase public mound architecture (Prindiville and Grove 1987), and one lower terrace (T-25) contained a walled sunken patio with the only Gulf Coast style table-top altar known outside of the Olmec heartland. Nearly every individual terrace was also the location of one Cantera phase residential structure. Although those structures generally lie today within the modern plow zone and have been heavily destroyed, the project was nevertheless able to study the differentiations that existed among the various house units in artifact content and subfloor burials. From those analyses, reviewed below, it is clear that Chalcatzingo demonstrates all of the criteria listed above for a chiefdom level society.

An intensive survey was made of the entire Amatzinac Valley. Forty-nine sites were recorded corresponding to the major period of occupation at Chalcatzingo, the Cantera phase. K. Hirth (1987:355-61, fig. 21.4, table 21.14) recognizes a five-tier hierarchy of those settlements: a regional center (one; Chalcatzingo), a large village (one), small villages (three), hamlets (fourteen), and isolated residences (thirty). In addition to his ranking of settlements, there is the additional criterion of public mound architecture, which occurred at four of the sites in addition to Chalcatzingo (see Hirth 1987:356), and may mark them as secondary centers to Chalcatzingo (Grove 1987c:421-22).

One Cantera phase house at Chalcatzingo, Plaza Central Str. 1 (Grove and Guillén 1987:26-28; Prindiville and Grove 1987:66-80), stands out as significantly different from the others (one of C. S. Spencer's criteria for chiefdom societies). Although the house's size, as defined by remnants of the stone foundation walls, may have been somewhat larger than the others (Prindiville and Grove 1987:table 6.1), the major difference between it and other houses is in the artifacts and features within and around the structure. Three times more subfloor burials (38) occur under P.C. Str. 1 than under any other excavated house and it is the only residence with subfloor burials interred in stone-capped slab-lined crypt graves (Merry de Morales 1987a, 1987b). Furthermore, P.C. Str. 1 is the only household unit that definitely includes an outside patio area flanked by a subsidiary structure (P.C. Str. 2).[1] The patio appears to have been a workshop area for exotic materials (jade and iron ore; Grove 1987c:422), the only one of its kind found at the site. Finally, P.C. Str. 1 is the only house associated with major public architecture, the 70 m long platform mound designated P.C. Str. 4.[2]

The best data set for the identification of social differentiation among the population at Chalcatzingo comes from the remains of that actual population in burial contexts. The total data set for the site's burials is easily accessible in an appendix to the Chalcatzingo site report (Merry de Morales 1987a). Readers are invited to use those data to follow this discussion more carefully or to arrive at their own conclusions independently. The Cantera phase burial data are reviewed and reexamined here to arrive at an understanding of what archaeological features distinguished the highest social ranks at Chalcatzingo,[3] acknowledging at the same time that we are discussing the burials as if they reflected one moment in time rather than an accumulated time span of two hundred years and are dealing only with the nonperishable manifestations of possible social differences. Those data do not strongly support the commonly held assumption that quantity of grave goods necessarily indicates an elite status.

Although Str. 1 is different from the other houses and was probably the residence of the highest-ranked family, it is important to realize that the house's 38 subfloor burials include the entire spectrum of grave types, burial positions, and grave goods found among the 115 Cantera phase burials recovered from 8 additional Cantera phase house areas, public architecture, and other contexts during the excavations. Obviously, therefore, there is no one-to-one correspondence between burial location in the elite house and other assumed elite grave markers. The Str. 1 burials are thus in a general sense a microcosm of the site's burial population and an appropriate sample to begin this analysis, which essentially follows the pattern of a taxonomy based on the following criteria: location, embellishment of burial pit, and grave goods, correlated with age, sex, and burial position.

Location

Several areas of the site were obviously special, for they contained public architecture. The site's uppermost terrace, the Plaza Central, is the location of the largest such construction, P.C. Structure 4, a 70 m long earthen platform mound (Grove and Guillén 1987:29-31; Prindiville and Grove 1987:63), as well as one residential structure, P.C. Str. 1 and its subsidiary building, P.C. Str. 2. A sunken walled patio and table-top altar occur on Terrace 25 (Fash 1987). Numerous burials were found in both areas. Several smaller stone-faced platform structures occur on other terraces (Prindiville and Grove 1987:64-66), but are not discussed here because no burials were found associated with them (see note 2).

Grave Embellishment

Among the burials in P.C. Str. 1, two basic grave types can be distinguished: stone-embellished graves and unembellished graves. The embellished graves include eight capped crypts (Burials 3, 5, 26, 28, 33, 34, 36, 37) and one burial (35) with stones placed at the pelvis and feet. Because they are restricted to special contexts, stone crypt graves may be a major elite burial marker. In addition to P.C. Str. 1, stone crypts were found at only two other locations at Chalcatzingo: P.C. Str. 4, the site's major public architecture (two crypts, Burials 39, 40); and Terrace 25, in association with the sunken patio and table-top altar (Burials 94, 95, 105, 114).

Graves partially embellished with stone had a slightly less restricted distribution and were found associated with house structures on T-21 (Burial 78), T-23 (79, 84), T-37 (136), S-39 (142, 143), and in nonhouse contexts on the Plaza Central (51), in the T-25 sunken patio (100, 110), and in Cave 4 on the Cerro Delgado (156, 157).

It has been argued that the purposeful addition of stones to outline all or part of a grave made it inherently special because additional labor was expended (e.g., Merry de Morales 1987b:98). While that is perhaps a valid assumption at sites lacking local stone resources, such as La Venta, Tabasco (which also has crypt graves; see Feature A-3-a, Drucker 1952:67-73), from a purely economic standpoint such a labor investment at Chalcatzingo was very minor. An average of fifteen stones per sq m litter the site's surface (Grove, Hirth, and Buge 1987:13), making stone readily accessible to anyone. The presence or absence of stone embellishments to graves therefore was clearly based upon social rules beyond mere labor investment.

In two instances the crypts of P.C. Str. 1 were positioned such that they appear to have been purposeful pairs (Merry de Morales 1987b:104-7). Within one pairing, Burials 33 and 3 each contained distinctive major offerings. The Burial 3 crypt was within the plow zone and poorly preserved. The skeleton was that of an adult. Two ceramic vessels (one a *cantarito* or small bottle), a mano, and a stone head from a monument (Mon. 17) were present as grave furniture. Crypt Burial 33 lay directly beneath 3, oriented perpendicular to it. Within that crypt were a small ceramic *cantarito* placed within a shallow bowl, a piece of a jade bloodletter, groupings of smoothed pebbles, and a greenstone "were-jaguar" figurine (Thomson 1987:fig. 17.1).

Unfortunately, poor skeletal preservation made identification of gender nearly impossible for any of the site's burials. While we recognize the perils in attempting to identify gender through presumed "female" and "male" artifacts, the grinding stone and bloodletter dichotomy present in grave pair

3-33 may be gender related. The two artifacts never co-occur in any burial assemblage and may serve to identify 33 as male (bloodletter) and 3 as female (grinding stone; see also Tolstoy 1989:111). If such identifications are valid, they demonstrate that both females and males could receive crypt burials.

The second crypt pair, Burials 5 and 34, were likewise perpendicular to one another. Burial 5 was a juvenile, while 34 was a young adult. This is significant, for it indicates that crypt burials were not restricted to adults. Furthermore, those two burials did not have the same vessel types as grave goods, indicating a possible dichotomy in ceramic offerings. The juvenile had been interred with one vessel, a gray ware bowl, while the crypt of the young adult lacked offerings associated with the body but had two white double-loop handle censers placed on the exterior of the crypt.

Age and sex distinctions and burial position cross-cut noncrypt burials, as they do the house's crypt burials. The remaining burials beneath Str. 1 included four crypts (all adults, one merely a skull burial) and noncrypt burials of twenty-four adults, four young adults, and two infants. Both infants had been interred with an adult, and in each instance both the adult and infant were in flexed positions. The flexed positioning of these infant-adult pairs is interesting because the extended burial position is by far the most common in the Chalcatzingo sample. Among the eight P.C. Str. 1 crypts, apart from the skull burial, six individuals were extended and one was flexed. That basic 6:1 extended-to-flexed ratio fairly accurately mirrors the Cantera phase burial sample of one hundred extended and fifteen flexed, except that twelve of the site's fifteen flexed Cantera phase interments were found beneath Str. 1. The remaining three flexed interments were located on T-9A (59), T-11 (66), and the T-25 patio (93).

Stone Monuments

The occurrence of a stone statue head, Mon. 17, in the interior of Burial 3's crypt is another significant correlate identifying crypt graves as elite. Monumental art is clearly associated with high-ranked individuals, who had the power and means to command its creation. Much of that art is portraiture of certain specific elite individuals, in most instances probably the site's chief. Formative period monuments were frequently mutilated by decapitation, and such acts probably took place at the death of a center's chief (Grove 1981). The inclusion of the decapitated monument head within the crypt grave strongly suggests that Burial 3 is the grave of the individual portrayed in the monument. Therefore, it is also important that Burial 3 may have been a female, for it demonstrates that at least one woman in the society was important enough to warrant a stone monument. The only definite female depicted in the known corpus of monumental art at Chalcatzingo appears in bas-relief on Mon. 21 (Grove and Angulo 1987:fig. 9.21). At this time, however, there are no other data suggesting that she is the woman portrayed on Mon. 17 and/or the person of Burial 3.

Other Grave Goods

Among the more distinctive grave goods within the crypts were jade (green-stone) artifacts, white double-loop handle censers, and *cantaritos* placed in shallow bowls (e.g., Merry de Morales 1987b:95-96, fig. 8.1). Because of their placement in crypts, those objects may be candidates as markers of an elite or high-ranked individual, but that assumption must be critically examined. All of those traits are therefore briefly discussed in turn below.

Jade. An additional correlate between elite and crypt graves is provided by Chalcatzingo Burials 39 and 40, stone crypt interments found atop the 70 m long Cantera phase earthen platform mound, P.C. Str. 4. Those two burials contained significantly greater quantities of jade than any other burials found on the site. At the time of their interment both individuals were wearing jade ear-spools and necklaces of jade beads. Burial 39 also had an associated jade celt, while Burial 40 had a concave iron ore mirror pectoral, an artifact generally assumed to be an elite marker (see discussion of Tlatilco, below).

Nevertheless, there is no strong association between crypt burials and jade objects elsewhere at the site. In contrast to those richly endowed burials in P.C. Str. 4, only two of Str. 1's eight crypt graves contained greenstone objects: Burial 28 had a single bead and broken pieces from a large jade earflare, and Burial 33 (the "pair" with 3) had been interred with a were-jaguar figurine and the top of a bloodletter. Thus, six crypts did not contain jade objects. However, four noncrypt interments did. Burial 16 had a pendant, 32 had both a pendant and the tip of a jade bloodletter, and 12 and 23 had single beads.

There is some correlation between jade in burial association and burial location. Jade grave goods were largely restricted to the Plaza Central area, the location of the large platform mound, P.C. Str. 4, and the elite house, P.C. Str. 1, and are minimal at other areas of the site. Three house subfloor burials on T-24 did have associated jade: Burial 87 had a jade fragment, Burial 89 a pendant, and Burial 91 a small jade disc and serpentine fragment. Jade ear-spool fragments were found with burials on T-4 (54) and T-37 (136), and single jade beads were found in the mouths of two burials in P.C. Str. 2 (43, 47) and two burials in the T-25 patio area (108, 111).

It is probable that some jade objects had greater perceived value than others, particularly value of a symbolic nature. Two basic categories of jade (and other greenstone) artifacts can be defined from among the grave goods: jewelry and nonjewelry (figurines, celts, bloodletters). The jewelry category can be further subdivided into beads and nonbead (ear-spools, pendants) jewelry. In addition, within those categories three possibly meaningful levels of burial jade can be ascertained.

The first level is the wearing of large quantities of jade jewelry at the time of interment. This level fits only the individuals in Burials 39 and 40, atop the large platform mound, while—as Merry de Morales notes (1987b:98)—

the jade associated with the burials of P.C. Str. 1 is generally small artifacts and broken fragments of larger artifacts and does not match the richness of jade offerings of Burials 39 or 40 in terms of either quality or quantity. The third level is the presence of a single bead in an interment. Few of those beads are of the same quality as the necklace beads worn in Burials 39 and 40. Those more common beads probably had the least value of any jade objects and would have required less labor to manufacture compared to the more intricate ear-spools, pendants, and bloodletters.

Furthermore, the basic symbolic value of single beads was also less than that of those other objects. As Merry de Morales (1987b:99) notes, only a few limited individuals had the wealth to enable them to take a quantity of valuable jade out of circulation by having it buried with them. The jade found in most burials was small or broken pieces and of ostensibly lesser economic value.

Cantaritos with Shallow Bowls. Interestingly, the only ceramics with the crypts of the two individuals of high rank buried on P.C. Str. 4, and within P.C. Str. 1's crypt Burial 33 (which contained the greenstone were-jaguar figure and a bloodletter) consisted in each instance of a small ceramic jar, a *cantarito*, sitting within a small shallow bowl. In comparison to the otherwise elaborate nature of those graves and their contents, the relatively plain *cantarito* and shallow bowl seem insignificant from an etic perspective. However, those two small vessels must have been important markers on the basis of their association with the other elite markers. As a directly associated pair they occur in only one other instance, as the sole ceramics of Str. 1's Burial 10 (a noncrypt interment that also included grinding stones and thus was possibly a female). The distribution of this offering type was therefore restricted to P.C. Strs. 1 and 4, apparently found with both males (33) and females (10), but not restricted to crypt burials.

It is important to also note that a similar ceramic pair occurs as the only ceramics in a grave in the northeast platform of La Venta's Complex A, so-called Offering 5 (Drucker, Heizer, and Squier 1959:162-64, fig. 41). That grave is partly embellished with stone and in addition to the *cantarito* and shallow bowl includes "strings" of jade beads and pendants. Those contexts at La Venta and Chalcatzingo serve to demonstrate that the basic quantity and quality of ceramic objects do not correlate with the other burial indicators of high rank and that certain objects had some encoded ideological or symbolic value not otherwise obvious to us today.

House subfloor graves on T-20 (73), T-23 (81), and P.C. Str. 2 (49) include both *cantaritos* and shallow bowls, but those vessels were placed in separate areas within the grave and are not purposely paired as in the high-status graves. *Cantaritos* also occur with other vessel forms or singly in crypt Burials 3, 28, and 36 and noncrypt interments 4, 32, 38 (P.C. Str. 1), 42, 45, 47 (P.C. Str. 2), 62 (T-9A), 84 (T-23), 127-128 (T-27), 142 (S-39), and 156 (Cave 4). Significantly, no *cantaritos* were found in any of the eighteen Cantera phase graves in association with the patio and altar on T-25.

It is possible that we are dealing with three different perceived levels of *cantarito* offerings: a *cantarito* placed in a shallow bowl as a high status marker (n=4), a bowl and a *cantarito* in the grave but separated (n=3), and a *cantarito* without a bowl (n=14). The latter two levels may be correlated with some rank value too subtle to understand with the data at hand.

Double-Loop Handle Censers. Three P.C. Str. 1 crypt burials contained white double-loop handle censers, 26 (n=1), 28 (n=1), and 34 (n=2). The charred interior base of most of those censers and their occasional positioning on the exterior of crypts (34) suggests that copal incense was burned in them during the burial ceremony, a ritual apparently reserved for only certain members of the society. However, such censers are not restricted to the higher-ranked crypt graves but also occur with non-stone-embellished burials in Str. 1 (2, 4, 30), with four burials in adjacent Str. 2 (41, 45, 47, 49), and with two burials in the special T-25 patio-altar area (106; stone-embellished 110). In addition, they occur in a subfloor grave on T-23 (83) and in a burial in Cave 4 (156) on the Cerro Delgado. There are six co-occurrences of censers and *cantaritos* in the same grave, five in burials beneath P.C. Str. 1 and 2 (4, 28, 45, 47, 49), and the sixth with Burial 156 in Cave 4.[4]

Discussion

Location of the burial in elite/public contexts is taken as a first criterion of elite status, and all of the crypt burials were within public/elite structures (P.C. Str. 4, Str. 1, and the T-25 patio). From this correlation, other markers of elite rank emerge—the presence of high-quality jade jewelry worn by the deceased in quantity and a *cantarito* placed in a shallow bowl. Those three markers co-occur in two instances, Burials 39 and 40 in P.C. Str. 4. Out of 115 Cantera phase burials, those two individuals stand out as probably possessing the highest rank in the society. They must have been persons of recognized power to have claimed burial or to have been accorded space within the platform mound itself. Within P.C. Str. 1, three individuals also stand out as high-ranked: Burial 3 (crypt, *cantarito*, and stone statue head), Burial 33 (crypt, were-jaguar figurine, bloodletter, and *cantarito* in a shallow bowl), and Burial 28 (crypt, jade earflare fragments, jade bead, censer, and *cantarito*).

Beyond those, there are few other obvious co-occurrences of markers that allow the recognition of different social ranks. Although rankings can be created for the other burials on the basis of those and other criteria, there is no evidence to indicate that such ranks correspond to the actual social divisions of the Cantera phase society. In fact, because temporal control on the burials is so general, it is impossible to ascertain whether the five high-ranked burials discussed above really reflect ranks at one moment in time, which—except for paired burials—is doubtful, or perhaps reflect the variability of markers of high-ranked individuals over several generations.

Importantly, burials within crypts were not restricted to only one sex or one age category. Both males and females appear to have been accorded crypt burials, as were young adults and one juvenile, indicating that the elite rank was ascribed. While jade worn in quantity may have been a marker of high status, jade otherwise seems to have varying levels of significance and in burial contexts shows a simple but important continuum: (1) quantities of high-quality jade objects (2); (2) small items of unbroken jade or large pieces of broken jade (9); (3) jade beads (6; usually lesser quality); (4) no jade. The presence of jade apparently is not in and of itself a marker of high rank.

It is often assumed that the quantity of grave offerings can be correlated with social rank. The Cantera phase data demonstrate, however, that the quantity of ceramic vessels associated with graves was extremely variable. Quantity actually shows a slight inverse correlation with two other elite markers: stone embellished graves and jade. Of Str. 1's thirty-eight burials, one (noncrypt) had nine vessels, three had six vessels (one crypt, with jade; two noncrypt), one had five (noncrypt), one had four (noncrypt), three had three (one crypt, two noncrypt), nine had two (three crypt, only one with jade; six noncrypt), five had one (all noncrypt), and fifteen had none (three crypt, twelve noncrypt). Two noncrypt burials (147, 148) on terrace S-39, at the southwest edge of the site, had the greatest quantity of pottery, ten vessels each.

The analysis has shown that no clear differentiation of social ranks emerges from the Chalcatzingo burial data. Although P.C. Str. 1 appears to be a special dwelling in terms of associated artifacts, location on the large plaza across from the platform mound, and the number and presence of elite grave attributes such as crypts and jade, the very fact that the thirty-eight subfloor burials reflect the spectrum of grave types, grave goods, and burial positions present within the larger Cantera phase burial sample indicates that the similarities in burial attributes between Str. 1 and other houses on the site are as important as the differences.

The way in which those attributes are somewhat differentially distributed between site areas may ultimately help us to understand chiefly intrasite obligations and other social ties within the community at Chalcatzingo. For example, three burials with a few small jade pieces were found at the house structure on T-24, at the opposite end of the site from P.C. Str. 1. What other ties can be ascertained between the T-24 house and P.C. Str. 1? S. S. Burton's (1987:316-18) analysis of Chalcatzingo's lithic industries has identified two distinct assemblages and their differential distribution on the site. Her Group B lithics, primarily obsidian (with little chert), were characteristic of only two house areas, P.C. Str. 1 and T-24. Both houses thus shared lithic tool kits richer in obsidian and with a greater quantity of shaped tools; that linkage between the chief (Str. 1) and the people of T-24 may also be minimally reflected in the presence of jade with three T-24 burials. The smaller jade objects or beads in other areas may reflect gifts from the chief to others in the society, while *cantaritos* and double-loop handle censers could reflect ties of another nature. Furthermore, because three times more individuals are buried beneath P.C. Str. 1 than beneath any other house, it is conceivable that people from other houses, of varying ranks but with special ties to the chief, were brought there for burial.

Finally, although it would be worthwhile to consider briefly whether Chalcatzingo's elite markers are restricted to that site or are relevant to central Mexico as a whole, comparative data for the Middle Formative period are essentially lacking. We can tentatively state that some of the markers discussed above are not restricted to Chalcatzingo. G. G. Vaillant (1935:175, fig. 8) uncovered crypt graves and associated jade offerings at El Arbolillo in the Basin of Mexico, and E. Merlo Juarez (n.d.) has reported an elaborate jade-rich crypt grave at Zinacantepec, Puebla.

The Early Formative and Tlatilco

It is now instructive to look at what preceded Chalcatzingo's Middle Formative ranked society, on both a regional and local level. From this it may be possible to see evidence for social evolution within the archaeological record. During the Early Formative period, Chalcatzingo was within the "Tlatilco culture sphere," a geographic region encompassing the southern Basin of Mexico and the state of Morelos in which the archaeological burial assemblages are distinguished by a specific complex of ceramic vessels and figurines.

Amate phase Chalcatzingo (1200-800 B.C.) was one of ten small settlements in the Amatzinac Valley. With the exception of Chalcatzingo, classified by K. Hirth (1987:349-50, table 21.12) as a small village, the settlements were hamlets (4) and isolated residences (5). Thus, it is clear that a simple chiefdomlike settlement hierarchy was present. However, the hierarchy does not present a completely accurate picture of the contrast between Chalcatzingo and other valley settlements during the Amate phase. Chalcatzingo is the only site known in the valley with stone-faced public architecture (Prindiville and Grove 1987:63, 65), a trait rare anywhere in the central highlands.

The Amatzinac Valley settlement hierarchy is also probably not typical of the majority of the Tlatilco culture sphere, particularly in site frequency and size (the largest Amatzinac Valley settlement is ranked by Hirth as a "small village"), because the valley is relatively arid, has little accessible water, and is even today a marginal area for agriculture (Grove, Hirth, and Buge 1987:8-9). In contrast, the valleys of central and western Morelos, with their large rivers, fertile alluvial bottomlands, and high natural humidity, were far more favorable locations for early agriculturalists, as borne out by the greater quantity and size of Tlatilco culture sites in those valleys.

It is possible that central Morelos is the cultural heartland of Tlatilco culture. Although some research has been conducted in those valleys (summarized in Grove 1974b), few areas have been so extensively surveyed that a settlement hierarchy becomes readily apparent. Grove's impression, from over a decade of work in those valleys, is that a three- or four-level hierarchy is present along each major river valley, with one large village (quite possibly with public architecture) and at least two other settlement levels: smaller villages and hamlets. It is highly probable that in Morelos the major valley systems generally equated with the regions of individual chiefly control.

The Basin of Mexico presents a far more difficult analytical unit in terms of distinguishing a regional settlement hierarchy because much of the area today lies beneath Mexico City. Thus, surface surveys have identified only nineteen Early Formative sites (Sanders, Parsons, and Santley 1979:94-96, maps 5-7), all in the middle and southern area of the basin. Unquestionably, the best-known site from the period is Tlatilco, where brickyard workers in the late 1930s began unearthing Early Formative graves with associated ceramics (e.g., Covarrubias 1943, 1950), most of which were sold on the antiquities market. Somewhat later, actual archaeological excavations were carried out periodically in the general area denominated as Tlatilco (e.g., Porter 1953; Piña Chan 1958; Tolstoy 1989:101-2, fig. 6.7). At the time most of that work was undertaken, priority was given to the salvage of burials rather than to excavations that might also have identified house areas and other features. Thus, other than the observation by Porter (1953:34) of possible "clay surfaced structures," the possibility that the Tlatilco graves might have been subfloor burials remains unresolved. However, Tolstoy has been carefully reanalyzing the Tlatilco data and has recently shown that the Tlatilco burials for which there are good records occur in groupings suggesting that they may indeed represent house subfloor burial clusters (e.g., Tolstoy 1989:102, fig. 6.7).

The Tlatilco graves originally gained fame through the quantity, elaborateness, and variety of the ceramic vessels and figurines found as burial offerings. Unfortunately, some of those were labeled "Olmec," a misidentification that has skewed interpretations of central Mexican prehistory for decades (e.g., Grove 1989). Those distinctive ceramics are not restricted to Tlatilco but are also common at contemporaneous sites in the southern Basin of Mexico and Morelos, permitting (as noted earlier) the definition of a "Tlatilco culture sphere." At all such sites the grave offerings exhibit a great deal of variation in quantity, quality, and vessel type.

Based upon his reanalysis of the Tlatilco grave lots, P. Tolstoy (1989:101-19) has reached the conclusion that rank distinctions were "reflected in the quality and quantity of offerings, in the depth and preparation of the grave, and in the position of the body" and has noted (1989:110) that grave depth shows a positive correlation with the quantity of objects. Artifacts he has identified as indicators of social rank (1989:108, 110, table 6.4 footnote a) include iron ore mirrors as the defining characteristic of his "Rank 1," 8+ objects (including necklaces, greenstone objects, shell, clay masks, pendants, whistles, etc.) but no mirrors as markers of his "Rank 2," 3-7 such objects as identifying "Rank 3," and 2 or fewer objects as "Rank 4." Despite his ranking, he states (1989:108) that "these indicators do not exhibit uniformly strong associations with one another. This suggests that other important and, in part, hidden factors contribute to their distributions."

Tolstoy's analysis is obviously post-facto by necessity. Although questions can be raised regarding when certain markers appear (e.g., jade, which probably occurs only late in the Tlatilco sequence), his analysis of ranking can be used as a comparative base for analyzing changes over time. In comparing the Early Formative markers of rank as exemplified at Tlatilco one by one with those of late Middle Formative Chalcatzingo, some similarities are present, but the overall contrast is even more striking.

Comparisons

Two exotic materials at both Chalcatzingo and Tlatilco appear to have served as elite markers—iron ore mirrors and jade. They were perhaps obvious markers then as now, because they were easily observable, overt symbols of rank. Their value comes in part from the fact that their raw materials are obtainable only by long-distance exchange. P. Tolstoy (1989: table 6.4) noted twelve instances of iron ore mirrors at Tlatilco, but at Chalcatzingo only the high-ranking Burial 40, also associated with quantities of quality jade beads, had two iron ore mirrors. Tolstoy's analysis does not provide co-occurrences of mirrors with jade, and jade quantities are not given. Importantly, a second criterion identified by Tolstoy for Tlatilco— quantity of grave goods—seems to have become unimportant by Cantera phase times at Chalcatzingo, to the extent that there is almost an inverse correlation between quantity of ceramic vessels and jade and crypt graves (as noted above). At Chalcatzingo particular forms of vessels—not their quantity—helped differentiate rank. The jade-rich crypt Burials 39 and 40 had only *cantaritos* placed within shallow bowls, as did crypt Burial 33, which also had the greenstone were-jaguar figurine. Two of the crypt graves beneath P.C. Str. 1 contained no ceramics at all, and at no time does there appear to be any clear correlation between quantity of burial offerings and rank in any of the graves at Chalcatzingo.

Although burial depth appears to correlate with Tolstoy's four "ranks" at Tlatilco, and also during the Classic period at the Tlajinga compound at Teotihuacan (Storey 1985:525), no such correlation exists at Chalcatzingo, where some of the highest ranked graves were relatively shallow in relation to the house floor or ground surface (e.g., Burials 3, 39, 40).

At Chalcatzingo the presence of a crypt grave was an important marker of elite status since those graves occurred only in the public/elite areas of the site. There is no evidence, however, that any Tlatilco graves were stone embellished (see Tolstoy 1989:111).

Tolstoy (1989:110) has suggested that burial position may have been important at Tlatilco, noting that bodies in an extended dorsal position had approximately twice the number of objects and were usually found in deeper graves than those buried in other positions. The majority of the Chalcatzingo burials are extended dorsally, but, as mentioned, fifteen Cantera phase burials were flexed, and twelve of those were found beneath P.C. Str. 1, together with high-ranked crypt graves. It was originally thought that flexed burials might have been of lower rank because they received the least variety of offerings (e.g., Merry de Morales 1987b:101-4). However, three facts call that assumption into question: (1) there is no association between rank and quantity of grave goods, and some crypt burials also lack grave goods; (2) the only two P.C. Str. 1 burials receiving single jade beads were noncrypt flexed burials; (3) one crypt burial (26) had been interred in a flexed position.

The Tlatilco and Chalcatzingo data compare only poorly. At Chalcatzingo a major criterion for rank was location with respect to public/elite structures, and such data are missing for Tlatilco. Nevertheless, assuming that there is some continuity and comparability of the data, some conclusions can be drawn from these two sites in terms of change through time in the marking of social rank in grave preparation. If Tolstoy's analysis has some validity, a major point of change has been the evolution from quantity of grave goods, depth of grave, and burial position as the primary criteria for social rank to stone embellishment of graves and a greater reliance on artifacts that carry an ideological burden, such as particular vessel forms and combinations (rather than quantity).

The Gulf Coast Olmec

Having reviewed the data from Chalcatzingo and Tlatilco, it is worthwhile now to see how those data correspond to archaeological evidence of an elite group in Gulf Coast Olmec culture. It has been common for Mesoamerican archaeologists to view the Olmec as more advanced than other Formative period societies. While most researchers consider the Olmec to have been a chiefdom-level society, at least two archaeologists who have worked in the area, M. D. Coe (Coe and Diehl 1980:147) and P. Drucker (1981), believe the Olmec had a state-level society.

In our opinion the Gulf Coast archaeological record for elite markers shows a pattern in the Early Formative that, apart from monumental art, is very little different from that of central Mexico or other areas of western Mesoamerica. Although as yet there have been no large-scale regional surveys, from the basic data available we can speak of a settlement hierarchy of three or four tiers, centered on major settlements such as San Lorenzo. Apart from a Bajio phase platform reported by Coe and Diehl (1980) at San

Lorenzo, good archaeological evidence for public architecture is lacking. If such structures existed, they remain to be identified.

At San Lorenzo, artifacts that are taken to indicate the presence of high-ranking persons include some iron ore mirror fragments, a very few greenstone pendants, and some serpentine "workshop debris" in the San Lorenzo phase (1150-900 B.C.; Coe and Diehl 1980:242-45). Unfortunately, there are no good contextual data showing that these objects occur in restricted distributions or in elite/public areas of the site. Regrettably, burials are also lacking in the San Lorenzo sample.

The Middle Formative (900-500 B.C.) Gulf Coast record of a ranked society is far more definitive. The elaborate constructions and burials of Complex A at La Venta show an elite controlling great expenditures of human labor and marking their rank with iron ore, jade artifacts, and embellished graves. In addition, high-ranking individuals seem to have expressed their social position by using an increasingly complex symbol system that was manifested on greenstone artifacts (e.g., decorated celts) and monumental art. That system included symbols of power that associated the elite with supernatural powers. One major problem with the Gulf Coast archaeological record is that our current knowledge of the Middle Formative period is derived almost entirely from one small area of one Olmec center, Complex A at La Venta (Drucker 1952; Drucker, Heizer, and Squier 1959). We still have little concept of the total society at La Venta, although recent work there by Rebecca Gonzalez promises to rectify that situation (see also Rust and Sharer 1988).

Even in the absence of any excavation data, there would be good evidence demonstrating the presence of an Olmec elite. That evidence is found in the basic feature that sets the Gulf Coast Olmec sites apart from their contemporaries in most other regions of Mesoamerica: monumental stone art. The majority of Early and Middle Formative monuments on the Gulf Coast glorified particular individuals through portrait carvings. Those monuments were carved from multiton pieces of stone brought over long distances at a great expense of human resources. Their presence at Olmec centers has probably been the major factor in creating the notion that Olmec society was somehow more advanced than other Mesoamerican chiefdoms, because it has long been assumed that there is a correlation between monumental art and state-level societies in other world areas.

Although Olmec monumental art has implications for Gulf Coast technology and labor output for esoteric needs, it is not archaeological evidence of a state-level society. That must be demonstrated by excavation data. The monuments do provide us with portraits of some Olmec elite and an idea of how those personages demonstrated their rights to rulership to their constituents, but that by itself does not categorize the Olmec elite as substantially different from elites elsewhere in Mesoamerica at this time. The creation of monumental art did not come about because Gulf Coast societies were socially more advanced than other chiefdoms, but because they had developed a conception of the relationship between the ruler and the cosmos involving identified chiefs and necessitating portrait depictions of those personages (Grove and Gillespie n.d.). That difference between the Gulf Coast and western Mesoamerica in the Formative period is repeated nearly a millennium later in the dichotomy between Classic Maya conceptions of identified rulership, which required monumental portraiture, and the conceptions of their central Mexican contemporaries, which did not. The monumental art at Chalcatzingo appears to date to the Cantera phase (Grove 1987c:426) and indicates that for a brief period the site's elite must have participated in that Gulf Coast worldview (Grove 1987b:435-40).

Conclusion

The presence of social ranking during the Middle Formative is seen in regional site hierarchies, public architecture, and, more importantly, intrasite residential differences and differences in burial treatment. The highest-ranking individuals, presumably the chiefs, can be readily identified by the co-occurrence of several of the postulated elite markers (burial in elite and/or public areas, crypt graves, and usually exotic items of perceived high value, including jade, iron ore mirrors, and *cantaritos* in shallow bowls). Beyond this highest rank, however, there is no further clustering of rank markers to allow us consistently to identify recognized lower ranks. Instead, they occur in a variety of groupings, revealing a social continuum and not social categories, which matches the ethnographic description of a chiefdom. Furthermore, if such marked social categories were found, it would not guarantee that we were dealing with actual social ranks; there are many other possible reasons for marking some persons as different from others.

Notes

1. Prindiville and Grove (1987:66) note that some subsidiary buildings or patios at other house areas could have been destroyed by erosion or plowing or missed by the project's sampling methods.

2. It is possible that the several Cantera phase stone-faced rectangular platform structures, not discussed in this chapter because they did not yield any burials, could have been foundations for elite residences (Prindiville and Grove 1987:64-66). That is particularly true of T-25 Str. 2 (Fash 1987:92), but for the others that possibility remains purely conjectural.

3. Merry de Morales (1987b:96-100) carried out a ranking of the burials using similar criteria.

4. Burial 156 in Cave 4 had three markers: stone embellishment, censer, and *cantarito*, plus an obsidian bloodletter. Those markers plus the fact that caves were sacred places to ancient Mesoamericans and the "extraordinary" nature of Cave 4 with its Cantera phase mud brick floor (Grove and Guillén 1987:54, figs. 4.38, 4.39) suggest Burial 156 was a special individual of relatively high rank.

13. Social Differentiation at Teotihuacan

George L. Cowgill

AS other chapters in this volume make clear, not all important social distinctions, in ancient Mesoamerica or anywhere else, can be characterized adequately by means of a single one-dimensional scale from low to high. It is not simply that archaeologists must rely more than we would like on signs of wealth as a proxy for role, status, or power. Wealth is always intertwined with these other variables but, except possibly in some "big man" societies, the relationship is never one-to-one. This is perhaps particularly so with regard to social mobility. In many societies, myths that inborn differences make aristocrats the only people suited for power and position and make commoners suited only to serve aristocrats are belied by blue bloods fallen on hard times and by plebeian upstarts in high places. In the United States, incidentally, the reverse is the case: the myth of universal equality of opportunity obscures unequal advantages that depend on wealth and family connections as well as on race, ethnicity, and gender.

However, there is more to it than mobility; there are often persons of high status who take little part in running the society and people of humble status but considerable power (often exercised behind the scenes rather than in visible high office). We could profitably consider examples such as the tendency of Roman senators to protect family status and wealth by *not* launching sons on senatorial careers (Hopkins and Burton 1983) or the finely tuned sensitivities to discrepancies of birth, office, and wealth in Victorian England, developed at length by novelists such as Charles Dickens and Anthony Trollope.[1] Closer to home, John Chance (1988) has contrasted eighteenth-century native elites in different parts of Mexico in terms of cross-cutting dimensions of wealth and political power.

Some discrepancies between native theory and practice are deliberate attempts at obfuscation; others simply happen. In any case, they always complicate and often confuse dealings with a society by its own members. The task of understanding is even harder for archaeologists, but discarding oversimple models of ancient societies is a large step in the right direction. We should distinguish at least the following.

1. Membership in a particular class (in extreme cases, a caste) is characterized by eligibility or ineligibility to hold certain offices, follow certain occupations, or display a certain lifestyle. In cases where eligibility was not translated into actuality, it seems virtually hopeless to recover it archaeologically. However, while only a fraction of persons eligible for a particular office or occupation may actually have held the office or followed the occu-

pation, distinct lifestyles may really have been followed by most members of different classes, especially if there were effectively enforced sumptuary rules. It may become possible to identify such styles (as opposed to simple quantitative differences in wealth) archaeologically—by differences in residences, locations of residences, household furnishings, and household refuse.

2. Actually holding a particular office and/or following a particular occupation is related to the way the society was organized. What were the recognized offices and the hierarchy or hierarchies of office? To what extent were priestly, military, administrative, judicial, and other offices distinct? Offices are best distinguished archaeologically by differences in dress, regalia, and other signs or symbols of office. These may accompany officeholders after death as grave goods, and they are often shown in art. There may be special burial practices for holders of certain offices, including burial in particular locations. Also, offices that are distinct may be exercised in certain types of structures (e.g., temples, palaces, courts of law).

Diverse occupations, of course, are recognizable to the extent that they leave behind relatively abundant amounts of distinctive and imperishable tools or discarded by-products. Osteological markers of certain activities are another possible line of evidence, so far little used.

3. A third variable is simply generalized wealth. Archaeologists have found this easiest to deal with. One can characterize burials or refuse associated with particular structures or neighborhoods in terms of some reasonable assumptions about the cost or "preciousness" of various categories of objects. Graves and structures themselves can be characterized according to their size, quality, and location. The difficulties with such variables are the fact that the relative costliness of things is not always as clear as we would like and the fact, emphasized above, that sheer wealth may not be a very sensitive indicator of class or high office. Nevertheless, in the present state of our knowledge, indices of wealth are very useful as long as we recognize that they depend on judgments that are somewhat uncertain and that they do not lead directly to insights about high offices and the organization of such offices.

The following discussion summarizes the current status of investigations bearing on questions of high offices, distinctive occupations, and wealth distributions at Teotihuacan. I adopt a cautious tone that may suggest that less is known than is the case. To be sure, questions loom larger than certainties, but we do know a good deal, and there is a very great deal more that can be learned by pursuing further many lines of investigation that we have scarcely begun.

Rulership at Teotihuacan

The office of rulership itself, or headship of the state, has proven curiously elusive at Teotihuacan, in contrast to its high visibility in Classic period

Maya inscriptions and monuments. The Aztecs also celebrated rulers in monumental art (as in carvings on the hill of Chapultepec), identified their pictures by name glyphs, and sometimes (as on the Stone of Tizoc) showed them capturing enemies. In the sixteenth century, Spanish chroniclers described societies throughout Mesoamerica that were headed by single individuals who, upon accession, normally held office as long as they were able. To be sure, there was often a process of selection from among a limited number of eligibles, rather than automatic inheritance of office through descent, and powers of heads of state were limited to varying degrees by the rights of other high-ranking persons. Our picture may be distorted to some extent by Spanish preconceptions. Nevertheless, it is clear that there was usually a single position, higher than all others in the political hierarchy, with no set limit of legitimate tenure.

This may well also have been the case at Teotihuacan. However, as yet the evidence is equivocal. Teotihuacan art—mural painting, decorated pottery, and small and large stone carvings—is notable for the absence of scenes in which some humans appear subordinated to others (R. Millon 1988; Pasztory 1988b). Humans are sometimes shown subordinated to deities, but not to one another. We also do not see scenes that center on a single person. Typically several persons are shown, often in procession, and all as similar to one another in the details of their postures, facial features, and costumes as freehand drawing allows. This is true not only of mural paintings (mostly known from interiors of dwellings), but also of decorations on ceramics and stone sculpture, most of which was in more public settings. Signs that might identify individuals are very rare and remain enigmatic.

The most notable example of signs that differentiate persons is the procession of figures wearing the "tassel headdress" reconstructed from looted mural fragments from the apartment compound called Techinantitla (Berrin 1988). This compound is larger than most at Teotihuacan (about 95 by 75 m, as reconstructed by René Millon [1988]). It is about 600 m east of the Moon Pyramid and somewhat outside the area with clear evidence of major pyramid groups associated with the Street of the Dead. Other than its unusual size and numerous murals, it is notable for being in a neighborhood where an above-average proportion of polychrome stuccoed and other fine wares was collected by the Teotihuacan Mapping Project surface survey.

Clara Millon (1973, 1988) first identified the tassel headdress, which she argued was associated with very high status at Teotihuacan and represented the Teotihuacan state when it appeared abroad (as on the shield carried by an armed figure on Stela 31 at Tikal). She did not, however, go so far as to identify it specifically with rulership, and René Millon (1988) has recently suggested that the figures shown at Techinantitla are more likely to be high-ranking military men (generals) rather than rulers. It is certainly true that Techinantitla, in spite of its size, is in an unlikely location for a royal palace.

Nevertheless, rulers may be celebrated in places other than their actual residences, and it is possible that the figures wearing the tassel headdress at Techinantitla may be rulers rather than generals.

One of the keys to understanding these figures will be reading the glyphs that accompany them. These could be personal names, but they might instead be names of groups that the individuals represented or to which they belonged, names of places, or something else. It is notable that one glyph group consists of a Feathered Serpent head on a mat, surmounted (as are the other glyphs in this procession) by a version of the tassel headdress. The mat sign is rare at Teotihuacan, but its association with rulership in the Maya area is suggestive (Langley 1986:273). Moreover, although it is very clear that the Feathered Serpent had multiple associations at Teotihuacan, David Grove (1987a) has recently argued that it was a sign of political authority earlier in Mesoamerica. This may have been one of its several meanings at Teotihuacan. Saburo Sugiyama (1989b) notes this possibility.

Grove (1987c) also argues that flaming torches were a symbol of political authority in early Mesoamerica. I do not know of any torch representations at Techinantitla. However, the "Maguey Priest" murals from Tlacuilapaxco (an apartment compound a short distance to the south) show what James Langley and I (personal communication, 1988) think may be bundles tied in the manner of torches. The interpretation of these objects is complex. They are clearly associated with autosacrifice by means of maguey spines and they are not flaming. Clara Millon (1988:199-200) argues that they are terraced plots of land that may also, through visual punning, have stood for tied bundles that were perhaps used in New Fire ceremonies at the completion of some cycle of time. She does not suggest that they had any special relationship to rulership.

Another occurrence of flaming torches at Teotihuacan is in the hands of a stone relief carving of a figure widely interpreted as the Great Goddess, found in a courtyard within the Calle de los Muertos Complex, a great walled assemblage of rooms, pyramids, and open spaces that straddles the Street of the Dead, south of the Sun Pyramid and north of the Ciudadela (Cabrera et al. 1982; Pasztory 1988b:70-71, fig. III.25a-b). This complex may well have been associated with high political authority, if not actual headship of the state (Cowgill 1983), and the prominent display of flaming torches here is intriguing. The Great Goddess is one of the most important deities at Teotihuacan and has multiple associations, but, so far as I know, no special association with rulership. I am not convinced that the carving in the Calle de los Muertos Complex actually is the Great Goddess, but this is a matter I cannot explore further here.

Outside of Teotihuacan flaming torches occur in such strongly Teotihuacan-related objects as the figure wearing Feathered Serpent dress on a stone relief from Soyoltepec in southern Veracruz (Sugiyama 1989b), and a figure wearing a version of the tassel headdress on the back of a pyrite-encrusted plaque from Kaminaljuyu (Kidder et al. 1946:fig. 175). Tied bundles also appear in the headdress of the figure on the left side of Tikal Stela 31. I am not sure that they stand for rulership at Teotihuacan, but I am virtually certain that those who carry them do so as a mark of fairly high office, possibly military.

Although the Ciudadela has been accepted for years as almost surely the seat of the heads of the Teotihuacan state, iconographic evidence for rulership there has been hard to come by. As Esther Pasztory (1988b) points out, mural paintings seem to have been nearly absent within the Ciudadela apartment compounds (one wonders if their place was taken by tapestries or other exceptionally fine perishable or portable objects, or whether functions served by murals in other residences were not relevant inside these compounds). Of course, if one of the meanings of the Feathered Serpent at Teotihuacan was political authority, then it is proclaimed more monumentally by the facades of the Feathered Serpent Pyramid (Temple of Quetzalcoatl) than anywhere else at Teotihuacan.

Recent excavations at the pyramid have revealed a previously unsuspected episode of large-scale human sacrifice associated with the pyramid's construction in the Miccaotli phase or very early in the Tlamimilolpa phase, around A.D. 150 to 250 (Cabrera et al. 1989, 1991; Sugiyama 1989a).[2] More than 120 individuals have been found, and the total is estimated to have been over 200. Of those excavated, 16 are relatively young individuals, with remains of weapons and not very rich dress. Another 72 also have the remains of weapons and are more richly dressed, with collars of cut red shell plates from which imitation human maxillae composed of teeth carved from shells are suspended. There are small variations from individual to individual—some have a few more or less trophy maxillae than others, the details of the red shell plates vary, a few have real human maxillae, and a few have maxillae of canids (possibly coyotes). Nevertheless, similarities greatly outweigh the differences. Pasztory (1989) notes that this parallels the lack of differentiation of figures in Teotihuacan murals.

There is little doubt that these individuals played military roles, although this does not exclude the possibility that they also had priestly functions. Their dress and grave goods suggest two ranks, one relatively low and the other most likely officers of intermediate level. It seems unlikely that these persons were at the top of the military hierarchy, because there are too many of them. They are found in multiple burials, both outside the pyramid and in the outer parts of its interior. Possibly they were captive enemies, but more likely they were loyal members of the Teotihuacan hierarchy.

Further inside the pyramid, an ancient looters' tunnel was found. The looters had removed the contents of two burial pits, also associated with the pyramid's construction. One of these pits was very large and situated on the central east-west axis of the pyramid. Because of the looting it is impossible to say how many individuals had been buried in them or to determine the full range of grave goods. From what the looters missed, however, it is clear that the offerings in these pits were richer than those in the previously described burials.

In 1989 our tunnel was extended to the exact center of the Feathered Serpent Pyramid, where another multiple burial, of some twenty individuals, was found at the ancient ground level, undisturbed by looters, but forming a confusing mass of intermingled bones, many in poor condition. Analyses of the remains are in too early a stage for detailed comments, but it is clear that, although many obsidian projectile points were also present here, the goods are much richer than and different from those in the outer mass burials. Thus, in a general way, burials become richer the closer one gets to the center of the pyramid, and presumably the status of the dead was also higher toward the center. Some of those at the center may have been of extremely high status.

Nevertheless, no one individual in this central mass burial stands out at once as special. Possibly evidence for such a person will emerge when we have had time to study the material more closely. It is also possible that there was such a person in the badly looted pit a short distance west of the center, and perhaps we shall never be able to resolve this question. For the present, we can only say that there were some very rich burials within the Feathered Serpent Pyramid, evidence for at least three (and probably more) levels of richness, but no certain evidence of any single individual of supreme importance. Perhaps the multitudes were sacrificed to accompany a dead ruler, but it is also possible that they were sacrificed for the deity to whom the pyramid was dedicated.

Several scholars (e.g., Cowgill 1983; R. Millon 1988; Pasztory 1988b) have postulated an early period of centralized and possibly autocratic rule at Teotihuacan, associated with its rapid expansion in the first century A.D., its domination of the Basin of Mexico, the construction of the Sun Pyramid, and the beginning of the monumental complex of temples and other structures along the Street of the Dead. They have seen the Ciudadela and the Feathered Serpent Pyramid as the culmination of this tendency, although Pasztory (1988b) stresses that the images on the pyramid avoid any direct references to personality or to military conquest. A later platform obscures much of the front facade of the pyramid. It was perhaps built not long after the pyramid itself, and it may be one of the markers of rejection of autocratic rule. René Millon (1988:112) suggests that "perhaps a successor to the early great leader probably buried in the center of the Sun Pyramid established despotic rule and so tyrannized those in the upper strata of Teotihuacan society that when the opportunity arose, it provoked a reaction strong enough ultimately to lead to an abiding limitation on the power of the ruler."

Millon (1988:112) feels that perhaps powerful ideological and institutional checks on the glorification of personal power were established early in Teotihuacan's history, not long after construction of the Ciudadela and the Feathered Serpent Pyramid. This would imply the existence of an effective collective leadership in the upper strata of Teotihuacan's society. He suggests that "one form a reaction against despotic rule might have taken would have been to turn the sacred qualities of rulership into restrictions." An alternative he considers less likely is that rulers might have been limited to a single term of office, for a specified number of years. This may not be so unlikely. Rome became a great empire in the usual sense of that term (a state controlling a very large territory and ethnically heterogenous populations) while it was still a republic governed by elected consuls who ruled in pairs for periods of a year (although, normally, they could be reelected after an interval). Nevertheless, I do not argue that rotating short-term rule was surely the case at Teotihuacan, only that it is a possibility to be seriously considered.

The exceedingly low symbolic profile of strong individual rulers at Teotihuacan has to be seen in connection with the tendency of the art, noted by many scholars and with particular cogency by Pasztory (1988a), to proclaim homogeneity and collective values in a society that was clearly quite heterogenous, with distinct ethnic neighborhoods and great actual differences in wealth. Was there strong personal rulership at Teotihuacan all along, systematically downplayed in the messages of murals and sculpture? This seems a possibility although, even so, a very great contrast with the Classic Maya and many other Mesoamerican societies would remain. It seems more likely that, at least from not long after the construction of the Ciudadela soon after A.D. 200, rulership at Teotihuacan was subjected to limitations unusual in Mesoamerica. This may have been facilitated by the fact that Teotihuacan does not seem to have undertaken conquests after that time, yet was strong enough that it was not threatened by others. Both conquests and invasions can aid rulers seeking to enlarge their power. Conquests provide new territories and resources that a ruler can control directly or use to reward loyal subordinates, and emergency powers granted in response to an invasion crisis may not be relinquished afterward. Without either, Teotihuacan rulers may have found it very hard to break free of highly sacralized aspects of their roles and the sort of restrictions postulated by René Millon.

Other Offices and Hierarchies

To what extent was there a distinction between priestly and military offices at Teotihuacan? Sometimes it seems as if little distinguishes military and priestly figures in the murals except that the former carry weapons and the latter typically carry bags and strew something, presumably the contents of the bags. L. Manzanilla (1988) argues that Teotihuacan society was organized and controlled by hierarchies conceived in overwhelmingly religious terms. E. Pasztory (1989) suggests that the military may have been less important for large-scale conquests or campaigns than for small-scale or ceremonial activity, as much for symbolic as for practical purposes, representing the grandeur of the Teotihuacan state both to its own population and to foreigners. Such a largely ceremonial role, albeit one in which bloody human heart sacrifices were prominent, is consistent with the possibility that military and priestly offices were not sharply distinguished. Nevertheless, I wonder if further analysis will reveal distinctive differences, other than the weapons and the bags, in priestly and military dress and symbols.

There are a number of pyramid and platform complexes quite far from the Street of the Dead, notably in square N6W3 of the Mapping Project system, near the far northwestern margin of the city. Some of these are quite sizable and suggest the possibility of priestly hierarchies that were relatively independent of the central authority, although that is not their only plausible interpretation (see Cowgill et al. 1984 for further discussion).

To the extent that trade was important at Teotihuacan, there must have been traders. However, some writers (e.g., Santley 1983) have exaggerated the role of trade in Teotihuacan society, and its true importance remains to be determined. Manzanilla (1988) doubts that a distinct class of merchants existed. Clearly foreign goods found their way into Teotihuacan, and Teotihuacan goods appear elsewhere in Mesoamerica. However, I know of no evidence for merchant neighborhoods or for a distinctive merchant lifestyle, except in the "merchants'" barrio on the eastern edge of the city, where Mapping Project collections and excavations and more recent excavations by Evelyn Rattray have found relatively high proportions of ceramics from the Gulf Coast and the lowland Maya area. Rattray also found a number of unusual circular structures. Laurette Séjourné (1959:30-37) has argued for merchants at the Zacuala Palace apartment compound, interpreting a figure with a pack-basket as the Aztec god of merchants, Yacatecuhtli. However, the figure in question carries a maize stalk in one hand and maize cobs in the basket, and the associations are clearly agricultural. In my opinion, the importance of trade and the extent to which a self-conscious class of merchants existed at Teotihuacan are among the questions that require much more study.

Crafts at Teotihuacan

This section notes some recent studies of craft activities at Teotihuacan, concentrating on those that emphasize identification of workshops and evidence bearing on modes and relations of production.

Michael Spence has published a number of papers on the obsidian industry (see especially Spence 1967, 1981, 1984, 1987). John Clark (1986) argues that the importance of Teotihuacan's obsidian trade has been exaggerated. His criticisms apply far more to the claims of Robert Santley (e.g., 1983, 1984) than to Spence's work, which is much closer to the data.

Spence has considerably reduced his earlier estimates of the number of workshops, but this does not imply a proportionate reduction in his estimate of the scale of the industry, since most of the sites now regarded as doubtful were never considered to be among the major production sites.

Evelyn Rattray and the late Paula Krotser have published on manufacture and distribution of certain ceramic groups at Teotihuacan (Krotser and Rattray 1980), and Krotser (1987) has studied levels of specialization among Teotihuacan potters. Work in progress by Mary Hopkins (1989) looks at changes in standardization of several utility wares over time, comparing wares made by specialized potters with other wares believed to have been made by persons who were not specialists. James Sheehy is studying the production of San Martín Orange utility ware at the site of Tlajinga 33, where this ware was produced by specialists (Widmer 1987). Charles Kolb (1977, 1986, 1988b, 1988c, 1988d, 1988e) has published a series of studies on various wares, and Evelyn Rattray (1981) and Louana Lackey (1988) have published on Thin Orange, a ware made in southern Puebla and imported by Teotihuacan in great quantity.

Margaret Turner (1987a, 1987b) has studied the lapidary industry of Teotihuacan, based largely on Teotihuacan Mapping Project data, especially a project excavation at Tecopac, a lapidary workshop in Square N3E5 on the northeastern margin of the city.

Martin Biskowski (1986) has begun a study of the Teotihuacan groundstone industry.

Markers of Differential Status or Wealth and Their Spatial Patterning

We know very little of early residences at Teotihuacan. From Late Tlamimilolpa times (ca. A.D. 300 to 400) onward, the vast majority of the population lived in architecturally substantial apartment compounds, built of walls with concrete facing and stone rubble filling. There is a widespread impression that most compounds were about 60 m on a side. This is true of many, but there is much variation. Most have not been excavated, and the actual areas of many are not entirely clear. However, according to Teotihuacan Mapping Project estimates, as indicated by the "interpretations" sheets of René Millon et al. (1973), the median area was about 43 by 43 m (ca. 1,830 sq m), and nearly a quarter of them were not larger than 30 by 30 m (900 sq m), while another quarter were over about 56 by 56 m (3,100 sq m), with a few covering more than a hectare (100 by 100 m). Size is not closely linked to status. Among the largest compounds are Techinantitla, whose occupants were of very high status, and Tlamimilolpa (Linné 1942), of rather low status.

Because smaller compounds must have usually housed fewer people than larger ones, the statistics for people are different from the statistics for structures. I estimate very roughly that somewhere around a quarter of the population lived in compounds smaller than about 45 by 45 m (2,000 sq m) and another quarter in compounds larger than 67 by 67 m (4,500 sq m).

The Mapping Project found occasional localities with significant amounts of Teotihuacan ceramics and other artifacts on the surface but no evidence of substantial architecture. Some of these may represent refuse or places where special activities were carried out, but others may have been architecturally insubstantial residences. In any case, judging from the low proportion of all Teotihuacan materials collected by the Mapping Project that came from such localities, only a very small proportion of the city's population could have lived outside of substantial structures. This need not imply that most of the population were relatively well off; it is more likely that many people of quite low wealth and status lived in substantially built compounds. Tlajinga 33, in a potters' barrio, is an example (Widmer 1987).

René Millon (1976:227-28, 1981:214) has argued for at least six status levels at Teotihuacan. The very highest is represented by occupants of the Ciudadela palaces. The second highest, probably numbering several thousand, would have included most of the priestly and administrative hierarchy and was undoubtedly subdivided into distinct levels (Millon 1981:214).

Millon envisages a major gap between these highest two strata and those below them, represented by many of the apartment compounds. Although he does not elaborate on the reasons for thinking that such a gap existed, it seems likely that he was thinking of a pronounced contrast between those who held high or moderately high office (and their households) and those who did not. Within the broad intermediate grouping (Millon explicitly avoids the term "middle class" because of its inevitable connotations in association with modern industrialized societies) he sees three levels, represented, from highest to lowest, by the Zacuala Palace, Teopancaxco, and Xolalpan. He bases this on a study by himself and Clara Millon "using such variables as size of rooms, use of space, decoration, construction techniques, burials, offerings, and other relevant data" (Millon 1976:227). Below this, compounds such as La Ventilla B and Tlamimilolpa probably were occupied by people of a sixth, relatively low, status level. Presumably Tlajinga 33 would also belong to this level. More recently, Millon (1981:214) has suggested that the people of lowest status probably did not live in apartment compounds, but in small insubstantial adobe structures. This indicates a seventh, not very numerous, level at the very bottom.

There are considerable contrasts between different apartment compounds, and there is no doubt that occupants varied considerably in wealth, status, and social roles. It is also clear, as Millon points out, that many Teotihuacan neighborhoods are not very homogeneous. Judged by criteria such as construction quality and evidence of mural paintings, there is a *tendency* for the proportion of wealthier households to decrease as one moves further from the Street of the Dead and for the proportion of poorer households to increase, but it is only a tendency. Some structures with apparently wealthy occupants are found quite far from the center, while some people of rather low status probably lived near the center.

The matter is further complicated by internal variation within compounds. Most are large enough to have held several households, and those excavated consist of distinct apartments. Relations between the occupants of different apartments are unclear. Probably those within a compound were bound by kin ties or otherwise formed a well-defined social unit. Nevertheless, there were apparently considerable differences of wealth and status among the occupants of different apartments within a compound. This is suggested architecturally at some excavated compounds, such as Tetitla, where some apartments are spacious, with numerous murals, while others have smaller rooms, less solid construction, and little or no evidence of murals (Séjourné 1966).

Moreover, a few burials with numerous grave goods, some of high quality, occur even in compounds where the weight of evidence implies that the occupants were quite poor. Tlamimilolpa is an example (Linné 1942). This is also seemingly the case at Tlajinga 33, where there are quite rich burials early (Widmer 1987). To be sure, at that time the occupants may have been lapidaries, of higher status than the specialized potters who occupied the compound later. Nevertheless, the early architecture of the site is not elaborate and does not suggest that the workers in fine stone were very wealthy.

In contemporary societies, people who are quite poor may save and sacrifice for years to amass the resources for a lavish occasion, such as a wedding, a funeral, or a coming-of-age celebration. They often spend amounts that seem, to persons imbued with notions of thrift and something like the Protestant Ethic, shockingly out of proportion to their means. I suspect that something like this happened at Teotihuacan and that occasionally quite poor people amassed the resources to provide a rich burial for a person, perhaps a founder, of great importance to the compound. This may help to explain why fragments of jade, worked shell, other precious materials, and sherds of fine ceramic wares are found so widely scattered, albeit in small quantities, throughout so much of Teotihuacan. Given the size of the city, it is most unlikely that the wide occurrence of fine materials can be explained by ancient or modern redeposition or refuse dumping.

The occurrence of a few rich burials in apartment compounds whose occupants were generally of low status also points up the need to consider the whole range of burials associated with a compound, rather than isolated examples. Martha Sempowski (1982, 1987) has done this for three compounds for which there are reasonably good data: Tetitla, Zacuala Patios (neighboring Zacuala Palace but distinct from it), and La Ventilla B. She constructed a "complexity" index, a composite score based on quantity, variety, and quality of grave goods, and rated seventeen to eighty-one burials for each compound. Admittedly, one has to make the usual assumptions in treating the complexity index as a measure of rank, status, or wealth of the deceased, but the results are interesting. Besides making comparisons between the compounds, Sempowski studied changes over time and associations with age and sex. She found that differences in complexity scores within each compound were larger than the differences in average scores between compounds. In general, scores were higher for adults than for subadults, and on the average higher for males than for females. She notes that over time the variability of scores within each compound tends to decline, which she sees as a sign of increased social homogeneity within compounds (although it may possibly be an artifact of smaller samples for the final period).

There is great overlap between compounds in individual scores, but the average is highest for Tetitla and lowest for La Ventilla B, with Zacuala Patios in the middle. (In René Millon's [1976] discussion, La Ventilla B is tentatively assigned to his sixth level. Tetitla and Zacuala Patios would presumably be toward the top of his three intermediate levels.) The average level of La Ventilla B burials changed little over time, but in the final (Metepec) phase the average for Tetitla rose somewhat, while that for Zacuala Patios plummeted close to the La Ventilla B average. This suggests that, late in the city's history, the status of Tetitla occupants was rising and the social distance between it and the other two compounds was increasing. Such growing differences, if substantiated by further studies, could be among the factors leading up to the violent destruction of Teotihuacan's palaces and temples in the eighth century A.D. Study of larger numbers of burials from many compounds along the lines of Sempowski's work is badly needed. Adequate data from older excavations are hard to come by, but recent and future work should permit this.

A number of computer-aided analyses of Mapping Project data have attempted to derive indices of wealth and/or status, to plot their spatial distributions, to identify distinctive neighborhoods in the city, and to identify spatially dispersed but related sites (Sload 1977, 1982, 1987; Altschul 1981, 1987; Cowgill et al. 1984; Cowgill 1987). These are summarized very briefly here. One approach is to plot distributions of ceramic and other artifact categories that appear by their nature to have been precious, such as jade and other lapidary materials and finely decorated ceramics. These plots confirm that occurrences are not limited to central parts of the city or to the vicinity of monumental structures, but the scarcity of these materials in surface collections sets limits on interpretations, since it is hard to tell whether nonoccurrences are meaningful or sampling accidents.

Another line has been to look for empirical associations between more common ceramic and artifact categories and sites or neighborhoods believed, for architectural or other reasons, to have been occupied by households of high or low status or to represent temples or other special structures. Early results of this approach have been interesting (see especially

Cowgill et al. 1984), but somewhat limited by the need to rely on rather broad initial classifications of materials. A long-term project of more detailed restudy of Mapping Project collections of ceramics and lithics has been completed,[3] and we hope before long to carry out spatial analyses with this much improved data base.

Conclusion

Implicit in this and other discussions of Mesoamerican elites is the contrast between "emic" and "etic" approaches. If our objectives are emic, we search for evidence about the categories and other concepts most salient to members of the society being studied. If our approach is etic, we seek to construct categories and other concepts that we ourselves find most useful for our purposes, whatever those purposes may be.

From an emic viewpoint, we ask whether members of Mesoamerican societies tended to think of themselves as comprised primarily (though probably with a few exceptions, such as slaves, criminals, deviants, and certain kinds of outsiders) of two classes, sharply differentiated from one another but internally fairly homogeneous. My impression, although it is not based on close study of data on any non-Teotihuacan society, is that this is probably a fairly accurate characterization of how many (very possibly nearly all) Mesoamerican societies viewed themselves. For example, it is noteworthy that, among the Aztecs, it did not seem to be difficult for the Spanish to elicit native terms that can be translated, apparently without doing them violence, as "commoners" and "nobles." Furthermore, we are told that there were different schools for the sons of each class, and this suggests some fairly powerful ways for inculcating different lifestyles, as well as preparing youths for different kinds of careers.

There are hints that the thought typical of Teotihuacanos may possibly have made a less sharp and two-valued conceptual distinction between "nobles" and "commoners." At any rate, distinctions between superiors and subordinates are not patent in what we know of Teotihuacan pictures and symbolism. On the other hand, Teotihuacan representations are as notable for what they do not show as for what they do show. For example, we do not know of a single scene directly showing the act of human sacrifice, but it is shown metaphorically in a scene where coyotes tear the heart from a deer (C. Millon 1988:218-21), and processions of celebrants brandishing what are unmistakably bloody hearts impaled on knives are well known. Thus, the absence of scenes of overt subordination/superordination in Teotihuacan art need not mean that such differences were unimportant in Teotihuacan thought. Furthermore, many of the elements of the elaborate costumes in which Teotihuacanos were shown may well have been, to their viewers, highly salient marks of status and/or office. Thus, I conclude, perhaps over-cautiously, that at present it is difficult to say whether or not Teotihuacanos tended to think of their society as divided into exactly two well-defined classes. The other possibilities are that they tended to deny any sharp distinction between social categories or that they thought of fundamental distinctions among three or more categories.

From an etic viewpoint, in any complex society there are bound to be many gradations in actual power, prestige, and wealth, and the positions of individuals must change over time. If offices are normally held for life, the rate of such changes will presumably be slower than if there is circulation in and out of offices, and changes will be fastest if such circulation is obligatory. In all societies, however, there is surely some degree of social mobility, whether it is emically acknowledged or not; and increases or decreases in wealth will facilitate upward or downward mobility in power, office, and status, whether or not that is emically thinkable.

For Teotihuacan, there is ample evidence, from an etic point of view, that a simple dichotomy between elite and commoner is oversimple. However, vast amounts need to be learned about the relative numbers of persons or households of different status, their spatial distributions, rates of mobility, how different offices were conceived and related to one another, and just how and to what extent the diverse dimensions of class and office (emic) and wealth and power (viewable both emically and etically) interacted with one another.

One of the many questions that might be asked concerns the relative proportions of persons who held positions intermediate between the very high and the average. If, empirically, there were intermediate positions (on any of the above dimensions) that were occupied by considerably fewer people than those either higher or lower, we could say that, apart from emic considerations, there was an etic sense in which the society was composed of distinct classes.[4] At present we cannot answer this question; it is only one of many that can be posed about Teotihuacan society.

Notes

1. I thank Susan Evans for having provided a generous supply of the novels of Anthony Trollope for the Teotihuacan Archaeological Research Center.

2. These excavations have been carried out as projects of the Instituto Nacional de Antropología e Historia, under the direction of Arqlgo. Rubén Cabrera C. Since 1988, I have been associate director. The expertise of Saburo Sugiyama has been especially valuable throughout. Vital financial support has come from the National Geographic Society and the National Endowment for the Humanities.

3. These studies have been supported by grants to various individuals and institutions from the National Science Foundation, the National Endowment for the Humanities, the Wenner-Gren Foundation, the American Council of Learned Societies, the Social Sciences and Humanities Research Council of Canada, and the Ivey Foundation.

4. Formally, this is analogous to the empirical question of whether, in a particular archaeological assemblage, the frequencies of scores on some descriptive variable exhibited by objects show a distribution with more than one well-defined peak (or mode). Such multimodalities are often the best clues we have for inferring emically salient artifact categories. In the case of social classes, there are many additional lines of relevant evidence, as I have suggested above. It is perhaps hard not to interpret discontinuities in social variables as evidence for emically

distinct social categories, but a "social pyramid" in which frequencies decline monotonically as one moves from average to highest status also does not seem inconsistent with emic class distinctions.

14. Royal Families, Royal Texts: Examples from the Zapotec and Maya

Joyce Marcus

ALL the well-known cultures of late prehispanic Mesoamerica—Aztec, Mixtec, Zapotec, and Maya—were characterized by the hierarchical arrangement of classes known as social stratification. As one reads the archaeological literature on these cultures, however, one finds considerable confusion about the number of social strata involved. For example, we have some articles claiming three, four, five, or even more social classes for the Maya, and others arguing that the Classic and Postclassic Maya had an "emerging middle class."

Such reconstructions are inaccurate in light of what is known ethnohistorically, and the source of confusion is not hard to find. Many archaeologists are trying to reconstruct the Maya based on our Western, secular, commercial society, rather than on Spanish eyewitness accounts of actual Mesoamerican states. Each time such archaeologists find a house or a burial that appears to be different from previous examples, they create a new class for ancient society.

In this paper I attempt to cut through some of this confusion by looking at ethnohistoric accounts of two indigenous Mesoamerican states, the Zapotec of Oaxaca and the Maya of the Yucatan Peninsula and Southern lowlands. By referring to other ancient Mesoamerican societies such as the Mixtec and Aztec, I also attempt to show what terms like "stratum," "class," "elite," and "wealth" meant in the context of such states.

Stratification

As disappointing as it may seem to some of my colleagues, no known Mesoamerican state had more than two strata: an upper stratum of hereditary nobility and a lower stratum of commoners. Confusion has arisen because each stratum had within it significant differences in rank, role, and profession. The upper stratum had within it a ruler, royal family members, major nobility, and minor nobility. The lower stratum could have traders, farmers, landless serfs, and slaves. None of these differences in rank or profession, however, was as significant as the institution that provided the gulf between the two strata: *class endogamy*.

Within the upper stratum, minor nobility could marry major nobility, and major nobility could marry members of royal families; they were not, however, supposed to marry commoners. Within the lower stratum, slaves could marry farmers, and farmers could marry traders; none could marry nobles, although some rulers took commoner mistresses. Thus, the two strata were kept separate. A successful trader, no matter how wealthy, remained a commoner; a minor noble, regardless of economic circumstances, remained a member of the hereditary nobility. This, at least, is how the Indians themselves viewed the system as working.

Archaeologists have often confused this situation by picturing the ancient Aztec or Maya as having socioeconomic classes like those of our society. They did not, and our society is not a good analogy for theirs. Think, for a moment, of British society, which has both socioeconomic classes and vestiges of hereditary nobility. Some of the wealthiest members of British society today are rock musicians of humble birth. Regardless of their wealth, these commoners can never hope to accede to the throne as do members of the hereditary nobility.

Thus, for ancient Mesoamerica, we should use the term "elite" in one of the ways given by George Marcus (1983a:8): "*Elite* literally meant the elect—persons formally chosen in some social process—and, particularly in a theological context, those chosen by God." For Mesoamerican states, the elite were not those chosen by men, but the hereditary nobles whose ancestors had been chosen to rule because they were supernatural rather than mortal.

The Ideology of Stratification

Mesoamerican stratification was reinforced by the belief that the nobility and commoners had separate origins far back in time. Nobles frequently claimed descent from supernatural forces or nonhuman beings, while commoners were seen as descending from other commoners, or from "mud men" or "stone men" who had emerged from fissures in the earth.

The Mixtec nobility, for example, claimed descent from certain trees growing along the river at Apoala, a rather small, unprepossessing locality in northern Oaxaca that was forever known as the "birthplace of the Mixtec rulers." A 1593 passage (Reyes 1593 [1976]) recounts this divine descent as follows:

It was a common belief among the native Mixtec speakers that the origin and beginnings of their pagan gods and rulers was in Apoala, a town in the Mixteca, which in their language is called *yuta tnoho*, which is "river where the rulers come from," because they are said to have split off from some trees that grew out of that river and that have special names. They also call that town *yuta tnuhu*, which is the "river of the lineages," and this is the more appropriate name and the one that fits it best.

In contrast, Mixtec commoners, the "original inhabitants," emerged from fissures and crevices in the earth's surface and were considered to be stone or mud people (Mary Smith 1973b:68-69). These commoners were said to have been conquered by those who came from Apoala, the hereditary rulers

(Reyes 1890:i-ii). The ancient Mixtec elite were stratum-endogamous, but usually community-exogamous. Commoners, on the other hand, were both stratum- and community-endogamous (see Spores 1965, 1967, 1983).

In addition to a belief in the separate origins of Mixtec nobility and commoners, the Mixtec language itself was used to reinforce the differences between nobility and commoners. For example, in Mixtec there was a completely separate set of terms for the body parts of the ruler and for the body parts of a commoner (see Marcus and Flannery 1983:table 8.1). Mixtec also displayed a rich variety of expressions to distinguish royal marriages from those of mere commoners. Expressions for royal marriage included "to sanctify or purify the empire;" "the nobleman drinks pulque;" "the nobility joins hands"/"the nobility shares tribute;" and "the royal celebration of the mat" (Alvarado 1593 [1962]; Reyes 1593 [1976], 1890; Mary Smith 1973a). The expression for "royal dowry" included the term for chocolate (*dzehua*), a beverage said to have been restricted to the nobility. These and other Mixtec expressions were used to associate the nobility with (1) purity, cleansing, and sanctity; (2) special beverages, such as pulque and chocolate, served in special drinking vessels; (3) the woven mat as a symbol of authority; and (4) the receipt of tribute from commoners.

Another significant attribute associated with Mixtec nobility was generosity. This was extremely important because it masked the actual asymmetrical relations that existed between nobles and commoners. Although all Mesoamerican societies displayed unequal access to goods and to positions in the sociopolitical hierarchy, both nobles and commoners used language indicating that it was "good" to be governed by nobles because they were "generous people."

Social Mobility

Adding to the confusion that the term "middle class" provides, some archaeologists have argued that "wealth" and "achievement" provided "social mobility" in late prehispanic Mesoamerica. In fact, stratification based on noble birth and class endogamy impeded such mobility. The ancient Zapotec acknowledged that wealth, unlike stratum membership, was a fleeting rather than permanent condition. In one sixteenth-century dictionary of the Valley Zapotec language (Córdova 1578b), there is a simile in which the Zapotec compare wealth to a river that runs hard during the rainy season, but dries up during the dry season (*penitixenicicanicalayna*). This expression is not unlike our "feast or famine," which emphasizes a variable state rather than a permanent status.

Determining the degree of advancement through achievement that took place within ancient Mesoamerican societies is a worthy research endeavor, but one that is difficult to address for any period before Spanish contact. The Aztec system provides some evidence for advancement through military and political service, but most cases involve minor nobility becoming major nobility, not actual commoners crossing the line from lower to upper stratum. Certainly we do not have many documented cases in which true commoners became members of the nobility by accumulating wealth.

This being the case, how convincingly could we show that a Late Classic Maya tomb was that of a "middle class" individual? Some commoners undoubtedly achieved success through skill, craftsmanship, or service, and may even have been chosen to serve in the palace of the nobility, but nothing we know about Mesoamerica suggests that they would have constituted a third class-endogamous stratum. And having been born of mud, or having emerged from below the surface of the earth, they could never belong to the stratum of people descended from supernatural beings. This being the case, I would strongly argue that we should not apply to the Maya terms such as "middle class," which are more appropriate to societies like our own.

Writing and the Elite

In this paper I look at two Mesoamerican stratified societies, the Maya and the Zapotec. Both societies had hieroglyphic writing, which was used as a tool of the upper stratum. Neither society was "literate" in the sense in which we use the term, because the ability to read and write was a jealously guarded skill restricted to a subset of the elite class and the scribes who served them. Far from being shared with commoners, the ability to write was one of the things that reinforced the gulf between the rulers and the ruled. As we shall see, most writing was concerned with, and controlled by, the elite.

Maya Nobles and Commoners: Separate Descent

The upper stratum of Postclassic Maya society consisted of *almehen*, a term that has been glossed as "noble," but which also means "illustrious individual by lineage" or "offspring with known descent in both the male and female line." When the ancient Yucatec Maya wished to disparage the Itza, who came from outside the region to occupy Chichen Itza, they called them "those without mothers and fathers" (Roys 1933:178)—meaning that the Itza could not trace their noble descent in both male and female lines as could the Yucatec Maya nobility. Other important Maya terms, such as *ah chibal*, refer to "royal blood" or "noble lineage" (Martínez Hernández 1929:86), while *ix ikal* refers to "royal women."

By maintaining the belief that as a group they had enjoyed a separate, divine descent, Maya royalty remained the only individuals who could serve as mediators between the secular commoners, on the one hand, and the divine supernatural beings (including the rulers' ancestors), on the other. Given such a powerful origin myth, the position of royalty and nobles was sanctified, made secure, and considered unalterable. The world order depended on the members of each stratum believing that they had separate origins, with that of the upper stratum being divine. Reciting myth and participating in special rites served to establish and reenact the sacred links between the rulers and the divine.

Maya nobility were closely linked to supernatural forces, especially the sun and the moon. Despite the demise of Maya nobility following the conquest, this myth is still preserved among some contemporary Maya groups. For example, the Mopan Maya of Belize retain a story of the Sun and Moon on earth and how they came to occupy the heavens. They say Sun wooed a girl; they were the first couple to have sexual relations. After spending a while on earth, the Sun, his wife, and his brothers ascended to the sky, where his wife became the Moon, and his brothers became the morning and evening stars (Thompson 1930, 1965). Thus, those that once had dwelt on earth ascended to assume their permanent positions in the sky as planets or stars.

In addition to the sun and moon, Maya nobility were closely linked to a variety of other celestial phenomena. Lightning ([hats'] chac) was an extremely powerful supernatural, closely allied to wind, rain, and the sky itself. Two-headed serpents (chan, can) and four lightnings (chaco'ob) were associated with four winds and the four world directions. As I have emphasized elsewhere (e.g., Marcus 1973, 1976a, 1978, 1983c), ca'an (sky, heaven, paradise) and can (four, gift, snake, serpent) are highly charged symbolic words that could refer to four regional capitals, to the rectangular universe, or to the four-sided heavens—the abode of the powerful supernaturals. Those Maya terms were also used to refer to the abode of the royal family, the palace (ca'anal na, "the enlarged, exalted house on high"). In his terrestrial domain, the Maya ruler was thought to live much as the supernaturals did in their celestial dome, since he was the link between the domain on high (ca'anal) and the earth below (Marcus 1978, 1983c, 1987).

Another extremely important characteristic of a Maya noble was generosity. The term almehen meant not only "noble," but also "generous." The longer expression almehen ol referred to the "warm-hearted," "good-hearted," "generous" nature of the noble (e.g., Martínez Hernández 1929:119).

In contrast, commoners (yalba uinic; or townspeople, pach kah uinic) were thought to have been made from clay (books of Chilam Balam), earth (Relaciones de Yucatan 1898-90:Bk I:79), or earth mixed with dry grass (López de Cogolludo 1688 [1867-68]:Bk 4, chapter 7). Such lowly terrestrial origins contrasted with the celestial origins of the royalty and nobility.

There is one Postclassic Yucatec Maya term that could lead to some future confusion about the presence of "middle-class Maya." The sixteenth-century Motul dictionary gives one term, azmen uinic, defined as "hombre entre principal y plebeyo, de mediano estado" (Martínez Hernández 1929:69). However, there is no evidence that this is a reference to a third stratum of Maya men and women, people who intermarried neither with royalty nor with commoners. I see at least three possible explanations for the term.

1. It could refer to a male member of the minor nobility. There were undoubtedly many such nobles who were too far removed from the direct line of royal descent ever to rule, but who would have enjoyed privileges not shared by commoners. (See the Zapotec term *tija joana*, below.)

2. It could refer to a male commoner who held some significant elected or appointed office. In many Mesoamerican states, respected commoners were elected by their peers or appointed by the ruler to positions of responsibility. "Ward heads" such as the Aztec *calpixque*, or "tribute collectors" such as the Zapotec *golaba* and the Aztec *tequitlatoque* are examples (e.g., Córdova 1578b [1942], Zorita 1941). Despite the prestige of their offices, such men remained commoners and married commoner women.

3. A third possibility is that the term refers to someone of mixed ancestry. Although male rulers took only elite women as their official, legitimate wives, some took commoner women as concubines. The offspring of such a union would be ineligible to rule (since he could not reckon elite descent in both his father's and mother's lines), but might have enjoyed greater prestige than a commoner. However, if this were what the term refers to, one would expect the Colonial Spaniards simply to have translated it "son of a noble father and a commoner mother."

In sum, we shall probably have to wait until we find more contexts for the term *azmen uinic* before we can accurately interpret it.

Zapotec Nobles and Commoners: Separate Descent

The upper stratum of Zapotec society consisted of two groups of lineages. The first of these was the royal lineage, *tija coqui*, "the lineage of the rulers." The second group contained all other hereditary elite and was designated *tija joana*, "the lineage of the nobles." As with the Maya, a frequent term applied to the Zapotec noble was *penipaalana*, "a generous person," "a magnanimous person, liberal in expenditures"—a label that indicates how the commoners regarded and addressed the nobility (Córdova 1578b [1942]:244, 253, 283). Commoners expected to receive feasts and to attend rituals hosted by these "generous persons." As mentioned above, such references mask the fact that, as a result of the labor of their commoners, the nobles could afford to be generous.

People of the Zapotec lower stratum, the commoners, were designated by the term *tijapeniqueche* meaning "lineage of the townspeople" (*tija* = lineage, *peni* = people, *queche* = town).

Various sumptuary rules distinguished the upper stratum. Only elite Zapotec were permitted to eat deer meat, rabbits, and turkeys (Zárate 1581 [1905]:200); the commoner diet is reported to have been restricted to lizards, snakes, beans, maize tortillas, fruits, chile, tunas (prickly pear fruits), nopales (prickly pear pods), and a variety of "greens" (*quelites*) (Canseco

1580 [1905]:149-50; Zárate 1581 [1905]:200, 204). While excavated middens suggest that the diet of the commoners was not quite this limited, these ethnohistoric documents do give us an idea of what the rules of stratification were.

Drinking chocolate beverages was also restricted to the Zapotec elite (RMEH 1928:vol. 2:129-30). Nobles were permitted to wear cotton clothing, sandals, feathered shirts, lip-plugs, feather headdresses, gold and precious stone necklaces, and other jewelry; commoners were forced to wear maguey clothing and not permitted to wear jewelry (Zárate 1581 [1905]:199-200). Zapotec commoners also used a set of "reverential verbs" when addressing the nobility (Córdova 1578a [1886]:55, 95).

An important similarity between the Maya and Zapotec was that both were concerned with establishing the deeds, genealogies, marriages, and conquests of their rulers through permanent records carved in stone. Let us now turn our attention to the first appearance of writing in those two areas and then look at the ways in which writing became a tool in the hands of the elite.

The Origins of Mesoamerican Writing

Writing made its appearance at the chiefdom level of sociopolitical development in three areas: among the Zapotec of the Valley of Oaxaca (600-500 B.C.), among the (possibly Zoque-speaking) groups occupying the Gulf Coast of Mexico (100 B.C.-A.D. 100), and among the Terminal Preclassic Maya (A.D. 1-300) (Marcus 1976c). In contrast, many other Mesoamerican chiefdoms (and even later states) neither developed writing nor borrowed it, although they were in contact with groups who possessed it.

Although limited writing (and very elaborate iconography) characterizes a number of the aforementioned chiefdoms, it was at the later state level that writing truly flourished. The change from a ranked society (where there is shared descent from apical ancestors) to a stratified society (whose members can demonstrate separate descent) was one of the essential changes in ancient Mesoamerican societies from A.D. 1 to 400. Such a fundamental ideological change was made more permanent by being engraved in stone, made more intelligible by that message being conveyed in both the art and the writing, and made more sacred by linking the ruler to supernatural creatures and supernatural powers.

The Control of Writing by the Royal Administrators

What were the topics that most interested the rulers of early Mesoamerican states? Most Classic Maya and Zapotec hieroglyphic texts display a limited range of themes: (1) establishing divine descent and royal genealogies; (2) recording personal events in the life of the ruler and his immediate family (e.g., his birth, accession to the throne, marriage, military feats, death); (3)

recounting intercommunity raids, battles, or conquests; and (4) recording the formation of alliances, both marital and military.

What kinds of information do not appear in these monuments? Not included are censuses, discussions of land use, economic policies, tribute exacted, labor service, and events that occurred in the lives of commoners. Other prehispanic states did keep such records—the Aztec, for example, with paper books and the Inca with knotted cords called *kipu*. Tribute and census records were more often the concern of bureaucratic states or empires like these, which in some ways provide a contrast to the Zapotec and Maya states under consideration here.

Maya Royalty and Royal Texts

Maya royalty devoted a significant amount of energy linking themselves to royal ancestors, to powerful supernaturals, and to deeds befitting powerful lords. To this end, they employed both writing and iconography on their monuments.

Iconography and writing complement each other. Iconography is used to create a permanent visual picture, while writing is used to present a verbal caption or descriptive statement. For example, on their stone monuments Maya lords are shown with the ideal physiognomy and posture of their culture. The ruler carries a set of standardized paraphernalia appropriate to his office. He is usually identifiable by his serenity, his attire, the artifacts he carries, and his size and placement in the scene; his depiction is the opposite of portraiture, for he is without imperfections. In contrast, commoners are frequently depicted in a more naturalistic fashion, often lacking serenity and having imperfect features. The accompanying text usually provides the specifics: one or more dates, the name of the ruler, one or more of his titles, and the nature of the event, such as the date of his accession to the throne or his capture of a sacrificial victim.

To show the humiliation of a noble who had been taken prisoner, the Maya artist carved an individual with holes in his ears (to show that he had once worn ear-plugs, now removed—for example, on Stela 12 from Piedras Negras), usually depicting him nude or nearly so (a particularly humiliating situation for the elite, who normally were burdened with layers of beautifully woven fabrics and elaborate feather garments), with his arms bound behind his back with rope. Instead of the serene faces that nobles displayed, captives were shown with grimaces; instead of the formal postures of victorious elite, captives were shown in unnatural, awkward, and contorted body positions (see Marcus 1974b). The hieroglyphs that provide the details of the deeds of the captor are usually more numerous, larger in size, and in high relief, while those describing the captive are fewer, smaller, and incised.

For example, the presentation of bound captives is shown on Lintel 4 and Stela 12 from Piedras Negras, while the taking of captives is shown on such

Fig. 14.1. Lintel 8 at Yaxchilan, Mexico: on the right, Bird Jaguar is shown capturing Jeweled Skull; on the left, a lesser lord is shown capturing another named prisoner. Carved area measures 0.78 m by 0.87 m (redrawn by Kay Clahassey from T. Proskouri-akoff 1963:fig.1).

monuments as Stela 3 from La Mar; Lintels 8 and 45 from Yaxchilan; and Lintels 1, 2, and 3 from Bonampak. Prisoners were depicted as human pedestals beneath the feet of victorious lords; bound captives were trod upon by their captors. When ascending or descending the steps of their palaces or temples, some Maya rulers actually stepped on the body of a captive carved on the stairway. Such prisoner stairways are known from several sites, including Yaxchilan, Tamarindito, and Dos Pilas. This prac-tice of rulers' treading on the bodies of victims destined for sacrifice is also known from stairways leading up to Building M at the Zapotec capital of Monte Alban (Marcus 1974b:plate 9).

Lintel 8 at Yaxchilan (fig. 14.1) depicts the capture of two prisoners (Proskouriakoff 1963:150-52). On the right, Bird Jaguar, the Yaxchilan ruler, is shown taking Jeweled Skull (whose name is given on his right thigh). The captive to the left has his name on his left thigh. The text on the upper left begins with the date 7 Imix 14 Tzec followed by the verb "was captured," and then the name "Jeweled Skull." On the upper right, the text continues with the glyph meaning "his prisoner," the name "Bird Jaguar," and the emblem glyph of Yaxchilan. The text in the center (above the heads of the prisoners) begins with the title "captor," followed by the name of the captive at left, then by three hieroglyphs that identify the "lesser lord" standing to the left of the captives.

Another iconographic device underscoring the elite/nonelite dichotomy is the size disparity of the figures. Many Maya rulers are shown greater than life-size, while commoners and captives are smaller than life-size (for example, Stela 1, Dos Pilas; Stelae 29 and 33, Naranjo). Thus, when rulers and captives are juxtaposed, the disparity in size conveys very effectively who is on top and who is not.

While some iconographic elements had a wider distribution, the Maya nobility had a monopoly on writing. This meant that the nobility had control of history, determining the content of the monuments by commissioning the scribes and lapidaries to write and carve texts. The nobles were trained in special schools, educated by other nobles who were often priests. Nobles learned to read and to understand some of the complexities of rituals, calendric cycles and events, and astronomical phenomena.

In contrast, commoners were forced to consult lower-status diviners (*ah kunal*, *ah chilan*, *ah kin nek*), who aided them in important decisions involving events such as marriage and child naming. Diviners intervened on behalf of the commoners, helping them to reach wise decisions by consulting calendric books and almanacs, that the commoners could not read, or by using divining materials such as maize kernels, beans, and small stones. The latter were sometimes painted blue, the color associated with offerings and sacrifice (Landa [1566] in Tozzer 1941:117, 154 [note 775], 130 [note 608]). During special rites, diviners contacted the supernatural for advice about the future.

Since writing was an elite prerogative, only the Maya upper stratum—not the society as a whole—can be characterized as literate. The preservation of elite endogamy, the perpetuation of a belief in divine descent, the conduct of exclusive rites, the wearing of restricted attire and paraphernalia, and the control of access to all written records were critical to the maintenance of the Maya state.

Another strategy of the elite was to link the origins of writing and the skill to use it with the supernatural (M. Coe 1977). If writing was sacred, then it was acceptable that only the nobility, with their separate divine descent, would have access to it. An iconographic example linking writing to the supernatural is shown on an incised bone from Burial 116 at Tikal. Burial 116, below Temple I, contained the body of Ruler "Double-Comb," who took office in A.D. 682 and died sometime after A.D. 711 (C. Jones 1977; C. Jones and L. Satterthwaite 1982). On the incised bone is a hand with a writing brush emerging from the open mouth of a heavenly serpent

Fig. 14.2. Incised bone discovered in ruler "Double-Comb's" tomb (Burial 116) beneath Temple I at Tikal: emerging from the open jaws of a heavenly being is a hand holding a brush (redrawn by Kay Clahassey from M. D. Coe 1977:fig.3).

(fig. 14.2). The fantastic creature is sacred, and so are both the hand and the message the scribe will write. Indeed, that same serpent was linked to royalty, nobility, and the high priest. One of the Yucatec Maya terms for the high priest himself was *ahaucan,* "Lord Serpent," a person who had special control of writing:

In him was the key of their learning and it was to these matters that they dedicated themselves mostly. . . . They provided priests for the towns when they were needed, examining them in the sciences and ceremonies, and committed to them the duties of their office, and [set] the good example to people and provided them with books and sent them forth. And they employed themselves in the duties of the temples and in teaching their sciences as well as in writing books about them. (Landa [1566] in Tozzer 1941:27)

Maya royalty recorded their personal histories on their stelae, often setting them up in lines in chronological order to be read from left to right (for example, at Piedras Negras and Calakmul), with each monument covering events during a five-, ten-, or twenty-year span. In such cases, each of the stelae has a shallow history. This history recorded on stelae can be contrasted with the Maya use of another medium, the wall panel, which records events that occurred in the much more distant past. Such wall panels were often used at Palenque (for example, in the Temple of the Cross, Temple of the Foliated Cross, and Temple of the Sun) to convey a history that had considerably more time depth and included occurrences we would classify as mythological or legendary because of their association with ancient dates. References to earlier rulers, and/or to a sequence of biological ancestors, occupy parts of these wall panels, but they need to be viewed with skepticism because some are associated with ancient myths.

Zapotec Royalty and Royal Texts

Early in the history of the Zapotec state centered at Monte Alban, ca. 100 B.C.-A.D. 200, one of the themes the elite chose to emphasize was the territorial limits of their realm. These limits were defined by hieroglyphs of communities subjugated along their borders (Marcus 1976b, 1980, 1983b, 1984). Another early theme was the taking of important captives from either tribute-paying towns or militarily subjugated places.

At Early Classic Monte Alban (A.D. 200-450), Zapotec monuments tended to be huge monoliths that could be viewed from a great distance, usually depicting the Zapotec ruler greater than life-size, much like the Maya rulers on stelae at Quirigua, Calakmul, and other sites. Following the decline of Monte Alban, after ca. A.D. 600, two of the prominent themes on stone monuments became royal marriages and royal genealogies. Some of these records were placed in royal residences or tombs (e.g., Marcus 1980:61-63, 1983a:191). Both royal marriage and divine descent were typically depicted on small slabs, designed to be read close up. The small size of these slabs, and of the hieroglyphic writing itself, contrasts with the larger monuments of the Early Classic.

The decision of the Zapotec elite to discontinue carving huge monuments for public display and to stop setting them up close to monumental public buildings is interesting. Many of the smaller and more private royal records were created to be kept in the antechambers of tombs. After the decline of the hilltop capital at Monte Alban, a number of smaller valley-floor centers, such as Cuilapan, Zaachila, Mitla, Matatlan, Lambityeco, and Macuilxochitl, began to use these small slabs to record the marriages and genealogies of their local dynasties (Marcus 1980, 1983a). These monuments may indicate a growing interest on the part of the dispersed Zapotec nobility in maintaining strong links to the royal families of the earlier Classic, as well as reasserting their claim to special rights and privileges. Many of these genealogical slabs occur in towns whose local nobility had been excluded from the written record during Monte Alban's apogee. With Monte Alban's control waning, a whole new set of opportunities opened up for the local dynasties scattered throughout the Valley of Oaxaca, one of which was royal marriage alliance.

Zapotec royal marriage was often depicted by a man and woman sitting or kneeling on individual mats or on "hill signs," facing each other and usually holding bowls or bags (Marcus 1983a:fig. 7.4). Above the marital pair was an iconographic motif A. Caso (1928) called the "celestial jaws," clearly a stylized mandible with teeth. The hieroglyphic names of the couple were usually given, as well as the names of relatives or immediate ancestors.

The celestial jaws apparently conveyed the divine descent of the Zapotec nobility. In some highly conventionalized depictions it is difficult to see the jaw and teeth (Marcus 1983a:fig. 7.3), but on a monument attributed to Zaachila (Marcus 1983a:fig. 7.4) one can clearly see the open celestial jaw, its teeth, some possible marine shells, and a royal ancestor handing a necklace to one of his earthly descendants.

Fig. 14.3. Fragment of a Zapotec genealogical slab, showing the celestial jaws motif (top center), which conveys divine descent to the two couples below. Exact provenience unknown; but believed to be from Matatlan, dating stylistically to A.D. 600-900. Size: 0.53 m by 0.62 m (drawn by Mark Orsen).

Another genealogical slab (fig. 14.3), apparently from Matatlan, shows an elderly couple below the celestial jaws. Descending from those jaws is a plant with leaves. The bearded male and his female companion wear elaborate feather headdresses. Atop her feather headdress is an apparent bird, and she holds a staff with leaves and a bird's head. Below this seated couple is another couple: a male (only his head remains) beneath the bearded male and a female beneath the woman. This slab gives us the names of the seated couple and their relatives beneath them. Only the woman in the lower right corner lacks a speech scroll.

Another example of the celestial jaws conveying divine descent is seen in a circular stone reported to have been found in the district of Zimatlan, in which a couple sits atop a "hill sign" (fig. 14.4). Also supplied are Zapotec calendric names and dates, both derived from the *pije* or 260-day ritual calendar. Rather than a plant, in this case, we see a bird descending from the celestial jaws.

Thus, like the Maya elite, the Zapotec nobility were linked to the sky (*quiepaa*), to celestial birds, and to supernaturals. For the Zapotec, the opening to *quiepaa* or heaven was an open fleshless mandible; for the Maya,

Fig. 14.4. Circular stone, reportedly from La Ciénaga near Zimatlan (Valley of Oaxaca) showing the celestial jaws motif with a bird descending; a man (left) and woman (right) are seated atop a hill sign. The hieroglyphic names and dates are drawn from the Zapotec pije or 260-day ritual calendar. Size: 0.43 m in diameter (drawn by Mark Orsen).

the lower world was reached through an open fleshless mandible. For example, the famous sarcophagus lid in the tomb beneath the Temple of the Inscriptions at Palenque shows the deceased ruler in "suspended animation" within the fleshless jaws of the underworld (see Morley, Brainerd, and Sharer 1983:fig. 4.23).

Royal women played prominent and changing roles in the Zapotec state. From A.D. 200 to 500, royal women were shown paired with their spouses in tomb murals at Monte Alban (Marcus 1983d:fig. 5.10) and in stone sculpture elsewhere. After A.D. 600, royal women from different dynasties were shown in marriage scenes that apparently linked valley-floor centers. Such a pattern of royal marriage alliance also characterized the Classic Maya state, particularly with regard to the secondary centers below regional capitals (Marcus 1973, 1976a, 1983c).

The Manipulation of Writing by the Maya Elite

Originally used as a tool for reinforcing the birth, death, marriage, conquests, and right to govern of legitimate rulers, writing could also become a tool of the usurper. At various times in Maya history, there were breaks in the official line of succession, resulting in a scramble for power among younger brothers, brothers-in-law, and even more distant relatives of the deceased ruler. Usurpers often used monumental texts to rewrite history and solidify their claim to the throne they had seized.

The taking of office was often the first moment at which a ruler's records were carved (Marcus 1976a, 1987). This meant that his name was usually not mentioned in any text until after he had acceded to the throne. Usurpers, or nobles not really in the direct line of succession, could use their accession monuments to alter both their birth dates and their credentials.

An example of the retrospective placement of birth dates comes from the Palenque ruler originally called "Sun Shield" or "Propeller Shield" (Ruz Lhuillier 1954b; Kubler 1969:22; Marcus 1974a, 1976a; Berlin 1977). His supposed birth date of March 6, A.D. 603 (9.8.9.13.0 8 Ahau 13 Pop) is a "round" date that may have been selected many years after the fact, perhaps at the time of his accession to the throne. The first text that records this ruler was actually carved when he was already supposedly fifty-seven years old; there are no earlier monuments to verify his date of birth. Propeller Shield, like many Maya rulers, had an opportunity to backdate his birth, either to pretend that he was born before other candidates for succession or to make himself more senior in wisdom and experience.

An awareness of this practice of backdating may help us to solve one of the major (if little discussed) problems with Propeller Shield of Palenque: the disparity between his claimed age and his presumed skeleton. The hieroglyphic inscription on his sarcophagus lid claims that he died in A.D. 683 at the age of eighty. Yet the skeleton in the sarcophagus, on the basis of a study of suture closings and other standard physical anthropological measures of age, is that of a man between forty and fifty years of age (Dávalos Hurtado and Romano Pacheco 1973:253) or perhaps even barely forty when he died (Ruz Lhuillier 1977:293). Propeller Shield's first monumental text was carved around 9.11.6.16.11 (7 Chuen 4 Chen), some twenty-four years before his death, allowing him ample opportunity to push back his birth date, and even his date of accession, for political reasons. At the time of this first monument, he was supposedly already fifty-seven years old—an age the physical anthropologists would say he had not even attained at his death in 9.12.11.5.18 (6 Etz'nab 11 Yax). While there are other possibilities (for example, the individual in the sarcophagus might not be the one mentioned on the lid), it seems likely that Propeller Shield deliberately exaggerated his age.

Nor was Propeller Shield the only ruler to do so. His son took office 132 days after his father's death, when he was supposedly forty-eight. The son's successor was purportedly fifty-seven years old at his accession. Later Palenque rulers supposedly took office at the ages of forty-three and fifty-two (Ruz Lhuillier 1977).

The lack of fit between these advanced ages recorded in hieroglyphic texts and the physical anthropological data on the elite skeletons at Palenque and elsewhere led Alberto Ruz Lhuillier (1977) to ask the rhetorical question: "did the Maya have a gerontocracy?" He had trouble accepting the idea, since the skeletal evidence did not show the Maya elite living to such advanced ages. He concluded that the Maya rulers were not living into their eighties and nineties. The Maya monument carvers were exaggerating the ages of some rulers, perhaps for some of the reasons suggested above. Significantly, these cases of deliberate backdating appear to follow gaps in the direct line of succession.

The case of the Palenque ruler is not unique. Other rulers are reported to have lived well into their nineties (for example, at Yaxchilan, where Proskouriakoff [1963] noted that she could find no clear birth or accession date for Shield Jaguar). In all these cases, we are missing monuments that record a *contemporaneous* record of the birth date: the ruler thus had the opportunity to select an advantageous date (Marcus 1974a, 1976a, 1987).

One possible goal of manipulating the facts in a monumental text was to claim descent from past rulers who were, in fact, not one's own direct ancestors. Such false genealogical claims were more likely to occur when a ruler died without a direct heir, making the line of succession less clear. There may have been many elite candidates whose factions supported them, and the winner was probably encouraged to solidify his claim to the throne by rewriting his genealogy. In such cases, the door would have been open to a more distant relative who had the skill to usurp the throne.

One ruler who seems to have acceded to the throne following a gap in succession was Shield Jaguar of Yaxchilan. His death was recorded on various lintels (Lintel 27, for example) as A.D. 742 (9.15.10.17.14 6 Ix 12 Yaxkin; Proskouriakoff 1963, 1964). There was another ten-year gap until his successor Bird Jaguar took over in A.D. 752 (9.16.1.0.0 11 Ahau 8 Tzec on Stela 11). Bird Jaguar's accession monument records the date of that event, provides an apparent depiction of Shield Jaguar and his wife, and also appears to show the transfer of power from Shield Jaguar to a younger man, presumably a descendant.

Who ruled Yaxchilan during the ten-year gap between the end of Shield Jaguar's reign and the beginning of Bird Jaguar's? Was Bird Jaguar, in fact, not the direct descendant of Shield Jaguar? If he was, why did he not succeed him immediately? Was he merely too young at the time? Did a regent, unspecified on any monument, rule for him until he was old enough? Or do the gaps in succession before and after Shield Jaguar reflect periods when there were no clear heirs, times when more distant relatives of the previous ruler struggled for power? Our problem in answering these questions underscores the fact that the ancient Maya put on their monuments only what each ruler wanted future nobles to believe, sometimes deliberately altering his true age and genealogy.

Another possible example of a dispute over succession is recorded on Lintel 3 at Piedras Negras and dates to A.D. 757 (9.16.6.10.19; Marcus 1976a:85-87). An emissary from Yaxchilan named Bat Jaguar traveled by canoe to Piedras Negras, where he met with other nobles to discuss the naming of a new ruler. When the Piedras Negras ruler died a few days later, a new ruler acceded to the throne, presumably with Bat Jaguar's approval.

Such examples show that the Maya elite had the capacity to write and, perhaps more importantly, to rewrite history, making modifications as they saw fit. Their control of writing and monument carving set them apart as a stratum, allowing them to select the subject matter and even to change the dates of important events. Like Itzcoatl, the fourth Mexica ruler, who burned the ancient books after he took office in A.D. 1427 in order to write a new and "official" history, the Maya elite were not trying to record the truth, but to decide what the official version of truth would be.

Zapotec Militarism and State Art

Just prior to the emergence of the state and during its peak years, art and writing were manipulated by the Zapotec elite. They created impressive buildings with stone monuments depicting themes designed to show the state's power and the extent of its realm. These carvings included hundreds of sacrificial victims, the names of tribute-paying as well as subjugated communities, and the display of bound captives with their arms tied behind their backs. On still other slabs the Zapotec ruler is shown with a staff, spear, or elaborate feather headdress, seated on a throne or receiving emissaries.

Of the (approximately) fifteen stone monoliths publicly displayed in Monte Alban's Main Plaza during Period IIIa, at least six depict bound, high-status captives standing atop hill signs that evidently recorded their place of origin (Caso 1928; Marcus 1976b, 1983d). One of these is Stela 8, in which a man with elaborate headdress (but little in the way of other garments) stands on a hill sign containing a human head and mandible that identify his hometown (fig. 14.5). At the left are glyphs giving either his calendric name or date of capture. Bound captives on other stelae are shown in animal costume, often as jaguars. Zapotec rulers, like their Maya counterparts, are sometimes shown seated on a jaguar-skin throne or wearing jaguar pelts.

Stela 4 from Monte Alban shows an elaborately dressed Zapotec lord named "8 Deer," thrusting his spear into a hill sign on which he also stands

Fig. 14.5. Stela 8 at Monte Alban: a prisoner with arms bound behind his back stands atop a hill sign containing a human head and mandible indicating the name of his hometown; this stela and others in the South Platform commemorate Monte Alban's victories, A.D. 200-450. Size: 2.30 m by 1.75 m (drawn by Mark Orsen).

(fig. 14.6). Next to his spear is a footprint, a widespread Mesoamerican convention meaning "travel;" thus, this conquest may have involved a trip to a distant part of the Zapotec realm.

Fig. 14.6. Stela 4 at Monte Alban, showing the Zapotec lord "8 Deer," with an elaborate headdress containing elements of Cocijo (Lightning), thrusting his spear into a hill sign, a well-known convention for conquest from the later Mixtec codices. Size: 1.90 m by 0.78 m (drawn by Mark Orsen).

Such militaristic themes characterized the *early* centralized state of the Zapotec. As noted, following the decline of Monte Alban, communities on the valley floor concentrated on genealogical registers that showed divine descent and royal marriage, while the previous militaristic themes disappeared. For the Maya, both militaristic and genealogical themes persisted throughout the sequence, although militaristic themes predominated during the 200 years before the collapse.

Summary

Ethnohistoric evidence indicates that the Zapotec and Maya, like most Mesoamerican states, had only two class-endogamous social strata. The upper stratum included the ruler, the royal family, and major and minor hereditary nobility. For the purposes of this volume, these were the elite, those "elected by the divine supernaturals" to rule. The lower stratum consisted of commoners and slaves; even when commoners were respected craft specialists or wealthy traders, they could not expect to marry members of the nobility or accede to the throne.

The separation of these two strata was ideologically justified by the belief that, while commoners were born of mud or earth, the elite had descended from supernatural beings. Elite birth conferred many privileges not available to commoners, including special kinds of clothing, food, beverages, burial rituals, and a wide range of sumptuary goods. On the other hand, the elite were supposed to be generous to commoners.

The elite used language to distinguish themselves from commoners. When addressing members of the nobility, commoners had to employ a special vocabulary and a set of reverential verbs and verb endings. Hieroglyphic writing was at least partly based on the spoken language. It was also monopolized by the elite: only members of the upper stratum and their trained scribes could write. The texts and associated iconography of royal monuments were used (1) to reinforce the preordained cosmos and world order, (2) to link the upper stratum to royal ancestors and supernatural beings, (3) to legitimize the right to rule with deeds appropriate to royalty (such as the capture of enemies, the sacrifice of captives, and certain kinds of divination and ritual bloodletting), and (4) to put on record the marriages or military alliances between elites by carving them in stone. There is ample evidence to suggest that writing was a tool that could be manipulated to serve the ruler's goals. Some rulers apparently backdated their births, destroyed the monuments of previous rulers, and rewrote history; they probably also exaggerated their conquests and glossed over defeats and occasional usurpations of power.

We should be skeptical of papers that try to portray the Maya or Zapotec as literate societies with three, four, or even more social classes. These were typical prehispanic states with two class-endogamous strata, whose writing was just one of a number of elite monopolies, and our own Western society does not provide a good analogy for them.

Acknowledgments

Part of this work was made possible by a research grant from the National Endowment for the Humanities (RO-21433-75-460). I would also like to thank Henry Wright for his insightful comments on an earlier draft of this paper and Kay Clahassey and Mark Orsen for preparing the illustrations.

15. Late Postclassic and Colonial Period Elites at Otumba, Mexico: The Archaeological Dimensions

Thomas H. Charlton and
Deborah L. Nichols

WHEN Hernan Cortes entered the Basin of Mexico in 1519, it was the geopolitical core of the largest prehispanic state in Mesoamerica, the Aztec empire. Aztec society was structured in a complex hierarchy (summarized in table 15.1). As with other agrarian states, the most important class distinction was between nobility and commoners. A vaguely defined class of merchants and elite artisans had an intermediate status. Class status was largely—but not entirely—hereditary. It was legitimized through religion and law. Certain types of clothing and ornamentation could be worn only by the nobility (Anawalt 1980), nobles were judged in different courts than commoners (Offner 1983), and members of the nobility were the recipients of tribute. Within each class there were, however, differences in wealth, reflected in the size of landholdings (Gibson 1964:268; Harvey 1984) and variations in the proportion of the population constituting the nobility (e.g., 20 percent in Tenochtitlan [Davies 1987:121], 19 percent in Huexotzingo [Dyckerhoff and Prem 1976:160], and 7 percent in Tlaxcala [Davies 1987:121]). At the apex of Aztec society was the nobility (*hue tlatoani* or *señores universales*) of the Triple Alliance centers—Tenochtitlan, Texcoco, and Tacuba. Through warfare and alliance they had gained control of the other polities in the basin and had extended their domain to more distant places. After the early fifteenth century, formerly independent city-states in the basin, each with its own ruling elite (*tlatoani*), had become semiautonomous administrative units within the Triple Alliance. These provincial elites, however, continued to play important roles in local and regional integration. Although the Spanish conquest broke the power of the Triple Alliance and replaced it with hispanic central government, local Indian elites (*caciques*) continued to mediate between the Spanish administration and the Indian population through the *cabecera-sujeto* unit (the head town of a region with tributary settlements; Gibson 1964). Further reductions in the power of the caciques occurred in the mid-1500s with the introduction of the hispanic system of electing Indian officials and paying them salaries in lieu of allowing them to collect tribute in goods and services (Gibson 1964; Charlton 1986).

Table 15.1: Aztec Social Structure

Nobility		
	Rulers	*tlatoani* (sing.)
	"Chiefs"	*tecutli* (sing.)
	"Sons of nobles"	*pilli* (sing.)
Intermediary		
	Merchants	*pochtecatl* (sing.)
	Luxury artisans	*tolteccatl* (sing.)
Commoners		
	"Free commoners"	*macehualli* (sing.)
	Rural tenants	*mayeque* (sing. and pl.)
	Slaves	*tlacotli* (sing.)

After Berdan 1982:46.

Indian elites continued to play important roles during the Colonial period as mediators between their communities and the Spaniards, who sought labor, land, and surplus production (Tutino 1976; Charlton 1986). However, the general trend was toward an increasingly homogeneous Indian class: "All in all, colonial rule tended to deemphasize heredity (ascription) as a criterion for Indian prestige and authority, and instead stressed initiative and personal capabilities (achievement), . . . a common pattern in conquest societies" (Berdan 1982:180).

Although Aztec elites are richly described in ethnohistoric documents, these sources often reflect a bias toward the imperial elites of the largest urban centers (Hodge 1984; Michael Smith 1987a). Colonial documents contain a much wider array of information on all social classes in both urban and rural settings; however, these sources reflect Spanish interests, and thus the data are selective. Furthermore, after the Spanish conquest changes in the indigenous social structure occurred rapidly with the loss of the military, administrators, priests, and *pochteca* (merchants). Thus, a fuller understanding of social stratification in peripheral areas of the basin (and provincial centers) must be approached archaeologically. Before discussing the archaeological evidence for Late Aztec and Colonial elites at the peripheral city-state capital of Otumba in the eastern Teotihuacan Valley, we shall outline some archaeological correlates of elite presence.

Archaeological Correlates of Ranking and Stratification in Central Mexico

As Chase and Chase note in their introduction to this volume, the archaeological identification of elites is part of a larger issue of defining the degree and nature of social ranking and stratification. It can be approached from several different levels (e.g., regional, community, household, and individual).

At the regional level, zonal settlement patterns provide indications of an elite class through evidence of population size, settlement stratification or hierarchies, and site function (Sanders and Price 1968). During Late Aztec times in the Basin of Mexico, the total population of 1,000,000 was distributed in settlements ranging from farming hamlets of fewer than 100 persons to the imperial capital of Tenochtitlan, with its resident population of 150,000-200,000, none of whom were farmers (Calnek 1976; Sanders, Parsons, and Santley 1979). The settlement hierarchy resembled a log-normal rank-size distribution (Blanton 1976) that, due to the decline in the Indian population during the Early Colonial period, shifted to a primate pattern with Mexico City dominating the region (Charlton 1986).

At the community level, the existence of elites can be inferred from several lines of evidence—size, degree of nucleation, and apparent planning, as at Tenochtitlan, with its mirror-image pattern of house lots, canals, and streets, or at Colonial *congregación* settlements with their central plazas and grid plans. Differential access to areas within a community segregates elites from others (Blanton 1978). At most Aztec provincial centers in the Basin of Mexico, the major temples, marketplace, and palace form a nucleated core that is easily distinguishable from the rural periphery. "In some respects this physical configuration of small centers reproduces in miniature and in a much more simplified form the settlement configuration of Greater Tenochtitlan" (Sanders, Parsons, and Santley 1979:163).

The scale of architecture is one of the best archaeological indicators of the size and organization of the labor force controlled by elites. The functions of public buildings (e.g., the absence of palaces in chiefdoms; Sanders 1974) also reflect the nature of the elite. Another line of evidence is the organization and scale of food and craft production. Richard Fox (1977), in fact, has argued that the centralization of preindustrial elite power can be measured by the dependence of urban-dwellers on rural food production and by the extent of occupational specialization within urban communities. Tenochtitlan and Colonial period Mexico City are excellent illustrations of Fox's premise about the degree of urban dependence on rural food production (see Parsons 1976 for a discussion of Aztec chinampa production). The extent of occupational specialization within urban communities is archaeologically represented in the physical segregation of craft specialists (Sanders 1974) and in manufacturing patterns, as M. W. Spence (1985) has shown for rural Aztec obsidian production. The presence of a specially delimited space for markets may indicate elite control or supervision, while central warehouses and storage facilities offer a means of assessing the scale of tribute collection.

At the household level, differences in wealth are a useful measure of stratification. Michael Smith (1987b) has recently identified a series of likely archaeological indicators, which are a function of the household's access to goods and services. These include differences in the size and quality of housing, which also permits identification of finer divisions within the elite class. Excavations at Cihuatecpan (Evans in preparation), for example, revealed the remains of a *tecpan* or village chief's (*tecuhtli*) house. In Colonial times, cacique houses were likely to be larger than those of other Indians, to incorporate Spanish architectural characteristics, and to be located at the center of nucleated Colonial period communities (Haskett 1988:44-48).

Certain types of household artifacts, according to Smith, also reflect class status. Elites are apt to have a larger quantity and greater diversity of food items. There are also differences in the size and types of cooking vessels, perhaps because staple foods (such as maize) were prepared differently by elite and commoner households. During the Colonial period, Indian elites mediated between the conservative villagers and the Spaniards and probably had greater access than most Indians to Spanish goods like ceramics, metal, and glass. Thus, the presence of elites can be defined by the presence of such items in quantities that fall between those found at Spanish sites and those at Indian communities (Charlton 1976; Seifert 1977).

Other types of artifacts should also occur in higher proportions in elite households. These include serving vessels, because of their use in household consumption rituals, paraphernalia associated with public religious observances, such as elaborate censers, and nonutilitarian luxury goods, such as jewelry. At the Aztec town of Huexotla in the eastern Basin of Mexico, E. M. Brumfiel (1987a) found proportionately fewer serving vessels and even fewer decorated serving vessels in the rural zone compared to the nucleated core of the site, where the elites probably resided. Both Smith (1987a) and Brumfiel (1987b) have discussed the importance of controlling the production and exchange of these goods for enhancing elite power in Aztec society. Finally, elite households are likely to have a greater diversity and quantity of materials goods. However, as Smith cogently notes, discard practices must be considered in the interpretation of these artifact patterns.

The individual level is the most difficult one to deal with archaeologically in the absence of written records (like Maya stelae) and perishable items like clothing (Anawalt 1980). Iconographic analysis of stone sculpture (e.g., Olmec altars) and mural paintings (such as those at Teotihuacan) is a fruitful approach, because a consistent set of symbols should be associated with political power (J. Brown 1981)—such as the crown and throne in Europe, litters in Mississippian chiefdoms, and headdresses of Mesoamerican rulers. Indian caciques, for example, were permitted to "carry swords or firearms, to wear Spanish clothing, to ride horses or mules with saddles or bridles, or in other ways to demonstrate their status within Indian society" (Gibson 1964:155), although other markings of status, such as polygyny, were ended by the Spanish.

In addition to iconography, burial patterns are a very important basis for inferring social ranking in the archaeological record. J. A. Brown (1981)

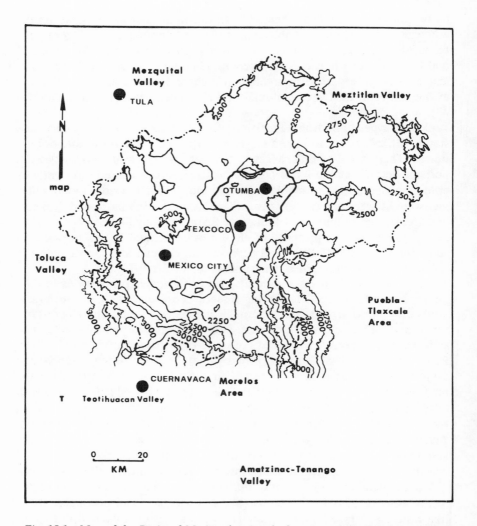

Fig. 15.1. Map of the Basin of Mexico showing the location of the Teotihuacan Valley and Otumba (after J. L. Lorenzo 1968:54, fig. 1).

notes five dimensions to be considered in the analysis of mortuary patterns: (1) complexity in the treatment of the corpse; (2) position and construction of the interment facility; (3) extent and duration of the funeral; (4) differences in material contributions to mortuary ritual; and (5) selective human sacrifice. In the Templo Mayor excavations, for example, elaborate clay and obsidian funerary urns were recovered. Two were found near cremation pits, and the figure depicted on one is probably Moctezuma Ilhuicama. Additionally, one stone-lined pit contained eleven Tlaloc effigies, jade beads, copal, and the skulls of thirty-four children (G. S. Stuart 1981). Elites should also be a distinct minority class in patterns of mortality and pathology (J. Brown 1981). Greater stature and fewer pathologies have been observed among elites in various preindustrial skeletal populations, and R. Storey (1985) has been able to document a high mortality rate among the occupants of a low-status Teotihuacan apartment compound.

This brief review indicates the kinds of archaeological data that can be used to infer social status differentiation in central Mexico, although each is associated with interpretive problems. Furthermore, survey and excavation data from the Late Aztec and Colonial periods do not include all types of data relevant to a definition of elite presence. Nevertheless, we feel that adequate evidence is available to study elite presence in the Basin of Mexico during the Late Horizon and Colonial periods. Data collected using other procedures will be necessary to confirm, modify, or reject some of the interpretations we make here.

The Otumba City State: A Brief Description

The Otumba city-state area is located in the eastern Teotihuacan Valley in the northeastern Basin of Mexico. The archaeological site of the city-state center of Otumba (TA-80) is located at the edge of a gently sloping piedmont just above the Middle Teotihuacan Valley alluvial plain, 12 km east of Teotihuacan (figs. 15.1 and 15.2). Settlements subordinate to Otumba, along with interspersed *calpixqui* districts that paid tribute directly to the Triple Alliance, are found on the piedmont to the north, east, south, and southwest of Otumba (Evans 1980). According to C. Gibson (1964), the symmetrical arrangement of *sujetos* around a *cabecera* is most characteristic of those regions, such as Chalco and the Teotihuacan Valley, some distance from the distorting factors of the lake system.

Previous Research

Both the site of Otumba and substantial portions of the city-state area have been surveyed (see fig. 15.3; Sanders 1965; Mather 1968; Charlton 1975, 1978b, 1987, 1988; Sanders, Parsons, and Santley 1979). Surface collections have been made at most sites and excavations have been carried out at irrigation features in Otumba and at Aztec, Colonial, and Republican period residences in some of the dependent settlements (Charlton 1973, 1975, 1977, 1978a; Evans 1985, in preparation; see also Tolstoy 1958:72; Mather 1968). Documentary sources provide additional data on the Otumba city-state (Evans 1980; Charlton 1986).

Although all previous projects touched on the topics of prehispanic and Colonial elites, none focused specifically on it. Most data were collected to provide information on the chronology and extent of settlement patterns. Nevertheless, we believe data from those projects can be used to evaluate the utility of the proposed archaeological correlates of elites.

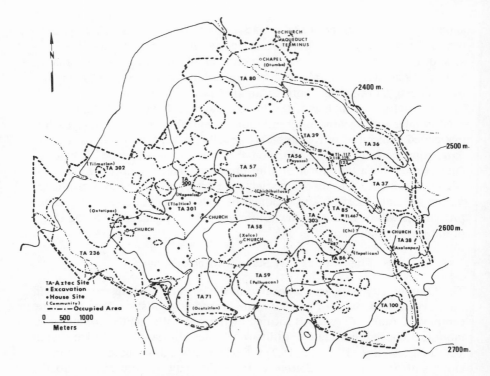

Fig. 15.2. Map of part of the Otumba city-state area showing the location of subordinate sites.

The Data

The ceramic and artifactual data used in this paper were collected during Charlton's Colonial project (1973). Dale D. Brodkey (1978) intensively analyzed them in an examination of Aztec and Postconquest settlement patterns within one part of the Otumba city-state area, including the center. We are indebted to her for careful analyses and plotting of the ceramic and artifactual data.

Survey data derive from several sources. The city-state center of Otumba has been surveyed twice, first by W. G. Mather in 1963 (Mather 1968) and most recently by T. H. and Cynthia L. Otis Charlton in 1987 (Charlton 1987, 1988). On the basis of the studies carried out, it is possible to identify two major residential areas: a nucleated core and a zone of dispersed residences (figs. 15.4 and 15.5). In addition, there is a series of manufacturing areas interspersed among the residential areas but primarily associated with the southeast section of the zone of dispersed residences. The total area is about 190 ha. The nucleated core covers about 20 percent of the area (38 ha). The site of Otumba lies in three topographic zones. The northern zone is an area of deep Middle Valley alluvial soil. The middle or peninsular zone is similar to the northern zone, although the soil is not as deep.

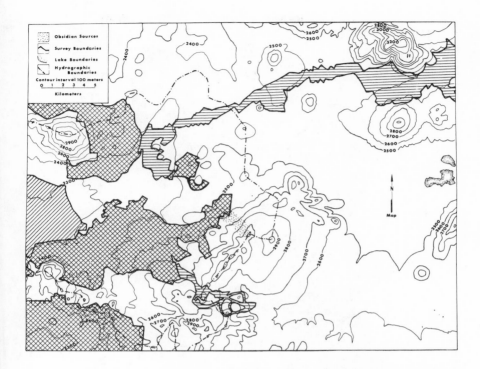

Fig. 15.3. Map of surveyed areas in the eastern Teotihuacan Valley: diagonal hatching, city of Teotihuacan survey; diagonal cross-hatching, Teotihuacan Valley and Texcoco area surveys; horizontal hatching, trade route surveys.

The southern zone is the northeastern section of a long ridge extending from the eastern edge of the valley. There the soil is variable in depth but is usually quite shallow. The nucleated core of the site lies primarily in the southern zone but extends to the peninsula and the north.

Identification of the Elite in Aztec and Early Colonial Otumba

The nucleated core of the site, with exposed plaster floors and rock walls, focuses on the juncture of the two now deeply entrenched branches of the Barranca del Muerto. At this juncture, on the tip of the peninsula and directly to the south, are two large mounds, either of which could be the remains of a Late Horizon temple pyramid. Associated with these mounds are large elevated areas with heavy rubble scatter. We believe these to be the remains of elite (*tlatoani*) residences. In addition, the rest of the nucleated core has extensive areas of continuous habitations and medium to heavy artifact densities.

Since the nucleated core differs on the surface from the surrounding zone of dispersed residences, we suggest that the core contained the residences of several levels of elite in the Otumba city-state center. These would have included the *tlatoani* (native ruler), the nobles, traders, and luxury artisans.

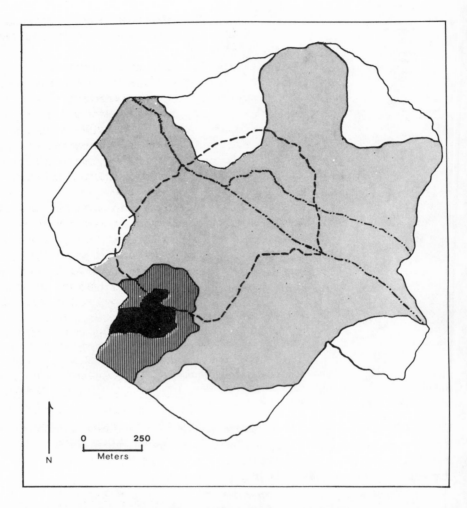

Fig. 15.4. TA-80, interpolative map based on Aztec sherd totals in each collection: white, <300; gray, 300-599; vertical hatching, 600-849; black, 850-1200; core defined by dashed line; barrancas by dash and double dot line.

If this is so, then, on the basis of our earlier discussion, we might expect the core to have higher and the periphery lower artifact densities. In addition, we would expect specific differences between the two residential areas to include higher frequencies of nonutilitarian artifacts, trade ceramics, figurines, and decorated serving wares in the core as opposed to the periphery. Similar patterns of variation should also occur between Otumba and its dependent sites, with more of each category being found at Otumba, definitely in the core and possibly in the periphery.

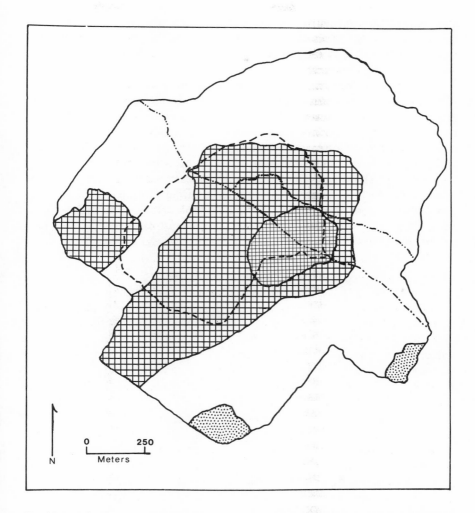

Fig. 15.5. TA-80, interpolative map of collection clusters based on the relative amounts of Aztec II, III, and IV Black-on-Orange sherds in each collection. Stippled areas, no Aztec II; small cross-hatching, Aztec II emphasis; large cross-hatching, Aztec III emphasis; white, Aztec IV emphasis. Site division symbols same as in Figure 15.4.

Materials Studied

In this paper we compare the frequency of occurrence of the several ceramic and artifact categories within Otumba (TA-80, core and periphery), and at the dependent sites (TA-36, TA-37, TA-38, and TA-39) on the ridge top to the southeast. The categories are Aztec ceramic totals, decorated Black-on-Orange serving vessels, trade ceramics (Huastec, Chalco-Cholula, and Gulf Coast), and nonlocally produced hollow figurines. The materials used were derived from thirty-four surface collections made by Charlton from 1967 to

1969 within the archaeological site (TA-80; 10 core; 24 periphery) of the Otumba city-state center and from collections made in 1968 and 1969 at the four dependent sites to the southeast (TA-36, [34], TA-37, [60], TA-38, [56], and TA-39, [41]; see fig. 15.2).

All surface collections were selected with the intent of obtaining complete areal coverage in all sections of each site. Dense areas were not deliberately selected or light areas avoided. At Otumba the distinction between core and periphery was not used to locate collections. The only categories of ceramics not collected were simple Plain Orange body sherds, handles, and supports. All collections were made using teams of comparable size and training. The time spent making each collection was standardized. The areas from which the collections were taken varied to some extent but were generally focused on definite and indefinite structures (mounds) within these sites. The collection techniques ensure a reasonable degree of comparability between the collections (Charlton 1981).

Preliminary Analyses

Using the analyzed collections we have compared (1) the total number of Aztec ceramics, (2) the number of Black-on-Orange serving vessels (14th-17th centuries; totals and by phases II, III, and IV), (3) the number of Late Horizon and Early Colonial indigenous trade wares, and (4) the number of elaborate hollow figurines (Otis Charlton, in press) occurring at each site and at the core and periphery at Otumba. In addition, we also examined the frequencies of majolicas, porcelains, glazed earthenwares, and olive jars.

We made statistical comparisons using upper-tailed unpaired t-tests and the one-tailed Mann-Whitney test (Siegel 1956:116-27; Moroney 1960:227-36). These were selected as parametric and nonparametric tests to determine whether or not to reject the null hypothesis that there were no differences in the quantities of the items found in collections from sites whose occupants differed in socioeconomic status and in political power. The alternate hypothesis was that higher-status individuals would have greater access to these materials, which would be reflected by differences in the collections.

For Otumba (TA-80) we carried out a cluster analysis using the percentages of Aztec II, III, and IV sherds to evaluate our tripole graph based on those same data. We then plotted the spatial distribution of the defined clusters and the total Aztec ceramics in each collections on interpolative maps (figs. 15.4 and 15.5). All statistical procedures were carried out using NCSS 5.0 (Hintze 1987). All mapping was done using MAPIT 2.0 (Kalush 1987). We are presenting the results here as preliminary, but highly suggestive. Additional fieldwork (7/88-5/89) and laboratory analyses (ongoing) will be carried out to test many of them.

Preliminary Results: The Late Horizon and Early Sixteenth Century

General-Vessel Consumption Rates. To determine if there were differences in the total quantity of ceramics occurring in the core and the periph-

Table 15.2: Summary Test Results: Ceramic Totals

	TA-80 Core	TA-80 Periphery
TA-80p	t prob. .1145x	--------.-.------
	z prob. .0994x	--------.-.------
TA-36	t prob. .0038+	t prob. .0003+
	z prob. .0001+	z prob. .0002+
TA-37	t prob. .0026+	t prob. .0001+
	z prob. .0000+	z prob. .0000+
TA-38	t prob. .0024+	t prob. .0001+
	z prob. .0000+	z prob. .0000+
TA-39	t prob. .0076+	t prob. .0034+
	z prob. .0004+	z prob. .0007+

+ =as predicted; x=no difference.

ery at Otumba, we compared the size of samples from the two residential areas (table 15.2). Collections from the core do tend to be larger than those from the periphery. However, this difference is not confirmed statistically. An interpolative map of the collection totals (Aztec only; fig. 15.5) indicates that small collections occur in scattered areas of the periphery and in one case in the edge of the core. Collections from most of the site, including both the core and the periphery, are roughly equivalent in total size.

However, when comparisons are made between Otumba and the dependent sites located on the ridge to the southeast (TA-36, TA-37, TA-38, and TA-39; see table 15.2), collections at Otumba are significantly larger than those at any of the four dependent sites. There is no significant variation in collection size among the dependent sites.

Black-on-Orange Serving Vessel Consumption Rates. In general, the overall number of sherds from Black-on-Orange serving vessels in a collection correlates strongly with the total size of that collection (> .78 at TA-80 core, TA-36, TA-37, and TA-39; < .54 at TA-80 periphery and at TA-38 [-.0035]). Within Otumba, collections from the core have a significantly greater number of such sherds than collections from the periphery (table 15.3). In addition, the core has significantly more Black-on-Orange sherds than all of the four dependent sites, while the periphery has significantly more than all but one, TA-39, the closest site (Mann-Whitney z score probability indicates no difference).

When Black-on-Orange ceramics are broken down into style phases (Aztec II, III, and IV; see table 15.4), it becomes clear that the differences between the core and periphery with respect to frequency of this type are time dependent. Aztec II and especially Aztec III Black-on-Orange sherds are significantly more abundant in the core than in the periphery. The reverse situation may be true for Aztec IV sherds, which occur more frequently in the periphery of Otumba than in the core according to the t-test

Table 15.3: Summary Test Results: Black-on-Orange Totals

	TA-80 Core	TA-80 Periphery
TA-80p	t prob. .0244+	---------.-.------
	z prob. .0236+	---------.-.------
TA-36	t prob. .0003+	t prob. .0003+
	z prob. .0000+	z prob. .0002+
TA-37	t prob. .0008+	t prob. .0060+
	z prob. .0000+	z prob. .0063+
TA-38	t prob. .0006+	t prob. .0027+
	z prob. .0000+	z prob. .0020+
TA-39	t prob. .0039+	t prob. .0868x
	z prob. .0001+	z prob. .0116+

+=as predicted; x=no difference.

(there is no difference according to the Mann-Whitney test z score probability).

A map plot (fig. 15.5) of three collection clusters based on the percentages of Aztec II, III, and IV Black-on-Orange sherds present in each collection, and one cluster where no Aztec II sherds occur, suggests that the periphery was occupied later than the core in the middle sixteenth century. In fact the peninsula, where one of the large pyramidal structures occurs, has virtually no Aztec IV Black-on-Orange ceramics. We believe that during those years, when Aztec IV designs developed, the elite residents of the core were moving, at Spanish request, to the Colonial community of Otumba, relocated to the north of the Aztec site. A church, monastery, and aqueduct were functioning there by 1550.

By removing Aztec IV Black-on-Orange ceramics (1540-1620?; Charlton in press) from the Late Horizon ceramic complex, it becomes clear that the elite of Otumba were alive, well, and prospering in the core from the founding of the site through the fifteenth century, with proportionately more Black-on-Orange serving dishes there than in the periphery. This conclusion differs from that reached by E. M. Brumfiel (1987a) for Huexotla. Such a difference may result from Texcoco's overshadowing of Huexotla or from Brumfiel's incorporation of Aztec IV Black-on-Orange sherds as part of the Late Horizon and early-sixteenth-century ceramic complex.

Comparisons of the occurrence of Aztec II Black-on-Orange sherds in Otumba and the four dependent sites tend to confirm the distinctiveness of Otumba and its core during Aztec II. All sites have significantly fewer Aztec II sherds than does the core. Two sites, TA-37 and TA-39, when compared with the periphery, however, show no significant differences in the quantities of Aztec II ceramics present.

With one exception, TA-39, all dependent sites have significantly fewer Aztec III Black-on-Orange sherds than either the core or the periphery at

Table 15.4: Summary Test Results: Black-on-Orange Totals by Phase

		TA-80 Core			TA-80 Periphery		
		II	III	IV	II	III	IV
TA-80p	t prob.	.0409+	.0042+	.9491*	------	------	------
	z prob.	.0063+	.0045+	.0754x	------	------	------
TA-36	t prob.	.0143+	.0005+	.0221+	.0239+	.0004+	.0000+
	z prob.	.0001+	.0000+	.0040+	.0099+	.0001+	.0000+
TA-37	t prob.	.0292+	.0013+	.0151+	.2699x	.0098+	.0000+
	z prob.	.0022+	.0000+	.0045+	.2930x	.0073+	.0000+
TA-38	t prob.	.0079+	.0007+	.1299x	.0012+	.0006+	.0002+
	z prob.	.0000+	.0000+	.1171x	.0000+	.0001+	.0000+
TA-39	t prob.	.0303+	.0003+	.2116x	.3152x	.0343+	.0008+
	t prob.	.0011+	.0000+	.1064x	.1830x	.0007+	.0001+

+ =as predicted; x=no difference; *=opposite predicted.

TA-80. (Aztec III ceramics at TA-39, the dependent site closest to Otumba, showed no significant differences in frequency from the Aztec III ceramics in the periphery at Otumba.) These differences continue with Aztec IV Black-on-Orange ceramics. Dependent sites have frequencies of Aztec IV Black-on-Orange ceramics significantly lower than the periphery and the core at Otumba with two exceptions: TA-38 and TA-39 have frequencies of Aztec IV designs similar to those at the core in Otumba.

Obviously, the greatest differences at Otumba and the dependent sites in the distribution of Black-on-Orange pottery occurred with Aztec III ceramics. These differences support the consolidation of an elite at Otumba during the Late Horizon, out of a less-differentiated Early Aztec period (Aztec II). By the middle of the sixteenth century, the elite had moved from the core to the relocated community of Otumba to the north. However, some population remained in the periphery at Otumba and in some of the dependent sites during the sixteenth century.

Trade Ware Consumption Rates. We also carried out similar comparisons of the frequency of occurrence of trade wares (Gulf Coast, Huastec, and Chalco-Cholula Polychromes) at Otumba and within the four dependent sites (table 15.5). Within Otumba, there is a significant difference between the core and the periphery in the amount of trade wares present, a greater amount being recorded for the core, as we might expect.

Comparisons between Otumba and the dependent sites indicate that all but one had significantly fewer trade ware sherds than either the core or the periphery at Otumba. TA-37, the one exception, showed no significant difference from the periphery at Otumba in the frequency of trade wares (the Mann-Whitney z score probability does not confirm this).

Hollow Figurine Consumption Rates. Hollow figurines date from the Late Horizon and were constructed using very sophisticated molding tech-

Table 15.5: Summary Test Results: Trade Ware Totals

	TA-80 Core	TA-80 Periphery
TA-80p	t prob. .0146+	-------.-.------
	z prob. .0045+	-------.-.------
TA-36	t prob. .0021+	t prob. .0009+
	z prob. .0000+	z prob. .0001+
TA-37	t prob. .0050+	t prob. .0626x
	z prob. .0001+	z prob. .0429+
TA-38	t prob. .0029+	t prob. .0047+
	z prob. .0000+	z prob. .0043+
TA-39	t prob. .0040+	t prob. .0181+
	z prob. .0000+	z prob. .0281+

+=as predicted; x=no difference.

niques. They seem to have been manufactured outside of the Otumba area and thus represent a local import (Otis Charlton in press). Within Otumba we found no significant differences in the frequency of their occurrence in the core and the periphery (table 15.6). Furthermore, with the possible exception of TA-38, none of the dependent sites have significantly fewer fragments of hollow figurines than either the core or the periphery at Otumba. Since this figurine type is commonly used in domestic household contexts and not in public display, it may not have served to differentiate between the elite and the commoners, or between urban and rural populations.

Summary of the Late Horizon and the Early Sixteenth Century. It is readily apparent that an indigenous elite can be defined for Otumba on the basis of indigenous architecture, zoning, ceramic distributions, and artifact distributions. It is interesting to note, however, that there is no evidence that this elite appropriated imported Spanish ceramics from Europe or China at this time. Most such wares, along with others, occur later and in the periphery of the site, not at the core. By 1550, most of the elite undoubtedly were living in the new town of Otumba. Since only limited peripheral survey is possible, we have few archaeological data from this area. The kinds of archaeological data available on elites during the Colonial period after 1550 come from sites other than the relocated town of Otumba.

Preliminary Results: The Colonial Period, 1603-1820

Excavated and survey data within the Otumba area come from known Indian communities. Some of these are still occupied today while others were abandoned at various times between 1603 and 1820. Numerous isolated rancho settlements scattered throughout the area provide additional data on status during this period. These were, in some instances, on lands still controlled by Indian communities at the end of the Colonial period (Charlton 1991).

Table 15.6: Summary Test Results: Hollow Figurine Totals

	TA-80 Core	TA-80 Periphery
TA-80p	t prob. .3079x	-------.-.------
	z prob. .5580x	-------.-.------
TA-36	t prob. .0840x	t prob. .1788x
	z prob. .1225x	z prob. .2314x
TA-37	t prob. .3102x	t prob. .5157x
	z prob. .2537x	z prob. .4941x
TA-38	t prob. .0402+	t prob. .0943x
	z prob. .0642x	z prob. .2273x
TA-39	t prob. .2911x	t prob. .4906x
	z prob. .2532x	z prob. .4567x

+ =as predicted; x=no difference.

When the artifact assemblages for the Indian communities of the seventeenth and eighteenth centuries are examined, it is very obvious that majolicas occur in exceedingly low quantities. During the same time, however, many of the ranchos have greater quantities of the same materials. It is tempting to suggest that the Indian elites who controlled these lands at the time would have used a ceramic assemblage that included more majolicas than the Indian communities but fewer than those found at Spanish-occupied sites. This indeed is the argument used by D. J. Seifert (1977). However, we need more precise data on the occupants of the various ranchos before being certain of its applicability. Other artifacts such as metal tools and glass containers remain scarce at all sites in this area until after the 1810 Revolution.

Conclusion

Preliminary examination of the archaeological materials from pre- and post-conquest sites in the Otumba area of the Basin of Mexico provides some insights into the sequence of development and decline of the indigenous elite of the city-state. The major differentiation within Otumba and between Otumba and its dependent sites occurs during the Aztec III period of the Late Horizon. Unlike the elite of Huexotla, the elite at Otumba seems to have developed later and to have benefited and prospered during this period of major expansion of the Triple Alliance. It is obvious that many different social, economic, and political factors were operative in a number of local contexts during the Late Aztec period. We are currently carrying out fieldwork at Otumba and in a number of dependent communities to clarify the processes operative there. Local economic specialization seems to have played a key role in the trajectory of Otumba's political development (Nichols and Charlton 1988).

The archaeological evidence suggests that after the conquest members of the elite left the core and moved to the relocated community of Otumba to the north. Subsequent to this removal and their incorporation into the hispanic governmental organization, we have few archaeological data from the town of Otumba. Instead, we must rely tentatively upon the materials from seventeenth- and eighteenth-century ranchos and Indian communities, which show clear-cut differences in the percentages of majolicas in the ceramic assemblages. Differential access to these hispanic-produced wares may reflect status differences among Indians during the Middle and Late Colonial period. Historical archaeological research needs to be carried out to examine this hypothesis.

Acknowledgments

The surface collections on which this paper is based were made from 1967 to 1969 in a project approved by INAH and supported by the Associated Colleges of the Midwest through a Non-Western Studies Faculty Research Fellowship (1967), the University of Iowa through an Old Gold Summer Faculty Research Fellowships (1968), and the National Science Foundation (Research Grant GS-2080, 1968-72). Current research at Otumba, carried out under a *permiso* from INAH, is supported by the National Science Foundation through Research Grants BNS-871-8140 (Dartmouth College, Deborah L. Nichols PI) and BNS 871-9665 (University of Iowa, Thomas H. Charlton PI) and by the National Endowment for the Humanities through Research Grant RO-21705-88 (University of Iowa, Thomas H. Charlton PI). Deborah L. Nichols received additional research support from the Claire Garber Goodman Fund and the Dartmouth Class of 1962. Thomas H. Charlton also received support from the University of Iowa through a Faculty Developmental Assignment. All figures were prepared by Cynthia L. Otis Charlton. Professor Michael Chibnik at the University of Iowa generously shared his expertise in statistical analyses. The authors gratefully acknowledge all support received.

The late Dale Deborah Brodkey participated in the analyses of the survey materials from 1970 to 1973. She prepared a manuscript dealing with the reinterpretation of Aztec settlement patterns and summarized the results of the analyzed surface collections. Her analyses and summaries served as a primary basis for this paper. Thomas H. Charlton appreciates her help and support during the early years of his Colonial Project and regrets that her untimely death has precluded her active participation in the publication of the results of that project.

16. "The Elite" and Assessment of Social Stratification in Mesoamerican Archaeology

Stephen A. Kowalewski, Gary M. Feinman, and Laura Finsten

THE collaborators on our project have been interested in social or class stratification in prehispanic Mesoamerica and elsewhere for a long time (Blanton et al. 1981; Kowalewski and Finsten 1983; Kowalewski et al. 1986). We have been stimulated by our readings in political economy, participation in multidisciplinary study groups, and interaction with social anthropologists who work in Oaxaca. We all agree that stratification is a key issue, though our individual approaches have differed on this more than on any other issue. On social or class stratification—what is the best definition of the problem, what theoretical approach to take—we vary from time to time along a range from soft-core Marxist to new home economist to (accusingly) the hard-core naive. Undoubtedly, we disagree and change our frames of reference because stratification is one of the long-standing fundamental issues of the social sciences.

The point of this paper is that current treatments of stratification in Mesoamerican archaeology do not come up to the theoretical or empirical standards of other social sciences. This failure is not because the archaeological record is impoverished. The archaeological record is rich in the material remains of social resources. But by relying on weak models with little precise reference to common, in-the-ground data, Mesoamerican archaeologists have failed to exploit the power of what is at their feet—reliable testimony of the distribution of things and how that distribution changed over time, space, and in relation to other things in the world. Mesoamericanists can make a contribution to studies of stratification, but it will probably not be through a concentration on the elite of prehispanic times.

Our opinion on the utility of the concept of an elite for Mesoamerican archaeology has already leaked out in the last paragraph. The term "elite," as currently understood in anthropology and other disciplines, has severely limited operational utility for those who deal with archaeological data. It refers to individuals and groups with the power or authority to control or greatly influence major social institutions. Archaeological methods usually cannot reliably identify people who control institutions. Nor can archaeology say much about how an elite operated. Archaeology cannot identify the elite very well because the things it is able to observe are different from the social relationships of elite behavior. Archaeology can make significant contributions to the study of stratification, especially in documenting variation and change in the distribution of material social resources. But this objective differs in empirical feasibility and theoretical rationale from the more dubious effort of identifying, from some thousand-year-old archaeoethnographic vantage point, a Mesoamerican elite pulling levers of power.

The "Elite" Concept and Contemporary Mesoamerican Archaeology

Among many Mesoamericanists today, the "elite" concept may disguise an older, deeply embedded culture-historical theory, one in which society was thought to be directed by norms or rules and now is said to be directed by the will of a few lords.

The culture-historical or eclectic theoretical approaches that dominated Mesoamerican archaeology until the 1960s still have many adherents. Culture history maintains cultures and traits as primary units of analysis. For culture-historians, cultures or ethnic groups have identifiable traditions, customs, norms, and values. Cultures are superorganic, existing above and determining the behavior of individuals. Culture history is especially dominant among Mesoamericanists who tend toward art history, literature, and humanist scholarship generally akin to classical archaeology in the Old World. Our objections are not to the careful investigation of regional or societal sequences of change—a necessary task for anthropological archaeology. Rather, we criticize the all-too-frequent Mesoamericanist infatuation with personages, diffusing traits and influences, and undifferentiated, mentalist conceptions of past cultures.

After the 1960s, another approach—cultural ecology—gained adherents among Mesoamerican archaeologists. Cultural ecology combines environmental differences with population growth to produce progressive cultural evolution. Some archaeologists remain impressed with cultural ecology; others are not.

Of course, this disciplinary history is quite familiar to most readers. Our reason for review is to place recent interest in ancient Mesoamerican elites in a historical perspective. The current Mesoamericanist focus on elites, and on political events generally (e.g., Helms 1979; Renfrew and Cherry 1986; several authors in Drennan and Uribe 1987; Culbert 1988; Freidel and Schele 1988a), is in large part a reaction to the excessive environmental determinism of cultural ecology. It is understandable exploration of territory not well covered by the earlier approaches. Yet, although the political approach has produced valuable insights, we wish to raise some cautions regarding what the perspective might easily become. In this developing political approach there are already some troublesome tendencies.

For some recent proponents, "elite interaction" threatens to become the buzz-word and explanatory burden-bearer, replacing the equally nebulous "cultural influences" and "population pressures" of earlier theories. The function of such concepts is to reduce and make more manageable the material that the observer must handle, a necessary part of any theoretical approach. But one should neither reify (in this case literally!) abstractions that have little likelihood of being examined empirically nor artificially narrow one's field of inquiry to one or two arbitrarily selected "crucial" variables.

After the groundless abstractions of previous approaches, the interest in politics and elites is understandable as an attempt to put actors back onto the Mesoamerican scene. But a potential danger in this political approach is the temptation to conclude that kings rule society and cause change, in place of culture for the culture historians and population pressure or the physical environment for rigid cultural ecologists. The political approach in recent archaeology seems to have many of the inclinations toward Great Man theorizing, king-listing for king-listing's sake, and disassociation from total social history that characterized old-style political history. Again, archaeological enquiry should be directed across the breadth of the archaeological record, toward understanding or explaining total social systems as they change over the long run. The focus on elites as the key explanatory concept may neglect bottom-up social processes and economic or other forces over which the powerful have little control.

The political approach and focus on elites has other troublesome similarities with the culture-historical approach. Both are normative, maintaining that society is rather completely directed, in the one case by culture and in the other by rulers. In both approaches, the directing agents do not need to be accounted for or explained. We see a yawning abyss between now-abundant archaeological writing about elites and the demonstration of material flows and behavioral relationships between the proposed elite and other members of social systems. Further, there is little research on what proportion and what kinds of total material flows involved elites. This detachment of the elite from other social groups is what we mean when we say that the elite focus has a tendency to be somewhat ungrounded.

Ungrounded abstraction and neglect of other social groups may lead to rather empty explanatory propositions that bind up cause and effect in what may be nearly the same concept. Here are some examples of the less-than-scientific arguments about elite interaction and power that we have seen in the archaeological literature. They are simplified for the sake of brevity and anonymity. Archaeologists may be tempted to assert that elites universally act in their own interests to increase their power and status and to reproduce themselves. This may be fine as far as it goes, but it does not go beyond a descriptive, changeless functionalism (the equivalent of culture historians explaining values by tradition or child-training). Archaeologists have identified the elite by possession of certain markers, and then they reify the markers by explaining elite power as a function of their possession.

This comes close to saying that a decline in the availability of jade or copper trinkets caused the weakening of political authority. That may be heady structural theory, but it is suspicious logic. It is equivalent to saying that the wearing of tuxedos is a marker of elite status; therefore, the elite get their power through wearing tuxedos. Always looking to elite action as cause of first resort leaves explanatory models logically ungrounded and out of touch with other social, economic, and ecological forces.

What are the objectives of this new focus on the elite in Mesoamerican archaeology? Is the great attention to the elite, implicitly or explicitly, a working part of research designed to investigate the full range of a social system? If so, what are the other concepts in the approach? Or is the objective more specific and not so encompassing? Is the research question simply a matter of identification, finding the infallible indicator of elite-ness? Is the problem that goods previously thought to be elite actually occur commonly, that polychrome pottery has become debased by occurring too widely? Perhaps we should now only look for real silk instead of mass-produced designer tweeds (their past equivalents, of course) or only the most exquisite jade plaques—or should we return to the undebased gold standard?

Identifying the Elite Archaeologically

In sociology (Mills 1956), ethnography (G. Marcus 1983a), and social history (Jaher 1972), observers have prior indication about what an institution's important decisions are, who makes them, and who controls the levers of power. These kinds of studies are based on extensive interviews, surveys, cross-checking among informants, extensive contemporary periodicals, diaries, letters, biographies, and other sources. The investigator must go beyond public posturing and propaganda, into events and social interaction that actors often seek to make private. Good ethnographic and historical technique applied to power-wielding requires data collection that is in some sense systematic, that is, covering all of something or sampling it in a representative or arguably thorough way. Systematic, representative information about behavior that is private is not easy to come by.

Archaeologists do not observe people interacting in the halls and homes of power, at least not on any reliable, systematic basis. Occasionally, the archaeologist unearths figurines standing in a ritual scene, a wall mural depicting accession to power, the tomb of a ruler with retainer burials. But these occasional finds relating to public life do not amount to a systematic corpus, nor do they say much about the intense, often hidden, interaction described by C. Wright Mills or George Marcus.

The private behavior of the elite and their public symbols of formal status are two different things, conceptually and in practice. Archaeologists have usually identified elites in prehispanic Mesoamerica on the basis of unusual, costly, or exotic artifacts. Often these artifacts are highly visible in the archaeological record and (not necessarily the same thing) were highly visible when people were using them (i.e., they were public). Public symbols are not necessarily reliable indicators of acts of power performed in deliberate seclusion.

It is probably not safe to assume that even such a substantial investment as house architecture is a completely reliable reflection of membership in an elite. Tip O'Neill, former Speaker of the U.S. House of Representatives and a decision maker if there ever was one, lived in a modest row house in a working-class Boston neighborhood (though his office in the Capitol might be more telling—archaeologists sometimes have similar information, as at the Tikal Central Acropolis or Monte Alban's Main Plaza). Your dentist probably lives in a fancier house than Tip.

Dress, too, can give misleading signals. On the basis of dress, who would ever have thought that Tip O'Neill was more powerful than Dave Freidel? Similarly, we might not want to take every proclamation carved in stone at face value—after all, if a thing is true, why does it need a billboard?

These are familiar doubts. We don't mean that the material facades are lacking in meaning or that archaeologists cannot find badges of formal office or artifactual indicators of bureaucracy. In some circumstances archaeologists can find these things with enough regularity to amass representative collections. But we are skeptical of elite identifications when there is little confirmation from independent data, systematically, for the same individual or household cases. Confirmation by independent data requires control sometimes not sought by Mesoamerican archaeologists, especially those outside the scientific tradition. But control and context are necessary for claims of elite identification. Further, claims about elite identification or interaction across space require far larger, more representative, and better-documented samples than many Mesoamerican archaeologists are accustomed to dealing with. Likewise, one should have less-than-total confidence in cross-temporal comparisons involving the same indicators of elite status when the investigator fails to show that the indicators have the same meaning across time (why should indicators have the same meaning for very long in a social context as dynamic as elite membership?).

"Elite" is a social network and power term ill-suited for the kinds of information archaeologists can control. But archaeologists can deal systematically with other information that reveals social organization and the distribution of socially defined resources. F. Plog and S. Upham (1983), for example, discuss categories of information on social organization that archaeologists are likely to obtain. Specifically for Mesoamerica, Michael Smith (1987b) has explored how household possessions in ongoing social systems reflect relative wealth. He considers how archaeologists may relate the state in which they find things in the ground to past social systems. This research illustrates how valuable insights about past class stratification may be gained by theoretically informed analysis of systematic bodies of data of the kind that archaeologists typically treat. We are also encouraged by our analysis of the Valley of Oaxaca settlement pattern data, some of which we present later in this paper.

Using Historical Analogies

Studies of prehispanic Mesoamerican elites and class or social stratification suffer from a too-heavy reliance on analogies with social categories from sixteenth-century chronicles. M. Lind and J. Urcid's (1983) interpretation of houses and tombs at seventh-century Lambityeco in Oaxaca is a well-reasoned effort to relate postcontact chronicles to archaeological materials from the later periods. But many of the analogies in the literature have a much weaker relation to systematic archaeological data. In Mesoamerican archaeology, analogy-spinning is less costly and unfortunately more fashionable than the more rigorous procedures of testing hypotheses with archaeological data or building models from archaeological data for further refinement using other archaeological data.

Three kinds of debilitating problems make historical analogies, when untested with independent archaeological data, a weak form of understanding the past. First, Mesoamerica changed a great deal from Preclassic to Classic to Postclassic times. If sixteenth-century categories were as applicable to the Classic as they are to the Late Postclassic, it would be remarkable. Historical analogies fail to consider or account for the known major transformations of prehispanic times. Overreliance on analogy is a denial of history, a point made by Stephen Gould (1986) in regard to the place of paleontology in biology.

Second, most major, frequently cited sixteenth-century chronicles present a normative view. Other, more detailed sources indicate a more diverse distribution of social resources (e.g., Williams and Harvey 1988). Diversity in legal form and practice is an impressive theme of M. Bloch's *Feudal Society* (1961:e.g., 176ff., 255ff.). The same comment—that analogies may tend to project a normative view when what we desire to understand is diversity—applies to cross-cultural analogies. For example, cross-cultural studies suggest that archaic state societies were typically divided into formal statuses of rulers, ruled, and often an intermediate status group (e.g., Claesson and Skalnik 1978). But it is important to remember that individual cases typically depart from this general pattern. Societies more often than not have patterns more complex than this three-part system if one looks for variation in other dimensions besides formal status.

Third, while ethnographic and historical analogies have an important place in our studies, overemphasis on them seems to take archaeologists away from their primary data source: what is in the ground. Commonly occurring, in-the-ground objects reflect processes other than chronicles' normative view or formal status divisions. These archaeological data are uniquely relevant for what they have to say about variation and change over time in both informal and formal status distributions. To neglect this property of the archaeological record is to neglect the basic responsibility of preserving and interpreting all the information, the variability, in it.

The Importance of Systematic Data

Mesoamerican archaeology has always had its classical archaeology streak. Its tendencies toward personal aesthetic gratification inhibit scientific progress. Much has been written about the distinctions between scientific or anthropological vs. classical archaeology, usually about the higher-level, philosophy of science issues such as theory-building. Here we stress a more basic difference in research technique. This is the fundamental matter of making systematic observations, collecting data that form meaningful, definable sets, with procedures that can be understood widely and are in some sense replicable. All of something or a representative sample of something is far more valuable than a collection of things that have no unity. Systematic corpora of data are not the sine qua non of science, but they often function as a foundation, starting point, and a transgenerational legacy, providing common material for the formation and evaluation of new ideas. Examples include the naturalist's herbariums, the National Opinion Research Center's survey data, DNA sequence data, and in fact some classical archaeology compendiums. These data banks, of course, are not free from the biases of their times, but they are at least collected with the intent of being complete or representative of variability, over large numbers of observations, within a specified empirical context.

Since our discipline specializes in a finite archaeological record, one would think that data banks would be a primary resource for our field, and they are in some areas of the world. But Mesoamericanists can't sit still long enough to work on such tiresome things. Cooperating in the compilation of such material is not part of the training of most Mesoamericanists. Instead, they are encouraged to make grand statements on the basis of a few samples that are representative of little more than the last field season's work, prevailing academic fashion, and the standard bibliography. In their eagerness to follow each new, fashionable model they cite the very same old inadequate sources, whether the topic be commerce, peer polities, elites, religion, intensive agriculture, ballcourts, collapses, or invasions. How can the same bibliographies be useful for so many things? The answer is, of course, that most of the sources are not truly useful. Mesoamericanists simply have low standards for the relevance of information.

We don't see how complex societies can be understood without the advantages provided by large, systematically collected bodies of information. Systematic data collection by itself will not result in automatic progress on complex problems such as stratification (cf. Mills 1959). What Mesoamerican archaeology also needs are concepts linking archaeological data to significant theories. But theories about stratification cannot be built or tested without large-scale programs for systematic data collection.

Archaeological Evidence from the Valley of Oaxaca

In our opinion it is more productive to transform the concern about the elite into a broader problem of social or class stratification. This keeps us in touch with the rest of social science and forces us to look at total social systems.

In the following sections our purpose is not to describe the past social systems in the Valley of Oaxaca (for that, see Kowalewski et al. 1989). Rather, we indicate how complex, heterogeneous, and changing those systems were, and we do so mainly with methodological instead of substantive intent.

Having said that systematic data are important, we now critically discuss some from the Valley of Oaxaca Settlement Pattern Project (Kowalewski et al. 1989). But stroking such data does not produce warm feelings of contentment—rather, it makes one appreciate the theoretical and methodological challenges that students of political economy grappled with even before there were any Mesoamerican archaeologists. It's humbling. But here and there we see glimmers of hope, possibilities that specifically archaeological approaches might turn out to mean something.

We have seven classes of data to discuss: house architecture, residential terraces, mounded architecture, spatial arrangements, obsidian, ceramics, and human osteology. Of course, the last category is not from the settlement surveys. At present, these data are not yet sufficiently representative of the variability in prehispanic Oaxacan society to form a picture of class or social stratification changing over time. But they are sufficient to outline the dimensions of the problem.

House Architecture

We assume that households and individuals use the resources that they have to meet social goals. One such resource is a house and accompanying grounds. House architecture thus has relative value across society as a means toward certain ends and as a reflection of household goals. It is a reflection of wealth (Michael Smith 1987b).

The size of household living space may vary with number of occupants, types of activities, wealth, and ostentation. R. E. Blanton (1978:97-98) has published histograms of room and patio areas for all well-preserved houses at Late Classic Monte Alban, the regional capital. Though the samples were incomplete, they were relatively large ($N = 56$ and $N = 104$). He concludes that the wide ranges and spread of cases apparent in these samples preclude models such as a simple three-tiered stratification.

Figure 16.1 is a histogram of room areas for all well-preserved houses at an Early Classic village ($N = 40$). We estimate that the village had a few

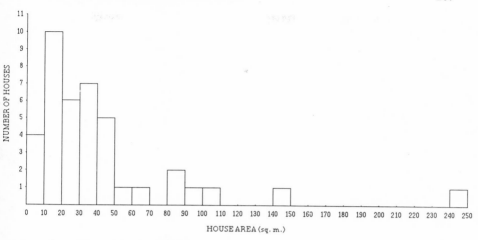

Fig. 16.1. Areas for Early Classic houses.

hundred people, and we place it in the lowly fifth rank of population centers at that time. Its house areas would fit into the lower third of Blanton's distribution of house areas at Monte Alban. At face value one might conclude that households at the small village disposed of fewer resources than the average at the capital. However, because of preservation and excavation biases at Monte Alban, the Monte Alban house distribution data favors the ancient city's larger houses and does not adequately represent the smaller ones. Before generalizations can be made about house sizes and wealth in Early Classic Oaxaca, better and larger samples will be needed.

Residential Terraces

House lot size is another way in which household resources may vary, reflecting wealth, range of activities, and household size. In the Valley of Oaxaca prehispanic houses and lots visible on the surface are too infrequent to produce representative samples. But hilltop towns where virtually everyone lived on an artificially created terrace were common. Abundant surface and excavation evidence demonstrates the terraces' residential function. They are delineated spaces created for household needs. We measured some 9,000 residential terraces, making every effort to record complete samples at each site that had well-preserved terraces.

Unfortunately, the terraced sites usually had a minority of the valley's population, so the data are not representative of the whole society. Since many sites are multiphase occupations, we discuss here a well-controlled sample, which includes all Early Classic terraced sites with measurable terraces in the Tlacolula and Ocotlan survey areas (Kowalewski et al. 1989). This amounts to 1,499 terraces in 13 sites. The sites range in size from small villages to a second-rank town.

The terrace areas for all 13 cases combined are shown in figure 16.2. If households typically used one terrace, as is likely in most but not all cases, then a majority of households disposed of less than 150 sq m for their lots.

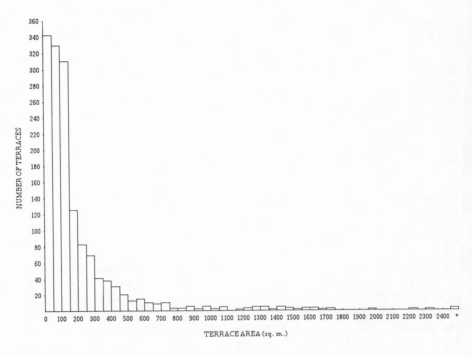

Fig. 16.2. Areas for all Early Classic terraces.

But 35 percent of terraces have areas above this mode. In addition, many of these terraces would be on the high end of the Monte Alban terrace-size distribution.

Marked differences in the forms of the distribution of terrace sizes are apparent among the 13 sites. Some sites are more heterogeneous than others. Each site has a strong, positively skewed distribution (the mean is considerably greater than the median). P. D. Allison (1978) has drawn attention to the positively skewed distribution of incomes today and discusses statistical indices and curves for comparing them (see also Courtland Smith 1980, Menard 1986). One of the measures used to describe income distributions is the coefficient of variation (CV, simply the standard deviation divided by the mean). For our 13 sites the CV ranges from 0.5 (least heterogeneous) to 2.0 (most heterogeneous), with most falling around 1.0 to 1.4. Keep in mind that we are not covering the full range of variation in Oaxacan terrace sizes for the Early Classic. Our sample excludes Monte Alban and Jalieza, which in the Early Classic were first-rank regional centers with larger mean terrace areas than the means for the sites in our sample. Jalieza had a mean terrace size of 699 sq m, with a CV of 2.8. Larger sites thus appear to have greater absolute ranges of variation and greater variability.

CVs for income distributions in developed and underdeveloped countries range from 0.7 to 1.0 (Atkinson 1970), so actually these prehispanic distributions seem to have more variability. Obviously, incomes and house lots are not the same things and there may be various reasons why terrace sizes are so variable, but our conclusion is really methodological. Analysts must be prepared for this complexity and range of variability. Two or three modes will not leap forth from histograms to present themselves as formal classes.

Mounded Architecture

Mounded architecture may represent wealth, ostentation, or control over labor. However, as shown by excavations at many sites, functional differences make interpretation complex. In Oaxaca pyramid mounds mark the remnants of temples, public buildings, palaces, elaborate residences, and ballcourts. If one assumes that all of these functions imply elite activities, in the loose sense, then the distribution of mounded architecture may be useful.

There are complicating factors. The availability of full-coverage survey information allows us to study some of these. Earlier configurations may be covered by later construction. A subregion with a relatively high frequency of mounds in one phase may have a low frequency compared to other subregions in the next. Mound volumes also vary by topographic location, on the alluvium versus in the piedmont. Certain types of sites, especially the hilltop terraced sites, vary systematically in the numbers and sizes of mounds. A further complication is that mound-building dropped off dramatically in the Late Postclassic throughout the region. There are strong subregional differences in the frequencies of mounds, suggesting that high-status positions were distributed in varying concentrations, that the nature of high-status activities varied over the region, or that it was the material manifestations—the mounds—that varied while the frequency of elites and their activities was about the same. Clearly, given the nature of this variation, one would be making a mistake by using mounded architecture as a simple measure of social status.

Although the Valley of Oaxaca mounds tend to be community, and not household or individual, products, their distribution may offer clues about the form of the social distribution of individual or household status. In our analysis of central places we used the number of mounds as an indicator of a settlement's civic/ceremonial importance. Histograms of central places by numbers of mounds are usually strongly skewed, with a long tail toward the upper end of the distribution. From the Late Formative through the end of the prehispanic sequence, we used these histograms and other information to form between four and six hierarchical levels of civic/ceremonial centers. The divisions are sometimes arbitrary, but other architectural and spatial characteristics often provide independent confirmation of the number-of-mounds criterion. When we plotted the centers on a map by level in the hierarchy, we could form a rough picture of spatial aspects of upper-order activities. As we point out below, this hierarchy is not always coterminous with hierarchies formed by measures other than mounded architecture. The hierarchical character of mound distributions and their lack of isomorphism with several of the other variables that reflect community position in the past suggest that hierarchies of individual or household positions will also be fairly complex.

Spatial Arrangements

Control over space (access and proximity) is a socially manipulated resource. Inaccessibility may be enhanced to screen administrative functions from public scrutiny. However, interpreting spatial arrangements and proximity is not straightforward, since the costs of transportation and communication may be borne by either partner in an exchange. D. Gregory and J. Urrey (1985) provide case studies on the use of regional space and class stratification in a modern context. Also, in an analytical sense, spatial associations are a valuable means for recognizing new relationships between potential wealth or status items.

For Monte Alban, R. E. Blanton (1978:98-100) discusses in detail the closure of the Main Plaza in the Classic period. There is similar evidence for the creation of privacy and barriers to traffic flow at the lesser political-religious centers in the valley from as early as the Middle Formative (Monte Alban Early I).

Proximity to civic/ceremonial centers is in some cases correlated with other measures of wealth. For example, average terrace areas are larger for Monte Alban's subdivisions near the Main Plaza and smaller in the more distant subdivisions of the city. This is significant since the larger terraces actually tend to occur on the steeper upper slopes, where construction would have been more difficult than on lower slopes.

Is a similar relationship between proximity to site center and terrace area evident at other sites? For the 13 Early Classic sites in the sample we used earlier from Tlacolula and Ocotlan, terraces with mounds or immediately adjacent to mounds were usually much larger than average. But perhaps more interesting is the range of differences from site to site in near-mound versus away-from-mound terrace areas. Near-mound terraces average from 55 percent smaller to 186 percent larger than away-from-mound terraces. Similarly, there is quite a spread (from 2 percent to 28 percent) in the proportion of a site's terraces that are in favorable, near-mound positions. Our use of a dichotomous variable should not imply a two-level social system. Apparently, the size and role of the town in the regional system and the range of special activities carried out on some terraces are additional variables that are associated with house lot size and affect the relationship between house lot size and proximity to mounded architecture.

Generally, at all sites (not just terraced sites), elaborate residences tend to cluster around administrative plazas through the Classic period. But elaborate residences are more dispersed in the Postclassic. At Mitla, for example, there are several Late Postclassic elaborate residences from 1 to 4 km removed from the main palaces. Change over time in spatial arrangements is a significant datum for interpretation of social structure.

The spatial distribution of funerary urns is an instructive case. Excavations show that urns occur as tomb furniture and date mainly to the Classic period. They are probably best interpreted as symbols of important deceased ancestors (J. Marcus 1983e). Our regional surveys have turned up four more facts about the funerary urns. They are much more frequent at Monte Alban than anywhere else. Urns are a distant second in frequency at secondary administrative centers. At Monte Alban and the secondary centers, they are most frequent near the site centers. And urns are most frequent in towns near the alluvium as opposed to towns of equal administrative or population rank farther back in the hills. On the basis of these facts, we have suggested that the greatest elaboration of funerary ritual involving urns was in connection with the state and with solidifying title to high-quality alluvial land by means of traditional Zapotec inheritance and ancestor worship. Such inherited estates were crucial, long-lasting foundations of the Monte Alban state.

We may not be correct in this interpretation. Further testing with other archaeological data will be necessary. But notice the analytical importance of spatial contexts. And to reach even this point we had to have excavations of hundreds of burials, iconographic study, sixteenth-century historical sources, an interpretation of the indicator (urns) in terms of cultural meaning, systematic information on spatial distribution of urns at both the community and regional scales, and a detailed analysis of long-term change in settlement systems. Without research at different scales, and the analysis to put facts together, the framing of nontrivial hypotheses about stratification will be uninformed and undisciplined.

Obsidian

Obsidian is a scarce good in the Valley of Oaxaca. Every piece was imported; there are no local sources. One might expect obsidian to be a good indicator of wealth. But there are complications. The highest densities appear to be at work areas, so these should be considered differently from the rest of the distribution. Then there are problems with function. Survey evidence and historical accounts show that it was used in temple ritual; historical sources also describe use in war clubs. The temple contexts thus might be considered differently, and we have to allow for the possibility of higher densities in military sites. These conditions preclude a straightforward interpretation of obsidian distributions.

The Late Postclassic period has the most obsidian; at that time, the five largest central places and several work areas account for the bulk of the obsidian we found. At Monte Alban and in other important centers, obsidian work areas were typically situated away from the civic/ceremonial centers of sites. The concentration of obsidian in five major centers as opposed to one (Monte Alban or San José Mogote) in earlier times, its relative dispersal away from the centers of major sites, and the persistent low frequencies at smaller settlements seem to provide important clues about the distribution of wealth.

Ceramics

Differential access to pottery can be examined using the findings of the regional survey. Most of our analysis has so far looked at ceramics at the community and higher levels, though there is some information on household variability. We have examined regional type distributions; number of types per site as a reflection of access to a variety of pottery wares, shapes, and decorative styles; and site-to-site variation in overall "fanciness" of pottery as indicated by a production step measure (Feinman 1980).

Probably the costliest pottery in ancient Oaxaca was the Mixtec style polychrome of the Late Postclassic. From excavations one might expect it to be a general marker of wealth. But polychrome distribution maps from the regional survey show it to be rather limited to the central and eastern parts of the valley, though widespread at various sites in those areas. In the western and southern valley, polychrome is rare, and other costly types— red-on-cream and graphite-on-orange—take its place. The lesson here is that, before one uses a pottery type as an indicator of household wealth, one needs to know its distribution both within the population and within the region.

In the Valley of Oaxaca, overall frequencies of pottery and types per site decline with distance from production centers. Historically (and perhaps in prehispanic times), people in areas with poorly developed markets made greater use of gourd or wooden containers as substitutes for pottery or produced simple, unelaborated ceramics. We have interpreted this pattern from both consumer and producer perspectives. This type of economic marginality shows up in access to pottery and in the frequency of less common artifact categories. In some phases, impoverished pottery and other artifact inventories also have been noted in the most demographically developed areas in the interior of the region. To test alternative explanations, we think further study of these patterns is required, using more reliable and representative artifact inventories.

The variable "number of ceramic types per site" usually has a statistical distribution more normal than the positively skewed distributions of other variables we examined. This may be due in part to the artificial constraints of a ceramic typology. Nevertheless, we have observed considerable variation in access to different types of pottery. Only some of the variation appears to be due to collection biases and sample size. A large portion of the variation is probably due to the position of communities in the regional system and to the diverse range of activities at various sites.

Average production-step measures from site to site vary surprisingly little (Finsten 1983). In Monte Alban IIIA, IIIB, IV, and V, the standard deviations in the number of types per site for all administrative and/or nonadministrative sites range between only 1 percent and 30 percent of the mean. However, we think that refinements in collecting and analysis would increase variation. This is an area in which more work could prove fruitful.

Human Osteology

Skeletal evidence of nutritional state, stress, and trauma may reflect position in social structure. D. C. Hodges (1986) has begun analysis on 556 individual burials from 14 sites in the Valley of Oaxaca. The results thus far are suggestive of significant variation and surprising continuities, depending on the specific measure and how data are aggregated. The data are not yet in a form where we can evaluate alternative patterns and interpretations.

Co-Occurrence of Indicators

How do these indicators co-vary? Analytical problems such as those we pointed out above are compounded when we study the mutual association of indicators. Decisions made in data collection and analysis, at the simpler levels and especially in terms of patterns and meanings of co-occurrence, are theory-laden. Future research on stratification in Oaxaca will require more careful attention to conceptual and analytic commitments that must be made in the data collection and analysis process ("inadvertent sociological theory"—Carter 1971).

We only have limited household-scale analysis, most of which is at the hilltop terraced sites. The greatest variation in terrace sizes and in pottery and other items found on individual terraces is at Monte Alban, followed to a much lesser degree by several secondary centers, and third by a few towns more involved than others in craft production and exchange. Narrower ranges of variation in terrace sizes, smaller terraces, and rather paltry artifact inventories are typical of terraced sites not at the top of the administrative hierarchy or not outstanding in craft production and exchange.

Most of our analysis has focused on variation between communities. Intercommunity variation is relevant in a discussion of social stratification. This analysis has measured degrees of heterogeneity between communities of the same as well as different sizes, and heterogeneity in the strength of relationships between indicators. If indicators vary in their degree of relationship over time and space at the community scale of analysis, then one should be ready for at least as much variation when analysis turns to the household scale.

We examined correlations among proximity to high-quality farmland, proximity to other central places, number of mounds, population size, number of ceramic types, and obsidian counts. Generally (though not always), the first two variable were not statistically associated with anything else. Obsidian counts are practical only for the Late Postclassic and correlate strongly with the other variables that define the top five or six centers.

Mounds, population, and types per site tend to be significantly associated with each other, but with varying degrees of strength. These three indicators, especially mounds and population, are generally correlated and they are good measures of the position of a community in a regional hierarchy of centers.

The association among mounds, population, and ceramic types is generally stronger in the later Formative but weakens during the Classic. In the Late Postclassic, below the level of the top six sites, the associations are weak. These trends reflect more complexity or functional segregation in the later phases. Subregional partitions vary considerably from regional patterns, suggesting functional distinctions between centers in different subregions. Again, further studies using household samples will have to be aware of these dimensions of variation.

Heterogeneity—among communities, over time, and among different indicators—is a strong element in the distribution of these social resources. In our opinion, to understand this degree of heterogeneity we shall need a theoretical framework more sophisticated than simple "elite/commoner" or "rulers/craft-specialists/ruled" schemes.

Methodological Conclusions

The problems of measurement and interpretation inherent in archaeological data are formidable but often surmountable. What does an obsidian blade distribution mean? How can we talk about access to the means of production when we don't know what land or fields went with which households? If occupation is customarily an important variable, what do we do when we can't systematically assign occupations to households? Where is our stratified, random, in-depth sample of households for the whole society? Many of these are archaeological problems that are probably resolvable in the long run; others we shall have to work around.

The distributions of various indicators of unequally held social resources illustrate certain features of prehispanic Oaxacan society. Where the measures are not artificially or functionally constrained to a narrow range (ceramics and obsidian), distributions tend to be skewed, with a long tail to the right, so that there are many people with a small amount of something and increasingly fewer people with larger amounts. There is typically a great range of variation from a point above the lower mode to the highest values.

There is nothing in these distributions themselves that speaks for a two- or three-class system, but we stress that division of such distributions is largely a theoretical, not an empirical, matter.

The distribution of social resources varied considerably across the region, among functionally different communities, and over time. Documenting change over time in the distribution of material resources may in the long run be archaeology's best contribution to stratification studies.

Let Us Not Reinvent the Wheel: Lessons from Sociology

The data just discussed do not compel an interpretation from the sixteenth-century chronicles; it is even less likely that ancient Oaxaca was directly analogous to medieval, modern, industrial, or postindustrial Europe or America. But when we try to interpret the information, when we try to discuss how Oaxaca society changed over time, how it is like and unlike the postconquest periods, we find we are faced with the same theoretical and analytical problems as sociologists who study class in industrial societies.

What is the basis of individual position? This has been a fundamental question for American empiricist sociology since the 1930s (Goldhamer and Shils 1939; T. Parsons 1940; K. Davis 1942; K. Davis and W. E. Moore 1945). What is the unit of analysis: the individual, the household, the family, or a larger unit? Some researchers treated stratification as a problem in the correct ranking of individuals according to their qualities—the status-attainment model; others continued attempts to use broader categories or groups (Cox 1945). Is there a unitary social structure—that is, a common ladder? Or is it a conflict among groups, with fewer rules and common goals? What matters over the long run, individuals or aggregates? What determines change? A major cleavage in stratification studies has been between functionalist and conflict theories. To a lesser extent, anthropological writers fall into one or the other camp, but the sociological literature provides a richer theoretical debate free of the clutter of archaeological technicalities.

Should we opt for community (Warner, Meeker, and Eells 1949) or "national" (Pfautz and Duncan 1950) social structure? H. W. Pfautz and O. D. Duncan have criticized W. L. Warner's anthropological study of class in America both for rigid adherence to method without sufficient attention to conceptual implication and for problems in the wider applicability of community-based results. Mesoamericanists should be familiar with the latter criticism.

How can Grand Theory be connected to observable objects? Should we even bother with Grand Theory? How do we know that indicators indicate what they are supposed to indicate? L. F. Carter (1971:13), for example, writes that "informed speculation about the linkages between our theoretical constructs and indicators can lead to more explicit testing strategies, as well as richer social theory." This is the same point we previously made concerning the investigation of the meaning of archaeological indicators. What are the crucial as opposed to the lesser determiners of position? How does one demonstrate answers to such questions?

To what extent do analytical methods inextricably mirror theory? There are alternative analytical approaches (Hatt 1950), but they are not theory-neutral (e.g., Cosier 1975, on the shift from cross-tabulation to regression methods in status-attainment studies). Status-attainment research by the late 1960s was establishment sociology, claiming itself to be a practical, empirical paradigm unfettered by unrealistic schemes of Great Sociological Thought. But it came under attack for embodying an implicit theory of free-market capitalism (Beck, Horan, and Tolbert II 1978, 1980; Horan 1978 vs. Hauser 1980). E. O. Wright, M. B. Katz, and others (Wright and Perrone 1977; Katz et al. 1982) have shown that American social stratification data could be linked to an explicitly Marxist framework. More recently, R. Goldman and A. Tickamyer (1984) have provided a twist on the structural vs. status-attainment debate, arguing that certain indicators, structures, and approaches were actually appropriate for one time and not another in the development of the American class system in the last century.

The importance of systematically collected data is underscored by the status-attainment vs. structural debate. Both sides often use exactly the same National Opinion Research Council data, yet they arrive at different conclusions. What is interesting to us about this is its similarity to a controlled experiment. The data are the same and the quantitative methods are essentially the same (and almost replicable). Yet different conceptual frameworks produced the diametrically opposed results.

This rapid check—it is hardly a thorough history—of issues in stratification research illustrates themes that should also be under discussion in studies of stratification in prehispanic Mesoamerica. We ought to be cognizant of questions already considered in the rest of the social sciences so that we can avoid reinventing the wheel (and having it come out square). Of the themes mentioned here, perhaps the most important for Mesoamerican archaeology in its current state is the need to connect concepts to systematic bodies of observations. We would leave a more lasting scientific legacy if we were able to do that.

Conclusions

We should be aware of method and theory in the study of stratification in complex societies outside of Mesoamerican archaeology. All such studies—contemporary, historical, or archaeological—thrive when they have alternative operative theories and large samples representing the variety of social positions with multiple indicators for a total social system. Mesoamericanists have neither many systematic data nor operant theory. We have not progressed much past the stage of loose analogy, we have not been critically self-conscious of the class and other biases we bring to our research from our own backgrounds, and we have not contributed much to general knowledge by exploiting the archaeological record for its perspective on long-term change in material distributions. If Mesoamerican archaeologists are going to contribute to the general knowledge regarding stratification, they will have to raise their standards of data adequacy, hypothesis testing, and quality of theoretical discourse.

Mesoamericanists can make progress in the scientific study of social systems. Encouraging research programs have been underway in the Valley of Mexico, where Elizabeth Brumfiel (1976, 1986, 1987b, 1988) has been sampling a variety of communities, and in Morelos, where Michael Smith (1986, 1987b) has been studying social stratification.

A more systematic, archaeologically oriented approach that employs and develops theories and concepts compatible with archaeological data is certainly possible. The examples illustrated in the body of this paper show a few ranges and distributional shapes for some social resources and a bit about how these varied. Although these illustrations are perhaps promising, we would be the first to say that we have not developed the conceptual frameworks necessary to advance these tentative observations into a full-scale research design.

Acknowledgments

We are grateful for the support given to the Valley of Oaxaca Settlement Pattern Project by the National Science Foundation, the Social Science Research Council, the Canadian Social Science and Humanities Research Council, the City University of New York, Purdue University, the University of Arizona, the University of Georgia, the University of Wisconsin, and Arizona State University. Authority to carry out fieldwork, and valuable assistance, was granted by the Instituto Nacional de Antropología e Historia and the Centro Regional de Oaxaca, directed by Manuel Esparza, Rogelio González, and Ma. de la Luz Topete V. This paper owes much to our colleagues Richard Blanton, Patrick Horan, Arthur Murphy, Henry Selby, and Alex Stepick. Thanks to Linda Nicholas for drafting the figures. We thank the many members of our field and lab crews and the Oaxacans over whose land we walked.

17. Ranking and Stratification in Prehispanic Mesoamerica

William T. Sanders

ARCHAEOLOGISTS have always displayed a lively interest in the reconstruction of prehistoric institutions. As our techniques have evolved we have become increasingly confident, and I would say more effective, in the achievement of this goal. Our concepts of the structure and function of ancient societies are derived from the ethnographic literature, from living or historically well documented cultures. Unfortunately, there is a regrettable looseness in the use of terminology derived from these studies. In part the blame rests on the shoulders of ethnographers, but the major onus lies in archaeologists' consistent misuse of it.

Granted, there is a range of opinion among ethnographers in the definition of basic social terms, typological and processual. In this paper I rely very heavily on usage found in the writings of G. P. Murdock (1949), M. Fried (1967), E. Service (1965) and P. C. Lloyd (1965). I am not arguing here for great precision in terminology, but some broad areas of agreement are necessary if we are to make meaningful cross-cultural comparisons.

The focus of the symposium was the nature of the Mesoamerican elite, but one obviously cannot discuss the elite without reference to the total social system of which the elite formed a part. The implication of the term "elite" is clear; it refers to a segment of a social system that enjoys measurably more prestige, power, and/or wealth than the society at large. Specific social systems differ in the degree to which these three variables function. In general, in the smallest and structurally simplest societies, high-status positions involve considerable prestige, little power, and virtually no significant wealth; in the most evolved systems, all three are important determinants of elevated status. Fried explains this range as due to a shift from the principle of ranking to stratification. He sees power as evolving from a condition where it derives almost entirely from prestige to one where wealth, in the form of control of strategic resources (in most preindustrial societies meaning agricultural land), is a major determinant of power.

In the simpler ranked societies, whatever power accompanies the higher-status positions is derived primarily from the role of ritual leadership. As the society gets larger, the roles of war leadership and internal dispute regulation become increasingly important and augment this limited power. Frequently, these roles become a source of wealth in the form of tribute, access to slaves, and gifts from litigants. An added source of wealth, which occurs as part of the process, is increased food production of the elite household itself, through the mechanism of polygyny, and clientage. In the more evolved cases of ranked societies, there may be some incipient stratification at the very top, based on the control of prime agricultural land, often cropped by slave labor. Many West African polities at the time of European contact had features similar to what we would call a highly evolved ranked society. Most of the population was organized into large expanded corporate groups (based on kinship), who owned tracts of agricultural land. There is evidence of differential political power within each group (i.e., the head was a political and ritual leader, but the only difference in access to land within the group was directly related to household size—specifically, the number of wives). There is also little evidence for major differences among lineages in terms of access to agricultural land. On the other hand, the ruling family owned private land, farmed by war captives. In the more complex African states (Benin, for example), the privilege extended downward to include other high-ranking individuals.

At the opposite end of the continuum are fully stratified societies. The particular form of stratification may vary from society to society; I have encapsulated this variety in the following alternative types.

1. A small segment of the society owns all or most of the agricultural land, and a large class of people is landless, working on the lands of the elite. In this case wealth, in land, is the major factor that produces political power and the major element in the system of stratification.

2. All holdings are family owned, but because of the rule of partible inheritance such holdings are small and vary little in size. The source of wealth lies, not in differential ownership of land, but in access to revenues (i.e., labor and or goods). This is the key variable in K. Wittfogel's *Oriental Despotism* (1957).

3. Economic resources other than land generate wealth and create a third source of power, such as trade and production of technology. These factors particularly operate in what we would call urban communities.

Terms like "ranking" and "stratification" are often used interchangeably by archaeologists and are equated with the terms "chiefdom" and "state." This has created considerable confusion in the literature. These last two terms should be used only in reference to political organization: the structure of power. There is, of course, a broad correlation of the chiefdom (as a political form) with ranking (as a principle of status differentiation), and the state with stratified society, but these correlations (particularly the latter) are not precise. I would define chiefdoms as political systems in which political statuses are based solely or predominantly on kinship. States could be defined not only as systems where the exercise of force is legitimized, as E. Service suggests, but (considering the fact that states probably derived from chiefdoms, in structural terms) as political systems in which specialized institutions of power, separate from kin-rank-based structures, have evolved; in the early stages of state formation, these occur side by side with the older structure. In fact, I would argue (but this needs to be tested) that kin-based institutions remain significant until stratification evolves to the conditions described above. The term "social class," following this argument, should only be used in reference to social systems wherein stratification is highly evolved, where the strata involve substantial self-interest.

A major problem for archaeology has been, and continues to be, the identification of material culture features that enable us to trace the evolution of society from ranked to stratified, from chiefdoms to states. With respect to ranking/stratification, the best guide to the degree of differentiation of an ancient society in power, prestige, and wealth is the ability of high-status individuals to use labor. In the case of 9N-8, a house compound excavated at Copan, the lord of the household was able to mobilize manpower 40 times over a period of 125-150 years for new building construction alone, the annual work projects ranging from 1,000-8,000 man days of labor. To this must be added architectural maintenance, building and maintenance of paved courtyards, daily household services, and tax payments in agricultural and craft production.

With respect to the differentiation of political power from kin-based structures, the evidence lies primarily in public architecture. In simpler hierarchical societies, the center of a polity either consists primarily of buildings directly used by the household of the chief (in most cases little different in function from those of lower-status households, only larger in size) or includes structures of ideological significance for the entire society, such as temples or tombs of previous office-holders. As the political power expands, the new institutions require housing, and the architecture of the center should reflect these expanded activities.

In my opinion, archaeological data for Preclassic Mesoamerica suggest the presence of only ranked societies and chiefdoms, of varying degrees of complexity and size. Even in the Classic period, ranked societies and chiefdoms persisted in most areas. By definition, such societies are characterized by a continuum in status differentiation—clearly defined social classes were absent. Stratified societies and states emerged in some areas during the Classic period and continued through the Postclassic. These societies varied considerably in terms of degree of stratification and complexity of the state institutions. Several Mesoamericanists have characterized such societies as having a basically simple structure with two well-defined classes, a ruling elite and a peasantry, a position I have presented and still endorse (Sanders and Price 1968).

Copan, one of the Classic Maya sites, is a typical example of this simple two-class society. D. L. Webster and A. Freter (1990a) estimate the total population of the Copan polity at its peak at between 18,000 and 24,000; the elite class made up 10 percent of this number, the balance being commoners. On the basis primarily of the scale, quality, and functional variability of architecture (but also including a variety of other data: burial, artifactual, and skeletal), this population falls into two basic levels. At the top some households clearly had more access to goods, particularly the services of skilled and unskilled labor beyond their own demographic resources. This segment made up 10 percent of the total population. An additional 10 percent were clients who resided with this class (i.e., their houses were attached directly to their patron's residential compound). In the case of Group 9N-8, perhaps the largest and most powerful of these households (other than the royal household), the approximately two hundred people who resided in the chiefly compound included members of a core kin group of variable rank. Some were craft specialists and possibly merchants; others were ritual specialists; still others were more probably unrelated clients or distant kin, who played the role of servants, and agricultural workers. Smaller households of this strata of Copan's population had as few as thirty to forty members. These smaller households lacked the complexity and degree of internal differentiation of 9N-8. Households of the much larger lower strata ranged in size from nuclear families to households slightly overlapping the lower end of the elite range in size.

The power of the royal lineage was measurably greater than that of the rest of the elite strata, in scale, quality, and internal differentiation of associated architecture. We are identifying the Main Group at Copan (what used to be called the Ceremonial Center) along with the residential groups attached to the sides of the Acropolis (in an area called Los Cemeterios in the literature) as the royal residential compound (see fig. 9.1). Most of the population of the Copan polity resided in residential compounds dispersed throughout the valley.

East of the palace compound and connected to it by a causeway is a densely settled urban area, locally referred to as Sepulturas, where forty residential groups resided, of which ten were the compounds of the mentioned elite families. This is where Group 9N-8 is located. West of the palace is a similar concentration of seventy-two residential units (El Bosque), of which eleven can be assigned to the elite class. The spatial arrangement here, however, is strikingly different than at Sepulturas. All but three of the higher-ranking residences are either adjacent or attached to the royal compound or arranged along a processional avenue leading into it. The great majority of the households in El Bosque were lower-strata units. It is tempting to conclude that the entire ward of El Bosque consisted of direct dependents, clients, and members of an expanded kin group of the royal lineage.

Recently completed excavations (Webster and Freter, personal communication, 1988) and dating of obsidian artifacts provide partial support for the model: substantial population decline occurred here in the century following the collapse of centralized rule at Copan, whereas in the Sepulturas barrio noble families maintained and even expanded their population and power until at least the year A.D. 1000—two centuries after the collapse.

The varied sources of data mentioned above—plus ethnographic analogy with the present-day Maya peasantry in highland Guatemala and Chiapas and ethnohistoric data for the Maya area in general—suggest that Copanec society was structured along kinship lines, probably based on patrilineal descent. The heads of elite households were probably leaders of large, internally ranked, expanded kin groups; and kinship, throughout Copan's history, was the most powerful single factor in patterning social relationships. As in many of the West African societies, the leaders probably acted as a council for the rulers; much of the politics at Copan involved a constant jockeying for power and position among the various elite lineage heads, with respect to each other and in relationship to the royal lineage.

In terms of broad evolutionary models, Copan was primarily a ranked society. But, as in many of its West African counterparts, incipient stratification was clearly present as well, most obviously at the very top. The expanded royal lineage must have had considerable power, resting in part on the differential control of prime agricultural land in the Copan Valley. Some of the more powerful lineage heads, on the basis of the degree of access to labor for construction (such as that of 9N-8), almost certainly were in a similar position.

Most of the elite lineage heads, based on the same criteria, were more like the West African lineage heads and acted as stewards of lineage lands. The architectural evidence from the royal compound also suggests that, at the time of its florescence, the structure had sufficiently departed from that of a chiefdom, so that one would characterize eighth-century Copan as a state. There is also increasing evidence that even the incipient stratification clearly present at Copan and the state were late phenomena and lasted perhaps 100 years.

Full-time craft specialization at Copan was present, but only in the form of clientage, involving prestige goods. More mundane technology was produced part-time, by peasant households.

Most Mesoamerican societies during the Classic and Postclassic probably were similar to eighth-century Copan. The decree of stratification versus ranking, however, must have ranged rather widely. Many polities during this period are probably best described as chiefdoms and others as states. In the case of the more stratified and statelike systems, the simple two-class structure was probably characteristic.

The only known exceptions to this two-level class structure were found at the capitals of a few unusually large central Mexican states such as Tenochtitlan-Tlatelolco and probably Teotihuacan and Tula. At Tenochtitlan-Tlatelolco, documentary data indicate the presence of a large middle class of full-time craft specialists, professional warriors, bureaucrats, priests, and merchants, a development clearly related to the enormous size of the city, in turn the product of the wealth and power generated by its administrative

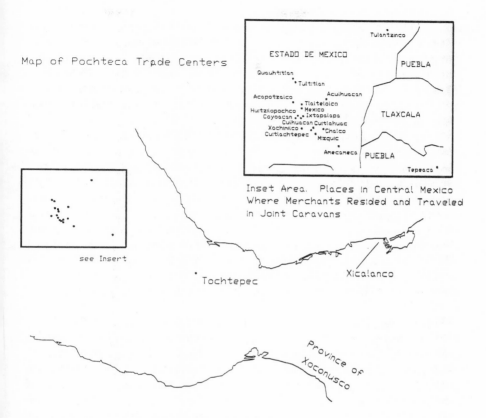

Map of Pochteca Trade Centers

ESTADO DE MEXICO

Tulantzinco

PUEBLA

Quauhtitlan
Tultitlan
Acapotzalco   Aculhuacan
          Tlaltelolco
Huitzilopochco Mexico
Coyoacan   Ixtapalapa   TLAXCALA
        Cuihuacan Cuitlahuac
Xochimilco
Cuitlachtepec   Chalco
        Mizquic
          Amecameca   PUEBLA
                    Tepeaca

Inset Area. Places in Central Mexico
Where Merchants Resided and Traveled
in Joint Caravans

see Insert

Tochtepec

Xicalanco

Province of Xoconusco

Fig. 17.1. Map of pochteca trade centers in Mesoamerica.

role as the capital of a large political system embracing some 5 to 6 million people.

This paper illustrates these points with a description of the *pochteca* as a specialized group of merchants involved in long-distance trade (fig. 17.1). An important distinction must be made between a situation in which some level of occupational specialization was present, a feature of all ranked and stratified societies, and one that led to the formation of a clearly defined social class. The kind of occupational specialization I have briefly described for Copan was typical of Mesoamerica and did not lead to a class of people, intermediate in prestige, wealth, and power, between the elite and the peasantry.

The *pochteca* of central Mexico (see fig. 17.1), in contrast, did constitute a true middle class, overtly expressed by a distinctive name, unique rituals associated with a patron god, and dress. As a class they were characterized by large size, an intermediate social position, and a guildlike organization, with a wide range of internal statuses. Major trading expeditions lasted for months and even years. All of these features suggest full-time specialization. Added to them were privileges such as juridical sovereignty, the right to send their children to the *calmecac* (the school of the elite class), the management of the major urban markets of Tenochtitlan-Tlatelolco, ownership of private land, and exemption from corvée labor. Some of these privileges were shared with the noble class or with professional warrior chiefs promoted from the commoner class (Acosta Saignes 1945; Sahagun 1946; Chapman 1959; Dibble and Anderson 1959).

Sahagun has provided us with our most detailed account of the *pochteca*, offering many insights as to their status and activities. When I first read this account many years ago, I was not aware of the obvious fact that his informants were from Tlatelolco, one of the five wards of the Aztec capital in 1519, whose residents were politically subordinate. The tone, purpose, and content of his informants' account is transparently political. The Tlatelolcan merchants were members of a conquered society and were obviously trying to emphasize their special and close association with the Aztec state and ruler. The history of the growth of the class and the extraordinary detailed account (which at times sounds like an epic) of a major expedition during the reign of Ahuitzotl represent an attempt to document this special relationship.

During the period from 1376, when Acamapichtli became the first Tenochca sovereign, until 1473, Tlatelolco was a semiautonomous state, with its own *tlatoani* or ruler. Sahagun was given the names of merchant leaders during the reigns of four successive *tlatoani* of Tlatelolco. Two leaders are given for each reign, suggesting the presence of two *calpullec* or wards of merchants. He also describes the growth of the class in terms of an increase in the variety of products brought back and, derivatively, the geographic expansion of their activities. During the reign of Axayacatl, Tlatelolco was directly incorporated into the Aztec state and administered by a Aztec governor. By the reign of Ahuitzotl, his successor, the number of merchant wards of the dual city had risen to seven.

At this point, the merchants present the epic narrative noted previously, a detailed description of a single expedition that reveals many facets of the operation of long-distance trade in the final decades of the Aztec empire.The special relationship with Ahuitzotl is carefully spelled out; they act as trading agents for the king, play the role of ambassadors to foreign rulers, and serve as intelligence agents in areas outside the empire. Highly formal meetings with the king are described at the inception and termination of the expedition, at which times the merchant leaders are addressed as kin by Ahuitzotl.

The political functions are so heavily stressed in this narrative that some writers have lost sight of the primarily entrepreneurial aspect of *pochteca* economy and have even described them as an arm of the state. B. Isaac (1986) has challenged this notion and I agree with his criticism. He goes too far, however, when he argues that the political roles played in the account may refer to a unique historical event. His argument leaves unexplained why the Tlatelolcan *pochteca* were so meticulous in presenting the account, and he ignores the following statement at the end of it:

And when Auitzotzin of Tenochtitlan died, Moctezuma, who was also a native of Tenochtitlan [*sic*] was then installed as ruler. In the same manner he continued the customs, followed the way, honored well the calling of the merchants, the vanguard merchants. He especially honored the principal merchants, the disguised merchants, those who bathed slaves, the slave dealers. He set them right by his side, even like the noblemen, the rulers; like all who had died, who had governed the cities of Mexico [and] Tlatilolco, he rendered them honor.[1] (Dibble and Anderson 1959:Bk 9:23)

This statement clearly indicates that the informants were describing the inception of a new role and that they continued to play it up to the time of the Spanish conquest. The *pochteca*, however, even at the end, were not primarily an arm of the state, but rather a class of urban professional middlemen. Much of their exchange had little or no connection with the mother city—they moved expensive prestige goods from city to city for the use of the upper class over much of Mesoamerica.

In this respect, their role was more comparable to a modern merchant marine. Since the role of the merchants has been the source of much debate (see Calnek 1978; Carrasco 1978), I quote and translate the following passage from Sahagun in full.

These merchants wander over all the country, dealing, buying in one part and selling in another that which they have purchased, these merchants wander through all of the settlements that are on the seacoast and inland, they do not neglect things to search for and places to travel, in parts buying, and in others selling. They do not avoid any place to search for things that they can buy and sell, not because the land may be very hot, nor because it is very cold, nor because it is very mountainous do they neglect to pass through it or turn it upside down[2] searching for what in the place is precious or profitable to buy and sell. These merchants suffer much for their work and dare enter every land (even though it be of enemies) and are very astute in dealing with those people, learning their language, dealing with them with kindness to make themselves attractive to the people through their friendliness. They discover where feathers and precious stones are, and gold; they buy them and carry them to sell where they know they are highly valued; also they ascertain where exquisite and precious animal skins are found, and sell them where they are highly valued. They also deal in precious vases made in diverse ways and painted with diverse designs, according to the custom of the land, some with lids made of turtle shell and spoons of the same material to froth the cacao, others with lids of diverse colors and figures, made in the manner of a tree leaf, and other precious frothing sticks to froth the cacao. (Sahagun 1946:vol. 1:53-54)

One interesting question is the size of this class. I assume here that, when a ward of Tenochtitlan-Tlatelolco is identified as a merchant ward, all or most of the residents were in fact *pochteca*. In small central Mexican states, wards comparable to those of the capital in size were made up of various kinds of specialists—and in some cases this was true even at the Aztec capital (Carrasco 1978; Rojas 1986). The problem is complex, but the term *calpulli*, translated in Spanish as *barrio*, functioned on a variety of spatial levels, as corporate groups of varying and inclusive sizes.

I believe this range in size is explained by the fact that, in its original form and perhaps a form persisting in rural communities, it was a segmentary lineage. Segmentary lineages have a highly flexible structure; they can be adapted to a rural and urban context and to the size and structure of the latter. As society becomes more stratified, they can also shift in structure from a kinlike to a patron-clientage type of internal relationship. In a center such as Tenochtitlan-Tlatelolco, with its 160,000-200,000 people, the size and scale of its urban economy would permit a process by which the maximal-level units functioned as units of economic specialization.

At the time of the Spanish conquest, there were approximately 100 *calpullec* (Rojas 1986); thus, the average size calculates at 1,600-2,000 people. If the seven wards of *pochteca* were of average size, this means a population of 11,000-14,000 people, of which perhaps 20-25 percent would be economically active males. The number of the latter might be smaller because many merchants, being of intermediate social status, would have had several wives and household servants. Furthermore, Sahagun's informants list a number of other towns in central Mexico with resident *pochteca*. Each ward at the Aztec capital, and the merchants from each city, formed a corporate guild, but there was also an overall organization centered at Tenochtitlan, and merchants from all these centers traveled together in large caravans. The total population of active males, who were members of the superguild, may have been as high as several thousand and the total population belonging to the class perhaps 15,000-20,000, surely the largest and internally most complex economic institution in the history of Mesoamerica. In addition to the superguild centered at Tenochtitlan, other central Mexican states, notably Cholula, had significant numbers of professional merchants.

Although I have found no references to the actual size of the caravans, Sahagun's statement that they crossed hostile territory and went fully armed would suggest considerable size—possibly several thousand, considering the fact that most Mesoamerican states were able to muster fighting forces that size.

Further confirmation as to the magnitude of trading activities was the need to establish colonies of *pochteca* at foreign towns to service the caravans, what Anne Chapman (1959) incorrectly calls "ports-of-trade." The most interesting example is the town of Tochtepec on the piedmont of the central Gulf Coast near the Oaxaca/Veracruz border. Caravans traveled to Tochtepec, where *pochteca* from each of the participating states resided and provided the merchants with supplies and, most importantly, information. There they split into two groups, one going to the south Gulf Coast, with a terminus at Xicalango. In the *Relación* of Chinantla, Tochtepec is described as a town of Mexicans and as the capital of the tributary province, where a garrison and an Aztec governor resided, who apparently was the supreme judicial official for the province (Paso y Troncoso 1905).

From this point on, caravans went armed to the teeth, and the *pochteca* had a reputation for bellicosity. This aspect of *pochteca* culture is of considerable interest, and it dovetails with a number of features of their subculture that indicate that Sahagun's Tlatelolcan informants were attempting to equate their class with the professional warriors, many of whom originally were, like the merchants, of commoner status and of an intermediate social position. The account of the conquest of Ayotlan and their turning over of the conquered territory to Ahuitzotl is part of this ploy and its political purpose is clear (the event provides additional support for my argument about the large size of the caravans). Further confirmation lies in the unusually detailed account of the banquet celebrating the completion of a trading expedition, to which warriors and nobles were invited: purchased slaves were sacrificed by the priests at the Templo Mayor and their bodies were eaten at the feast. The parallel to the warrior dedicating his captive to the sustenance of the gods is obvious. This equation is further supported by the merchants' statement that a specialized group, the slave merchants, were particularly favored by Ahuitzotl.

Finally, the following extraordinary quote from Sahagun completes the equation of merchant with warrior:

But if only sickness took one, if he died there in Anauac, they did not bury him. They only arranged him on a carrying frame. Thus did they adorn the dead: they inserted a feather labret in his lips, and they painted black the hollows about his eyes; they painted red about the lips with ochre, and they striped his body with white earth. He wore his paper stole, each end reaching his armpit. And when they had adorned him, then they stretched him on the carrying frame; they bound him there with the carrying frame cords. Thereupon they bore him to a mountain top. There they stood him up; they leaned the carrying frame against a post. There his body was consumed. And they said that indeed he had not died, for he had gone to heaven; he followed the sun. And just so was it said of those who had died in war; they said that they followed the sun; they went to heaven. (Dibble and Anderson 1959:Bk 9:24)

Another occupational specialized group, closely related economically to the *pochteca*, were the *tlameme* or professional burden bearers. This particularly central Mexican phenomenon was directly related to the large-scale political and commercial systems in that area. Obviously, a specialized stratum of this type could only emerge where the market for their services demanded it. R. Hassig (1985) presents the most detailed analysis. *Tlameme* clearly constituted an occupationally differentiated population: those in Tenochtitlan-Tlatelolco, at least, were full-time professionals, and contracts in terms of payments, schedules, load weights, and distances traveled per day were highly formalized. Possibly those in the capital were clients attached directly to merchants' households and were members of the merchant ward.

Tlameme were hired for single-day journeys or contracted for the entire long-distance trip. Apparently, loads transported within the empire were handled by contracted labor from local towns along the route, and each set of *tlameme* would travel for a single day. This procedure permitted larger loads to be handled and hence reduced costs. I suspect that these were part-time local peasants, but Hassig does not address this question.

For expeditions headed beyond the borders of the empire, *tlameme* were contracted from the home city, carried much lighter loads (23 kilos), and accompanied the merchants throughout the trip. These carriers must have been away from home for periods of a year or more. In the decades immediately after the Spanish conquest, the going rate for long-distance carriers, in terms of wage, was 100 cacao beans a day, which in the 1540s was worth approximately 1/2 reale in Spanish currency. At the same time, a fanega (46 kilos) of maize, which would have been the staple food of the *tlameme* as well as the rest of the Mesoamerican population, had a cash value of 3-4 reales in the market place. Thus, a *tlameme* would have to work 6-8 days to earn a fanega of maize. Assuming that he was a long-distance carrier, that he was absent approximately one year from his home city, and that he worked 300 days of a calendar year, he could earn between 37.5 and 50 fanegas of maize (1,752-2,300 kilos) for the trip. With this he could cover his family maize requirements and provide 100 percent surplus for meeting his other technological needs, via purchases in the marketplace, taxes, and ceremonial obligations. Payments by the merchants to such *tlameme* at the end of the trip could have been made after the disposal of goods in the Tenochtitlan-Tlatelolco market or on the basis of surpluses of grain produced in fields owned by the merchants and farmed by local peasants. A 23-kilo load consisted of 24,000 cacao beans. At this rate of payment, if the burden bearer brought cacao from the trip, as the final product to be disposed of in the marketplace, the load would have sufficed to support him and his family only 240 man days and, of course, provide no profit for the merchant. It is pretty clear from this that the full-time *tlameme* could not have brought even the less rapidly consumed luxury foodstuffs from such considerable distances. On the other hand, cacao was brought, as imperial tax, from areas as distant as Xoconusco. In this case, however, the cost of transport would be underwritten as part of the tax obligation of subject lords along the route; presumably, larger loads were carried by part-time *tlameme* to reduce this cost. The use of part-time *tlameme* labor would even permit the shipment of cacao from considerable distances as an item of trade. The average distance traveled per day by *tlameme* was minimally 20 km. Even a load of 23 kilos, brought from a distance of 300 km would only cost 3,000 cacao beans (30 days x 100 beans per day wage) and leave a load of 21,000 beans for sale in Tenochtitlan.

In confirmation of this point, it is clear from Sahagun's account that generally only goods of extremely high value were carried by the full-time *tlameme* on these long-distance expeditions and returned to the market-place in the home city. He mentions as exports fine textiles, gold and rock crystal jewelry, and slaves, all sold to the elite in foreign areas. In return the burden bearers brought jade, turquoise mosaics, seashells, coral, tropical bird feathers, and ocelot skins, all goods of considerable value in the markets of central Mexico. Of particular interest, however, is Sahagun's statement that the merchants also exported obsidian artifacts from central Mexico, even on these long-range expeditions, another demonstration of the high efficiency of the production and transport capabilities of this one mundane item (see Sanders and Santley 1983). He specifically says that obsidian was sold to the common people. The goods could have been carried by the slaves mentioned as exports, making the exchange significantly more profitable.

On the basis of the Spanish accounts (particularly from Sahagun and Zorita 1941) we know that a number of craft groups at Tenochtitlan-Tlatelolco also enjoyed elevated status, particularly the goldsmiths, lapidaries, and feather workers, and the city was full of occupational specialists producing more mundane goods. While it is impossible to provide even a rough estimate of the size of these elements and of the bureaucratic, warrior, or priestly classes, considering the simple fact that much of the population of the city consisted of non-food-producing specialists, these elements were large enough and economically specialized and stratified enough to constitute true social classes (Calnek 1976).

One possible clue to the size of the professional warrior class residing in the city in 1519 is found in a statement by the Anonymous Conqueror (Conquistador Anónimo 1941:45):

The principal lord of this great temple was Montezuma and he had them guarded[3] here as I will tell you; and he had besides a garrison [*guarnición*] of 10,000 men of war, all selected as men of valor, who guarded and accompanied his person. When there was a riot or rebellion in the city or its surroundings, they or a part of them went forth ahead; if for some reason more people were needed they were assembled quickly in the city and its nearby area.

The phrase "selected as men of valor" and the reference to them as a "garrison" that "accompanied his person" suggests strongly that the Anonymous Conqueror is referring to the professional warriors. They would obviously be experienced warriors, but also fairly young, so the ratio to total membership per family or household would be relatively high. Those of highest rank, however, would have had a polygamous household and household servants—and the ratios would then have been higher. In any case, the total population involved would be a substantial element in the urban population and would have served as a large clientele for the merchants' goods. It should be noted that the Anonymous Conqueror is one of the most conservative sources with respect to numbers.

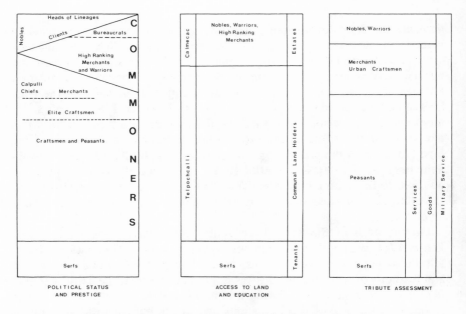

Fig. 17.2. Three ways to model social stratification in the prehispanic Basin of Mexico.

For the combined urban and rural population of the Basin of Mexico, the diagrams in figure 17.2 show three ways of ordering the system of stratification. Diagram 1 is based upon political power. We know that warrior nobles from the lower class, who had recently received the associated honors, were still considered *macehualtin* or commoners and often held political offices in the Aztec imperial bureaucracy, as well as taxation rights over specific rural *calpullec*. Some merchants, in their roles as market supervisors and judges, can also be considered members of the political bureaucracy. Many *pipiltin* or nobles by descent, who did not themselves inherit land or hold public offices, were craftsmen attached to their kin's households; hence, their political status would be lower than that of most commoner warriors and some merchants. Diagram 2 stratifies the population in terms of access to agricultural land and to educational opportunities; here the stratification is more apparent. The third diagram is derived from Zorita's statement about tribute obligations; again the stratification is clearer, but, in contrast, in this diagram the urban craftsmen, probably those producing mundane goods as well as elite, are equal to the merchants in status.

In a recent paper (Sanders and Webster 1988), D. L. Webster and I have argued, based on a model of preindustrial cities by Richard Fox (1977), that urbanization in Mesoamerica was energetically limited in all areas of agricultural and craft production, and most importantly in transport. With perhaps one exception (obsidian) long-distance trade could only involve goods that had considerable value and hence were accessible only to the upper and middle levels of society—primarily the former. A large differentiated class of merchants, like the *pochteca*, could only evolve in a situation where this consuming class was also large. A sizable number of *pochteca* customers were residents of Tenochtitlan-Tlatelolco; others were from central Mexican states.

In central Mexico, in 1519, the primary customer area for the *pochteca* guild's ultimate sales, there was a population of approximately 2 to 2.5 million people, excluding the metropolitan area of greater Tenochtitlan (Sanders 1976). Applying the Copan data on ranking and stratification to this figure, some 10 percent of the population or 200,000 to 250,000 people would have been the primary beneficiaries of the *pochteca*'s trading activities. In greater Tenochtitlan, with 400,000 people, well over half of the population would have been clientele. Added to these figures would be the local elite outside of the central Mexican area that received the services of the *pochteca*.

The major theoretical point being made here is that institutional complexity relates to the scale of the human activity being administered or serviced; the emergence of a large, internally complex economic institution, like the *pochteca* guild, could occur only in the demographic and political setting of central Mexico in the fifteenth century. Finally, only with a large mercantile class and its related economic elements, the *tlameme* and elite craft specialists who processed the raw products brought by the merchants, could a significant, well-defined middle class emerge in a setting as energetically and technologically limited as prehispanic Mesoamerica.

Notes

1. There are several references to the *pochteca* as bathers of slaves destined for sacrifice. This may be directly related to the fact that the slaves were purchased, not captured in battle, and that they were unacceptable to the gods until ritually prepared.

2. The verb used here is "trastornarla."

3. The verb form here is "guardadas." The reference is to the priesthood attending the temples of the great enclosure.

18. The Concern with Elites in Archaeological Reconstructions: Mesoamerican Materials

George E. Marcus

I must admit that I have been both attracted to and quite daunted by the task of contributing something to this volume on the analytical value, or even the possibility, of a systematic perspective on elites in Mesoamerican archaeology. What is attractive is the opportunity to think again about research on elites in a context much more challenging than the requirements of ethnographic inquiry on such subjects (see Marcus 1983a). This is also an opportunity for me to think beyond the very constrictive boundaries of what has been conventionally taken in the social sciences as the sources of elite theory—writings such as those of the Italians V. Pareto and G. Mosca, and more recently of C. Wright Mills (1956)—to a new set of theoretical sources that, while not going by the label "elite theory," indeed meet some of the unfulfilled goals of this line of research. I refer to the work of the French social theorists Michel Foucault and Pierre Bourdieu, who, while never focusing on the concept of elites nor on elite groups in particular, have nonetheless had the most trenchant things to say about power and status hierarchies and the practices that sustain them under varying historical circumstances.

What is daunting is that I know very little about advances in archaeological theory and practice since the mid-1960s (when, as an undergraduate, I had a career interest in archaeology), and I know even less about the complex and sophisticated tradition of Mesoamerican archaeology, save for my reading of the diverse set of excellent papers presented at the American Anthropological Association symposium from which this volume derives. Furthermore, I have to agree at least with the spirit of the conclusion expressed in the very spirited paper of Kowalewski, Feinman, and Finsten that chooses a somewhat different direction from the theme of the volume: "In sum, 'elite' can be a convenient label in loose speech, but it has no analytical value in work with archaeological data. Now we can put the concept back into the secondary refuse." These authors, who factor quantitative techniques that are sensitive to the massive bits-and-pieces nature of archaeological data over the impetuosity of analogy, put their faith in stratification, on which sociologists have presumably been able to establish an empirical terra firma, in contrast to the murky ground on which the related concept of elites has been developed.

I do indeed agree that elite theory and research as they have been explicitly developed in sociology have limited analytic power in archaeology, as they also have in ethnography. It is certainly true that theoretical play with the concept of elites will not allow Mesoamerican archaeologists to refine with any precision the simple two-class (noble-commoner) framework that has dominated reconstructions (Chase and Chase, introduction, this volume). Perhaps the quantitatively sophisticated sociological literature on stratification might be of more use in suggesting ways of interpreting mass assemblages of artifact types and distributions, although, despite appearances of rigor and precision, this literature has been plagued by as many conceptual indeterminacies at the interpretive end as has the elite literature and thus is probably not as deserving of the preferential respect that Kowalewski, Feinman, and Finsten so freely give to it in their paper. But surely archaeologists want more from their data than the very limited range of questions, essentially about social architecture, that quantitative stratification studies in sociology can address, however important these questions are.

In their joint introduction and individual papers, the Chases themselves do very well with the concept of elites, while recognizing clearly the limitations of its potential as a guide or framework for the fine-grained analysis of mass assemblages of archaeological data. They deliver a needed overview critique of the simplistic assumptions and questions that have guided research on the identification of elites in Mesoamerican societies and modestly push for an agenda of new issues. For example, based on their findings at Caracol, they complicate the simple noble-commoner scheme by establishing the presence of intermediate elite groups (perhaps marking the existence of an additional broad stratum or class) in society that are based on ritual and occupational specializations. It is debatable whether the Chases' labeling of these groups with such a Eurocentric and modernist term as "bourgeoisie" is appropriate, but there can be no doubt that their focus on such distinctive elite (or status, to use Max Weber's term) groups of ambiguous social origins is therapeutic in opening up new questions generally about elites in Mesoamerican societies. The existence of such groups certainly will not be a surprise to any anthropologist or historian who has studied classic kingships and aristocratic societies globally. However, what the analytic emphasis on such intermediate groups does is to shift the focus in research on elites and stratification from a search for precise indices in the material record of the presence or absence of elite status markers to the more difficult and interesting questions of the relationships among different kinds of elites in the construction of a particular institutional order. In trying to work intensively on the intermediate class of specialists, the Chases at least open up broader questions about the relationships among varied elite groups without, however, suggesting what a theory of such relationships, appropriate for the kinds of materials on which archaeologists have to rely, might be like.

In addition, the Chases point to the very important contributions that the analysis of architectural styles and iconography can make to our understanding of social relationships in Mesoamerican societies and of elite ideology, as expressed through images, and the grounded practices of control and discipline that ensure the production of such ideology through material media. The value of approaching Maya (mainly elite) history through iconography is amply demonstrated in David Freidel's paper, "Children of the First Father's Skull." I myself would have stressed the importance of art-historical materials in archaeological elite research even more, if only because culture theory in this realm has been so lively in recent decades (viz., the influence of structuralist and semiotic approaches first on literature and then on visual arts and, more recently, of deconstructionist and critical theory methods through the same route). It has brought a certain discipline, standards of interpretation, and an intellectual complexity to the symbolic analysis of images and architecture, a preoccupation that perhaps deservedly had declined in interest for "scientific" archaeologists because of the highly idiosyncratic and speculative manner in which it had been conducted.

In fact, most of the papers in this volume exemplify the ambition of classic elite research to go beyond questions of social stratification to say things about specific relationships of power and domination and about how status distinctions are systematically produced. These are matters of content, more than form, and are rarely subject to direct observation in any context of elite research. In this sense, all elite research, ethnographic and historical as well as archaeological, operates by means of methodological reconstruction. Elite research at its best, even when at work among contemporary subjects who seclude themselves from or grant only limited access to ethnographers, operates from analogy, disciplined inference, and the discernment of provisional patterns that are subject to continual revision through new or challenging data collections. While, in particular, much about elite lifeways and interrelationships is denied archaeological reconstruction (except through the key use of ethnohistory, iconographic analysis, and the like), the papers in this volume demonstrate that an interest in such matters can and should be eminently empiricist in nature. It need not be pursued through interpretive practices that are wildly speculative or irresponsible, especially given the real advances that have been made in the consideration of the nature of power and status hierarchies in societies of all kinds through the writings of theorists such as Michel Foucault (especially *Discipline and Punish*, 1979) and Pierre Bourdieu (especially *Distinction*, 1984).

In the remainder of this brief essay, I want only to reiterate and clarify, for the sake of application to archaeology, some of my earlier conclusions about the value of the tradition of elite theory and research, known and identified as such in Euroamerican social science, for ethnographic style inquiries on this subject. Beyond this, I have some admittedly (and apologetically) programmatic things to say about the value of a body of theory that has, it seems to me, superseded the existing tradition of elite theory and given elite studies a new lease on life. In terms of theory construction, this body of theory might, in certain of its formulations, even have a special affinity for the materialist base from which archaeology must develop its interpretations; in fact, I have already come across interesting applications and influences from these theories in archaeological scholarship, which, if not of theoretical relevance to concerns with Mesoamerican elites, are at least of use as a comparative case with which to probe and substantively develop further the line of questioning initiated in this volume.

Earlier Conclusions about the Value of the Tradition of Elite Theory and Research Reprised

In my earlier consideration of the development of ethnographic studies of elites (1983a), I developed the following major points:

1. In assessing the value of an elite focus as an analytical approach in any relevant domain of inquiry (sociological, historical, ethnographic, archaeological, etc.), nothing is more important to keep in mind than both the particular context in the development of Western social theory in which the concept of elites as well as elite theory arose and the specific set of historic circumstances that theoretical concerns with elites have addressed, since, I would argue, that it is in these historical and cultural contexts particularly that the use of elite theory, as it explicitly exists in the social sciences, is most cogent and analytically powerful. In short, the theory of elites explicitly developed in Western social theory makes most sense within the confines of the specific history of modernity, from the sixteenth century to the present, largely in the framework of the nineteenth-century development of European states and industrial societies and, by the late twentieth century, of a world system. To abstract elite theory from its specific historic and cultural referents in the attempt to constitute it as *generic* social theory is a perilous undertaking at best.

2. In its contemporary uses as an everyday term of both lay and social scientific reference, and as the basis for a systematic body of theory and research, the concept of elites has without doubt been most important in the former sense, as an "odd-job" word in L. Wittgenstein's terms (as "a convenient label of loose speech" in Kowalewski, Feinman, and Finsten's). Clear in what it signifies, but ambiguous as to its precise referents, the concept of elites in general usage locates cause and agency in social events by evoking the image of a ruling, controlling few while remaining intractably vague about the precise identity, organization, or social embeddedness of such persons.

I argue that this shaping of the concept in an elusive form had a very specific historic determination and function in Western societies, as they underwent a long transformation from the ancient regimes of feudal Europe into the mass societies and liberal nation-states of modernity. Before the nineteenth century, the word "elite" had restricted meanings, being overshadowed by the abundance of explicit categories of rank, which affirmed in language a premise of inequality inherent in feudal society in nineteenth-century Europe; the gradual decline and disappearance of the older, varied distinctions of rank marked an ideological uneasiness about any kind of fixed inequality, especially if it was identifiable as residing in actual, enduring groups of powerful and privileged individuals. In social thought fundamental ambiguity arose about where and by whom superordinate authority ought to be exercised. Yet, to contemporary observers, concentrations of power, wealth, and elevated status were not less evident as phenomena of the new orders just because the structural nature of these concentrations was difficult to perceive and discuss. General uncertainty persisted in nineteenth-century Europe and America about how to refer to these unquestionably permanent features of society, which had become, in effect, ideological unmentionables.

During this period, "elite" came into much wider usage, along with the concept of class and a collection of terms used to identify impersonal institutions (especially the state, bureaucracy, the economy, and the market). At different levels of abstraction, these concepts stood for sources of causal agency behind the events in the new orders and, more importantly, enabled those who spoke about society to continue to refer to evident inequalities while remaining vague about their precise empirical status.

What distinguishes "elite" from such alternative terms as "class" and "the state" is that the former focuses one's imagery at a much lower level of abstraction than do the latter. It evokes the image of identifiable groups of persons rather than impersonal entities such as formal organizations and mass collectivities. Furthermore, the concept of elites carries with it the notion that such groups are the major source of change within relevant levels of social organization—local, regional, societal, and international—and that they are the force behind institutional processes in which others—the masses, nonelites—participate with them. The concept suggests that the organization of these powerful groups can be mapped and described. This is unlike alternative concepts of agency such as class or the state, which are useful precisely to the extent that they remain empirically unelaborated entities.

3. Small wonder, then, that the theory and research tradition following (or paralleling) this history of the term "elite" has focused, to the exclusion of other issues, upon the delineation of the empirical status of an elusive concept. Elite theory and research have been largely about the social architecture of elites, rather than process, lifestyle, and strategies of status differ-

entiation. Also, because the concept of elites represents, more than class or institutional agency, a very sensitive challenge to the notion that entrenched inequality in a highly visible, personal form did not (or should not) develop in liberalizing and democratizing social orders, it is not surprising that the narrowly empirical concerns of elite theory and research with the identity, extent, and embeddedness of elites within social organization—as well as with the degree of monopolization or restraint in their exercise of power— have been inextricably tied to more general radical and conservative critiques of mass liberal society. In fact, the inherent normative dimensions and ideological contexts of elite theory and research have often overtaken their modest, narrowly empirical goals of adequately describing power structures within modern and modernizing societies over the past two centuries.

4. Specifically, classical elite theory is associated with the nineteenth-century Italian theorists Pareto and Mosca. Just as changes in the way "elite" was used as an everyday word occurred in the wake of historic changes in European societies, so elite theory arose as an alternative way of conceiving the general workings of nineteenth-century European capitalist societies. In his later works, Marx conceived the sociological implications of capitalist economic processes in terms of the abstract social entities they generated—classes. As Anthony Giddens has suggested (1973:118), by fixing his discussion at this level of abstraction, Marx left undeveloped a treatment of the connections between economic and political power. The theories of Pareto and Mosca can be seen as a supplement—but a very critical one—to the more ambitious, totalizing Marxian theory.

Seemingly, Pareto and Mosca reduced the level of abstraction in Marx to a more hardheadedly empirical, realist level. Whether in fact the concept of elites they introduced was any less theoretically abstract than the Marxian concept of class, or any easier to see in action, is beside the point; it has appeal as more tangible in human terms than the later work of Marx, which dealt with relations among systems rather than between persons. Furthermore, if Marx is seen as aligned with a particular antibourgeoisie position in European politics, then Pareto's and Mosca's supplements-as-critique to Marx can also be read as a political rebuttals to left-wing analyses of society and the political implications they contained. Elite theory was interpreted in this way (largely though the work of Robert Michels) in twentieth-century fascism, but it also served later critiques (throughout the work of C. Wright Mills) of the state and monopoly capitalism.

The point to emphasize, then, about the development of concerns with elites as a theory is that they have devolved very much as a part-theory, in reaction and as a supplement to more encompassing and abstract schemes of nineteenth-century Western social theory. Elite theory stands or falls empirically on whether or not the salience, or even the existence, of a postulated elite group can be demonstrated. As might be expected, most of the latter-day theoretical refinements on Pareto and Mosca in the social sciences have been typological experiences, sorting out the differences among related concepts such as class, stratification, elite, and status group for their operational use and testing in specific projects of research. To my mind, the most satisfying of these theoretical exercises in typology has been that of Giddens (1974).

5. A pronounced interest in research on elites developed in Anglo-American social science following World War II. In its empirical concerns, this research was strongly influenced by the theories of Pareto and Mosca; in taking as its major issue how, and to what degree, elites influenced social processes, it remained fixated on a question raised but unresolved by the ambiguous usage of the concept of elites in nineteenth-century social discourse. This research was much concerned with the threat that the surge of authoritarian regimes and overt elitist doctrines as part of European fascism (with which classic elite theorists became associated) posed for democracy and political liberalism. So it is important, finally, to understand that the tradition of elite research in the social sciences developed in a very specific ideological context that lent it relevance and significance.

6. In developing a distinctly ethnographic concern with elites against this particular development of elite theory and research in the social science, I emphasized the importance of distinguishing elites and elite groups, as identifiable subjects appropriate for a participant-observation/fieldwork method of research, by defining them in relation to particular institutional processes, rather than in terms of a broad concept of class affiliation or stratification. For me, elite groups are the shadow, informal organizations that run formal, mostly public organizations in any society. Although anthropologists have done a lot of conceptual work on "nongroups," networks, factions, and the like that could meet the need of defining such informal structures of elite organization, I was more interested in the questions of content that have largely been missed or weakly treated by the explicit tradition of elite theory and research: first, the nature of the relationship between elites and the institutions they control, and the connection between this relationship and the masses of nonelites to whom elites are largely invisible but over whose lives they have considerable direct and indirect power though institutional processes, bureaucracy, rule-making, and the like; and second, the worldviews shared and debated by elites within their intimate, even tribal, subcultures of power tied to institutional positions. (Do specific elites "see" society at large in any detail, or do they see only as far as institutional politics take them, no matter how far-reaching may be the effects of decisions made within their institutional domains and the games that elites, by definition, make of the latter?) These are essentially cultural questions about power and status, and about the *practices* that produce and reproduce them. Nothing in elite theory, so labeled, or, for that matter, in much of Anglo-American social theory could assist me in ad-

dressing these sorts of issues. Fortunately, there exist very ambitious recent theories, if not precisely about elites in the social architectural sense of much explicit elite theory, then about the bedrock matters of domination, power, and status. These, to which we now turn, not only have helped me with formulating questions about the content of elite culture in which, as an ethnographer, I have been interested, but also provide, I believe, a surer ground for archaeological inquirers into elites.

Elite Theory by any Other Name . . .

The 1960s witnessed a virtual renaissance in the ambitious production of Western social theory, reminiscent of the major theoretical systems of the nineteenth and early twentieth centuries (e.g., those of Marx, Weber, and Durkheim, which remain the enduring intellectual capital of most contemporary social sciences) and originating in the same homelands of these earlier systems—France and Germany. Analogous to the mediating role that Talcott Parsons historically occupied in relation to the influence of these classic theorists on American scholarship, Anthony Giddens (1976, 1979) has served as the major early interpreter and synthesizer of the new continental theorists for Anglo-American social science. However, by the late 1970s and 1980s, the works of these theorists had been widely read (and misread) in England and the United States, pulled apart and put back together again in a multitude of idiosyncratic ways according to the interests of disciplines as diverse as philosophy, history, literary and art criticism, political science, history, law, sociology, and anthropology.

In this renaissance of social theory the writers I judge most important in the revival of elite studies—who provided a set of very rich concepts and strategies of analysis for addressing anew the subjects of power, domination, and status differentiation in relation to microscopically observed cultural processes—are Michel Foucault and Pierre Bourdieu. Other theorists writing in the 1960s or given renewed attention then (such as A. Gramsci and L. Althusser in the Marxist tradition, and J. Habermas out of Frankfurt School critical theory) helped provide a theoretical hold on the content of elite studies, but none offered the sustained, conceptually focused perspectives on power and status formation in social life provided by Foucault and Bourdieu.

Very different in their styles as thinkers and in the projects they pursue, Foucault and Bourdieu are of similar interest to scholars concerned with elites because of their microscopic treatments of the "practices" (Bourdieu's term) and "technologies" (Foucault's term) of regimes of domination or, as noted, of the subcultures of elites that control and administer institutional orders that in turn organize the daily lives of the general population of any sociopolitical entity. The work of both has been very much interested in "the order of things" (to use the translated title of one of Foucault's early books, *Les mots et les choses*). Foucault and Bourdieu both have a fascination with "reading" the power and status implications of structured environments, architecture, modes of representation, devices, techniques of producing objects, and the movement of objects in exchange and the manner in which they acquire value, rather than with behaviors directly observed, decision-making processes, or literal interpersonal transactions among particular subjects. This salient materialistic aspect of what they choose to observe might make them particularly attractive to archaeologists, who also try to "read" the power and status implications from the assemblages of artifacts, objects, writing and representation systems, and architectural structures that they recover.

In their own historic context of creation, Foucault's and Bourdieu's theories are very much intended to provide an account of modernity, just as were the great nineteenth-century systems of theory at an earlier historic moment. However, unlike the supplemental-reactive character of elite theory, the works of Foucault and Bourdieu are fully worked out global accounts. In the mode of nineteenth-century systematic social theory, both Foucault and Bourdieu employ a traditional-modern contrast, or its equivalent, to demonstrate the unique ways in which power and status hierarchies are constituted in modernity. Both seem to explore the implications of an increasingly (and now almost totally) rationalized social order of modernity. Ironically, the most suggestive ideas in Foucault and Bourdieu for the archaeology of elites in complex state or imperial systems come not from their treatments of baseline "tradition" (as in Bourdieu's discussion of exchange systems among the Algerian Kabyls in *Outline of a Theory of Practice*, 1977) or the premodern past (as in Foucault's account of criminal punishment under European kingships in the early part of *Discipline and Punish*, 1979), but from their accounts of power and status in the fully rationalized sociocultural systems of modernity.

Their discussions of processes of domination may not fit conditions in, say, Mesoamerican state societies, but they provide a set of analytical images or a framework for envisioning elite domination in extremis that might fruitfully be used to construct hypotheses with which to interrogate archaeological materials, much in the way that K. Wittfogel's flawed and gradually discredited hypothesis from *Oriental Despotism* (1957) about the power implications of so-called hydraulic civilizations served, even as it was being critiqued (by archaeologists who, intentionally or not, misinterpreted Wittfogel), to refine and advance archaeological knowledge of a variety of complex political systems. In a sense, Wittfogel as well as Foucault and Bourdieu targeted the pervasive nature of domination by elites in modernity. The latter are more subtle, less grossly ideological, but the theories of all three stand as extreme ideal types waiting for application to archaeological materials through modification and refinement.

Even the briefest overview of the theories of Foucault and Bourdieu is both beyond the scope of this paper and (given their absence as influences in any of the papers of this volume) inappropriate. Therefore, before concluding, I shall merely note one study on Egypt by Whitney Davis (in press) that effectively interweaves influences from Bourdieu and, more indirectly, from Foucault, among other relevant contemporary theorists. Davis is using a fund of intellectual capital to tailor concepts to archaeological evidence about domination that might be suggestive for elite studies concerned with Mesoamerica.

Whitney Davis: "Representation, Legitimation, and the Emergence of the Ancient Egyptian State"

In his paper (in press), Davis addresses the remarkable uniformity of images in "official" art produced under the Egyptian state from the third millennium B.C. until its dissolution after the conquest of Alexander in 332 B.C. He probes the form and history of the canon governing artistic representation typical of Egyptian tomb-painting and temple wall-relief. While taking into account the varied interests of artists, patrons, and viewers, in this paper, he focuses precisely on questions of discipline and invariance that make possible the ideological legitimation of elite interests. His larger theoretical question—central to elite studies—involves the practices (ideological and otherwise) that produce and ensure successful domination, here through image production. Skillfully weaving theoretical resources, Davis relies most heavily on Bourdieu's ideas about the constitution of official representations that not only conceal interestedness from the masses but from the elites themselves, and, secondarily, on Max Weber, Frederic Jameson, and, indirectly, Michel Foucault (who is more of an influence in other papers by Davis).

Remarkably, the identity of the elite—the prime question of traditional elite research—remains murky; what the paper does offer is a carefully controlled speculative reading of ideology formation inferred from the production of images. Davis interrogates not elite behaviors, but elite practices of discipline, surveillance, and control. Classic iconographic interpretation from art history is merged in a novel way with the concerns of sociological analysis. Bourdieu (the primary theoretical influence) is useful precisely in showing Davis where to look for evidence of domination among discourses or representations and how to ask questions of process about it. In this case, the relationship between a controlling elite (patrons) and the specialists who produced the images is of central focus (as it probably would be for Mesoamerica, given the material in intermediate classes of elite specialists that the Chases have introduced and emphasized).

A Concluding Note

Even if it were granted that a reasonable case has been made here for the revival of elite studies around aspects of major recent initiatives in social theory, a revival that is especially relevant to archaeological analysis and reconstruction, one would still want a much more specific context of research to develop such studies. I believe the practice (or, more accurately, the hope) of subsuming specific data or materials on human subjects under a general or universal theory, couched in an abstract conceptual language free of the complications of any specific context, has had its day in the social sciences (its heyday, of course, having been the Parsonian synthesis). Therefore, any use of a set of concepts pulled from Foucault and Bourdieu and reshaped for a specific body of material makes sense only in a framework of controlled comparison. Of course, this assertion is not new within any particular area of anthropological concern, archaeological or ethnographic: the power of argument in all the papers of this volume derives from careful temporal and spatial statements of comparison within Mesoamerica. I am thinking more of controlled global comparisons, which have not been well developed in anthropology outside of evolutionary frameworks (e.g., the work of J. Friedman and M. Rowlands of the mid- and late 1970s).

Much more modestly applied than evolutionary guidelines of comparative work in archaeology, systematic comparisons among premodern kingships—the terms of comparison being shaped by concepts such as those of Bourdieu and Foucault—would provide the grounding by which elite practices of domination and status differentiation could be clarified in Mesoamerica. For example, a comparative dialogue between Whitney Davis' account of the disciplined production of images in Egypt and David Freidel's account of the iconography of Mayan kingship might be mutually enhancing. Given the very lively new work done by social and cultural anthropologists on kingship all over the world, free of the traditional evolutionary program and thoroughly steeped in post-1960s trends in social theory (e.g., the work of Marshal Sahlins and Valerio Valeri on Hawaii, Gillian Feeley-Harnik on Malagasy, Luc de Heusch on Africa, Nicholas Dirks on India, and Stanley Tambiah on Thailand), the necessary, secondary comparative framework awaits for ambitious and responsible reconstructions of elite practices of domination and technologies of discipline that are "readable" within the institutional complexes of Mesoamerican societies. The promise of elite studies within Mesoamerican archaeology, then, seems to me to depend very much on their contextualization within the current remaking of our comparative understanding of the histories and sociologies of kingships.

19. An Archaeological Assessment of Mesoamerican Elites

Diane Z. Chase and Arlen F. Chase

ANY consideration of elites is by definition an examination of an elusive concept. Even in modern nations, arguments abound as to who exactly constitutes an "elite" and how the term should be applied within different situations. It is difficult to identify living elites, let alone long dead ones. Yet that is exactly what we have sought to do within this book—identify past elites based upon a body of extremely incomplete—and "dead"—archaeological data. The task is an important one, however, because elites have direct relevance to social, political, and economic organization and to the degree of stratification in any society. Needless to say, differences of opinion have arisen. But it is precisely in these disagreements that the value of this book lies—for such disputes point to larger questions concerning the makeup of ancient Mesoamerican society as well as the ways in which archaeological interpretations are made.

This volume illustrates the lack of agreement on the identification, number, and significance of elites in Precolumbian society. Some of this discord is due to differing methodological approaches. It is clear from the papers presented, however, that all of Mesoamerica did not have equal numbers or percentages of elites through time. It is also apparent that viewing the variations and patterns in the distribution of elites over time and space *is* significant in terms of Mesoamerican prehistory and cultural dynamics. Thus, it is inappropriate to suggest or assume that a singular socio-cultural situation existed throughout prehistoric Mesoamerica.

Given the differing theoretical and methodological approaches—as well as the widespread areas considered by the authors of the chapters—it may surprise some that any patterns or agreements emerge from the contributions in the volume. While there is overlap among the various papers by virtue of the simple fact that all consider the topic of elites, in actuality each paper is unique with regard to area, focus, and data base. Different approaches to the archaeological record, analogy, and ethnohistory have also colored the interpretations that are offered. Yet the papers can be grouped into two basic schools of thought concerning the composition of Mesoamerican society.

This chapter is distinct from the preceding discussion by G. Marcus, which focuses on the historical perspective of elites, in that it is specifically archaeological in focus; however, it considers issues that go beyond a mere consideration of elites and Mesoamerica. In order to facilitate discussion, several broad topics are highlighted: archaeological method and theory; the role of analogy; the segmentary state model;[1] history versus archaeology; continuity, disjunction, and stratification in the archaeological record; and elite dynamics.

Archaeological Method and Theory

The very use of the word "elites" implies the existence of societal opposites within a given culture—those who have privilege and power and those who do not. While the term is sometimes used in other ways (cf. U.S. Southwest; Cordell and Gummerman 1989; Upham et al. 1989), it is often assumed to correlate with stratified societies (cf. Fried 1967:184-226). A consideration of elites necessarily gives rise to two distinct interpretative realms: the identification of stratification and the ways in which this information affects the wider political, economic, religious, and social system(s). The recognition of societal levels is a prerequisite to the interpretation of hierarchical political structure. Yet such recognition is not as easy as it sounds, for it must be premised on archaeological data, only partially preserved and only partially recovered. What must be asked is how do we derive our interpretations for the existence of societal levels? Is it from ethnography? Is it from anthropological theory? Is it from ethnohistory? Is it from archaeology?

To get at questions of stratification and political organization archaeologically is a herculean effort. Specifically, how are questions relating to these realms operationalized in the archaeological record? A primary assumption is that elites are a group with unequal access to basic resources as compared to the rest of society (cf. Fried 1967:186) and that they will be identifiable archaeologically in terms of material remains. It is generally assumed that this inequality may be seen in household items, refuse, constructions, and funerary activities, as well as in evidence for better health and diet. But any assessment of the archaeological data is difficult and is often guided by models and paradigms that are derived from other disciplines, data, times, and continents. It is in the framework(s) used for interpreting archaeological remains that differences of opinion are found. Yet the archaeological data themselves can place parameters on the kinds of interpretations that can or cannot be made.

Certain kinds of archaeological research designs and data are better suited than others to answering questions about complexity. Survey will provide some idea as to what kinds of remains are present and whether or not they might be hierarchically organized; in some instances, survey will permit predictions of what will be found beneath the ground surface. Whether survey can directly indicate workshop areas and other data relevant to complexity is dependent on the part of Mesoamerica in which one works. Drier environments in Mesoamerica have sites with a substantial surface visibility of artifactual remains; this fact has permitted greater latitude in higher-level interpretations (Charlton and Nichols; Kowalewski et al.). Test-pits provide an idea of the range of archaeological materials that may be found in an area, but, because of their small size and limited cultural associations, they do not usually provide data that directly bear on behavioral interpretations (cf. A. Chase and D. Chase 1990). Intensive excavations often reveal much about complexity because of the detailed chronological and spatial information that may be gained relating to construction events and past activities; but, because of limited resources and the time and effort involved in such horizontal stripping or vertical penetrations, the end result can be a very small sample from what may be a very large site. While some combination of the above techniques is obviously advisable, practical considerations often make it impossible to carry out the ideal research design. The whole situation is compounded further depending on whether or not a site or a region is under study; failure to consider data in a regional (or wider) perspective may lead to inaccurate characterizations.

Ample consideration must be given to the relationships among theory, method, and data (cf. Sabloff 1986:116). Not all research questions can be answered with the same strategy of investigation. Intensive work may be necessary to answer some desired questions; however, once undertaken, investigations might also uncover additional data that suggest controversies where simpler correlations were once possible. Such is the nature of scientific inquiry.

In spite of the multitude of problems in simply approaching the archaeological record, most researchers—regardless of the nature of the data base—seek to address the most difficult considerations. This obviously complicates the situation as well. Still further chasms exist in attempts at archaeological interpretation. We all enter into conceptualizations about archaeological data based on our own experiences and understandings. And a major debate is presently ensuing in archaeology about the very nature of archaeological interpretation and whether or not such interpretations have any validity or merely represent our best efforts at fantasizing about the past (cf. Trigger 1989a:379-382, 386-396).

But, regardless of the approach, archaeology does provide us with answers. Problems occur only when there is insufficient realization of three basic items: (1) that different questions may require different research strategies; (2) that all models must be tested; and/or (3) that there may be no cultural universals.

The archaeologically based papers in this volume show substantial variation in research methodology. All provide some discussion of method and theory. Some researchers (Cowgill; Haviland and Moholy-Nagy; Webster) focus on single sites with large data bases. Others compare two or more sites (D. Chase; Grove and Gillespie; Pendergast; Tourtellot et al.)—trying to gain an insight into variability in the archaeological remains relating to elites over time and space. Yet others (A. Chase; Freidel; Kowalewski et al.) look at multiple sites within a region or even broader area to try to analyze relationships. Further variation exists in the primary data base that is utilized. Most papers are based on excavation data. Some, however, focus on surface survey (Charlton and Nichols). Some use analogy to other ethnographic societies (Fox et al.; Henderson) or ethnohistory (Charlton and Nichols; D. Chase; J. Marcus; W. Sanders) as alternative sources for models or data. Various classes of archaeological data are used—residences, architecture, burials, skeletal information, artifacts, and iconography. The focus of the papers also varies: while most papers dealt with power and wealth, some authors were alternatively concerned with a historical perspective of elites (G. Marcus), stratification (Sanders; Kowalewski et al.), cosmology (Freidel), religion (D. Chase), trade (Hirth), and warfare (Freidel).

The Role of Analogy

It is one matter to collect data through mapping and excavation. It is quite another matter, however, to place these data within the matrix of past behavior and/or social organization. Archaeology, based as it is in material remains, does not often provide explicit evidence of past activity. To look at more than chronological and spatial ordering of material remains requires interpretation; behavior must be inferred. While some levels of interpretation may be relatively straightforward, others are more complex. Thus, while the inference that a group of people are sedentary agriculturalists may be easily made, inferring aspects of social organization can be substantially more complex and less certain.

Archaeologically, we are always seeking to model and explain behavior, but our synchronic models are generally derived from analogies to ethnographically known societies or general social theory. Analogies are drawn from a seemingly limitless variety of contexts; they are used in interpretations of Mesoamerican elites in a number of papers in this volume. But sometimes the models and/or analogies that are applied to a given body of archaeological data are inappropriate (cf. Wobst 1978).

Many models display an inherent theoretical brilliance, especially when viewed in terms of anthropological precepts. On the surface, they appear to provide solutions to puzzling archaeological situations. Yet difficulties often lurk below this surface. A major problem is the way in which analogies are employed to bolster a given model. In spite of substantial literature on the subject, there is little or no agreement on the appropriate criteria for selecting an analogy. Must an analogy be derived from a similar culture area? Should it be from a culture in a similar environment with a similar technological base? Or is there no framework that needs to be followed? In some cases it seems that no criteria are applied and that any analogy may be deemed to suffice for interpretation.

A primary consideration in the use of analogy is the degree to which known contemporary cultures can be assumed to reflect the total extant variety of past cultures. Alternative varieties of organization presumably existed and have been lost archaeologically. This is probably very true for societies in the New World that were decimated, upended, and regrouped by Europeans at contact. A secondary consideration is the degree to which cultural continuity is important in making an analogy. There is frequently a Western bias in comparative views of world civilizations (J. Marcus 1983c:470; Chang 1989:166). Like others in this volume (Kowalewski et al.), we feel that it is very inappropriate to apply Old World analogies for complex organization in the New World without substantial rationale. The New World and the Old World developed independently and without knowledge of each other for millennia. Surely, major cultural and organizational differences arose within each milieu. A tertiary consideration is the degree to which environment and technological achievements are important in making a comparison. Thus, in our opinion, it is unwise for the Mesoamerican archaeologist to look to very differently based African or Southeast Asian societies for analogies relating to complexity; this procedure will without doubt miscast the New World picture.

One other complicating factor exists. Simply stated, the problem is not solely the lack of standards for employing analogies, but that such analogies are simply applied and assumed to be explanatory, when in point of fact they have never been tested. Archaeological cultures must be viewed in the same culturally relative manner as living cultures. The application of ethnography, ethnohistory, and general analogies and models to archaeological data must be seen for what it is—as equally problematic as other aspects of archaeological interpretation and not as a simple panacea to a complex situation.

The Segmentary State

The Maya are referred to as a "segmentary state"—or by related terminology such as "regal-ritual"—in a number of the preceding papers (Fox et al.; Tourtellot et al.; Sanders; Webster). In the Maya region, the segmentary state model was pioneered by Robert Carmack (1973, 1981) and then further explored by John Fox (1978b, 1987) to explain not only highland Maya Quiche organization, but also that of other Maya areas. Both researchers premise a strict lineage form of social organization for the Quiche Maya based on Carmack's readings of the ethnohistoric documents. Fox (1987:4) explicitly states that "this marks the first time that segmentary lineages have been recognized in Mesoamerica."

Ethnohistoric research by others on the same documents used by Carmack to postulate lineages and feudalism has, however, revealed something quite different. Robert Hill and John Monaghan (1987:158-59), in their study of the organization of the Quiche community of Sacapulas, Guatemala, specifically refer to their disagreements with Carmack's and Fox's readings of the Quiche data. They (1987:29-34, 41-42, 159) document the fact that the very word that Carmack uses to infer a lineage structure for all of Quiche society—*chinamit*—was not an anthropological lineage at all, but rather "a territorial unit and not kin-based"; in fact, they show that this term is akin to the Aztec *calpulli*.

Thus, ethnohistoric and ethnographic work by Hill and Monaghan on boundary maintenance in Sacapulas has been able to demonstrate that the segmentary lineage structure postulated by Carmack and Fox did not exist for the Quiche Maya. Adam Kuper (1983:92) has gone so far as to suggest "that the lineage model, its predecessors and its analogs, have no value for anthropological analysis." Yet the attribution of such a system to the Quiche group has been picked up by other Mesoamerican archaeologists in search of alternative models and has been applied to a great many sites and regions. Sanders (this volume), in fact, now sees the *calpulli* as being a segmentary lineage (in contrast to Carrasco 1971:364, 368). The related concepts of segmentary state and regal-ritual center have also been applied to interpretations of Mesoamerican urbanism (cf. Sanders and Webster 1988 critiqued by Michael Smith 1989 and D. Chase, A. Chase, and W. Haviland 1990). In fact, many related concepts and models derived from Old World situations (cf. R. Fox 1977) have been introduced into Mesoamerica with questionable substantiation in the relevant archaeological, ethnohistoric, or ethnographic materials.

The concept of the segmentary state was formulated by Aidan Southall (1956, 1988). This unit was created for the Alur of eastern Africa, but Southall (1956:254-60) clearly implies that it has widespread usage elsewhere. For Southall (1956:251), a "segmentary state" is based on lineage or kinship arrangements within a pyramidal social structure in which the "powers exercised . . . are virtually of the same type at the several different levels"; in contrast, a fully developed state exhibits a "hierarchical power structure" because "such powers are delegated from the top of the structure" and "similar powers are not repeated at all levels." Southall's (1956:252) analytical distinction between the segmentary state and the more developed unitary state hinges on "Weber's concept of legitimacy"—"the prestige of being considered binding" rather than based on "motives of tradition or of expediency." To Southall (1956), a segmentary state exhibits neither a strong central authority nor a bureaucracy and is largely incapable of maintaining control over distant territory in terms of feuding, landholding, or fiscal relations. One key aspect of Southall's (1988:52) definition also includes the concept of flexible, changing boundaries because of the lack of political control outside of a core area.

Southall's description of a segmentary state does *not* fit the Late Classic Maya of the Southern, and presumably Northern, lowlands. Rather, the lowland Maya had a form of political organization that could be termed a "unitary state" following Southall's definitions, although we hesitate to utilize either of his bipolar categories.

While not denying that lineages were important to the Maya or that some segmentation may have occurred, a decentralized kinship-based system does not characterize the Classic and Postclassic Maya political order. Centralized bureaucracies were clearly in evidence at sites like Tikal and Caracol. At Tikal, by the Late Classic era the ruling elite probably acted as the main landholding corporation (D. Chase, A. Chase, and W. Haviland 1990:501), arguing for a centralized power and a nonsegmentary state. The settlement pattern at Caracol with its regularized distribution of plaza groups among and between the extensive terrace systems also indicates that local kin-based groups were not in control of settlement policy, but rather that a centralized bureaucracy was. Similar interpretations may be made for the Postclassic Maya of the Northern lowlands (Farriss 1984:148).

Hieroglyphic interpretations concerning categories of subsidiary lords would also indicate that power could be delegated by a given ruler, thus also contravening the definition of a segmentary state. At Caracol, the relationship between the supreme lord and the minor lord is clearly stated. The power is possessed by the ruler and delegated to the subordinate lord—clearly a form of legitimacy. This can be seen in statements both at Caracol proper (cf. the *sul* title in A. Chase, N. Grube, and D. Chase 1991) and at its outlying dependencies such as La Rejolla. Grube (personal communication, 1990) has noted that "sometimes it happens that a subordinate calls himself a sublord of an already deceased ruler by means of these possessed titles." Kornelia Kurbjuhn (n.d.) has similarly pointed out that a *sahal*—"a governor or deputy chief of a small, dependent site"—"must refer to a lifelong appointment independent of a specific ruler or his lineage." Thus, legitimacy formed a part of the Classic Maya political order. Following Southall, this would again reinforce the Classic Maya position as a unitary state.

Additional evidence relative to the unitary nature of Maya states can be mustered from the ethnohistoric evidence, at least from the Northern lowlands. Ralph Roys (1943, 1957) has dealt extensively with the social and political organization of the Northern lowlands. He (1943:35-36, 1957:4) acknowledges the widespread existence of lineages among the Maya, but fully admits that there are problems involved in understanding them, even going so far as to say that these groups "contained too many members and were too widely dispersed to be considered lineages in the anthropological meaning of the term." Reading Roys, one realizes that principles beyond kinship governed the Maya of the Northern lowlands (see also Haviland 1972).

Roys (1957:6) further defines three different kinds of territorial organization as being present in the Northern lowlands at the time of Spanish contact: (1) territories governed under the centralized rule of a single head of state, termed a *halach uinic*; (2) territories governed not by one ruler, but by a convocation of local *batab*s belonging to the same lineage; and (3) territories governed independently by many autonomous units. While a superficial reading of two of the forms of governance defined by Roys could be classified as segmentary in nature, comments by Nancy Farriss (1984:148) make it abundantly clear that these forms could in no way be construed as constituting a segmentary state, for all of Roys' forms recognized formal boundaries and were hierarchical in organization:

Two points about the geopolitical structure are relevant here. One is that the provinces were, for all the flux of political groupings and the varying degrees of cohesion, more than random collections of towns. They all possessed internal ties of some kind and provincial boundaries, which might be readjusted by war or arbitration but which were nonetheless recognized as boundaries. The other point is that these ties were for the most part hierarchical in nature, with a rank ordering of towns at the subprovincial level regardless of how unified or loosely organized the larger entity might be.

That such a political organization was once even more complicated can be seen in reports of two previous periods of political unification: first, under Chichen Itza and, later, under Mayapan (Roys 1943:58).

Although not always recorded, even earlier, Classic period, attempts at "empires" can be seen in the archaeological and epigraphic records of the Southern lowlands (A. Chase and D. Chase 1989; Schele and Freidel 1990). These same records indicate that the Maya of the Late Classic era had a clear conception of a bounded political and ritual unit. The determination of boundaries and boundary sites was very significant. In fact, Maya warfare often concerned itself with where the boundary of a given political unit was located (cf. Caracol and Naranjo; A. Chase, N. Grube, and D. Chase 1991).

In summary, then, while the segmentary state model may be of heuristic use in developmental considerations of complexity, it is misapplied to the Classic and Postclassic Maya data with which we are familiar. The archaeology, ethnohistory, and ethnography of the Maya provide evidence that is contrary to the tenets of this model. The nomothetic and unilinear aspects of the model must also be questioned. For these reasons, we believe it is unwise to equate the New World Maya with the Old World-derived model of a segmentary state.

History versus Archaeology

Because archaeology provides us with only the remnants of past activities, we often not only rely on analogy with living peoples, but also look toward historic information to augment the archaeological record. Only history and archaeology can provide the temporal perspective for studying change in human society (cf. Trigger 1989a:372ff, 1989b). Both disciplines are concerned with the chronological ordering of events; however, each has a data base with distinctive benefits and limitations. The written documents of history provide information on individuals and specific events that may be very detailed; however, written materials often contain the biases of individual recorders and can mirror their ethnocentrism. As indicated above, reconstructing behavior from the material record of archaeology is fraught with its own interpretative pitfalls. When used to address the same problem, history and archaeology sometimes yield different answers. In an ideal situation, history and archaeology would be combined in a conjunctive approach where neither discipline nor data base would dominate interpretation; rather, the different kinds of data could be tested against each other to gain a balanced picture. Unfortunately, in practice, this is rarely the case; when both history and archaeology are available, one is generally given precedence over the other.

In prehistoric Mesoamerica, a substantial amount of historic information is available (Nicholson 1975; J. Marcus 1976c). Written materials were created and used by certain Mesoamerican peoples (most notably the Maya; Culbert 1991); there are also European texts that discuss native American culture during the early years of contact. As with all historic material, an overarching question exists with regard to the reliability of these texts regardless of their origin or content. Indigenous hieroglyphic texts, for example, may overemphasize the significance of specific rulers; Spanish texts may ethnocentrically misinterpret native culture. Yet another consideration is whether one can directly correlate historic materials from one region of Mesoamerica with another. The *Popol Vuh* is a case in point (Tedlock 1985); this origin myth is based in the oral history of the highland Quiche Maya; however, it is assumed to be useful for explaining archaeological remains found throughout the Maya area (cf. Schele and Freidel 1990; Freidel, this volume)—regardless of the degree of cultural/temporal contact with the Postclassic/historic Quiche. Thus, historic materials must be evaluated not only for reliability, but also for their applicability to a particular culture or subgroup.

The papers in this volume use history and archaeology in various ways. For some, history is the primary data base (J. Marcus); others use archaeology in a critical comparison with history (D. Chase; Charlton and Nichols). William Sanders uses ethnohistory as a primary source of information on the Aztec; this permits a far more detailed understanding than is possible given the limited archaeological information. But it also means that his interpretations are generally not grounded in archaeology. Thomas Charlton and Deborah Nichols compare what is known ethnohistorically with what can be defined archaeologically for Postclassic central Mexico, attempting to explicitly test their assumptions. Diane Chase uses ethnohistory and Postclassic archaeology for the lowland Maya, noting problems in certain traditional interpretations based solely on the ethnohistoric data; this work also points to a multitude of problems both in assuming that history is correct and in directly applying ethnohistorically based models to much earlier archaeological societies. Joyce Marcus examines both native American and European history for the purpose of deriving interpretations of Precolumbian society. Despite her critique of Maya epigraphy as being unreliable, Marcus is staunch in her defense of Spanish historic sources as being correct concerning Precolumbian status distinctions. David Freidel alternatively focuses on the validity of the indigenous texts and iconography and their usefulness for the interpretation of the Precolumbian political situation.

The only paper in this volume to focus solely on history and writing is that of Joyce Marcus. She is also the most emphatic about the existence of a two-group or two-class society in Mesoamerica (consisting of a small group of nobles and a larger group of commoners that presumably included slaves), based on these historic materials. Virtually all of the papers dealing with archaeological data point to a difficulty in identifying two strict groups "on the ground." Some suggest that while there may have been two "ideal" groups as described ethnohistorically, the archaeology indicates more divisions within these larger groupings (A. Chase; D. Chase; Cowgill; Tourtellot et al.). Some note the possibility that there may be differences between what is said and what is actually done in a culture (cf. Cowgill; D. Chase; A. Chase and D. Chase). Our position (cf. D. Chase) is that if a simple two-class division does not mirror Late Postclassic Maya society archaeologically, it cannot be assumed to fit the earlier Classic Maya.

Models derived from historic sources, whether written by members of the culture or by those from outside, must be reviewed critically. Joyce Marcus has shown how a critical reading of hieroglyphic texts can cast doubt on their veracity. David Freidel, here and elsewhere (Schele and Freidel 1990), has demonstrated the usefulness of such texts for archaeological interpretation. The European historic documents used by a majority of the authors in this volume, while tantalizing in their detail, often present misleading worldviews of New World societies, for transcribers did not understand the intricacies of the events they were recording and attempted to explain things they did not understand in terms of their own worldview and language. Even carefully derived ethnohistoric interpretations concerning Precolumbian society should not be assumed to fit the archaeological situation. Archaeology can play a key role in assessing the validity of historic accounts; this condition holds whether one is analyzing epigraphy or ethnohistory.

The majority of the archaeological papers in this volume provide no direct support for a two-level division of ancient Mesoamerican society; in fact, some papers indicate archaeological evidence for more than two divisions. We feel that this archaeological information cannot be ignored. Three possibilities exist for resolving the presumed discrepancies between the archaeological and ethnohistorical interpretations: (1) the two-group division may have existed, but the subdivisions within the groups may actually have been more important than the hereditary classes themselves in terms of correlations with wealth; (2) the two-group division may have been the ideal situation in Mesoamerican society, but not in the reality of the sociopolitical organization; (3) indications in the ethnohistory for a middle group of people may adequately mirror the archaeological situation that sometimes dictates the existence of a relatively large middle group.

Continuity, Disjunction, and Stratification in the Archaeological Record

General theories of complexity have long attempted to wrest meaning from the archaeological record. Thus, the recognition of hierarchies of both sites in a given region and social groups at any one site was seen as important for arguments pertaining to stratification and social complexity. But how does one identify a social hierarchy archaeologically, especially at a single site? In the past, the primary way was to look at continuous and discontinuous distributions of presumed status indicators in the archaeological record. Discontinuous distributions of archaeological remains were seen as being markers of stratification and distinct status levels while continuous distributions were seen as being something less complex, specifically reflecting a ranked society or chiefdom. Papers in this volume suggest that there may be a problem with such an approach.

There is a difference of opinion with regard to what a lack of clear-cut archaeological status-related divisions means. Those working in the highlands (Sanders), in the southern peripheries (Henderson), and on early time horizons (Grove and Gillespie) tend to see the absence of clear-cut divisions in the archaeological record as implying a nonstate ranked society. John Fox and his coauthors think that the gradations seen in the archaeological record at Utatlan are reflective of an underlying egalitarian structure. Other researchers working both in the highlands (Cowgill; Kowalewski et al.) and the lowlands (A. Chase; D. Chase; Haviland and Moholy-Nagy), who also note a lack of clear-cut divisions in the data, often—but not always—focus on the idea of a state or greater complexity. George Cowgill, in fact, uses the gradations in the archaeological data of Teotihuacan to point to the existence of up to seven levels within three overall groups at that site—obviously a complex hierarchical situation. Thus, it can be inferred that the lack of sharp "class" distinctions in the archaeological data— or, alternatively, the recognition of a general gradation from the top to the bottom of a given society—does not necessarily indicate the level of a given social or political organization; such assemblages are just as likely to reflect great complexity as they are to reflect simpler societies.

There may be distinctive reasons for the existence of similar patterns in the archaeological record. The basic premise underlying the association of continuous distributions with nonstratified societies is that these mirror the individual ranking of people in a society relative to a chief and his lineage. However, a similar gradation in the archaeological data may result from interactions found in politically and economically more complex societies (C. Smith 1976; D. Chase and A. Chase 1988:75). Thus, additional information—such as a consideration of scale, integration, and horizontal and/or vertical differentiation (Blanton et al. 1981:17-22)—assumes significance in determining whether a continuous distribution reflects a ranked or a stratified society.

As has been indicated, the identification of stratification in a society archaeologically is premised in the idea that there will be apparent distinctions in material remains reflective of different status groups. The reality of the archaeological situation suggests that this may not be the case. It is often unclear which variables are critical in making divisions. How one structures one's questions will also have a bearing on the existence of either a disjunction or a continuum. A focus on a single variable will often result in clear-cut distinctions and divisions. A focus on multiple variables often leads to blurring in the categories under investigation, thus leading to the archaeological recognition of a continuum. Equally problematic are some descriptions of group differences that focus on material items, like distinctive dress, that are unlikely to survive in the archaeological record. William Sander's postulated Aztec merchant class may be quite evident from the ethnohistoric materials, but its recognition archaeologically would be problematic, especially given the variability encompassed in his description.

Regardless of the variables being considered, archaeologists encounter a conundrum when they must attempt to decide where to place divisions between groups. Even though there are often clear distinctions between the uppermost and lowermost segments of society, the actual societal divisions are generally less obvious in Mesoamerica. A similar situation exists in ancient Mesopotamia; C. C. Lamberg-Karlovsky (1989:257) notes that "the Sumerian population consisted of five distinct social classes," but at the same time writes that "lines of separation between the classes were far from clear."

Among all the variables that may be examined (such as artifact distributions, settlement patterns, and structural elaboration), it is the mortuary data base that provides a prominent portion of the information on status distinctions (cf. O'Shea 1984); yet it is also a part of the record that may be affected by nonstatus factors. A lack of distinctions in mortuary remains does not necessarily equate with a lack of status distinctions in society (Ucko 1969; Huntington and Metcalf 1979:122; Pearson 1982). In Mesoamerica, however, status distinctions do seem to be reflected in the archaeological record; skeletal remains can also be analyzed for differences in diet and health (Haviland and Moholy-Nagy; Pendergast).

The presence of intermediate status burials and residential groups archaeologically at several lowland Maya sites has led us to suggest the existence of some sort of middle level in Mesoamerican society. Members of these groups display intermediate aspects of wealth (cf. M. Smith 1987b) and are far more numerous than would generally be expected for any elite grouping. Arlen Chase's data from Caracol, Belize, demonstrate an increase in this middle group over time and the probable association of this growth with successful warfare. Diane Chase's work suggests that this middle group persisted into the Postclassic/Historic era. William Sanders sees the merchants of Aztec central Mexico becoming such a "middle" class.

If we were to explore over time the distributions of continuous and discontinuous variables archaeologically, as they relate to complexity in Mesoamerica, we predict that we would find the following general pattern in the archaeological remains over time: continuous distribution, discontinuous distribution, continuous distribution. Such a situation does not imply the rise and fall of a complex society. Rather, in our estimation, it reflects a nonstratified society that experiences the onset of stratification and the development of what may be termed an archaic state and then, finally, subsequent elaboration in that complexity as the political entity continues to exist. In this light, it is important to re-emphasize that continuous distributions of archaeological data can be representative of *both* simpler societies and complex ones.

Elites and the Dynamics of Mesoamerican Civilization

By definition, some sort of elite must have existed in past Mesoamerican societies. Some individual or group directed different aspects of any society and made decisions that were subsequently implemented. The archaeological data indicate that such individuals existed, minimally inferentially and sometimes directly in the archaeological record—as in the Maya case, where we see rulers portrayed and their histories recorded on monuments, and sometimes find their stupendous interments, like those of Pacal at Palenque and Ah Cacao at Tikal.

At many sites, however, the on-the-ground definition of the elite is extremely problematic, largely because their identification relies on understanding the extant archaeological diversity and assigning meaning to patterns that may be discerned. It is in the assignment of meaning to recognized archaeological patterns that most researchers have difficulty. Often they use analogies or general theoretical conceptualizations of societies and their evolution either to assign such meaning or to gain a framework for structuring their interpretation. Yet this approach to the archaeological data is fraught with problems and it minimizes the archaeological contributions to diversity, complexity, and change.

The papers within this volume provide a series of examples of how archaeological interpretation is accomplished. They also illustrate the problems faced by archaeologists when dealing with obtuse definitional matters. One area on which most authors would agree is that Mesoamerican elites were a "power elite" (cf. Mills 1956; Dahl 1969; Kornhauser 1969)—even though none of them use this terminology directly. The concept of a power elite was derived by C. W. Mills (1956) to discuss power in contemporary American society. This unified power group is composed of "top government executives, military officials, and corporate directors" (Kornhauser

1969:43).   A second, middle level of power includes a variety of interest groups. The largest, but least powerful group, is the "mass society." The ruling elite is a controlling group that is a minority of the population and that is not created by democratic process (Dahl 1969:37).

While there is no clear agreement about the size of the elite group and while there may be variation in their numbers temporally and spatially, they were a relatively small portion of the total Mesoamerican population. It is equally apparent that the elite made the political decisions, not the other members of society. What is in question in the Mesoamerican archaeological data is the number of other levels of power. Was there, for example, a middle level above the powerless masses? And did power relationships vary temporally and spatially? Thus, stating that ancient Mesoamerica provides excellent examples of power elites may be correct, but the interesting questions revolve around the composition of the elite relative to the rest of society and any variations in the system.

It is difficult to assess Mesoamerican social dynamics given the distinctive methodologies and perspectives that are used with regard to elites; however, some variation in both contemporary and temporal realms is evident. For example, the data from the Maya site of Caracol, Belize (A. Chase), demonstrate that during the Classic period an increasingly large middle-level group developed that had increased access to elite items over time. It is as yet unclear whether this was movement in a positive direction indicating a more efficient social or political system with more division of labor and adminstrative activities or, instead, a potential problem leading ultimately to societal breakdown given the greater access to, more knowledge of, and potentially greater degree of questioning of the social and political system. It is possible that the difficulty in defining a small elite group at Sayil (Tourtellot et al.) is representative of a similar transition. Contemporary variation in societal composition and organization is very evident in data from both the central Maya area (A. Chase; Haviland and Moholy-Nagy; Pendergast) and its peripheries (Henderson; Webster). Over time, the Maya data show surprising continuities (D. Chase). Similarly, temporal change and contemporary variation is discernable in highland Mexico (Charlton and Nichols; Cowgill; Grove and Gillespie; Kowalewski et al.; Sanders). This diversity among Mesoamerican sites still needs further exploration and explanation. However, by viewing elites dynamically we can start to view social and political structure. And the variety and change in such structure is the key to understanding Precolumbian Mesoamerican society.

Notes

1. The discussion relating to segmentary states that appears in this paper is derived from a presentation by A. Chase at the 89th Annual Meeting of the American Anthropological Association in New Orleans in December 1990 in a session titled "Maya Settlement Pattern Studies: New Methods and Interpretations" chaired by S. Jaeger and D. Walker. Robert M. Hill II subsequently provided additional sources on lineage theory. The authors, however, take full responsibility for the content of this statement.

Bibliography

ABRAMS, E. M.
1984a   "Replicative Experimentation at Copan, Honduras: Implications for Ancient Economic Specialization." *Journal of New World Archaeology* 6(2):39-48.
1984b   *Systems of Labor Organization in Late Classic Copan, Honduras: The Energetics of Construction.* Ph.D. diss., Dept. of Anthropology, Pennsylvania State Univ., Univ. Park.
1987   "Economic Specialization and Construction Personnel in Classic Period Copan, Honduras." *American Antiquity* 52(3):485-99.

ACOSTA SAIGNES, M.
1945   *Los Pochteca: Ubicación de los mercaderes en la estructura social tenochca.* Acta Antropológica I, Mexico City.

ADAMS, R. E. W.
1963   "A Polychrome Vessel from Altar de Sacrificios, Peten, Guatemala." *Archaeology* 16(2):90-92.
1970   "Suggested Classic Period Occupational Specialization in the Southern Maya Lowlands." In W. Bullard, ed., *Maya Archaeology, Papers of the Peabody Museum* 61:487-502, Cambridge, Mass.
1971   *The Ceramics of Altar de Sacrificios.* Papers of the Peabody Museum of Archaeology and Ethnology, vol. 63, no. 1, Harvard Univ. Cambridge, Mass.
1973   "Maya Collapse: Transformation and Termination in the Ceramic Sequence at Altar de Sacrificios." In *The Classic Maya Collapse*, pp. 133-64. *See* Culbert 1973.
1974   "A Trial Estimation of Classic Maya Palace Populations at Uaxactun." In *Mesoamerican Archaeology: New Approaches*, pp. 285-96. *See* Hammond 1974.
1977a   ed., *The Origins of Maya Civilization.* Univ. of New Mexico Press, Albuquerque.
1977b   *Prehistoric Mesoamerica.* Little, Brown and Co., Boston.
1981   "Settlement Patterns of the Central Yucatan and Southern Campeche Regions." In *Lowland Maya Settlement Patterns*, pp. 211-57. *See* Ashmore 1981a.

ADAMS, R. E. W., and R. D. JONES
1981   "Spatial Patterns and Regional Growth among Maya Cities." *American Antiquity* 46:301-22.

ADAMS, R. E. W., and W. D. SMITH
1977   "Apocalyptic Visions: The Maya Collapse and Medieval Europe." *Archaeology* 30:292-301.
1981   "Feudal Models for Classic Maya Civilization." In *Lowland Maya Settlement Patterns*, pp. 335-49. *See* Ashmore 1981a.

ALLISON, P. D.
1978   "Measures of Inequality." *American Sociological Review* 43(6):865-80.

ALTSCHUL, J. H.
1981   *Spatial and Statistical Evidence for Social Groupings at Teotihuacan, Mexico.* Ph.D. diss., Depart. of Anthropology, Brandeis Univ. Waltham.

1987   "Social Districts of Teotihuacan." In *Teotihuacán*, pp. 197-217. *See* Mc-Clung and Rattray 1987.

ALVARADO, F. de

1593   *Vocabulario en lengua mixteca, hecho por los Padres de la Orden de Predica-dores, que residen en ella, y ultimamente recopilado y acabado por el Padre . . Vicario de Tamazulapa, de la misma orden.*, Facsimile, ed., W. Jiménez Moreno. Instituto Nacional Indigenista and INAH (1962), Mexico City.

ANAWALT, P.

1980   "Costume and Control: Aztec Sumptuary Laws." *Archaeology* 33(1):33-43.

1981   "Costume Analysis and the Provenience of the Borgia Group Codices." *American Antiquity* 46(4):837-52.

ANDREWS, A. P., and F. ROBLES C.

1985   "Chichen Itza and Coba: An Itza-Maya Standoff in Early Postclassic Yucatan." In *The Lowland Maya Postclassic*, pp. 62-72. *See* A. Chase and P. Rice 1985.

ANDREWS, E. W., IV.

1969   *The Archaeological Use and Distribution of Mollusca in the Maya Lowlands.* Middle American Research Institute Publication 34, Tulane Univ., New Orleans.

ANDREWS, E. W., V.

1979   "Some Comments on Puuc Architecture of the Northern Yucatan Peninsula." In L. Mills, ed., *The Puuc: New Perspectives*, pp. 1-17. Central College, Pella, Ia.

ARNOLD, J. E., and A. FORD

1980   "A Statistical Examination of Settlement Patterns at Tikal, Guatemala." *American Antiquity* 45(4):713-26.

ASHMORE, W.

1981a   ed., *Lowland Maya Settlement Patterns*. Univ. of New Mexico Press, Albuquerque.

1981b   *Precolumbian Occupation at Quirigua, Guatemala: Settlement Patterns in a Classic Maya Center.* Ph.D. diss., Univ. of Pennsylvania.

1981c   "Some Issues of Method and Theory in Lowland Maya Settlement Archaeology." In *Lowland Maya Settlement Patterns*, pp. 37-70. *See* 1981a.

1988   "Household and Community at Classic Quirigua." In *Household and Community in the Mesoamerican Past*, pp. 153-69. *See* Wilk and Ashmore 1988.

ASHMORE, W., and R. J. SHARER

1978   "Excavations at Quirigua, Guatemala: The Ascent of a Maya Elite Center." *Archaeology* 31(6):10-19.

ATKINSON, A. B.

1970   "On the Measurement of Inequality." *Journal of Economic Theory* 2(3):244-63.

AVENDANO Y LOYOLA, A. de

1696   *Relación de las entradas que hize a la conversión de los gentiales Ytzaex.* Manuscript in the Newberry Library, Chicago.

AWE, J. J.

1985   "Archaeological Investigations at Caledonia, Cayo District, Belize." M.A. thesis, Trent Univ., Peterborough.

BALL, J. W.
1979 "Ceramics, Culture History, and the Puuc Tradition: Some Alternative Possibilities." In L. Mills, ed., *The Puuc: New Perspectives*, pp. 18-35. Central College, Pella, Ia.
1986 "Campeche, the Itza, and the Postclassic: A Study in Ethnohistorical Archaeology," In *Late Lowland Maya Civilization*, pp. 379-408. *See* Sabloff and Andrews 1986.
BARRERA VASQUEZ, A., et al.
1980 *Diccionario Maya Cordemex*. Ediciones Cordemex, Merida, Yucatan, Mexico.
BASCOM, W. R.
1984 *The Yoruba of Southwestern Nigeria*. Waveland Press, Prospect Heights, Ill.
BAUDEZ, C.
1978 "Archaeoastronomy at Copan: An Appraisal." *Indiana* 11:63-71. Gebr. Mann Verlag, Berlin.
1983 ed., *Introdución a la arqueología de Copan, Honduras*. Secretaría de Estado en el Despacho de Cultura y Turismo, Tegucigalpa, Honduras.
1986 "Iconography and History at Copan." In P. A. Urban and E. M. Schortman, eds., *The Southeastern Maya Periphery*, pp. 17-26. Univ. of Texas Press, Austin.
1989 "The House of the Bacabs: An Iconographic Analysis." In *The House of the Bacabs*, pp. 73-81. *See* Webster 1989a.
BAUDEZ, C., and P. BECQUELIN
1973 *Archéologie de Los Naranjos, Honduras*. Mission Archéologique et Ethnologique Francaise au Mexique, Etudes Mesoaméricaines 2, Mexico City.
BEAUDRY, M. P.
1987 "Interregional Exchange, Social Status, and Painted Ceramics: The Copan Valley Case." In *Interaction on the Southeast Mesoamerican Frontier*, pp. 227-46. *See* Robinson 1987.
BECK, E. M., P. M. HORAN, and C. M. TOLBERT II
1978 "Stratification in a Dual Economy: A Sectoral Model of Earnings Determination." *American Sociological Review* 43(4):704-20.
1980 "Social Stratification in Industrial Society: Further Evidence for a Structural Alternative." *American Sociological Review* 45(4):712-19.
BECKER, M.
1972 "Plaza Plans at Quirigua, Guatemala." *Katunob* 8(2):47-62.
1973 "Archaeological Evidence for Occupational Specialization among the Classic Period Maya at Tikal, Guatemala." *American Antiquity* 38:396-406.
1979 "Priests, Peasants and Ceremonial Centers: The Intellectual History of a Model." In *Maya Archaeology and Ethnohistory*, pp. 3-20. *See* Hammond and Willey 1979.
1982 "Ancient Maya Houses and Their Identification: An Evaluation of Architectural Groups at Tikal and Inferences Regarding Their Functions." *Revista Española de Antropología Americana* 12:111-29, Madrid.
1986 "Household Shrines at Tikal, Guatemala: Size as a Reflection of Economic Status." *Revista Española de Antropología Americana* 14:81-85, Madrid.
BEFU, H.
1977 "Social Exchange." *Annual Review of Anthropology* 6:255-82.

BELL, R., D. V. EDWARDS, and R. H. WAGNER
1969   *Political Power: A Reader in Theory and Research.* Free Press, New York.
BENSON, E.
1973   ed., *Mesoamerican Writing Systems.* Dumbarton Oaks, Washington, D.C.
1986   ed., *City-States of the Maya: Art and Architecture.* Rocky Mountain Institute for Pre-Columbian Studies, Denver.
BENYO, J. C., and T. L. MELCHIONNE
1987   "Settlement Patterns in the Tencoa Valley, Honduras: An Application of the Coevolutionary Systems Model." In *Interaction on the Southeast Mesoamerican Frontier,* pp. 49-64. *See* Robinson 1987.
BERDAN, F.
1978   "Tres formas de intercambio en la economía azteca." In *Economía política e ideología,* pp. 75-94. *See* Carrasco and Broda 1978.
1982   *The Aztecs of Central Mexico.* Holt, Rinehart, and Winston, New York.
1986   "Enterprise and Empire in Aztec and Early Colonial Mexico." In *Research in Economic Anthropology, Supplement 2,* pp. 281-302. *See* Isaac 1986a.
BERLIN, H.
1977   *Signos y significados en las inscripciones mayas.* Instituto Nacional del Patrimonio Cultural de Guatemala, Guatemala.
BERRIN, K.
1988   ed., *Feathered Serpents and Flowering Trees: Reconstructing the Murals of Teotihuacan.* Fine Arts Museums of San Francisco, San Francisco.
BISKOWSKI, M.
1986   "Metates and the Teotihuacan Socioeconomic System: A Preliminary Analysis." Manuscript on file, Dept. of Anthropology, Univ. of California, Los Angeles.
BLANTON, R. E.
1976   "The Role of Symbiosis in Adaptation and Sociocultural Change in the Valley of Mexico." In E. R. Wolf, ed., *The Valley of Mexico,* pp. 181-201. Univ. of New Mexico Press, Albuquerque.
1978   *Monte Alban: Settlement Patterns at the Ancient Zapotec Capital.* Academic Press, New York.
1985   "A Comparison of Early Market Systems." In S. Plattner, ed., *Markets and Marketing,* pp. 399-418. Monographs in Economic Anthropology, no. 4, Univ. Press of America, Lanham, Md.
BLANTON, R. E., and G. FEINMAN
1984   "The Mesoamerican World System." *American Anthropologist* 86:673-82.
BLANTON, R. E., S. KOWALEWSKI, G. FEINMAN, and J. APPEL
1981   *Ancient Mesoamerica: A Comparison of Change in Three Regions.* Cambridge Univ. Press, Cambridge.
BLANTON, R. E., S. KOWALEWSKI, G. FEINMAN, and L. FINSTEN
1981   "Patterns of Regional Inequality in the Prehistoric Valley of Oaxaca." Paper presented at 80th Annual Meeting of the American Anthropological Association, Los Angeles.
BLOCH, M.
1953   *The Historian's Craft.* Vintage Books, New York.
1961   *Feudal Society.* Univ. of Chicago Press, Chicago.
BOURDIEU, P.
1977   *Outline of a Theory of Practice.* Cambridge Univ. Press, Cambridge.

1984   *Distinction: A Social Critique of the Judgment of Taste.* Harvard Univ. Press, Cambridge, Mass.

BRAAKHUIS, H. E. M.
1987   "Artificers of the Days: Functions of the Howler Monkey Gods among the Mayas." *Bijdragen* (Vokendunde) 143(1):25-53 (The Netherlands).

BRODKEY, D. D.
1978   "Postconquest Settlement Patterns of the Otumba Area, Mexico." Manuscript in possession of the author.

BROWN, C. H.
1991   "Hieroglyphic Literacy in Ancient Mayaland: Inferences from Linguistic Data." *Current Anthropology* 32(4):489-496.

BROWN, J. A.
1981   "The Search for Rank in Prehistoric Burials." In *The Archaeology of Death*, pp. 25-38. *See* Chapman, Kinnes, and Randsborg 1981.

BROWN, K. L.
1980   "Archaeology in the Quiche Basin, Guatemala." *Mexicon* 2(5):72-73.
1983   "Archaeology, Ethnohistory and the Quiche Maya: A Study of Social Organization." Paper presented at the 82d Annual Meeting of the American Anthropological Association, Chicago.
1985   "Postclassic Relationships between the Highland and Lowland Maya." In *The Lowland Maya Postclassic*, pp. 270-81. *See* A. Chase and P. Rice 1985.
1987   "Core or Periphery: The 'Highland Maya' Question." In *Interaction on the Southeast Mesoamerican Frontier*, pp. 421-34. *See* Robinson 1987.

BRUMFIEL, E. M.
1976   *Specialization and Exchange at the Late Postclassic (Aztec) Community of Huexotla, Mexico.* Ph.D. diss., Dept. of Anthropology, Univ. of Michigan, Ann Arbor.
1986   "The Division of Labor at Xico: The Chipped Stone Industry." In *Research in Economic Anthropology, Supplement 2,* pp. 245-79. *See* Isaac 1986a.
1987a   "Consumption and Politics at Aztec Huexotla." *American Anthropologist* 89(3):676-85.
1987b   "Elite and Utilitarian Crafts in the Aztec State." In E. M. Brumfiel and T. K. Earle, eds., *Specialization, Exchange, and Complex Societies*, pp. 102-18. Cambridge Univ. Press, Cambridge.
1988   "Factions, Class, and Inter-Ethnic Alliance at Late Postclassic Xaltocan." Paper presented at 46th International Congress of Americanists, Amsterdam.

BRUMFIEL, E. M., and T. EARLE
1987   "Specialization, Exchange and Complex Societies: An Introduction." In E. Brumfiel and T. Earle, eds., *Specialization, Exchange, and Complex Societies*, pp. 1-9. Cambridge Univ. Press, Cambridge.

BULLARD, W. R., Jr.
1960   "Maya Settlement Pattern in Northeastern Peten, Guatemala." *American Antiquity* 25:355-72.
1964   "Settlement Pattern and Social Structure in the Southern Maya Lowlands during the Classic Period." In *XXXV Congreso Internacional de Americanistas*, vol. 1. Mexico City.

BUNZEL, R.
1952   *Chichicastenango.* American Ethnological Society, Publication 22, J. J. Augustin, New York.
BURTON, S. S.
1987   "Middle Formative Lithic Industries at Chalcatzingo." In *Ancient Chalcatzingo*, pp. 305-20. *See* Grove 1987a.
CABRERA, R., I. RODRIGUEZ, and N. MORELOS
1982   eds., *Memoria del Proyecto Arqueológica Teotihuacan 80-82.* Instituto Nacional de Antropología e Historia, Mexico City.
CABRERA, R., S. SUGIYAMA, and G. COWGILL
1991   "The Templo de Quetzalcoatl Project at Teotihuacan: A Preliminary Report," *Ancient Mesoamerica* 2(1):77-92.
CABRERA, R., et al.
1989   "El Proyecto Templo de Quetzalcoatl." *Arqueología* 5:51-79. Instituto Nacional de Antropología e Historia, Mexico City.
CALNEK, E.
1972   "The Internal Structure of Cities in America, Pre-Columbian Cities: The Case of Tenochtitlan." *El proceso de urbanizacíon en América desde sus origenes hasta nuestros dias, Actas y memorias,* vol. 1. *XXXIX Congreso Internacional de Americanistas,* Lima.
1976   "The Internal Structure of Tenochtitlan." In E. R. Wolf, ed., *The Valley of Mexico,* pp. 287-302. Univ. of New Mexico Press, Albuquerque.
1978   "El sistema de mercado de Tenochtitlán," In *La economía política e ideología. See* Carrasco and Broda 1978.
CANSECO, A. de
1580   "Relación de Tlacolula y Mitla hecha en los Días 12 y 23 de Agosto respectivamente." In F. del Paso y Troncoso (1905), ed., *Papeles de la Nueva España: Segunda Serie, Geografia y Estadística,* vol. 4, pp. 144-54. Sucesores de Rivadeneyra, Madrid.
CARLSON, J. B.
1981   "A Geomantic Model for the Interpretation of Mesoamerican Sites: An Essay in Cross-Cultural Comparison." In E.P. Benson, ed., *Mesoamerican Sites and Worldviews,* pp. 143-211. Dumbarton Oaks, Washington, D.C.
CARMACK, R.
1968   "Toltec Influence on the Postclassic Culture History of Highland Guatemala." In *Archaeological Studies in Middle America.* Middle American Research Institute, Publication 26, Tulane Univ. New Orleans.
1973   *Quichean Civilization: The Ethnohistoric, Ethnographic and Archaeological Sources.* Univ. of California Press, Berkeley.
1976   *La estratificacíon quicheana prehispánica: Estratificacíon social en la Mesoamérica prehispánica,* Instituto Nacional de Antropología e Historia, Mexico City.
1977   "Ethnohistory of the Central Quiche: The Community of Utatlan." In *Archaeology and Ethnohistory of the Central Quiche,* pp. 1-19. *See* Wallace and Carmack 1977.
1981   *The Quiche Mayas of Utatlan.* Univ. of Oklahoma Press, Norman.
n.d.   Ethnographic Field Notes from the Central Quiche and Totonicapan Areas, 1966-76.

CARMEAN, K.
1990a   *The Ancient Households of Sayil: A Study of Wealth in Terminal Classic Maya Society.* Ph.D. dissertation, Dept. of Anthropology, Univ. of Pittsburgh.
1990b   "Architectural Labor Investment and Social Status at Sayil, Yucatan, Mexico." Paper presented at the 55th Annual Meeting of the Society for American Archaeology, Las Vegas, Nev.
CARNEIRO, R.
1970   "A Theory of the Origin of the State." *Science* 169:733-38.
CARRASCO, P.
1971   "Social Organization of Ancient Mexico." In *Handbook of Middle American Indians*, vol. 10, pp. 349-75. *See* Wauchope, Ekholm, and Bernal 1971.
1978   "La economía del México prehispánico." In *La economía, política e ideología*, pp. 13-76. *See* Carrasco and Broda 1978.
1982   "The Political Economy of the Aztec and Inca States." In G. Collier, R. Rosaldo, and J. Wirth, eds., *The Inca and Aztec States: 1400-1800: Anthropology and History*, pp. 23-40. Academic Press, New York.
CARRASCO, P., and J. BRODA
1978   eds., *La economía, política e ideología en el México prehispánico.* Editorial Nueva Imagen, Mexico City.
CARTER, L. F.
1971   "Inadvertent Sociological Theory." *Social Forces* 50(1):12-25.
CASO, A.
1928   *Las estelas zapotecas.* Secretaría de Educacíon Pública, Talleres Gráficos de la Nación, Mexico City.
CASO, A., and I. BERNAL
1965   "Ceramics of Oaxaca." In *Handbook of Middle American Indians*, vol. 3, pp. 871-95. *See* Wauchope and Willey 1965.
CHANCE, J. K.
1988   "Indian Elites in Colonial Mexico." Paper for Annual Meeting of the American Anthropological Association, Phoenix (November).
CHANG, K. C.
1989   "Ancient China and its Anthropological Significance." In *Archaeological Thought in America*, pp. 155-66. *See* Lamberg-Karlovsky 1989.
CHAPMAN, A.
1959   *Puertos de intercambio en Mesoamérica prehispánica.* Serie Historia III, INAH, Mexico City.
CHAPMAN, R., I. KINNES, and K. RANDSBORG
1981   *The Archaeology of Death.* Cambridge Univ. Press, Cambridge.
CHARLTON, T. H.
1973   *Post-Conquest Developments in the Teotihuacan Valley, Mexico, Part I: Excavations.* Report no. 5, Office of the State Archaeologist, Iowa City, Ia.
1975   "Archaeology and History: 1519-1969, The Emerging Picture in the Teotihuacan Valley." *Actas del XLI Congreso Internacional de Americanistas*, vol. 1, pp. 219-29. Mexico City.
1976   "Contemporary Central Mexican Ceramics: A View from the Past." *Man* (n.s.) 11:517-25.

1977　　"Report of a Prehispanic Canal System, Otumba, Edo. de Mexico: Archaeological Investigations, August 10-19, 1977." Manuscript submitted to INAH, Mexico City.

1978a　"Investigaciones arqueológicas en el Mucipio de Otumba, temporada de 1978: 1a parte: Resultos prelimares de los trabajos de campo, 1978." Manuscript submitted to INAH, Mexico City.

1978b　"Teotihuacan, Tepeapulco and Obsidian Exploitation." *Science* 200:1227-36.

1981　　"Otumba: Archaeology and Ethnohistory." Paper presented at the 46th Annual Meeting of the Society for American Archaeology, San Diego.

1986　　"Socioeconomic Dimensions of Urban-Rural Relations in the Colonial Period Basin of Mexico." In V. Bricker and R. Spores, eds., *Supplement to the Handbook of Middle American Indians: Ethnohistory*, vol. 4, pp. 122-31. Univ. of Texas Press, Austin.

1987　　"Otumba, México, Reconocimientos de superficie del sitio de TA-80, Otumba: Informe técnico parcial No. 1." Manuscript submitted to the Dirección de Monumentos Prehispánicos and to the Consejo de Arqueología, INAH, Mexico City.

1988　　"Reconocimientos de superficie del sitio de TA-80, Otumba: Informe técnico final." Manuscript submitted to la Dirección de Monumentos Prehispánicos and to the Consejo Arqueología, INAH, Mexico City.

1991　　"Land Tenure and Agricultural Production in the Otumba Region, 1787-1803." In H. R. Harvey, ed., *Land and Politics in the Valley of Mexico: A Two Thousand Year Perspective*, pp. 223-263. Univ. of New Mexico Press, Albuquerque.

in press　"The Aztec Collapse: An Archaeological Perspective: Early Colonial Period Ceramics of the Otumba Area, Mexico." In R. Santley, R. Diehl, and J. Parsons, eds., *Pattern and Process in Ancient Mesoamerica: Essays in Honor of William T. Sanders*. Univ. of Alabama Press.

CHASE, A. F.

1979　　"Regional Development in the Tayasal-Paxcaman Zone, El Peten, Guatemala: A Preliminary Statement." *Cerámica de Cultura Maya* 11:86-119.

1983　　*A Contextual Consideration of the Tayasal-Paxcaman Zone, El Peten, Guatemala*. Ph.D. diss., Dept. of Anthropology, Univ. of Pennsylvania, Philadelphia.

1985a　"Archeology in the Maya Heartland: The Tayasal-Paxcaman Zone, Lake Peten, Guatemala."*Archaeology* 38(1):32-39.

1985b　"Postclassic Peten Interaction Spheres: The View From Tayasal." In *The Lowland Maya Postclassic*, pp. 184-205. *See* A. Chase and P. Rice 1985.

1985c　"Troubled Times: The Archaeology and Iconography of the Terminal Classic Southern Lowland Maya." In *Fifth Palenque Round Table, 1983*, vol. 7, pp. 103-14. *See* Robertson and Fields 1985.

1990　　"Maya Archaeology and Population Estimates in the Tayasal-Paxcaman Zone, Peten, Guatemala." In *Precolumbian Population History in the Maya Lowlands*, pp. 149-165. *See* Culbert and Rice 1990.

1991　　"Cycles of Time: Caracol in the Maya Realm." In *Sixth Palenque Round Table, 1986*, pp. 32-43. *See* Robertson and Fields 1991.

in prep.　"Variations on a Theme: Three Early Classic Carved Stone Bowls."

CHASE, A. F., and D. Z. CHASE
1987a   *Glimmers of A Forgotten Realm: Maya Archaeology at Caracol, Belize.* Univ. of Central Florida, Orlando.
1987b   *Investigations at the Classic Maya City of Caracol, Belize: 1985-1987.* Monograph 3, Pre-Columbian Art Research Institute, San Francisco.
1989   "The Investigation of Classic Period Warfare at Caracol, Belize." *Mayab* 5:5-18.
1990   "Los sistemas mayas de subsistencia y patrón de asentamiento: Pasado y futuro." In L. Yañez-Barnuevo García and A. Ciudad Ruiz, eds., *Los mayas: El esplendor de una civilización*, pp. 38-48. Sociedad Estatal Quinto Centenario, Turner Libros, S.A., Madrid.
1992   "El norte y el sur: Política, dominios, y evolucion cultural maya." *Mayab.*
in press "Maya Veneration of the Dead at Caracol, Belize." In M. Robertson, ed., *Seventh Mesa Redonda de Palenque, 1989.* vol. 9. Pre-Columbian Art Research Institute, San Francisco.
CHASE, A. F., N. GRUBE, and D. Z. CHASE
1991   "Three Terminal Classic Monuments from Caracol, Belize." *Research Reports on Ancient Maya Writing*, no. 36. Center for Maya Research, Washington, D.C.
CHASE, A. F., and P. RICE
1985   eds., *The Lowland Maya Postclassic.* Univ. of Texas Press, Austin.
CHASE, D. Z.
1981   "The Postclassic Maya at Santa Rita Corozal." *Archaeology* 34(1):25-33.
1982   *Spatial and Temporal Variability in Postclassic Northern Belize.* Ph.D. diss., Dept. of Anthropology, Univ. of Pennsylvania, Philadelphia.
1985a   "Between Earth and Sky: Idols, Images, and Postclassic Cosmology." In *Fifth Palenque Round Table, 1983*, pp. 223-33. *See* Robertson and Fields 1985.
1985b   "Ganned But Not Forgotten: Late Postclassic Archaeology and Ritual at Santa Rita Corozal, Belize." In *The Lowland Maya Postclassic*, pp. 104-25. *See* A. Chase and P. Rice 1985.
1985c   "Less Is More: The Illusory Imbalance between Lowland and Highland Mesoamerican Theory." Paper presented at the 84th Annual Meeting of the American Anthropological Association, Washington D.C., December.
1986   "Social and Political Organization in the Land of Cacao and Honey: Correlating the Archaeology and Ethnohistory of the Postclassic Lowland Maya." In *Late Lowland Maya Civilization*, pp. 347-377. *See* Sabloff and Andrews 1986.
1988   "Caches and Censerwares: Meaning from Maya Pottery." In *A Pot for All Reasons*, pp. 81-104. *See* Kolb and Lackey 1988.
1990   "The Invisible Maya: Population History and Archaeology at Santa Rita Corozal, Belize." In *Precolumbian Population History in the Maya Lowlands*, pp. 199-213. *See* Culbert and Rice 1990.
1991   "Lifeline to the Maya Gods: Ritual Bloodletting at Santa Rita Corozal." In *Sixth Palenque Round Table, 1986*, pp. 89-96. *See* Robertson and Fields 1991.
CHASE, D. Z., and A. F. CHASE
1981   "Archaeological Investigations at Nohmul and Santa Rita, Belize: 1979-1980." *Mexicon* 3(3):42-44.

1982 "Yucatec Influence in Terminal Classic Northern Belize." *American Antiquity* 47(3):596-614.

1986a "Archaeological Insights on the Contact Period Lowland Maya." In M. Rivera and A. Ciudad, eds., *Los mayas de tiempos tardíos*, pp. 13-20. Sociedad Española de Estudios Mayas y Institutio de Cooperación Iberoamericana, Madrid.

1986b *Offerings to the Gods: Maya Archaeology at Santa Rita Corozal.* Univ. of Central Florida, Orlando.

1988 *A Postclassic Perspective: Excavations at the Maya Site of Santa Rita Corozal, Belize.* Monograph 4, Pre-Columbian Art Research Institute, San Francisco.

1989 "Routes of Trade and Communication and the Integration of Maya Society: The Vista from Santa Rita Corozal." In H. McKillop and P. Healy, eds., *Coastal Maya Trade*, pp. 19-32. Occasional Papers in Anthropology no. 8, Trent Univ., Toronto.

n.d. "The Postclassic Maya." Manuscript in preparation.

CHASE, D. Z., A. F. CHASE, and W. A. HAVILAND

1990 "The Classic Maya City: Reconsidering 'The Mesoamerican Urban Tradition.' " *American Anthropologist* 92(2):499-506.

CHEEK, C., and M. SPINK

1986 "Excavaciones en el Grupo 3, Estructura 223 (Operacíon VII)." In *Excavaciones en el área úrbana de Copán I. See* Sanders 1986.

CLAESSEN, H .J. M., and SKALNIK

1978 eds., *The Early State.* The Hague, Mouton.

CLANCY, F. S., and P. D. HARRISON

1990 eds., *Vision and Revision in Maya Studies.* Univ. of New Mexico Press, Albuquerque.

CLARK, G.

1986 *Symbols of Excellence: Precious Materials as Expressions of Status.* Cambridge Univ. Press, New York.

CLARK, J. E.

1986 "From Mountains to Molehills: A Critical Review of Teotihuacan's Obsidian Industry." In *Research in Economic Anthropology, Supplement 2,* pp. 23-74. *See* Isaac 1986a.

COE, M. D.

1956 "The Funerary Temple among the Classic Maya." *Southwestern Journal of Anthropology* 12(4):387-94.

1973 *The Maya Scribe and His World.* Grolier Club, New York.

1975 "Death and the Ancient Maya." In E. Benson, ed., *Death and the Afterlife in Pre-Columbian America*, pp. 87-104. Dumbarton Oaks, Washington, D.C.

1977 "Supernatural Patrons of Maya Scribes and Artists." In *Social Process in Maya Prehistory*, pp. 327-47. *See* Hammond 1977.

1984 *Mexico.* 3d ed. Thames and Hudson, London.

1987 *The Maya.* 4th ed. Thames and Hudson, London.

1988 "Ideology of the Maya Tomb." In E. P. Benson and G. G. Griffen, eds., *Maya Iconography*, pp. 222-35. Princeton Univ. Press, Princeton.

COE, M. D., and R. DIEHL

1980 *In the Land of the Olmec.* Univ. of Texas Press, Austin.

COE, W. R.
1965   "Tikal, Guatemala and Emergent Maya Civilization." *Science* 147:1401-19.
1966   "Review of *Prehistoric Maya Settlements in the Belize Valley* by G. R. Willey, W. R. Bullard, Jr., J. B. Glass, and J. C. Gifford." *American Journal of Archaeology* 70:309-11.
1967   *Tikal: A Handbook of the Ancient Maya Ruins*. Univ. Museum, Univ. of Pennsylvania, Philadelphia.
1990   *Excavations in the Great Plaza, North Terrace, and North Acropolis of Tikal*. Tikal Report no. 14, Univ. of Pennsylvania, Univ. Museum, Philadelphia.

COGGINS, C. C.
1975   *Painting and Drawing Styles at Tikal: An Historical and Iconographic Reconstruction*. Ph.D. diss., Harvard Univ. Cambridge, Mass.
1979   "A New Order and the Role of the Calendar: Some Characteristics of the Middle Classic Period at Tikal." In *Maya Archaeology and Ethnohistory*, pp. 38-50. *See* Hammond and Willey 1979.
1980   "The Shape of Time: Some Political Implications of a Four-Part Figure." *American Antiquity* 45:727-39.
1983   *The Stucco Decoration and Architectural Assemblage of Structure 1-Sub, Dzibilchaltun, Yucatan, Mexico*. Middle American Research Institute Publication 49, Tulane Univ. New Orleans.
1986   "A New Sun at Chichen Itza." Paper presented at 2nd International Conference on Archaeoastronomy, Merida, Mexico.
1987   "Pure Language and Lapidary Prose." Paper presented at symposium New Theories on the Ancient Maya, Univ. of Pennsylvania, Univ. Museum, Philadelphia.
1990   "The Birth of the Baktun at Tikal and Seibal." In *Vision and Revision in Maya Studies*, pp. 79-97. *See* Clancy and Harrison 1990.

COGGINS, C. C., and O. C. SHANE III
1984   *Cenote of Sacrifice: Maya Treasures from the Sacred Well at Chichen Itza*. Univ. of Texas Press, Austin.

COHEN, A.
1979   "Political Symbolism." *Annual Reviews in Anthropology* 8:87-113.

CONQUISTADOR ANONIMO
1941   *Relación de algunas cosas de la Nueva España y de la gran ciudad de Temestitán. Escrito por un compañero de Hernán Cortés*. Editorial América, Mexico City.

CORDELL, L. S., and G. J. GUMMERMAN
1989   eds., *Dynamics of Southwest Prehistory*. Smithsonian Institution Press, Washington, D.C.

CORDOVA, J. de
1578a   *Arte en lengua zapoteca*. Reprinted by Morelis (1886), Pedro Balli, Mexico City.
1578b   *Vocabulario en lengua zapoteca*, Facsimile INAH (1942), Pedro Charte y Antonio Ricardo, Mexico City.

CORTES, H.
1971   *Hernan Cortes: Letters from Mexico*. Edited and translated by A. Pagden. Orion Press, New York.

COSIER, L. A.
1975   "Presidential Address: Two Methods in Search of a Substance." *American Sociological Review* 40(6):691-700.
COVARRUBIAS, M.
1943   "Tlatilco: Archaic Mexican Art and Culture." *Dyn* 4-5:40-46, Mexico City.
1950   "Tlatilco: El arte y la cultura preclasica del Valle de mexico." *Cuadernos Americanos* 3:149-62.
COWGILL, G. L.
1979   "Teotihuacan, Internal Militaristic Competition, and the Fall of the Classic Maya." In *Maya Archaeology and Ethnohistory*, pp. 51-62. *See* Hammond and Willey 1979.
1983   "Rulership and the Ciudadela: Political Inferences from Teotihuacan Architecture." In *Civilization in the Ancient Americas*, pp. 313-43. *See* Leventhal and Kolata 1983.
1987   "Métodos para el estudio de relaciones espaciales en los datos de la superficie de Teotihuacán." In *Teotihuacan*, pp. 161-89. *See* McClung and Rattray 1987.
COWGILL, G. L., J. H. ATSCHUL, and R. S. SLOAD
1984   "Spatial Analysis of Teotihuacan: A Mesoamerican Metropolis." In H. Hietala, ed., *Intrasite Spatial Analysis in Archaeology*, pp. 154-95. Cambridge Univ. Press, Cambridge.
COX, O. C.
1945   "Estates, Social Classes, and Political Classes." *American Sociological Review* 10:464-69.
CREAMER, W., and J. HAAS
1985   "Tribe versus Chiefdom in Lower Central America." *American Antiquity* 50(4):738-54.
CULBERT, T. P.
1973   ed., *The Classic Maya Collapse*. Univ. of New Mexico Press, Albuquerque.
1988   "Political History and the Development of Maya Glyphs." *Antiquity* 62(234):134-52.
1991   *Classic Maya Political History: Hieroglyphic and Archaeological Evidence*. Cambridge Univ. Press, Cambridge.
CULBERT, T. P., and D. S. RICE
1990   eds., *Precolumbian Population History in the Maya Lowlands*. Univ. of New Mexico Press, Albuquerque.
CULBERT, T. P., et al.
1990   "The Population of Tikal, Guatemala." In *Precolumbian Population History in the Maya Lowlands. See* Culbert and Rice 1990.
CURTIN, P.
1984   *Cross-Cultural Trade in World History*. Cambridge Univ. Press, Cambridge.
DAHL, R. A.
1969   "A Critique of the Ruling Elite Model." In *Political Power*, pp. 36-41. *See* Bell, Edwards, and Wagner 1969.
DALTON, G.
1977   "Aboriginal Economies in Stateless Societies." In T. Earle and J. Ericson, eds., *Exchange Systems in Prehistory*, pp. 191-212. Academic Press, New York.

1981   "Anthropological Models in Archaeological Perspective." In I. Hodder, G.
          Isaac, and N. Hammond, eds., *Pattern of the Past: Studies in Honour of
          David Clarke*, pp. 17-48. Cambridge Univ. Press, Cambridge.
D'ALTROY, T., and T. EARLE
1985   "State Finance, Wealth Finance, and Storage in the Inka Political Econ-
          omy." *Current Anthropology* 26:187-206.
DAVALOS HURTADO, E., and A. ROMANO PACHECO
1973   "Estudio preliminar de los restos osteológicos en la tumba del Templo de
          las Inscripciones Palenque." In *El Templo de las Inscripciones Palenque*,
          pp. 253-54. *See* Ruz Lhuillier 1973.
DAVIES, N.
1987   *The Aztec Empire: The Toltec Resurgence*. Univ. of Oklahoma Press, Nor-
          man.
DAVIS, K.
1942   "A Conceptual Analysis of Stratification." *American Sociological Review*
          7(3):309-21.
DAVIS, K., and W. E. MOORE
1945   "Some Principles of Stratification." *American Sociological Review*
          10(2):242-49.
DAVIS, W.
in press "Representation, Legitimation and the Emergence of the Ancient Egyp-
          tian State." To appear in a volume on African prehistory, edited by R.
          McIntosh and S. McIntosh. Univ. of Wisconsin Press, Madison.
DAVOUST, M.
1977   *Les chefs maya de Chichen Itza*. Angiers, France.
DIBBLE, C. E., and A. J. O. ANDERSON
1959   *Florentine Codex: Book 9-The Merchants*. School of American Research,
          Santa Fe, and Univ. of Utah, Salt Lake City.
DIEHL, R.
1983   *Tula: The Toltec Capital of Ancient Mexico*. Thames and Hudson, London.
DRENNAN, R. D.
1976   "Religion and Social Evolution in Formative Mesoamerica." In K. Flan-
          nery, ed., *The Early Mesoamerican Village*, pp. 345-68. Academic Press,
          New York.
1984   "Long-Distance Transport Costs in Pre-Hispanic Mesoamerica." *American
          Anthropologist* 86:105-12.
1987   "Regional Demography in Chiefdoms." In *Chiefdoms in the Americas*, pp.
          307-24. *See* Drennan and Uribe 1987.
DRENNAN, R. D., and C. A. URIBE
1987   eds., *Chiefdoms in the Americas*. Univ. Press of America, Lanham, Md.
DRUCKER, P.
1952   *La Venta, Tabasco: A Study of Olmec Ceramics and Art*. Bureau of Ameri-
          can Ethnology Bulletin 153, Smithsonian Institution, Washington, D.C.
1981   "On the Nature of the Olmec Polity." In E. P. Benson, ed., *The Olmec and
          Their Neighbors*, pp. 29-47. Dumbarton Oaks, Washington, D.C.
DRUCKER, P., R. F. HEIZER, and R. J. SQUIER
1959   *Excavations at La Venta, Tabasco, 1955*. Bureau of American Ethnology
          Bulletin 170, Smithsonian Institution, Washington, D.C.

DUNHAM, P.
1988   "Maya Balkanization and the Classic Florescence: Golden Age or Incipi-
        ent Collapse." Paper presented at 87th Annual Meeting, American An-
        thropological Association, Phoenix.
DuSOLIER, W.
1943   *A Reconnaissance on the Isla de Sacrificios, Veracruz, Mexico.* Notes on
        Middle American Archaeology and Ethnology no. 14, Carnegie Institution
        of Washington, Washington, D.C.
DYCKERHOFF, U., and H. J. PREM
1976   "La estratificación social en Huexotzinco." In P. Carrasco and J. Broda,
        eds., *Estratificación social en la Mesoamerica prehispánica,* pp. 157-77.
        INAH, Mexico City.
EARLE, T. K.
1987   "Chiefdoms in Archaeological and Ethnohistorical Perspective." *Annual
        Review of Anthropology* 16:279-308.
EDMONSON, M. S.
1979   "Some Postclassic Questions about the Classic Maya." In M. G. Robert-
        son, ed., *Tercera Mesa Redonda de Palenque,* vol. 4. Herald Printers, Mon-
        terey, Cal.
1982   *The Ancient Future of the Itza: The Book of Chilam Balam of Tizimin.* Univ.
        of Texas Press, Austin.
ESCOBEDO AYALA, H. L.
1991   *Epigrafia e Historia Politica de los Sitios del Noroeste de las Montañas Mayas
        durante el Clasico Tardio.* Tesis de Licenciado en Arqueologia, Universi-
        dad de San Carlos de Guatemala, Escuela de Historia, Guatemala.
ESTRADA, J. de
1955   "Descripción de la Provincia de Zapotitlán and Suchitepequez." *Anales de
        la Sociedad de Geografia e Historia de Guatemala* 28:68-84.
EVANS, S.
1980   *A Settlement System Analysis of the Teotihuacan Region, Mexico: A.D. 1350-
        1520.* Ph.D. diss., Dept. of Anthropology, Pennsylvania State Univ., Univ.
        Park.
1985   "Siguatecpan: An Aztec Period Rural Village in the Teotihuacan Valley."
        Paper presented at the 50th Annual Meeting of the Society for American
        Archaeology, Denver.
in prep. "Architecture and Authority in an Aztec Village." In H. R. Harvey, ed.,
        Land and Politics in the Valley of Mexico.
EVANS-PRITCHARD, E. E.
1940   *The Nuer.* Oxford Univ. Press, Oxford.
FARRISS, N. M.
1984   *Maya Society Under Colonial Rule.* Princeton Univ. Press, Princeton.
FASH, W. L.
1983a   "Deducing Social Organization from Classic Maya Settlement Patterns."
        In *Civilization in the Ancient Americas,* pp. 261-88. *See* Leventhal and Ko-
        lata 1983.
1983b   *Maya State Formation: A Case Study and Its Implications.* Ph.D. diss., Har-
        vard Univ., Cambridge, Mass.
1987   "The Altar and Associated Features." In *Ancient Chalcatzingo,* pp. 82-94.
        See Grove 1987a.

FEINMAN, G.
1980   *The Relationship between Administrative Organization and Ceramic Produc-
         tion in the Valley of Oaxaca, Mexico.* Ph.D. diss., Dept. of Anthropology,
         City Univ. of New York, New York.
FINSTEN, L.
1983   *The Classic-Postclassic Transition in the Valley of Oaxaca, Mexico.* Ph.D.
         diss., Dept. of Sociology and Anthropology, Purdue Univ., West Lafayette,
         Ind.
FLANNERY, K. V.
1968   "The Olmec and the Valley of Oaxaca: A Model for Inter-regional Inter-
         action in Formative Times." In E. Benson, ed., *Dumbarton Oaks Confer-
         ence on the Olmec*, pp. 79-110. Dumbarton Oaks, Washington, D.C.
1983a   "The Legacy of the Early Urban Period: An Ethnohistoric Approach to
         Monte Alban's Temples, Residences, and Royal Tombs." In *The Cloud
         People*, pp. 132-36. *See* Flannery and Marcus 1983a.
1983b   "Major Monte Alban V Sites: Zaachila, Xoxocotlan, Cuilapan, Yagul, and
         Abasolo." In *The Cloud People*, pp. 290-95. *See* Flannery and Marcus
         1983a.
FLANNERY, K. V., and J. MARCUS
1983a   *The Cloud People: Divergent Evolution of the Zapotec and Mixtec Civiliza-
         tions.* Academic Press, New York.
1983b   "The Origins of the State in Oaxaca." In *The Cloud People*, pp. 79-83, *See*
         1983a.
FLANNERY, K. V., and J. SCHOENWETTER
1970   "Climate and Man in Formative Oaxaca." *Archaeology* 23:144-52.
FOLAN, W. J., E. R. KINTZ, and L. A. FLETCHER
1983   *Coba: A Classic Maya Metropolis.* Academic Press, New York.
FOLAN, W. J., et al.
1982   "An Examination of Settlement Patterns at Coba, Quintana Roo, Mexico,
         and Tikal, Guatemala: A Reply to Arnold and Ford." *American Antiquity*
         47(2):430-36.
FORD, A.
1986   *Population Growth and Social Complexity: An Examination of Settlement
         and Environment in the Central Maya Lowlands.* Arizona State Univ. An-
         thropological Research Paper no. 35, Tempe.
FORD, A., and J. E. ARNOLD
1982   "A Reexamination of Labor Investments at Tikal: Reply to Haviland, and
         Folan, Kintz, Fletcher and Hyde." *American Antiquity* 47(2):436-40.
FOUCAULT, M.
1973   *The Order of Things: An Archaeology of the Human Sciences.* Random
         House, New York.
1979   *Discipline and Punish: The Birth of the Prison.* Random House, New York.
FOX, J. A., and J. S. JUSTESON
1986   "Classic Maya Dynastic Alliance and Succession." In V. Bricker and R.
         Spores, eds., *Supplement to the Handbook of Middle American Indians:
         Ethnohistory,* vol. 4, pp. 7-34. Univ. of Texas Press, Austin.
FOX, J. W.
1978a   "Chinautla Viejo (Mixcu): Un sitio estratégico en la frontera Cak-
         chiquel/Pokomam." *Anales de la Sociedad de Geografía e Historia* 51:13-25.

1978b   *Quiche Conquest*, Univ. of New Mexico, Albuquerque.
1980   "Lowland-Highland Mexicanization Processes in Southern Mesoamerica." *American Antiquity* 45:43-54.
1981   "The Postclassic Eastern Frontier of Mesoamerica: Cultural Innovation along the Periphery." *Cultural Anthropology* 22(4):321-46.
1987   *Maya Postclassic State Formation: Segmentary Lineage Migration in Advancing Frontiers*. Cambridge Univ. Press, Cambridge.
1988a   "Hierarchization in Maya Segmentary States." In B. Bender and J. Gledhill, eds., *State and Society: The Emergence and Development of Social Hierarchy and Political Centralization*. Allen and Unwin, London.
1988b   "Katun Confederation among the Early Postclassic Lowland and Highland Maya." Paper presented at the 46th International Congress of Americanists, Amsterdam, The Netherlands.
1989   "On the Rise and Fall of 'Tulans' and Maya Segmentary States." *American Anthropologist* 91:656-81.
1991   "The Lords of Light versus the Lords of Dark: The Postclassic Highland Maya Ballgame." In *The Mesoamerican Ballgame*, pp.213-238. *See* Scarborough and Wilcox 1991.
n.d.   "Factionalism among the Postclassic Quiche Maya: The Calendar for Competition and Cooperation." In E. M. Brumfiel and J. W. Fox, eds., *Factionalism and Political Development in the New World*. Cambridge Univ. Press, Cambridge.

FOX, R. G.
1977   *Urban Anthropology*. Prentice Hall, Englewood Cliffs, NJ.

FREIDEL, D. A.
1981   "The Political Economics of Residential Dispersion among the Lowland Maya." In *Lowland Maya Settlement Patterns*, pp. 371-82. *See* Ashmore 1981a.
1985   "New Light on the Dark Age: A Summary of Major Themes." In *The Lowland Maya Postclassic*, pp. 285-309. *See* A. Chase and P. Rice 1985.
1986a   "Maya Warfare: An Example of Peer Polity Interaction." In *Peer-Polity Interaction and the Development of Sociopolitical Complexity*, pp. 93-108. *See* Renfrew and Cherry 1986.
1986b   "Terminal Classic Lowland Maya: Successes, Failures, and Aftermaths." In *Late Lowland Maya Civilization: Classic to Postclassic*, pp. 409-30. *See* Sabloff and Andrews 1986.
1987   *Yaxuna Archaeological Survey: A Report of the 1986 Field Season*. Dept of Anthropology, Southern Methodist Univ., Dallas.

FREIDEL, D. A., and J. A. SABLOFF
1984   *Cozumel: Late Maya Settlement Patterns*. Academic Press, N.Y.

FREIDEL, D. A., and L. SCHELE
1988a   "Kingship in the Late Preclassic Lowlands: The Instruments and Places of Ritual Power." *American Anthropologist* 90(3):547-67.
1988b   "Symbol and Power: A History of the Lowland Maya Cosmogram." In E. Benson and G. Griffin, eds., *Maya Iconography*, pp. 44-93. Princeton Univ. Press, Princeton, N.J.
1989   "The Maya War Jaguar: Historical Invention and Structural Transformation." Paper presented at the SAA meetings, Atlanta, (April).

FREIDEL, D. A., and J. A. SABLOFF
1984   *Cozumel: Late Maya Settlement Patterns*. Academic Press, New York.
FRETER, A.
1982   "Was the 'Quiche State' a State?: A Reanalysis of the Utatlan Residence
         Zone Data." M.A. thesis, Univ. of Houston.
1988   *The Classic Maya Collapse at Copan, Honduras: A Regional Settlement Per-
         spective*. Ph.D. diss., Dept. of Anthropology, Pennsylvania State Univ.,
         Univ. Park.
FRIED, M.
1967   *The Evolution of Political Society*. Random House, New York.
FRIEDMAN, J., and M. ROWLANDS
1977   eds., *The Evolution of Social Systems*. Duckworth, London.
FRY, R. E.
1979   "The Economics of Pottery at Tikal, Guatemala: Models of Exchange for
         Serving Vessels." *American Antiquity* 44(3):494-512.
FRY, R. E., and S. C. COX
1974   "The Structure of Ceramic Exchange at Tikal, Guatemala." *World Archae-
         ology* 6:209-25.
FUENTES Y GUZMAN, F. A. de
1932-33 *Recordación Florida: Discurso historial y demonstracíon natural, material,
         military y publica del reino de Guatemala*. Biblioteca Goathemala, vols. 6-8.
         Guatemala.
GANN, T.
1900   "Mounds in Northern Honduras." In *Nineteenth Annual Report, 1897-1898,
         Bureau of American Ethnology*, pt. 2, pp. 661-92. Smithsonian Institution,
         Washington, D.C.
1918   *The Maya Indians of Southern Yucatan and Northern British Honduras*. Bu-
         reau of American Ethnology, Bulletin no. 64. Washington, D.C.
GENET, J.
1934   "Letter." *Maya Research* 1:136.
GERSTLE, A.
1987a   "Ethnic Diversity and Interaction at Copan, Honduras." In *Interaction on
         the Southeast Mesoamerican Frontier*, pp. 328-56. *See* Robinson 1987.
1987b   *Maya-Lenca Ethnic Diversity in Late Classic Copan, Honduras*. Ph.D. diss.,
         Dept. of Anthropology, Univ. of California, Santa Barbara.
GIBSON, C.
1964   *The Aztecs under Spanish Rule*. Stanford Univ. Press, Stanford, Ca.
GIDDENS, A.
1973   *The Class Structure of Advanced Societies*. Harper and Row, New York.
1974   "Elites in the British Class Structure." In P. Stanworth and A. Giddens,
         eds., *Elites and Power in British Society*. Cambridge Univ. Press, Cam-
         bridge.
1976   *New Rules of Sociological Method*. Basic Books, New York.
1979   *Central Problems in Social Theory: Action, Structure, and Contradiction in
         Social Analysis*. Univ. of California Press, Berkeley.
GOLDHAMER, H., and E. A. SHILS
1939   "Types of Power and Status." *American Journal of Sociology* 45(2):171-82.

GOLDMAN, R., and A. TICKAMYER
1984   "Status Attainment and the Commodity Form: Stratification in Historical Perspective." *American Sociological Review* 49:196-209.
GOULD, S. J.
1986   "Evolution and the Triumph of Homology, or Why History Matters." *American Scientist* 74:60-69.
GRAHAM, E., and D. M. PENDERGAST
1988   "Obsidian Hydration Dates from Tipu and Lamanai, Belize: Implications for the Assessment of Spanish Impact on Sixteenth-Century Maya Trade Networks." Manuscript on file, Dept. of New World Archaeology, Royal Ontario Museum.
GRAHAM, J. A.
1973   "Aspects of Non-Classic Presences in the Inscriptions and Sculptural Art of Seibal." In *The Classic Maya Collapse*, pp. 207-20. *See* Culbert 1973.
GREGORY, D., and J. URREY
1985   eds., *Social Relations and Spatial Structures*. St. Martin's Press, New York.
GROVE, D. C.
1974a   "The Highland Olmec Manifestation: A Consideration of What It Is and Isn't." In *Mesoamerican Archaeology: New Approaches*, pp. 109-28. *See* Hammond 1974.
1974b   *San Pablo, Nexpa, and the Early Formative Archaeology of Morelos.* Vanderbilt Univ. Publications in Anthropology 12, Nashville.
1981   "Olmec Monuments: Mutilation as a Clue to Meaning." In E. P. Benson, ed., *The Olmec and Their Neighbors*, pp. 49-68. Dumbarton Oaks, Washington, D.C.
1984   *Chalcatzingo: Excavations on the Olmec Frontier.* Thames and Hudson, London.
1987a   ed., *Ancient Chalcatzingo*, Univ. of Texas Press, Austin.
1987b   "Chalcatzingo in a Broader Perspective." In *Ancient Chalcatzingo*, pp. 434-42. *See* 1987a.
1987c   "Comments on the Site and Its Organization." In *Ancient Chalcatzingo*, pp. 420-33. *See* 1987a.
1987d   "Middle Formative Serpent Imagery: Early Symbols of Rulership." Paper for Annual Meeting of the American Anthropological Association, Chicago.
1987e   " 'Torches,' 'Knuckle Dusters' and the Legitimization of Formative Period Rulership." *Mexicon* 9(3):60-65.
1989   "Olmec: What's in a Name?" In R. J. Sharer and D. C. Grove, eds., *The Olmec and the Development of Formative Mesoamerican Civilization*, pp. 8-14. Cambridge Univ. Press, Cambridge.
GROVE, D. C., and J. ANGULO V.
1987   "A Catalog and Description of Chalcatzingo's Monuments." In *Ancient Chalcatzingo*, pp. 114-31. *See* Grove 1987a.
GROVE, D. C., and S. D. GILLESPIE
n.d.   "Ideology and Evolution at the Pre-State Level: Formative Period Mesoamerica." In A. Demerest and G. Conrad, eds., *Ideology and the Cultural Evolution of Pre-Columbian Civilizations*. School of American Research, Santa Fe.

GROVE, D. C., and A. CYPHERS GUILLEN
1987   "The Excavations." In *Ancient Chalcatzingo*, pp. 21-55. *See* Grove 1987a.
GROVE, D. C., K. G. HIRTH, and D. E. BUGE
1987   "The Physical and Cultural Setting." In *Ancient Chalcatzingo*, pp. 6-13. *See*
        Grove 1987a.
GRUBE, N.
1990   "A Reference to Water-Lily Jaguar on Caracol Stela 16." *Copan Note 68*.
        Copan, Honduras.
GUILLEMIN, J. R.
1977   "Urbanism and Hierarchy at Iximche." In *Social Process in Maya Prehis-
        tory*, pp. 227-64. *See* Hammond 1977.
HALSTEAD, P., and J. O'SHEA
1989   "Introduction: Cultural Responses to Risk and Uncertainty." In *Bad Year
        Economics*, J. Halstead and J. O'Shea, eds, pp. 1-7. Cambridge Univ.
        Press, Cambridge.
HAMMOND, N.
1974   ed., *Mesoamerican Archaeology: New Approaches*. Univ. of Texas Press,
        Austin.
1975   "Maya Settlement Hierarchy in Northern Belize." In *Contributions of the
        University of California Archaeological Research Facility*, no. 27, pp. 40-55.
        Los Angeles.
1977   ed., *Social Process in Maya Prehistory*. Academic Press, London.
1982   *Ancient Maya Civilization*. Rutgers Univ. Press, New Brunswick, N.J.
HAMMOND, N., and G. R. WILLEY
1979   eds., *Maya Archaeology and Ethnohistory*. Univ. of Texas Press, Austin.
HANSEN, E. C., and T. C. PARRISH
1983   "Elites versus the State." In *Elites*, pp. 257-77. *See* G. Marcus 1983a.
HANSEN, R.
1987   "Initial Explorations at Nakbe, Peten, Guatemala." Paper delivered at the
        86th Annual Meeting, American Anthropological Association, Chicago
        (November).
HARLAN, M. E.
1979   "An Inquiry into the Development of Complex Society at Chalcatzingo,
        Morelos, Mexico: Methods and Results." *American Antiquity* 44(3):471-93.
HARNER, M.
1975   "Scarcity, the Factors of Production and Social Evolution." In S. Polgar,
        ed., *Population, Ecology, and Social Evolution*, pp. 123-38. Mouton, The
        Hague.
HARRISON, P. D.
1969   "Form and Function in a Maya 'Palace' Group." In *Verhandlungen des
        XXXVIII. Internationalen Amerikanistenkongresses* 1:165-72. Stuttgart-
        Munich.
1970   *The Central Acropolis, Tikal, Guatemala: A Preliminary Study of the Func-
        tions of its Structural Components during the Late Classic Period*. Ph.D.
        diss., Dept. of Anthropology, Univ. of Pennsylvania, Philadelphia.
1981   "Some Aspects of Preconquest Settlement in Southern Quintana Roo,
        Mexico." In *Lowland Maya Settlement Patterns*, pp. 259-86. *See* Ashmore
        1981a.

1986   "Tikal: Selected Topics." In *City-States of the Maya*, pp. 45-71. *See* Benson 1986.

HARRISON, P. D., and B. L. TURNER
1978   *Pre-Hispanic Maya Agriculture*. Univ. of New Mexico Press, Albuquerque.

HARVEY, H. R.
1984   "Aspects of Land Tenure in Ancient Mexico." In H. R. Harvey and H. J. Prem, eds., *Explorations in Ethnohistory*, pp. 83-102. Univ. of New Mexico Press, Albuquerque.

HASKETT, R. S.
1988   "Living in Two Worlds: Cultural Continuity and Change among Cuernavaca's Colonial Indigenous Ruling Elite." *Ethnohistory* 35(1):34-59.

HASSIG, R.
1985   *Trade, Tribute and Transportation: The Sixteenth Century Political Economy of the Valley of Mexico*. Univ. of Oklahoma Press, Norman.

HATT, P. K.
1950   "Stratification in the Mass Society." *American Sociological Review* 15(2):216-22.

HAUSER, R. M.
1980   "On 'Stratification in a Dual Economy.' " *American Sociological Review* 45(4):702-12.

HAVILAND, W. A.
1963   *Excavation of Small Structures in the Northeast Quadrant of Tikal, Guatemala.*, Ph.D. diss., Dept. of Anthropology, Univ. of Pennsylvania, Philadelphia.
1965   "Prehistoric Settlement at Tikal, Guatemala." *Expedition* 7(3):15-23.
1966   "Maya Settlement Patterns: A Critical Review." *Middle American Research Institute Publication 26*, pp.21-47. Tulane Univ., New Orleans.
1967   "Stature at Tikal, Guatemala: Implications for Ancient Maya Demography and Social Organization." *American Antiquity* 32:316-25.
1968   "Ancient Lowland Maya Social Organization." In *Middle American Research Institute Publication 26*, pp. 93-117. Tulane Univ., New Orleans.
1970   "Tikal, Guatemala and Mesoamerican Urbanism." *World Archaeology* 2:186-98.
1971   "A View of Classic Maya Social Structure." Paper presented to Maya Seminar, Dept. of Anthropology, Harvard Univ. (March 24).
1972   "A New Look at Classic Maya Social Organization at Tikal." *Ceramica de Cultura Maya* 8:1-16.
1974   "Occupational Specialization at Tikal, Guatemala: Stoneworking-Monument Carving." *American Antiquity* 39:494-96.
1978   "On Price's Presentation of Data on Tikal." *Current Anthropology* 19:180-81.
1981   "Dower Houses and Minor Centers at Tikal, Guatemala: An Investigation into the Identification of Valid Units in Settlement Hierarchies." In *Lowland Maya Settlement Patterns*, pp. 89-117. *See* Ashmore 1981a.
1982   "Where the Rich Folks Lived: Deranging Factors in the Statistical Analysis of Tikal Settlement." *American Antiquity* 47(2):427-29.
1985   "Population and Social Dynamics: The Dynasties and Social Structure of Tikal." *Expedition* 27(3):34-41.

1988   "Musical Hammocks at Tikal: Problems with Reconstructing Household
           Composition." In *Household and Community in the Mesoamerican Past*, pp.
           121-34. *See* Wilk and Ashmore 1988.
in press   *Excavations in Group 7F-1: An Elite Residential Group of Tikal.* Tikal Re-
           port No. 22, Univ. of Pennsylvania, The Univ. Museum, Philadelphia.
HAVILAND, W. A., et al.
1985   *Excavations in Small Residential Groups of Tikal: Groups 4F-1 and 4F-2.*
           Tikal Report No. 19, Univ. of Pennsylvania, Univ. Museum, Philadelphia.
HEALY, P. F.
1987   "Ancient Honduras: Power, Wealth, and Rank in Early Chiefdoms." Pa-
           per presented at symposium on Wealth and Hierarchy in the Intermediate
           Area, Dumbarton Oaks, Washington, D.C.
HEALY, P. F., et al.
1983   "Caracol, Belize: Evidence of Ancient Maya Agricultural Terraces." *Jour-
           nal of Field Archaeology* 10:397-410.
HELMS, M. W.
1979   *Ancient Panama: Chiefs in Search of Power.* Univ. of Texas Press, Austin.
1987   "Thoughts on Public Symbols and Distant Domains Relevant to the Chief-
           doms of Lower Central America." Paper presented at symposium on
           Wealth and Hierarchy in the Intermediate Area, Dumbarton Oaks, Wash-
           ington, D.C.
HENDERSON, J. S.
1977   "The Valle de Naco: Ethnohistory and Archaeology in Northwestern Hon-
           duras." *Ethnohistory* 24(4):363-77.
1978   "El noroeste de Honduras y la frontera oriental maya." *Yaxkin* 2(4):241-
           53.
1987a   "Frontier at the Crossroads." In *Interaction on the Southeast Mesoamerican
           Frontier*, pp. 455-62. *See* Robinson 1987.
1987b   "Variations on a Theme: A Frontier View of Maya Civilization." Paper
           presented at symposium on New Theories on the Ancient Maya, Univ.
           Museum, Philadelphia.
HENDERSON, J. S., et al.
1979   "Archaeological Investigations in the Valle de Naco. Northwestern Hon-
           duras: A Preliminary Report." *Journal of Field Archaeology* 6(1):169-92.
HENDON, J.
1987   *The Uses of Maya Structures: A Study of Architecture and Artifact Distribu-
           tion at Sepulturas, Copan, Honduras.* Ph.D. diss., Dept. of Anthropology,
           Harvard Univ., Cambridge, Mass.
HICKS, F.
1986   "Prehispanic Background of Colonial Political and Economic Organiza-
           tion in Central Mexico." In R. Spores, ed., *Ethnohistory: Supplement to the
           Handbook of Middle American Indians*, vol. 4, pp. 35-54. Univ. of Texas
           Press, Austin.
HILL, R. M. II, and J. MONAGHAN
1987   *Continuities in Highland Maya Social Organization: Ethnohistory in Sacapu-
           las, Guatemala.* Univ. of Pennsylvania Press, Philadelphia.
HINTZE, J. L.
1987   *Number Cruncher Statistical System, Version 5.0, 2/87.* Kaysville, Utah.

HIRTH, K.
1984   ed., *Trade and Exchange in Early Mesoamerica*. Univ. of New Mexico Press, Albuquerque.
1987   "Formative Period Settlement Patterns in the Rio Amatzinac Valley." In *Ancient Chalcatzingo*, pp. 343-67. *See* Grove 187a.

HODDER, I.
1982   ed., *Symbolic and Structural Archaeology*. Cambridge Univ. Press, Cambridge.

HODGE, M. G.
1984   *Aztec City States*. Museum of Anthropology Memoir 18, Univ. of Michigan, Ann Arbor.

HODGES, D. C.
1986   *Agricultural Intensification and Prehistoric Health in the Valley of Oaxaca, Mexico*. Ph.D. diss., Univ. of Michigan, Ann Arbor.

HOPKINS, K. and G. BURTON
1983   "Ambition and Withdrawal: The Senatorial Aristocracy under the Emperors." in K. Hopkins, ed., *Death and Renewal: Sociological Studies in Roman History*, vol. 2, pp. 12-200. Cambridge Univ. Press, Cambridge.

HOPKINS, M. R.
1989   "On Paste Uniformity in Teotihuacan Cooking Pots." Paper of Annual Meeting of the American Anthropological Association, Washington, D.C.

HORAN, P. M.
1978   "Is Status Attainment Research Atheoretical?" *American Sociological Review* 43:534-41.

HOUSTON, S. D.
1987   "Notes on Caracol Epigraphy and Its Significance." Appendix II, *Investigations at the Classic Maya City of Caracol*. *See* A. Chase and D. Chase 1987b.
1989   *Maya Glyphs*. Univ. of California Press, Berkeley.

HOUSTON, S. D., and P. MATHEWS
1985   *The Dynastic Sequence of Dos Pilas, Guatemala*. Monograph 1, Pre-Columbian Art Research Institute, San Francisco.

HOUSTON, S. D., D. STUART, and K. TAUBE
1988   "Folk Classification of Classic Maya Pottery." *American Anthropologist* 91(3):720-726.

HUNTINGTON, R. and P. METCALF
1979   *Celebrations of Death*. Cambridge Univ. Press, Cambridge.

ICHON, A., et al.
1982   *Rabinal et la Vallée Moyenne du Rio Chixoy, Baja Verapaz-Guatemala*. Cahiers de la RCP 500. Centre National de la Recherche Scientifique, Institut d'Ethologie, Paris.

ISAAC, B. L.
1986a   ed, *Research in Economic Anthropology, Supplement 2: Economic Aspects of Prehispanic Highland Mexico*. JAI Press Inc., Greenwich, Conn.
1986b   "Notes on Obsidian, the Pochteca and the Position of Tlatelolco in the Aztec Empire." In *Research in Economic Anthropology, Supplement 2*, pp. 319-43. *See* Issac 1986a.

IVERSEN, E.
1971   "The Hieroglyphic Tradition." In J. R. Harris, ed., *The Legacy of Egypt*, 2nd ed., pp. 170-96. Clarendon Press, Oxford.

JAEGER, S.
1991   *Settlement Pattern Research at Caracol, Belize: The Social Organization in a Classic Maya Center*. Ph.D. diss., Dept. of Anthropology, Southern Methodist University, Dallas.

JAHER, F. C.
1972   "Nineteenth-Century Elites in Boston and New York." *Journal of Social History* 6(1):32-77.

JOESINCK-MANDEVILLE, L. R. V.
1987   "Yarumela, Honduras: Formative Period Cultural Conservatism and Diffusion." In *Interaction on the Southeast Mesoamerican Frontier*, pp. 196-214. *See* Robinson 1987.

JONES, C.
1969   *The Twin Pyramid Group Pattern: A Classic Maya Architectural Assemblage at Tikal, Guatemala*. Ph.D. diss., Dept. of Anthropology, Univ. of Pennsylvania, Philadelphia.
1977   "Inauguration Dates of Three Late Classic Rulers of Tikal, Guatemala." *American Antiquity* 42:28-60.
1984   *Deciphering Maya Hieroglyphs*. Univ. Museum, Univ. of Pennsylvania, Philadelphia.

JONES, C., W. R. COE, and W. A. HAVILAND
1981   "Tikal: An Outline of Its Field Study (1956-1970) and a Project Bibliography." In J. A. Sabloff, ed., *Supplement to the Handbook of Middle American Indians*, pp. 296-312. Univ. of Texas Press, Austin.

JONES, C., and L. SATTERTHWAITE
1982   *The Monuments and Inscriptions of Tikal: The Carved Monuments*. Tikal Report no. 33, pt. A, Univ. Museum Monograph 44, Univ. Museum, Philadelphia.

JONES, G. D.
1984   "Maya-Spanish Relations in Sixteenth Century Belize." *Belcast Journal of Belizean Affairs* 1(1):28-40. Belize College of Arts, Science, and Technology, Belize City.

JOYCE, R. A.
1988   "The Ulua Valley and the Coastal Maya Lowlands: The View from Cerro Palenque." In E. H. Boone and G. R. Willey, eds., *The Southeast Classic Maya Zone*, pp. 269-95. Dumbarton Oaks, Washington, D.C.

KALUSH, R. J., JR.
1987   *Mapit, Version 2.0*. Questionnaire Service Company, East Lansing, Mi.

KATZ, M. B., M. J. DOUCTE, and M. STERN
1982   *The Social Organization of Early Industrial Capitalism*. Harvard Univ. Press, Cambridge, Mass.

KELLEY, D. H.
1982   "Notes on Puuc Inscriptions and History." In L. Mills, ed., *The Puuc: New Perspectives: Supplement*, Central College, Pella, Iowa.

KENNEDY, N. C.
1980   *The Formative Period Ceramic Sequence from Playa de los Muertos, Honduras*. Ph.D. diss., Univ. of Illinois, Urbana.

1986   "The Periphery Problem and Playa de los Muertos: A Test Case." In *The Southeast Maya Periphery*, pp. 179-93. *See* Urban and Shortman 1986.

KIDDER, A. V., J. JENNINGS, and E. M. SHOOK
1946   *Excavations at Kaminaljuyu, Guatemala*. Carnegie Institution of Washington Publication 561, Washington, D.C.

KIRCHHOFF, P.
1952   "Mesoamerica." In S. Tax, ed., *Heritage of Conquest*, pp. 17-30. Free Press, Glencoe.

KOBISHCHANOW, Y.
1987   "The Phenomenon of Gafol and its Transformation." In H. Claessen and P. Van de Velde, eds., *Early State Dynamics*, pp. 108-28. Studies in Human Society, vol. 2, E. J. Brill, Leiden.

KOLB, C. C.
1977   "Technological Investigations of Mesoamerican 'Thin Orange' Ceramics." *Current Anthropology* 18:534-36.
1986   "Commercial Aspects of Classic Teotihuacan Period 'Thin Orange' Wares." In *Research in Economic Anthropology, Supplement 2*, pp. 155-205. *See* Isaac 1986a.
1988a   ed., *Ceramic Ecology Revisited, 1987*. BAR International Series 436 (ii), Oxford.
1988b   "Classic Teotihuacan Candeleros: A Preliminary Analysis." In *Ceramic Ecology Revisited*, pp. 449-646. *See* 1988a.
1988c   "Classic Teotihuacan Copoid Wares: Ceramic Ecological Interpretations." In *Ceramic Ecology Revisited*, pp. 345-448. *See* 1988a.
1988d   "Classic Teotihuacan Granular Wares: Ceramic Ecological Interpretations." In *Ceramic Ecology Revisited*, pp. 227-344. *See* 1988a.
1988e   "The Cultural Ecology of Classic Teotihuacan Period Copoid Ceramics." In *A Pot for All Reasons*, pp. 147-97. *See* Kolb and Lackey 1988.

KOLB, C. C., and L. LACKEY
1988   *A Pot for All Reasons: Ceramic Ecology Revisited*. Laboratory of Anthropology, Temple Univ., Philadelphia.

KORNHAUSER, W.
1969   " 'Power Elite' or 'Veto Groups'?" In *Political Power*, pp. 42-52. *See* Bell, Edwards, and Wagner 1969.

KOWALEWSKI, S. A., and L. FINSTEN
1983   "The Economic Systems of Ancient Oaxaca: A Regional Perspective." *Current Anthropology* 24(4):413-31; 25(1):128-29.

KOWALEWSKI, S. A., et al.
1986   "Implications of Macroregional Processes for Social Inequality." Paper presented at the 85th Annual Meeting of the American Anthropological Association, Philadelphia.
1989   *Monte Alban's Hinterland, Part II: Prehispanic Settlement Patterns in Tlacolula, Etla, and Ocotlan, the Valley of Oaxaca, Mexico*. Technical Report no. 23, Museum of Anthropology, Univ. of Michigan, Ann Arbor.

KOWALSKI, J. K.
1985   "Lords of the Northern Maya: Dynastic History in the Inscriptions." *Expedition* 27(3):50-60.

1989   "Who Am I among the Itza?: Terminal Classic Connections between Northern Yucatan and the Western Maya Lowlands and Highlands." In R. A. Diehl and J. C. Berlo, eds., *Mesoamerica after the Decline of Teotihuacan: A.D. 700-900*, pp. 173-85. Dumbarton Oaks, Washington, D.C.

KROCHOCK, R. J.
1988   "The Hieroglyphic Inscriptions and Iconography of the Temple of the Four Lintels and Related Monuments, Chichen Itza, Yucatan, Mexico." M.A. thesis, Univ. of Texas, Austin.
1991   "Dedication Ceremonies at Chichen Itza: The Glyphic Evidence." In *Sixth Palenque Round Table, 1986*, pp. 43-50. *See* Robertson and Fields 1991.

KROTSER, P. H.
1987   "Levels of Specialization among Potters of Teotihuacan." In *Teotihuacán*, pp. 417-27. *See* McClung and Rattray 1987.

KROTSER, P. H., and E. RATTRAY
1980   "Manufactura y distribución de tres grupos cerámicos de Teotihuacán." *Anales de Antropología* 17:91-104.

KUBLER, G.
1967   "The Iconography in the Art of Teotihuacan." In *Studies in Pre-Columbian Art and Archaeology*, no. 4. Dumbarton Oaks, Washington, D.C.
1969   "Studies in Classic Maya Iconography." In *Memoirs of the Connecticut Academy of Arts and Sciences*, vol. 18. Connecticut Academy of Arts and Sciences, New Haven.

KUPER, A.
1982   "Lineage Theory: A Critical Retrospect." *Annual Review of Anthropology* 11:71-95.

KURBJUHN, K.
n.d.   "Stela 5 of Piedras Negras and the Reign of Ruler III." Paper presented at the 1986 Mesa Redonda de Palenque.

KURJACK, E. B.
1974   *Prehistoric Lowland Maya Community and Social Organization: A Case Study at Dzibilchaltun, Yucatan, Mexico*. Middle American Research Institute Publication 38. Tulane Univ., New Orleans.

KURJACK, E. B., and E. W. ANDREWS V
1976   "Early Boundary Maintenance in Northwest Yucatan." *American Antiquity* 41:317-25.

KURJACK, E. B., and S. GARZA T.
1981   "Pre-Columbian Community Form and Distribution in the Northern Maya Area." In *Lowland Maya Settlement Patterns*, pp. 287-309. *See* Ashmore 1981a.

KURJACK, E. B., T. GARZA, S., and J. LUCAS
1979   "Archaeological Settlement Patterns and Modern Geography in the Hill Region of Yucatan." In L. Mills, ed., *The Puuc: New Perspectives*, pp. 36-45. Central College, Pella, Ia.

KURJACK, E. B., R. MALDONADO C., and M. G. ROBERTSON
1991   "Ballcourts of the Northern Maya Lowlands." In *The Mesoamerican Ballgame*, pp 145-159. *See* Scarborough and Wilcox 1991.

LACKEY, L. M.
1988   "Traditional Mexican Pottery Technology and Thin Orange Wares." In *A Pot for All Reasons*, pp. 119-211. *See* Kolb and Lackey 1988.

LAMBERT-KARLOVSKY, C. C.
1989   ed., *Archaeological Thought in America*. Cambridge Univ. Press, New York.
LANGLEY, J. C.
1986   *Symbolic Notation of Teotihuacan: Elements of Writing in a Mesoamerican Culture of the Classic Period*. BAR International Series 313, Oxford.
LAPORTE, J. P., and V. FIALKO C.
1987   "La cerámica del clásico temprano desde mundo perdido, Tikal: Una reevaluación," In P. Rice and R. Sharer, eds., *Maya Ceramics*, pp. 123-81. BAR International Series 345(i), Oxford.
1990   "New Perspectives on Old Problems: Dynastic References for the Early Classic at Tikal." In *Vision and Revision in Maya Studies*, pp. 33-66. *See* Clancy and Harrison 1990.
LAS CASAS, B. de
1909   *Apologética historia de las Indias*. 2 vols. Nueva Biblioteca de Autores Españoles, vol. 13, Madrid.
LEVENTHAL, R. M., A. A. DEMAREST, and G. R. WILLEY
1987   "The Cultural and Social Components of Copan." In K. Trinkaus, ed., *Polities and Partitions: Human Boundaries and the Growth of Complex Societies*, pp. 179-205. Anthropological Research Papers no. 37, Arizona State Univ., Tempe.
LEVENTHAL, R., and A. KOLATA
1983   eds., *Civilization in the Ancient Americas*. Univ. of New Mexico Press, Albuquerque.
LINCOLN, C. E.
1986   "The Chronology of Chichen Itza: A Review of the Literature." In *Late Lowland Maya Civilization*, pp. 141-96. *See* Sabloff and Andrews 1986.
LIND, M., and J. URCID
1983   "The Lords of Lambityeco and Their Nearest Neighbors." *Notas Mesoamericanas* 9:78-111.
LINNE, S.
1942   *Mexican Highland Cultures: Archaeological Researches at Teotihuacan, Calpulalpan, and Chalchicomula in 1934-35*. Ethnographical Museum of Sweden, n.s., no. 7., Sweden.
LLOYD, P. C.
1965   "The Political Structures of African Kingdoms: An Exploratory Model in Political Systems and the Distribution of Power." In *Political Systems and the Distribution of Power*, pp. 63-112. ASA Monograph 2, Tavistock, London.
LONGYEAR, J.
1952   *Copan Ceramics: A Study of Southeastern Maya Pottery*. Carnegie Institution of Washington Publication 597, Washington, D.C.
LOPEZ de COGOLLUDO, D.
1688   *Historia de Yucatán.*, 3d ed. (1867-1868), Mérida.
1971   *Los tres siglos de la dominación española en Yucatán, o sea historia de esta provincia* (facsimile of 2d ed., Campeche-Merida 1842-1845). Akademische Druck und Verlagsanstalt, Graz.

LORENZO, J. L.
1968   "Clima y agricultura en Teotihuacán." In J. Lorenzo, ed., *Materiales para la arqueología de Teotihuacán*, pp. 51-72. INAH, Serie Investigaciones no. 17, Mexico City.

LOTEN, H. S., and D. M. PENDERGAST
1984   *A Lexicon for Maya Architecture*. Archaeology Monograph 8, Royal Ontario Museum, Toronto.

LOUNSBURY, G. G.
1973   "On the Derivation and Reading of the 'Ben-Ich' Prefix." In *Mesoamerican Writing Systems*, pp. 99-143. *See* Benson 1973.

LOWE, J. W. G.
1985   *The Dynamics of Apocalypse*. Univ. of New Mexico Press, Albuquerque.

MCANANY, P. A., and B. L. ISAAC
1989   *Prehistoric Maya Economies of Belize*. Research in Economic Anthropology, Supplement 4. JAI Press Inc., Greenwich.

MCCLUNG, E. and E. RATTRAY
1987   eds., *Teotihuacán: Nuevas datos, nuevas sintesis, nuevos problemas*. Universidad Autónoma de Mexico, Mexico City.

MCVICKER, D.
1985   "The Mayanized Mexicans." *American Antiquity* 50(1):82-101.

MAJEWSKI, T., and K. L. BROWN
1985   "A Conjunctive Approach to Quiche Mayan Prehistory." In T. Majewski, ed., *Demographic and Ethnohistoric Research in the Colonial Americas*. Biblioteca Americana, Mexico.

MALLORY, J. K.
1984   *Late Classic Maya Economic Specialization: Evidence from the Copan Obsidian Assemblage*. Ph.D. diss., Dept. of Anthropology, Pennsylvania State Univ., Univ. Park.

MANZANILLA, L.
1988   "The Economic Organization of the Teotihuacan Priesthood: Hypotheses and Considerations." Paper for the symposium Art, Polity, and the Teotihuacan State chaired by J. Berlo, Dumbarton Oaks, Washington, D.C.

MARCUS, G.
1983a   ed., *Elites: Ethnographic Issues*. Univ. of New Mexico Press, Albuquerque.
1983b   " 'Elite,' as a Concept, Theory, and Research Tradition." In *Elites*, pp. 7-27. *See* 1983a.
1983c   "Elite Communities and Institutional Orders." In *Elites*, pp. 41-57. *See* 1983a.
1983d   "Introduction." In *Elites*, pp. 3-6. *See* 1983a.
1983e   "A Review of Ethnographic Research on Elites in Complex Societies." In *Elites*, pp. 29-39. *See* 1983a.

MARCUS, J.
1973   "Territorial Organization of the Lowland Classic Maya." *Science* 180:911-16.
1974a   *An Epigraphic Approach to the Territorial Organization of the Lowland Classic Maya*. Ph.D. diss., Dept. of Anthropology, Harvard Univ., Cambridge, Mass.
1974b   "The Iconography of Power among the Classic Maya." *World Archaeology* 6:83-94.

1976a   *Emblem and State in the Classic Maya Lowlands: An Epigraphic Approach to Territorial Organization.* Dumbarton Oaks, Washington, D.C.

1976b   "The Iconography of Militarism at Monte Alban and Neighboring Sites in the Valley of Oaxaca." In H. B. Nicholson, ed., *The Origins of Religious Art and Iconography in Preclassic Mesoamerica.* Latin American Center, Univ. of California at Los Angeles, Los Angeles.

1976c   "The Origins of Mesoamerican Writing." *Annual Review of Anthropology* 5:35-67.

1978   "Archaeology and Religion: A Comparison of Zapotec and Maya." *World Archaeology* 10:172-91.

1980   "Zapotec Writing." *Scientific American* 242:50-64.

1983a   "Changing Patterns of Stone Monuments, A.D. 600-900." In *The Cloud People*, pp. 191-97. *See* Flannery and Marcus 1983a.

1983b   "Conquest Slabs of Building J, Monte Alban." In *The Cloud People*, pp. 106-8. *See* Flannery and Marcus 1983a.

1983c   "Lowland Maya Archaeology at the Crossroads." *American Antiquity* 48(3):454-88.

1983d   "On the Nature of the Mesoamerican City." In *Prehistoric Settlement Patterns*, pp. 195-242. *See* Vogt and Leventhal 1983.

1983e   "Rethinking the Zapotec Urn." In *The Cloud People*, pp. 144-48. *See* Flannery and Marcus 1983a.

1983f   "Stone Monuments and Tomb Murals of Monte Alban IIIa." In *The Cloud People*, pp. 137-43. *See* Flannery and Marcus 1983a.

1984   "Mesoamerican Territorial Boundaries: Reconstructions from Archaeology and Hieroglyphic Writing." *Archaeological Review from Cambridge* 3(2):48-62, Cambridge (England).

1987   *The Inscriptions of Calakmul: Royal Marriage at a Maya City in Campeche, Mexico.* Technical Report 21, Univ. of Michigan Museum of Anthropology, Ann Arbor.

MARCUS, J., and K. V. FLANNERY
1983   "An Introduction to the Late Postclassic." In *The Cloud People*, pp. 217-26. *See* Flannery and Marcus 1983a.

MARTINEZ HERNANDEZ, J.
1929   *Diccionario de Motul: Maya Español.* Companía Tipografica Yucateca, Merida.

MATHER, W. G.
1968   "The Aztec State of Otumba, Mexico: An Ethno-Historical Settlement Pattern Study." M.A. thesis, Pennsylvania State Univ., Univ. Park.

MATHEWS, P.
1985   "Maya Early Classic Monuments and Inscriptions." In G. R. Willey and P. Mathews, eds., *A Consideration of the Early Classic Period in the Maya Lowlands*, pp. 5-54. Institute for Mesoamerican Studies Publication 10, State Univ. of New York at Albany.

1986   "Classic Maya Political Organization." Paper presented at a symposium: Patterns, Processes and the Mind: A New Look at the Dynamics of Maya History and Civilization, Kimbell Art Museum, Fort Worth (May 18).

MATHEWS, P., and J. S. JUSTESON
1984   "Patterns of Sign Substitution in Mayan Hieroglyphic Writing: The 'Affix
         Cluster'." In J. S. Justeson and L. Campbell, eds., *Phoneticism in Mayan
         Hieroglyphic Writing*, pp. 185-231. Publication 9, Institute for Mesoameri-
         can Studies, State Univ. of New York, Albany.
MENARD, S.
1986   "A Research Note on International Comparisons of Inequality of In-
         come." *Social Forces* 64(3):778-93.
MERLO JUAREZ, E.
n.d.   "Un enterramiento olmeca en Zinacatepec, Puebla." Manuscript on file at
         the INAH Centro Regional, Puebla, Mexico.
MERRY de MORALES, M.
1987a   "Appendix C: The Chalcatzingo Burials." In *Ancient Chalcatzingo*, pp. 95-
         113. *See* Grove 1987a.
1987b   "Chalcatzingo Burials as Indicators of Social Ranking." In *Ancient Chal-
         catzingo*, pp. 95-113. *See* Grove 1987a.
MICHELS, J. W.
1977   "Political Organization at Kaminaljuyu: Its Implications for Interpreting
         Teotihuacan Influence." In W. Sanders and J. Michels, eds., *Teotihuacan
         and Kaminaljuyu: A Study in Prehistoric Culture Contact*, pp. 453-467. Pen-
         sylvania State Univ. Press, Univ. Park.
MILLER, A. G.
1986   "From the Maya Margins: Images of Postclassic Power Politics." In *Late
         Lowland Maya Civilization*, pp. 199-222. *See* Sabloff and Andrews 1986.
MILLER, M. E.
1986a   "Copan: Conference with a Perished City." In *City-States of the Maya*, pp.
         72-109. *See* Benson 1986.
1986b   *The Murals of Bonampak.* Princeton Univ. Press, Princeton, N.J.
MILLER, M. E., and S. D. HOUSTON
1987   "The Classic Maya Ballgame and Its Architectural Setting: A Study in
         Relations between Text and Image." *Res*:47-66.
MILLON, C.
1973   "Painting, Writing, and Polity in Teotihuacan, Mexico." *American Antiq-
         uity* 38:294-314.
1988   "A Reexamination of the Teotihuacan Tassel Headdress Insignia." In
         Feathered Serpents and Flowering Trees, pp. 114-34 (also discussions of sev-
         eral murals, pp. 194-226). *See* Berrin 1988.
MILLON, R.
1973   *Urbanization at Teotihuacan: The Teotihuacan Map*, vol. 1, pt. 1. Univ. of
         Texas Press, Austin.
1976   "Social Relations in Ancient Teotihuacan." In E. R. Wolf, ed., *The Valley
         of Mexico*, pp. 205-48. Univ. of New Mexico Press, Albuquerque.
1981   "Teotihuacan: City, State, and Civilization." In V. Bricker and J. Sabloff,
         eds., *Supplement to the Handbook of Middle American Indians,* vol. 1, pp.
         198-243. Univ. of Texas Press, Austin.
1988   "Where *Do* They All Come From? The Provenance of the Wagner Murals
         from Teotihuacan." In *Feathered Serpents and Flowering Trees*, pp. 78-113.
         See Berrin 1988.

MILLON, R., R. B. DREWITT, and G. L. COWGILL
1973   *The Teotihuacan Map–Part Two: Maps*. Univ. of Texas Press, Austin.
MILLS, C. W.
1956   *The Power Elite*. Oxford Univ. Press, New York.
1959   *The Sociological Imagination*. Oxford Univ. Press, New York.
MOHOLY-NAGY, H., F. ASARO, and F. H. STROSS
1984   "Tikal Obsidian: Sources and Typology." *American Antiquity* 49(1):104-117.
MORLEY, S. G., G. W. BRAINERD, and R. J. SHARER
1983   *The Ancient Maya*. 4th ed. Stanford Univ. Press, Stanford, Ca.
MORONEY, M. J.
1960   *Facts from Figures*. 2d ed. rev. Penguin Books, London.
MURDOCK, G. P.
1949   *Social Structure*. MacMillan, New York.
MURRA, J.
1975   "El control vertical de un máximo de pisos ecológicos en la economía de las sociedades andinas." In J. Murra, ed., *Formaciones económicas y políticas del mundo andino*, pp. 59-115. Instituto de Estudios Peruanos, Lima, Peru.
NAVARRETE, C., J. CON U., and A. MARTINEZ M.
1979   *Observaciones Arqueológicas en Cobá, Quintana Roo*. Centro de Estudios Mayas, UNAM, Mexico.
NICHOLS, D. L., and T. H. CHARLTON
1988   "Processes of State Formation: Core versus Periphery in the Late Postclassic Basin of Mexico." Paper presented at the 53d Annual Meeting of the Society for American Archaeology, Phoenix.
NICHOLSON, H. B.
1960   "The Mixteca Puebla Concept in Mesoamerican Archaeology: A Re-examination." In A. F. C. Wallace, ed., *Men and Cultures*, pp. 612-17. Univ. of Pennsylvania, Philadelphia.
1971   "Religion in Pre-Hispanic Central Mexico." In G. F. Ekholm and I. Bernal, eds., *Handbook of Middle American Indians*, vol. 10, pp. 395-446. Univ. of Texas Press, Austin.
1975   "Middle American Ethnohistory: An Overview." In H. Cline, ed., *Handbook of Middle American Indians*, vol. 15, pp. 487-505. Univ. of Texas Press, Austin.
1982   "The Mixteca-Puebla Concept Revisited." In E. H. Boone, ed., *The Art and Iconography of Late Post-Classic Central Mexico*, pp. 227-49. Dumbarton Oaks, Washington, D.C.
NOGUERA, E.
1971   "Minor Arts in the Central Valleys." In G. F. Ekholm and I. Bernal, eds., *Handbook of Middle American Indians*, vol. 10, pp. 258-69. Univ. of Texas Press, Austin.
OFFNER, J. A.
1983   *Law and Politics in Aztec Texcoco*. Cambridge Univ. Press, Cambridge.
ORREGO, M.
n.d.   "Excavaciones en Chikin Tikal." Manuscript on file in Instituto de Antropología e Historia, Guatemala (1979).

O'SHEA, J. M.
1984   *Mortuary Variability: An Archaeological Investigation.* Academic Press, Orlando.

OTIS CHARLTON, C. L.
in press "Hollow Rattle Figurines of the Otumba Area, Mexico." In R. S. Santley, R. A. Diehl, and J. R. Parsons, eds., *Pattern and Process in Ancient Mesoamerica: Essays in Honor of William T. Sanders*, Univ. of Alabama Press.

PARSONS, J. R.
1976   "The Role of Chinampa Agriculture in the Food Supply of Aztec Tenochtitlan." In C. Cleland, ed., *Cultural Change and Continuity: Essays in Honor of James Bennett Griffen*, pp. 233-62. Academic Press, New York.

PARSONS, L., and B. PRICE
1971   "Mesoamerican Trade and Its Role in the Emergence of Civilization." In R. Heizer and J. Graham, eds., *Observations on the Emergence of Civilization in Mesoamerica*, pp. 169-95. Contributions of the Univ. of California Archaeological Research Facility, no. 11, Berkeley.

PARSONS, T.
1940   "An Analytical Approach to the Theory of Social Stratification." *American Journal of Sociology* 45(6):841-62.

PASO y TRONCOSO, F. del
1905   ed., "Relación de Chinantla." In F. del Paso y Troncoso, ed., *Papeles de la Nueva España*. Segunda Serie, Geografía y Estadística, vol. 4, Relaciones Geográficas de las Diócesis de Tlaxcala, Madrid.

PASZTORY, E.
1974   "The Iconography of the Teotihuacan Tlaloc." In *Studies in Pre-Columbian Art and Archaeology*, no. 15. Dumbarton Oaks, Washington, D.C.

1988a   "Abstraction and Utopian Vision at Teotihuacan." Paper for the symposium Art, Polity, and the City of Teotihuacan chaired by J. Berlo, Dumbarton Oaks, Washington, D.C.

1988b   "A Reinterpretation of Teotihuacan and Its Mural Painting Tradition." In *Feathered Serpents and Flowering Trees*, pp. 45-77. *See* Berrin 1988.

1989   "Military Might as Reality and Rhetoric at Teotihuacan." Paper for the symposium El Periodo Clasico, INAH, Museo Nacional de Antropología, Mexico City.

PEARSON, M. P.
1982   "Mortuary Practices, Society and Ideology: An Ethnoarchaeological Study." In *Symbolic and Structural Archaeology*, pp. 99-113. *See* Hodder 1982.

PEEBLES, C. S., and S. M. KUS
1977   "Some Archaeological Correlates of Ranked Societies." *American Antiquity* 42(3):421-48.

PENDERGAST, D. M.
1979   *Excavations at Altun Ha, Belize, 1964-1970*, vol. 1. Royal Ontario Museum, Toronto.

1981a   "An Ancient Maya Dignitary: A Work of Art from the ROM's Excavations at Lamanai, Belize." *Rotunda* 13(4):5-11.

1981b   "Lamanai, Belize: Summary of Excavation Results: 1974-1980." *Journal of Field Archaeology* 8(1):29-53.

1982a   *Excavations at Altun Ha, Belize, 1964-1970*, vol. 2. Royal Ontario Museum, Toronto.

1982b   "Lamanai 1982 (II): Headaches in Ottawa as Stella Remains Dateless." *Royal Ontario Museum Archaeological Newsletter*, n.s. no. 208, Toronto.

1984   "The Hunchback Tomb: A Major Archaeological Discovery in Central America." *Rotunda* 16(4):5-11.

1985a   "Lamanai, Belize: An Updated View," In *The Lowland Maya Postclassic*, pp. 91-103. *See* A. Chase and P. Rice 1985.

1985b   "Lamanai 1984: Digging in the Dooryards." *Royal Ontario Museum Archaeological Newsletter*, series 2, no. 6, Toronto.

1986a   "Under Spanish Rule: The Final Chapter in Lamanai's Maya History." *Belcast Journal of Belizean Affairs* 3 (1-2):1-7, Belize City.

1986b   "Stability through Change: Lamanai, Belize, from the Ninth to the Seventeenth Century." In *Late Lowland Maya Civilization*, pp. 223-49. *See* Sabloff and Andrews 1986.

1990a   *Excavations at Altun Ha, Belize, 1964-1970*, vol. 3. Royal Ontario Museum, Toronto.

1990b   "Up from the Dust: The Central Lowlands Postclassic as Seen from Lamanai and Marco Gonzalez, Belize." In *Vision and Revision in Maya Studies*, pp. 169-177. *See* Clancy and Harrison 1990.

PFAUTZ, H. W., and O. D. DUNCAN

1950   "A Critical Evaluation of Warner's Work in Community Stratification." *American Sociological Review* 15(2):205-15.

PICKENS, M.

1979   "The 'First Father' Legend in Maya Mythology and Iconography." In M. G. Robertson, ed., *Third Palenque Round Table, 1978, Part 2*, pp. 124-37. Univ. of Texas Press, Austin.

PINA CHAN, R.

1958   *Tlatilco*. In *Serie Investigaciones* 1, 2. INAH, Mexico City.

PIRES-FERREIRA, J. W.

1975   *Exchange Networks in Formative Mesoamerica, with Special Reference to the Valley of Oaxaca*. Museum of Anthropology Memoirs 7. Univ. of Michigan, Ann Arbor.

1976   "Shell and Iron-ore Mirror Exchange in Formative Mesoamerica with Comments on Other Commodities." In K. Flannery, ed., *The Early Mesoamerican Village*, pp. 311-26. Academic Press, New York.

1978a   "Mossbauer Spectral Analysis of Olmec Iron Ore Mirrors: New Evidence of Formative Period Exchange Networks in Mesoamerica." In D. Browman, ed., *Cultural Continuity in Mesoamerica*, pp. 101-54. Mouton, The Hague.

1978b   "Obsidian Exchange Networks: Inferences and Speculation on the Development of Social Organization in Formative Mesoamerica." In D. Browman, ed., *Cultural Continuity in Mesoamerica*, pp. 49-78. Mouton, The Hague.

1978c   "Shell Exchange Networks in Formative Mesoamerica." In D. Browman, ed., *Cultural Continuity in Mesoamerica*, pp. 79-100. Mouton, The Hague.

PIRES-FERREIRA, J. W., and K. FLANNERY

1976   "Ethnographic Models for Formative Exchange." In K. Flannery, ed., *The Early Mesoamerican Village*, pp. 286-92. Academic Press, New York.

PLOG, F., and S. UPHAM
1983   "The Analysis of Prehistoric Political Organization." In E. Tooker, ed.,
        The Development of Political Organization in Native North America, pp.
        199-213. American Ethnological Society, Washington, D.C.
POLLARD, H. P.
1987   "The Political Economy of Prehispanic Tarascan Metallurgy." *American
        Antiquity* 52(4):741-52.
POLLOCK, H. E. D.
1965   "Architecture of the Maya Lowlands." In *Handbook of Middle American
        Indians*, vol. 2, pt. 1, pp. 378-440. *See* Wauchope and Willey 1965.
1980   *The Puuc*. Memoirs of the Peabody Museum, vol. 19, Harvard Univ., Cam-
        bridge, Mass.
POLLOCK, H. E. D., et al.
1962   *Mayapan, Yucatan, Mexico*. Carnegie Institution of Washington Publica-
        tiion 619, Washington, D.C.
POPENOE, D. H.
1934   "Some Excavations at Playa de los Muertos, Ulua River, Honduras." *Maya
        Research* 1(2):61-85.
POPOL VUH
1971   *The Book of Counsel: The Popol Vuh of the Quiche Maya of Guatemala*.
        Translated by M. Edmonson. Middle American Research Institute Publi-
        cation 35. Tulane Univ., New Orleans.
PORTER, M. N.
1953   *Tlatilco and the Pre-Classic Cultures of the New World*. Viking Fund Publi-
        cations in Anthropology 19. Viking Press, New York.
PRICE, B. J.
1974   "The Burden of Cargo: Ethnographical Models and Archaeological Infer-
        ence." In *Mesoamerican Archaeology: New Approaches*, pp. 445-65. *See*
        Hammond 1974.
1978   "Secondary State Formation: An Explanatory Model." In R. Cohen and E.
        Service, eds., *Origins of the State: The Anthropology of Political Evolution*,
        pp. 161-86. Institute for the Study of Human Issues, Philadelphia.
PRINDIVILLE, M., and D. C. GROVE
1987   "The Settlement and Its Architecture." In *Ancient Chalcatzingo*, pp. 63-81.
        See Grove 1987a.
PROSKOURIAKOFF, T.
1955   "The Death of a Civilization." *Scientific American* 192:82-88.
1962   "The Artifacts of Mayapan." In *Mayapan, Yucatan, Mexico*, pp. 321-549.
        See Pollock et al. 1962.
1963   "Historical Data in the Inscriptions of Yaxchilan, pt. I." *Estudios de Cul-
        tura Maya* 3:149-67.
1964   "Historical Data in the Inscriptions of Yaxchilan, pt. II." *Estudios de Cul-
        tura Maya* 4:177-201.
1970   "On Two Inscription at Chichen Itza." In W. R. Bullard, ed., *Monographs
        and Papers in Maya Archaeology*, pp. 457-67. Papers of the Peabody Mu-
        seum, vol. 61, Harvard Univ., Cambridge, Mass.
PULESTON, D. E.
1983   *The Settlement Survey of Tikal*. Tikal Report No. 13. Univ. Museum Mono-
        graph 48. Univ. Museum, Univ. of Pennsylvania.

PYBURN, K. A.
1989   "Maya Cuisine: Hearths and Lowland Economy." In *Research in Economic Anthropology, Supplement 4*, pp. 325-44. *See* McAnany and Isaac 1989.
QUIRARTE, J.
n.d.   "Deer, Birds, and Ballplayers: A Study of Headdresses Represented on Maya Polychrome Vases." Paper prepared for the International Symposium on the Ballgame, (November 20-24, 1985). Tucson, Ariz.
RAMSEY, J. R.
1982   "An Examination of Mixtec Iconography." In J. S. H. Brown and E. W. Andrews V, eds., *Aspects of the Mixteca-Puebla Style and Mixtec and Central Mexican Culture in Southern Mesoamerica*, pp. 32-42. Middle American Research Institute Occasional Paper 4. Tulane Univ., New Orleans.
RANDS, R. L., and R. E. SMITH
1965   "Pottery of the Guatemalan Highlands." In *Handbook of Middle American Indians*, vol. 2, pp. 95-145. *See* Wauchope and Willey 1965.
RAPPAPORT, R.
1968   *Pigs for the Ancestors: Ritual in the Ecology of a New Guinea People*. Yale Univ. Press, New Haven.
RATHJE, W. L.
1970   "Socio-political Implications of Lowland Maya Burials: Methodology and Tentative Hypotheses." *World Archaeology* 1:359-74.
1971   "The Origin and Development of Classic Maya Civilization." *American Antiquity* 36:275-85.
1972   "Praise the Gods and Pass the Metates: A Hypothesis of the Development of Lowland Rainforest Civilizations in Mesoamerica." In M. Leone, ed., *Contemporary Archaeology*, pp. 365-92. Univ. of Southern Illinois Press, Carbondale.
1975   "The Last Tango in Mayapan: A Tentative Trajectory of Production-Distribution Systems." In J. A. Sabloff and C. C. Lamberg-Karlovsky, eds., *Ancient Civilization and Trade,* pp. 409-48. Univ. of New Mexico Press, Albuquerque.
1983   "To the Salt of the Earth: Some Comments on Household Archaeology among the Maya." In *Prehistoric Settlement Patterns*, pp. 23-34. *See* Vogt and Leventhal 1983.
RATTRAY, E.
1981   "Anaranjado delgado: Cerámica de comercio de Teotihuacán." In E. Rattray, J. Litvak, and C. Diaz, eds., *Interacción cultural en Mexico*, pp. 55-80. Universidad Nacional Autónoma de México, Mexico City.
RELACIONES DE YUCATAN
1898-1900 *Colección de documentos inéditos relativos al descubrimiento, conquista y organización de las antiguas psesiones españolas de ultramar*. Segunda Serie, vol. 11, Sucesores de Rivadeneyra, Madrid.
RENFREW, C., and J. F. CHERRY
1986   eds., *Peer-Polity Interaction and Socio-Political Change*. Cambridge Univ. Press, Cambridge.
REVISTA MEXICANA de ESTUDIOS HISTORICOS (RMEH)
1927-28 vols. 1 and 2 (*RMEH* suspended in 1929; resumed as *Revista Mexicana de Estudios Antropológicos* in 1939).

REYES, A. de los
  1593   *Arte en lengua mixteca . . . México.* Reprinted in Vanderbilt Univ. Publica-
           tions in Anthropology 14 (1976). Nashville.
  1890   "Arte en lengua mixteca." *Actes de la Société Philologique*, vol. 18, Paris.
RICE, D. S.
  1986   "The Peten Postclassic: A Settlement Perspective." In *Late Lowland Maya
           Civilization,* pp. 301-44. *See* Sabloff and Andrews 1986.
RICE, D. S. and D. E. PULESTON
  1981   "Ancient Maya Settlement Patterns in the Peten, Guatemala." In *Lowland
           Maya Settlement Patterns,* pp. 121-56. *See* Ashmore 1981a.
RICE, P. M., and D. S. RICE
  1979   "Home on the Range: Aboriginal Maya Settlement in the Peten Savan-
           nas." *Archaeology* 32(6):16-25.
RICE, P. M., et al.
  1985   "Provenience Analysis of Obsidian from the Central Peten Lake Region,
           Guatemala." *American Antiquity* 50:591-604.
RIESE, B.
  1989   "The Inscription on the Sculptured Bench of the House of the Bacabs." In
           The House of the Bacabs, pp. 82-87. *See* Webster 1989a.
ROBERTSON, M. G.
  1974   "The Quadripartite Badge–A Badge of Rulership." In M. G. Robertson,
           ed., *Primera Mesa Redonda de Palenque, Part 1,* pp. 77-93. Robert Louis
           Stevenson School, Pebble Beach, Ca.
  1986   "Some Observations on the X'telhu Panels at Yaxcaba, Yucatan." In E. W.
           Andrews V, ed., *Research and Reflections in Archaeology and History: Es-
           says in Honor of Doris Stone,* pp. 87-111. Middle American Research Insti-
           tute Publication 57. Tulane Univ., New Orleans.
ROBERTSON, M. G. and V. M. FIELDS
  1985   eds., *Fifth Palenque Round Table, 1983.* Pre-Columbian Art Research In-
           stitute, San Francisco.
  1991   eds., *Sixth Palenque Round Table, 1986.* Univ. of Oklahoma Press, Nor-
           man.
ROBERTSON, M. G., R. H. RANDS, and J. S. GRAHAM
  1972   *Maya Sculpture from the Southern Lowlands, the Highlands, and Pacific
           Piedmont, Guatemala.* Lederer, Street, and Zeus, Berkeley.
ROBICSEK, F., and D. M. HALES
  1981   *The Maya Book of the Dead: The Ceramic Codex.* Univ. of Virginia Art
           Museum, Charlottesville; distr., Univ. of Oklahoma Press, Norman.
ROBINSON, E. J.
  1987   ed., *Interaction on the Southeast Mesoamerican Frontier.* BAR International
           Series 327, Oxford.
ROBLES C., F., and A. P. ANDREWS
  1986   "A Review and Synthesis of Recent Postclassic Archaeology in Northern
           Yucatan." In *Late Lowland Maya Civilizations,* pp. 53-98. *See* Sabloff and
           Andrews 1986.
ROJAS, J. L. de
  1986   *México Tenochtitlan, economia, y sociedad en el siglo XVI: Crónica de la
           Ciudad de México.* El Colegio de Michoacán, Fondo de Cultura
           Económica México.

ROYS, R. L.
1933   *The Book of Chilam Balam of Chumayel.* Carnegie Institution of Washington Publication 438, Washington, D.C.
1943   *The Indian Background of Colonial Yucatan.* Carnegie Institution of Washington Publication 548, Washington, D.C.
1957   *The Political Geography of the Yucatan Maya.* Carnegie Institution of Washington Publication 613, Washington, D.C.
1962   "Literary Sources for the History of Mayapan." In *Mayapan, Yucatan, Mexico,* pp. 24-86. *See* Pollock et al. 1962.
1965   "Lowland Maya Society at Spanish Contact." In *Handbook of Middle American Indians,* vol. 3, pp. 659-78. *See* Wauchope and Willey 1965.

RUE, D.
1987   "Early Agriculture and Early Preclassic Maya Occupation in Western Honduras." *Nature* 326:6110.

RUST, W. F., and R. J. SHARER
1988   "Olmec Settlement Data from La Venta, Tabasco, Mexico." *Science* 242:102-4.

RUZ LHUILLIER, A.
1954a   "Exploraciones en Palenque: 1952." In *Anales del Institutio Nacional de Antropología e Historia,* vol. 6, no. 34, pp. 79-112. Secretaría de Educacíon Publica, Mexico City.
1954b   "La pirámide-tumba de Palenque." *Cuadernos Americanos* 74:141-59.
1969   *La costa de Campeche en los tiempos prehispánicos.* Serie Investigaciones, no. 18. INAH, Mexico, City.
1973   *El Templo de las Inscripciones, Palenque.* Colección Científica: Arqueología 7. INAH, Mexico City.
1977   "Gerontocracy at Palenque?" In *Social Process in Maya Prehistory,* pp. 287-95. *See* Hammond 1977.

SABLOFF, J. A.
1970   "Type Descriptions of the Fine Paste Ceramics of the Bayal Boca Complex, Seibal, Peten, Guatemala." In W. R. Bullard, Jr., ed., *Monographs and Papers in Maya Archaeology,* pp. 357-404. Peabody Papers vol. 61, Peabody Museum, Harvard Univ., Cambridge, Mass.
1973   "Continuity and Disruption during Terminal Late Classic Times at Seibal: Ceramic and Other Evidence." In *The Classic Maya Collapse,* pp. 107-32. *See* Culbert 1973.
1975a   "Changing Conceptions of the Ancient Maya and Their Neighbors." In S. Williams, ed., *The Maya and Their Neighbors,* pp. 12-19. Peabody Museum of Archaeology and Ethnology. Harvard Univ., Cambridge, Mass.
1975b   *Excavations at Seibal, Peten, Guatemala: Ceramics.* Memoirs of the Peabody Museum, vol. 13, no. 2. Harvard Univ., Cambridge, Mass.
1977   "Old Myths, New Myths: The Role of Sea Traders in the Development of Ancient Maya Civilization." In E. Benson, ed., *The Sea in the Pre-Columbian World,* pp. 67-97. Dumbarton Oaks, Washington, D.C.
1983   "Classic Maya Settlement Pattern Studies: Past Problems, Future Prospects." In *Prehistoric Settlement Patterns,* pp. 413-22. *See* Vogt and Leventhal 1983.

1986   "Interaction among Classic Maya Polities: A Preliminary Examination." In
        Peer Polity Interaction and Socio-political Change, pp. 109-116. *See* Renfrew
        and Cherry 1986.

SABLOFF, J. A., and E. W. ANDREWS V
1986   eds., *Late Lowland Maya Civilization: Classic to Postclassic.* Univ. of New
        Mexico Press, Albuquerque.

SABLOFF, J. A., and W. L. RATHJE
1975   "The Rise of a Maya Merchant Class." *Scientific American* 233(4):72-82.

SABLOFF, J. A., and G. TOURTELLOT
1991   *The Ancient Maya City of Sayil: The Mapping of a Puuc Region Center.*
        Middle American Research Institute Publication 60. Tulane Univ., New
        Orleans.

SABLOFF, J. A., and G. R. WILLEY
1967   "The Collapse of Maya Civilization in the Southern Lowlands: A Consid-
        eration of History and Process." *Southwestern Journal of Anthropology*
        23(4):311-36.

SABLOFF, J. A., et al.
1982   *Analyses of Fine Paste Ceramics.* Memoirs of the Peabody Museum, vol. 15,
        no. 2. Harvard Univ., Cambridge, Mass.

1984   *Ancient Maya Settlement Patterns at the Site of Sayil, Puuc Region, Yucatan,*
        Mexico: Initial Reconnaissance (1983). Latin American Institute Research
        Series, no. 14. Univ. of New Mexico, Albuquerque.

1985   *Settlement and Community Patterns at Sayil, Yucatan, Mexico: The 1984*
        Season. Latin American Institute Research Paper Series, no. 17. Univ. of
        New Mexico, Albuquerque.

SACAPULAS
1968   *Título de los Señores de Sacapulas* (1551). Translated by R. Acuna. Latin
        American Center, Univ. of California at Los Angeles, Los Angeles.

SAENZ de SANTA MARIA, C.
1940   *Diccionario Cakchiquel-Español.* Tipografía Nacional, Guatemala.

SAHAGUN, B. de
1946   *Historia general de las cosas de Nueva España.* Acosta Saignes, ed., Edito-
        rial Nueva España, SA, Mexico.

SAHLINS, M.
1972   *Stone Age Economics.* Aldine-Atherton, Chicago.

SANDERS, W. T.
1956   "The Central Mexican Symbiotic Region: A Study in Prehistoric Settle-
        ment Patterns." In G. Willey, ed., *Prehistoric Settlement Patterns in the New*
        World, pp. 115-27. Viking Fund Publications in Anthropology, New York.

1965   *Cultural Ecology of the Teotihuacan Valley.* Dept. of Sociology and Anthro-
        pology, Pennsylvania State Univ., Univ. Park.

1972   "Population, Agricultural History, and Societal Evolution in Mesoamer-
        ica." In B. Spooner, ed., *Population Growth: Anthropological Implications*,
        pp. 101-53. MIT Press, Cambridge, Mass.

1974   "Chiefdom to State: Political Evolution at Kaminaljuyu, Guatemala." In
        C. B. Moore, ed., *Reconstructing Complex Societies*, pp. 97-121. Supple-
        ment to the *Bulletin of the American Schools of Oriental Research*, no. 20.

1976   "The Population of the Central Mexican Symbiotic Region: The Basin of
        Mexico and Teotihuacan Valley in the Sixteenth Century." In W. M.
        Denevan, ed., *The Native Population of the Americas in 1492*. Univ. of
        Wisconsin Press, Madison.
1981a   "Classic Maya Settlement Patterns and Ethnographic Analogy." In *Low-
        land Maya Settlement Patterns*, pp. 351-369. *See* Ashmore 1981a.
1981b   "Ecological Adaptation in the Basin of Mexico: 23,000 b.c. to the Present."
        In J. A. Sabloff, ed., *Handbook of Middle American Indians: Supplement 1:
        Archaeology*, pp. 147-97. Univ. of Texas Press, Austin.
1986   ed., *Excavaciones en el area urbana de Copán, Honduras I*. Secretaría en el
        Despacho de Cultura y Turismo, Tegucigalpa, Honduras.

SANDERS, W. T., J. R. PARSONS, and R. S. SANTLEY
1979   *The Basin of Mexico: Ecological Processes in the Evolution of a Civilization*.
        Academic Press, New York.

SANDERS, W. T., and B. PRICE
1968   *Mesoamerica: The Evolution of a Civilization*. Random House, New York.

SANDERS, W. T., and R. SANTLEY
1983   "A Tale of Three Cities: Energetics and Urbanization in Pre-hispanic
        Central Mexico." In *Prehistoric Settlement Patterns: Essays in Honor of
        Gordon R. Willey*, pp. 243-91. *See* Vogt and Leventhal 1983.

SANDERS, W. T., and D. WEBSTER
1978   "Unilinealism, Multilinealism and the Evolution of Complex Societies." In
        C. Redman et al., eds., *Social Archeology: Beyond Subsistence and Dating*,
        pp. 249-302. Academic Press, New York.
1983   "The Copan Project: Phase 2: The First Three Years Annual Reports
        1981-1983." Manuscript in possession of authors.
1988   "The Mesoamerican Urban Tradition." *American Anthropologist* 90(3):521-
        46.

SANTLEY, R. S.
1983   "Obsidian Trade and Teotihuacan Influence in Mesoamerica." In A.
        Miller, ed., *Highland-Lowland Interaction in Mesoamerica: Interdisciplinary
        Approaches*, pp. 69-124. Dumbarton Oaks, Washington, D.C.
1984   "Obsidian Exchange, Economic Stratification, and the Evolution of Com-
        plex Society in the Basin of Mexico." In *Trade and Exchange in Early
        Mesoamerica*, pp. 43-86. *See* Hirth 1984.

SCARBOROUGH, V., and D. WILCOX
1991   *The Mesoamerican Ballgame*. Univ. of Arizona Press, Tucson.

SCHELE, L.
1976   "Accession Iconography of Chan-Bahlum in the Group of the Cross at
        Palenque." In M. G. Robertson, ed., *Segunda Mesa Redonda de Palenque,
        Part III*, pp. 9-34. Robert Louis Stevenson School, Pebble Beach.
1981   "Sacred Site and World View at Palenque." In E. P. Benson, ed.,
        Mesoamerican Sites and World Views, pp. 87-117. Dumbarton Oaks, Wash-
        ington, D.C.
1983   "Human Sacrifice among the Classic Maya." In E. P. Benson, ed., *Ritual
        Human Sacrifice in Mesoamerica*, pp. 7-48. Dumbarton Oaks, Washington,
        D.C.

1985   "The Hauberg Stela: Bloodletting and the Mythos of Maya Rulership." In *Fifth Palenque Round Table, 1983,* vol. 7, pp. 135-49. *See* Robertson and Fields 1985.

1986   "Architectural Development and Political History at Palenque." In *City-States of the Maya*, pp. 110-37. *See* Benson 1986.

1987   *Workbook of the Hieroglyphic Workshop.* Dept. of Art, Univ. of Texas, Austin.

n.d.a   "The Puleston Hypothesis: The Waterlily Complex in Classic Maya Art and Writing." On file, Dept. of Art, Univ. of Texas, Austin (1979).

n.d.b   "The Tlaloc Heresy." Paper presented at the symposium Patterns, Processes and the Mind: A New Look at the Dynamics of Maya History and Civilization, Kimbell Art Museum, Fort Worth, (May 18, 1986).

SCHELE, L., and D. FREIDEL
1990   *A Forest of Kings: Royal Histories of the Ancient Maya.* William Morrow, New York.

1991   "The Courts of Creation: Ballcourts, Ballgames, and Portals to the Maya Otherworld." In *The Mesoamerican Ballgame*, pp. 289-315. *See* Scarborough and Wilcox 1991.

SCHELE, L., and J. H. MILLER
1983   "The Mirror, the Rabbit, and the Bundle: 'Accession' Expressions from the Classic Maya Inscriptions." *Studies in Pre-Columbian Art and Archaeology*, no. 25. Dumbarton Oaks, Washington, D.C.

SCHELE, L., and M. E. MILLER
1986   *The Blood of Kings: Dynasty and Ritual in Maya Art.* Kimbell Art Museum, Fort Worth.

SCHELE, L., D. STUART, and N. GRUBE
1986-88 *Copan Notes.* Copan Mosaics Project and the Instituto Hondureño de Antropología e Historia, Copan, Honduras.

SCHNEIDER, H.
1979   *Livestock and Equality in East Africa: The Economic Basis for Social Structure.* Indiana Univ. Press, Bloomington.

1981   *The Africans: An Ethnological Account.* Prentice-Hall, Englewood Cliffs, N.J.

SCHOLES, F. V., and E. B. ADAMS
1938   *Don Diego Quijada, Alcalde mayor de Yucatán, 1561-1565, Documentos sacados de los Archivos de España*, 2 vols. Biblioteca Histórica Mexicana de Obras Inéditos, nos. 14-15, Mexico City, Antigua Librería Robredo.

SCHORTMAN, E. M., and P. A. URBAN
1986   "Introduction." In *The Southeast Maya Periphery*, pp. 1-14. *See* Urban and Shortman 1986.

SCHORTMAN, E. M., et al.
1986   "Interregional Interaction in the Southeast Maya Periphery: The Santa Barbara Archaeological Project 1983-1984." *Journal of Field Archaeology* 13(3):259-72.

SEIFERT, D. J.
1977   *Archaeological Majolicas of the Rural Teotihuacan Valley, Mexico.* Ph.D. diss., Dept. of Anthropology, Univ. of Iowa, Iowa City.

SEJOURNE, L.
1959   *Un palacio en la ciudad de los dioses: Exploraciones en Teotihuacán, 1955-58.* INAH, Mexico City.
1966   *Arquitectura y pintura en Teotihuacán.* Siglo Veintiuno, Mexico City.
SEMPOWSKI, M. L.
1982   *Mortuary Practices at Teotihuacan, Mexico: Their Implications for Social Status.* Ph.D. diss., Department of Anthropology, Univ. of Rochester, Rochester.
1987   "Differential Mortuary Treatment: Its Implications for Social Status at Three Residential Compounds in Teotihuacan, Mexico." In *Teotihuacán,* pp. 115-31. *See* McClung and Rattray 1987.
SERVICE, E.
1962   *Primitive Social Organization.* Random House, New York.
SHAFER, H. J., and T. R. HESTER
1983   "Ancient Maya Chert Workshops in Northern Belize, Central America." *American Antiquity* 48(3):519-43.
1986   "Maya Stone-Tool Craft Specialization and Production at Colha, Belize: Reply to Mallory." *American Antiquity* 51(1):158-66.
SHARER, R. J.
1977   "The Maya Collapse Revisited: Internal and External Perspectives." In *Social Process in Maya Prehistory,* pp. 532-52. *See* Hammond 1977.
1978   "Archaeology and History at Quirigua, Guatemala." *Journal of Field Archaeology* 5(1):51-70.
SIDRYS, R.
1976   "Classic Maya Obsidian Trade." *American Antiquity* 41(4):449-64.
SIEGEL, S.
1956   *Nonparametric Statistics for the Behavioral Sciences.* McGraw-Hill, New York.
SIEMENS, A. H.
1978   "Karst and the Pre-Hispanic Maya in the Southern Lowlands." In *Pre-Hispanic Maya Agriculture,* pp. 117-43. *See* Harrison and Turner 1978.
1982   "Pre-Hispanic Use of Wetlands in the Topical Lowlands of Mesoamerica." In K. Flannery, ed., *Maya Subsistence: Studies in Memory of Dennis E. Puleston,* pp. 205-25. Academic Press, New York.
SISSON, E. B.
1976   *Survey and Excavation in the Northwestern Chontalpa, Tabasco, Mexico.* Ph.D. diss., Dept. of Anthropology, Harvard Univ., Cambridge, Mass.
SLOAD, R. S. (GOTTSCHO)
1977   "Toward More Precise Status Categories at Teotihuacan, Mexico." *Newsletter of Computer Archaeology* 13:1-16.
1982   *A Study of Status and Function in the Xolalpan-Metepec Community in Teotihuacan, Mexico.* Ph.D. diss., Dept. of Anthropology, Brandeis Univ., Waltham, Mass.
1987   "The Great Compound: A Forum for Regional Activities." In *Teotihuacán* pp. 219-41. *See* McClung and Rattray 1987.
SMITH, A. L.
1950   *Uaxactun, Guatemala: Excavations of 1931-1937.* Carnegie Institution of Washington Publication 477. Washington, D.C.

1962   "Residential and Associated Structures at Mayapan." In *Mayapan, Yu-catan, Mexico*, pp. 165-320. *See* Pollock et al. 1962.

1982   *Excavations at Seibal, Peten, Guatemala: Major Architecture and Caches.* Memoirs of the Peabody Museum, vol. 15, no. 1. Harvard Univ., Cambridge, Mass.

SMITH, CAROL A.

1976   "Exchange Systems and the Spatial Distribution of Elites: The Organization of Stratification in Agrarian Societies." In C. Smith, ed., *Regional Analysis: Social Systems*, vol. 2, pp. 309-74. Academic Press, New York.

1983   "Regional Analysis in World-System Perspective: A Critique of Three Structural Theories of Uneven Development." In S. Ortiz, ed., *Economic Anthropology: Topics and Theories*, pp. 307-59. Univ. Press of America, Lanham, Md.

SMITH, COURTLAND

1980   "Community Wealth Concentration: Comparisons in General Evolution and Development." *Economic Development and Cultural Change* 28:801-18.

SMITH, MARY E.

1973a   *Picture Writing from Ancient Southern Mexico: Mixtec Place Signs and Maps.* Univ. of Oklahoma Press, Norman.

1973b   "The Relationship between Mixtec Manuscript Painting and the Mixtec Language: A Study of Some Personal Names in Codices Muro and Sanchez Solis." In *Mesoamerican Writing Systems*, pp. 47-98. *See* Benson 1973.

SMITH, MICHAEL E.

1986   "The Role of Social Stratification in the Aztec Empire: A View from the Provinces." *American Anthropologist* 88:70-91.

1987a   "Archaeology of the Aztec Economy: The Social Scientific Use of Archaeological Data." *Social Science History* 11(3):237-59.

1987b   "Household Possessions and Wealth in Agrarian States: Implications for Archaeology." *Journal of Anthropological Archaeology* 6:297-335.

1989   "Cities, Towns, and Urbanism: Comment on Sanders and Webster." *American Anthropologist* 91(2):454-60.

SMITH, R. E.

1957a   "The Marquez Collection of X Fine Orange and Fine Orange Polychrome Vessels." *Notes on Middle American Archaeology and Ethnology*, no. 131, pp. 135-86. Carnegie Institution of Washington, Washington, D.C.

1957b   "Tohil Plumbate and Classic Maya Polychrome Vessels in the Marquez Collection." *Notes on Middle American Archaeology and Ethnology*, no. 129, pp. 117-30. Carnegie Institution of Washington, Washington, D.C.

1971   *The Pottery of Mayapan.* Papers of the Peabody Museum, vol. 66, 2 pts., Harvard Univ., Cambridge, Mass.

SOUTHALL, A.

1956   *Alur Society: A Study in Processes and Types of Domination.* Heffer Press, Cambridge.

1988   "The Segmentary State in Africa and Asia." *Comparative Studies in Society and History* 30:52-82.

SPENCE, M. W.

1967   "The Obsidian Industry of Teotihuacan." *American Antiquity* 32:507-14.

1981   "Obsidian Production and the State in Teotihuacan." *American Antiquity* 46:769-88.
1984   "Craft Production and Polity in Early Teotihuacan." In *Trade and Exchange in Early Mesoamerica*, pp. 87-114. *See* Hirth 1984.
1985   "Specialized Production in Rural Aztec Society: Obsidian Workshops of the Teotihuacan Valley." In W. J. Folan, ed., *Contributions to the Archaeology and Ethnohistory of Greater Mesoamerica*, pp. 76-125. Southern Illinois Univ. Press, Carbondale.
1987   "The Scale and Structure of Obsidian Production in Teotihuacan." In *Teotihuacán*, pp. 429-50, *See* McClung and Rattray 1987.

SPENCER, C. S.
1987   "Rethinking the Chiefdom." In *Chiefdoms in the Americas*, pp. 369-89. *See* Drennan and Uribe 1987.

SPINDEN, H.
1913   *A Study of Maya Art*. Memoirs of the Peabody Museum, vol. 6. Harvard Univ., Cambridge, Mass.

SPINK, M.
1983   *Metates as Socioeconomic Indicators during the Classic Period at Copan, Honduras*. Ph.D. diss., Dept. of Anthropology, Pennsylvania State Univ., Univ. Park.

SPORES, R.
1965   "The Zapotec and Mixtec at Spanish Conquest." In *Handbook of Middle American Indians*, vol. 3, pp. 962-87. *See* Wauchope and Willey 1965.
1967   *The Mixtec Kings and Their People*. Univ. of Oklahoma Press, Norman.
1983   "The Origin and Evolution of the Mixtec System of Social Stratification." In *The Cloud People*, pp. 227-38. *See* Flannery and Marcus 1983a.

STEPHENS, J. L.
1969   *Incidents of Travel in Central America, Chiapas, and Yucatan*. Dover Publications, New York.

STONE, D.
1972   *Pre-Columbian Man Finds Central America*. Peabody Museum Press, Cambridge, Mass.

STOREY, R.
1985   "An Estimate of Mortality in a Pre-Columbian Urban Population." *American Anthropologist* 87:519-35.

STUART, D.
1985   "The 'Count of Captives' Epithet in Classic Maya Writing." In *Fifth Palenque Round Table, 1983*, vol. 7, pp. 97-101. *See* Robertson and Fields 1985.
1988   "Ten Phonetic Syllables." *Research Reports on Ancient Maya Writing*, no. 14. Center for Maya Research, Washington, D.C.
n.d.   "Epigraphic Evidence of Political Organization in the Usumacinta Drainage." Manuscript in possession of the author.

STUART, G. E.
1989   "City of Kings and Commoners." *National Geographic Magazine* 176(4):498-505.

STUART, G. E., and G. S. STUART
1976   *The Mysterious Maya*. National Geographic Society, Washington, D.C.

STUART, G. S.
1981   *The Mighty Aztecs*. National Geographic Society, Washington, D.C.

SUGIYAMA, S.
  1989a   "Burials Dedicated to the Old Temple of Quetzalcoatl at Teotihuacan,
          Mexico." *American Antiquity* 54:85-106.
  1989b   "Iconographic Interpretation of the Temple of Quetzalcoatl at Teotihua-
          can." *Mexicon* 11:68-74.
TAUBE, K.
  1985   "The Classic Maya Maize God: A Reappraisal." In *Fifth Palenque Round
          Table, 1983*, vol. 7, pp. 171-81. *See* Robertson and Fields 1985.
  1988   "A Prehistoric Maya Katun Wheel." *Journal of Anthropological Research*
          4(2):183-203.
TAX, S.
  1953   *Penny Capitalism in Guatemalan Indian Economy*. Institute of Social An-
          thropology Publication 16. Smithsonian Institution, Washington, D.C.
TEDLOCK, D.
  1985   *Popul Vuh: The Definitive Edition of the Mayan Book of the Dawn of Life
          and the Glories of Gods and Kings*. Simon and Schuster, New York.
THOMPSON, J. E. S.
  1930   *Ethnology of the Mayas of Southern and Central British Honduras*. Anthro-
          pological Series, vol. 17, no. 2. Field Museum of Natural History, Chicago.
  1931   *Archaeological Investigations in the Southern Cayo District British Honduras*.
          Anthropological Series, vol. 17, no. 3. Field Museum of Natural History
          Publication 301, Chicago.
  1942   *The Civilization of the Mayas*. Anthropology Leaflet 25, Field Museum of
          Natural History, Chicago (1st ed., 1927).
  1965   "Maya Creation Myths, Part I." *Estudios de Cultura Maya* 5:13-32.
  1966   *The Rise and Fall of Maya Civilization*. 2d ed. Univ. of Oklahoma Press,
          Norman (1st ed., 1954).
  1970   *Maya History and Religion*. Univ. of Oklahoma Press, Norman.
  1973   "Maya Rulers of the Classic Period and the Divine Right of Kings." In *The
          Iconography of Middle American Sculpture*, pp. 52-71. Metropolitan Mu-
          seum of Art, New York.
THOMPSON, J. E. S., H. E. D. POLLOCK, and J. CHARLOT
  1932   *A Preliminary Study of the Ruins of Coba, Quintana Roo*. Carnegie Institu-
          tion of Washington Publication 424, Washington, D.C.
THOMSON, C. W.
  1987   "Chalcatzingo Jade and Fine Stone Objects." In *Ancient Chalcatzingo*, pp.
          295-304. *See* Grove 1987a.
TOLSTOY, P.
  1958   "Surface Survey of the Northern Valley of Mexico: The Classic and Post-
          Classic Periods." In *Transactions of the American Philosophical Society*,
          n. s. 48, part 5. Philadelphia.
  1989   "Coapexco and Tlatilco: Sites with Olmec Materials in the Basin of Mex-
          ico." In *The Olmec and the Development of Formative Mesoamerican Civili-
          zation*, pp. 85-119. Cambridge Univ. Press, Cambridge.
TOURTELLOT, G.
  1982   *Ancient Maya Settlements at Seibal, Peten, Guatemala: Peripheral Survey
          and Excavation*. Ph.D. diss., Harvard Univ., Cambridge, Mass.
  1983   "An Assessment of Classic Maya Household Composition." In *Prehistoric
          Settlement Patterns*, pp. 35-54. *See* Vogt and Leventhal 1983.

1988a "Developmental Cycles of Households and Houses at Seibal." In *House-hold and Community in the Mesoamerican Past*, pp. 97-120. *See* Wilk and Ashmore 1988.

1988b *Excavations at Seibal, Department of Peten, Guatemala: Peripheral Survey and Excavation Settlement and Community Patterns*. Memoirs of the Peabody Museum, vol. 16. Harvard Univ. Cambridge, Mass.

1990 Paper presented at Fall 1989 Precolumbian Session, Dumbarton Oaks.

1990 "Burials: A cultural Analysis." In *Excavations at Seibal, Department of Peten, Guatemala*, vol. 17, no. 2, pp. 81-142. Memoirs of the Peabody Museum, Harvard Univ., Cambridge, Mass.

TOURTELLOT, G., and J. A. SABLOFF

1972 "Exchange Systems among the Ancient Maya." *American Antiquity* 37:126-35.

TOURTELLOT, G., et al.

1988 "Mapping Community Patterns at Sayil, Yucatan, Mexico: The 1985 Season." *Journal of New World Archaeology* 7(2/3):1-24.

TOURTELLOT, G., et al., with an appendix by M. P. SMYTH

1989 *Archaeological Investigations at Sayil, Yucatan, Mexico, Phase II: The 1987 Field Season*. Univ. of Pittsburgh Publications in Anthropology 1, Pittsburgh.

TOZZER, A. M.

1941 *Landa's Relacion de las Cosas de Yucatan*. Peabody Museum of Archaeology and Ethnology Paper 28. Harvard Univ., Cambridge, Mass.

1957 *Chichen Itza and Its Cenote of Sacrifice: A Comparative Study of Contemporaneous Maya and Toltec*. Memoirs of the Peabody Museum, vols. 11 and 12. Harvard Univ., Cambridge, Mass.

TRIGGER, B. G.

1989a *A History of Archaeological Thought*. Cambridge Univ. Press, Cambridge.

1989b "History and Contemporary American Archaeology: A Critical Analysis." In *Archaeological Thought in America*, pp. 19-34. *See* Lamberg-Karlovsky 1988.

TRIK, A. S.

1939 "Temple 22 at Copan." *Contribution to American Archaeology and History*, vol. 5, no. 27. Carnegie Institution of Washington, Washington, D.C.

1963 "The Splendid Tomb of Temple I, Tikal, Guatemala." *Expedition* 6(1):2-18.

TURNER, B. L., II

1978 "Ancient Agricultural Land Use in the Central Maya Lowlands." In *Pre-Hispanic Maya Agriculture*, pp. 163-83. *See* Harrison and Turner 1978.

TURNER, B. L., II, and P. D. HARRISON

1983 "Pulltrouser Swamp and Maya Raised Fields: A Summation." In B. Turner II and P. Harrison, eds., *Pulltrouser Swamp: Ancient Maya Habitat, Agriculture, and Settlement in Northern Belize*, pp. 246-70. Univ. of Texas Press, Austin.

TURNER, B. L., II, and W. JOHNSON

1979 "A Maya Dam in the Copan Valley, Honduras." *American Antiquity* 44(2):299-305.

TURNER, M. H.
1987a   "The Lapidaries of Teotihuacan, Mexico." In *Teotihuacán*, pp. 465-71. *See* McClung and Rattray 1987.
1987b   *The Lapidary Industry of Teotihuacan, Mexico*. Ph.D. diss., Dept. of Anthropology, Univ. of Rochester, Rochester.
TUTINO, J. M.
1976   *Creole Mexico: Spanish Elites, Haciendas, and Indian Towns, 1750-1810*. Ph.D. diss., Dept. of History, Univ. of Texas (Univ. Microfilms 77-3989, Ann Arbor).
UCKO, P.
1969   "Ethnography and Archaeological Interpretation of Funerary Remains." *World Archaeology* 1:262-80.
UPHAM, S., K. G. LIGHTFOOT, and R. A. JEWETT
1989   *The Sociopolitical Structure of Prehistoric Southwestern Societies*. Westview Press, Boulder.
URBAN, P. A. and E. M. SCHORTMAN
1986   eds., *The Southeast Maya Periphery*. Univ. of Texas Press, Austin.
VAILLANT, G. G.
1935   *Excavations at El Arbolilio*. Anthropological Papers of the American Museum of Natural History 35(2). American Museum of Natural History, New York.
VIEL, R.
1983   "Evolución de la cerámica en Copán: Resultados preliminares." In *Introducción a la arqueología de Copán, Honduras*, vol. 3, pp. 471-550. *See* Baudez 1983.
VILLACORTA, J. A.
1962   *Popol Vuh*. Ministerio de Educación Publica, Guatemala.
VOGT, E. Z.
1961   "Some Aspects of Zinacantan Settlement Patterns and Ceremonial Organization." *Estudios de Cultura Maya* 1:131-45.
1964   "Some Implications of Zinacantan Social Structure for the Study of the Ancient Maya." In *XXXV Congreso Internacional de Americanistas*, vol. 1, pp. 307-19. Mexico City.
1969   *Zinacantan: A Maya Community in the Highlands of Chiapas*. Harvard Univ. Press, Cambridge, Mass.
1983   "Ancient and Contemporary Maya Settlement Patterns: A New Look from the Chiapas Highlands." In *Prehistoric Settlement Patterns*, pp. 89-114. *See* Vogt and Leventhal 1983.
VOGT, E. Z., and F. CANCIAN
1970   "Social Integration and the Classic Maya: Some Problems with Haviland's Argument." *American Antiquity* 35:101-2.
VOGT, E., and R. LEVENTHAL
1983   eds., *Prehistoric Settlement Patterns*. Univ. of New Mexico Press, Albuquerque.
WALLACE, D. T.
1977a   "Archaeological Perspective." In *Archaeology and Ethnohistory of the Central Quiche*, pp. 106-9. *See* Wàllace and Carmack 1977.

1977b   "An Intra-Site Locational Analysis of Utatlan: The Structure of an Urban Site." In *Archaeology and Ethnohistory of the Central Quiche*, pp. 20-54. *See* Wallace and Carmack 1977.

WALLACE, D. T., and R. M. CARMACK
1977   eds., *Archaeology and Ethnohistory of the Central Quiche*. Institute for Mesoamerican Studies Publication 1. State Univ. of New York, Albany.

WARNER, W. L., M. MEEKER, and K. EELLS
1949   *Social Class in America*. Science Research Associates, Chicago.

WAUCHOPE, R.
1938   *Modern Maya Houses: A Study of their Archaeological Significance*. Carnegie Institution of Washington, Publication 502, Washington, D.C.

WAUCHOPE, R., G. ECKHOLM, and I. BERNAL
1971   eds., *Handbook of Middle American Indians*, vols. 10 and 11. Univ. of Texas Press, Austin.

WAUCHOPE, R. and G. R. WILLEY
1965   eds., *Handbook of Middle American Indians*, vols. 3 and 4. Univ. of Texas Press, Austin.

WEBB, M. C.
1975   "The Flag Follows Trade: An Essay on the Necessary Interactions of Military and Commercial Factors in State Formation." In J. A. Sabloff and C. C. Lamberg-Karlovsky, eds., *Ancient Civilization and Trade*, pp. 155-209. Univ. of New Mexico Press, Albuquerque.

WEBSTER, D. L.
1977   "Warfare and the Evolution of Maya Civilization." In *The Origins of Maya Civilization*, pp. 335-71. *See* R. Adams 1977a.
1979   *Cuca, Chacchob, Dzonot Ake: Three Walled Northern Maya Centers*. Occasional Papers in Anthropology no. 11. Dept. of Anthropology, Pennsylvania State Univ., Univ. Park.
1985a   "Recent Settlement Survey in the Copan Valley, Honduras." *Journal of New World Archaeology* 5(4):39-51.
1985b   "Surplus, Labor, and Stress in Late Classic Maya Society." *Journal of Anthropological Research* 41(4):375-99.
1988   "Copan as a Classic Maya Center." In E. H. Boone and G. R. Willey, eds., *The Southeast Classic Maya Zone*, pp. 5-30. Dumbarton Oaks, Washington, D.C.
1989a   ed., *The House of the Bacabs*. Studies in Pre-Columbian Art and Archaeology 29. Dumbarton Oaks, Washington, D.C.
1989b   "The House of the Bacabs: Its Social Context." In *The House of the Bacabs*, pp. 5-40. *See* 1989a.

WEBSTER, D. L., and E. M. ABRAMS
1983   "An Elite Compound at Copan, Honduras." *Journal of Field Archaeology* 10(3):285-96.

WEBSTER, D., W. FASH, and E. ABRAMS
1986   "Excavaciones en el Conjunto 9N-8, Patio A (Operacion VIII)." In *Excavaciones en el área urbana de copán I. See* Sanders 1986.

WEBSTER, D., and A. FRETER
1990a   "The Demography of Late Classic Copan." In *Precolumbian Population History in the Maya Lowlands*, pp. 37-61. *See* Culbert and Rice 1990.

1990b   "Settlement History and the Classic Collapse at Copan: A Refined
          Chronological Perspective." *Latin American Antiquity* 1(1):66-85.
WEBSTER, D. L., and N. GONLIN
1988   "Household Remains of the Humblest Maya." *Journal of Field Archaeology*
          15:169-90.
WEEKS, J. M.
1977   "Evidence for Metalworking in the Periphery of Utatlan." In *Archaeology
          and Ethnohistory of the Central Quiche*, pp. 55-57. *See* Wallace and Car-
          mack 1977.
1983   *Chisalin: A Late Postclassic Maya Settlement in Highland Guatemala*. BAR
          International Series 169, Oxford.
WIDMER, R. J.
1987   "The Evolution of Form and Function in a Teotihuacan Apartment Com-
          pound: The Case of Tlajinga 33." In *Teotihuacán*, pp. 317-68. *See* McClung
          and Rattray 1987.
WILK, R. R., and W. ASHMORE
1988   *Household and Community in the Mesoamerican Past*. Univ. of New Mex-
          ico Press, Albuquerque.
WILLEY, G. R.
1956   "The Structure of Ancient Maya Society: Evidence from the Southern
          Lowlands." *American Anthropologist* 58:777-82.
1974   "The Classic Maya Hiatus: A 'Rehearsal' for the Collapse?" In *Mesoameri-
          can Archaeology: New Approaches*, pp. 417-38. *See* Hammond 1974.
1978   *Excavations at Seibal, Peten, Guatemala: Artifacts*. Memoirs of the Peabody
          Museum, vol. 14, no. 1. Harvard Univ., Cambridge, Mass.
WILLEY, G. R., and R. M. LEVENTHAL
1979   "Prehistoric Settlement at Copan." In *Maya Archaeology and Ethnohistory*,
          pp. 75-102. *See* Hammond and Willey 1979.
WILLEY, G. R., R. M. LEVENTHAL, and W. FASH
1978   "Maya Settlement in the Copan Valley." *Archaeology* 31:32-43.
WILLEY, G. R., and D. B. SHIMKIN
1973   "The Maya Collapse: A Summary View." In *The Classic Maya Collapse*,
          pp. 457-501. *See* Culbert 1973.
WILLEY, G. R., et al.
1965   *Prehistoric Maya Settlements in the Belize Valley*. Papers of the Peabody
          Museum of Archaeology and Ethnology, vol. 54. Harvard Univ., Cam-
          bridge, Mass.
1975   *Excavations at Seibal, Department of Peten, Guatemala: Introduction*. Mem-
          oirs of the Peabody Museum, vol. 13, no. 1. Harvard Univ., Cambridge,
          Mass.
WILLIAMS, B. J., and H. R. HARVEY
1988   "Content, Provenience, and Significance of the *Codex Vergara* and the *Co-
          dice de Santa Maria Asuncion*." *American Antiquity* 53(2):337-51.
WINTER, M.
1984   "Exchange in Preclassic Highland Oaxaca." In *Trade and Exchange in
          Early Mesoamerica*, pp. 179-214. *See* Hirth 1984.
WITTFOGEL, K.
1957   *Oriental Despotism: A Study in Total Power*. Yale Univ. Press, New Haven.

WOBST, H. M.
1978   "The Archaeo-Ethnology of Hunter-Gatherers or The Tyranny of the Eth-nographic Record in Archaeology." *American Antiquity* 43(2):303-9.
WONDERLEY, A. W.
1981   *Late Postclassic Excavations at Naco, Honduras.* Ph.D. diss., Cornell Univ., Ithaca.
1985a   "Investigaciones arqueológicas en Río Pelo, Valle de Sula: Preclásico Tardío." Manuscript on file, Instituto Hondureño de Antropología e His-toria, Tegucigalpa.
1985b   "The Land of Ulua: Postclassic Research in the Naco and Sula Valleys, Honduras." In *The Lowland Maya Postclassic*, pp. 254-69. *See* A. Chase and P. Rice 1985.
1986a   "Materials Symbolics in Pre-Columbian Households: The Painted Pottery of Naco, Honduras." *Journal of Anthropological Research* 42(4):497-534.
1986b   "Naco, Honduras: Some Aspects of a Late Precolumbian Community on the Eastern Maya Frontier." In *The Southeast Maya Periphery*, pp. 313-32. *See* Urban and Shortman 1986.
1987   "Imagery in Household Pottery from 'La Gran Provincia de Naco.'" In *Interaction on the Southeast Mesoamerican Frontier*, pp. 304-27. *See* Robin-son 1987.
in press "Structures of Authority and Acquisition in the Late Postclassic Maya Lowlands." In P. J. Netherly and D. A. Freidel, eds., *Pathways to Power: New Models for the Political Economy of Precolumbian Polities.*
WOODBURY, R. B., and A. S. TRIK
1953   *The Ruins of Zaculeu, Guatemala.* United Fruit Co., New York.
WREN, L., and P. SCHMIDT
1991   "Elite Interaction During the Terminal Classic Period: New Evidence from Chichen Itza." In *Classic Maya Political History*, pp. 199-225. *See* Culbert 1991.
WRIGHT, E. O., and L. PERRONE
1977   "Marxist Class Categories and Income Inequality." *American Sociological Review* 42(1):32-55.
WRIGHT, H. T.
1986   "The Evolution of Civilization." In D. J. Meltzer et al., eds., *American Archaeology: Past and Future*, pp. 323-65. Smithsonian Institution Press, Washington, D.C.
ZARATE, B. de
1581   "Relación de Guaxilotitlan." In *Papeles de la Nueva España*, vol. 4, pp. 196-205. *See* Paso y Troncoso 1905.
ZORITA, A. de
1941   "Breve y sumaria relación de los señores y maneras y diferencias que habia en la Nueva España . . ." In J. Garcia Icazbalceta, ed., *Nueva colec-ción de documentos para la historia de México.* Editorial Salvador Chavez Hayhoe, Mexico City.

Index